Civilizational Imperatives

A VOLUME IN THE SERIES

THE UNITED STATES IN THE WORLD

founded by Mark Philip Bradley and Paul A. Kramer

edited by Benjamin Coates, Emily Conroy-Krutz, Paul A. Kramer, and Judy Tzu-Chun Wu

A list of titles in this series is available at cornellpress.cornell.edu.

Civilizational Imperatives

Americans, Moros, and the Colonial World

Oliver Charbonneau

Cornell University Press
Ithaca and London

First published 2020 by Cornell University Press

Printed in the United States of America

Library of Congress Cataloging-in-Publication Data

Names: Charbonneau, Oliver, 1984– author.
Title: Civilizational imperatives : Americans, Moros, and the colonial world / Oliver Charbonneau.
Description: Ithaca [New York] : Cornell University Press, 2020. | Series: The United States in the world | Includes bibliographical references and index.
Identifiers: LCCN 2020009191 (print) | LCCN 2020009192 (ebook) | ISBN 9781501750724 (hardcover) | ISBN 9781501750731 (pdf) | ISBN 9781501750748 (epub)
Subjects: LCSH: Muslims—Philippines—History—20th century. | Imperialism—History—20th century. | Philippines—Colonization— History—20th century. | United States—Foreign relations— Philippines. | Philippines—Foreign relations—United States.
Classification: LCC DS685 .C53 2020 (print) | LCC DS685 (ebook) | DDC 959.9/032—dc23
LC record available at https://lccn.loc.gov/2020009191
LC ebook record available at https://lccn.loc.gov/2020009192

For Victoria

Just by saying that something was so, they believed that it was. I know now that these conquerors, like many others before them, and no doubt like others after, gave speeches not to voice the truth, but to create it.

Laila Lalami, *The Moor's Account*

Contents

Figures

Acknowledgments

A first book is a journey across unfamiliar terrain. At the risk of belaboring a clumsy topographical metaphor, many people helped map the territory ahead, often providing gentle course correction. The various individual and institutional supports I received while writing this book were integral to its completion. My gratitude extends beyond my facility with the language, but I will try to convey it anyhow.

Civilizational Imperatives began as a conversation with Frank Schumacher in early 2010. Frank helped shape my understanding of U.S. history and pushed me to extend my lines of analytical inquiry. His breadth of knowledge, generosity of spirit, and professional guidance made this project possible. I am grateful to have him as a mentor and friend. Numerous other faculty members in the History Department at the University of Western Ontario (and affiliate colleges) also helped move me down the path from feckless layabout to competent historian. Carl Young, Robert McDougall, Francine McKenzie, William Turkel, Robert Wardaugh, Nancy Rhoden, Maya Shatzmiller, Laurel Shire, Robert Ventresca, and Renée Soulodre-La France are due gratitude for their insights and patience. Thanks also to my colleagues at the University of Glasgow, who have made me feel extremely welcome in my new academic home.

Many historians from my (broadly defined) field lent support and guidance throughout the research and writing process. Ian Tyrrell gave thoughtful feedback on my first draft and encouraged me as I moved the project forward. His dedication to assisting young scholars is an inspiration. Anne Foster showed an early interest in *Civilizational Imperatives* and helped me better understand the academic editing process. Joshua Gedacht has shaped my thinking on Islamic Southeast Asia and been a great conference companion. Karine Walther tutored me on the particulars of finishing a book and provided a template for writing wide-ranging histories. Kristin Hoganson and Jay Sexton saw value in this endeavor and encouraged me to refine my ideas on transimperial exchanges. Beyond this, I am grateful to many others for their advice, support, and collegiality on various fronts. The following list is necessarily partial. Many thanks to Patricio Abinales, Christopher Capozzola, William Clarence-Smith, Boyd Cothran, Patricia Irene Dacudao, Julio Decker, Thomas Fleischman, Michael Hawkins, Daniel Immerwahr, David Huyssen, Margaret Jacobs, Patrick Kirkwood, Jonas Kreienbaum, Timothy Marr, Rebecca McKenna, Sarah Miller-Davenport, Marina Moskowitz, Karen Miller, Simon Newman, Hana Qugana, Dan Scroop, Kim Wagner, and Colleen Woods. Michael Adas unknowingly inspired the title of this book—my thanks to him as well.

Paul Kramer's many writings on U.S. imperialism in the Philippines shaped my understanding of the topic. His support for my research has been immensely gratifying. I am thankful to Paul for his guidance and for tolerating my digressive e-mails. Thanks also to the other series editors and the manuscript reviewers. At Cornell University Press, appreciation goes to Michael McGandy (who has more patience for first-time authors than we likely deserve), Meagan Dermody, and Susan Specter. Bill Nelson provided great maps at reasonable rates.

Helpful staff members at the Bentley Historical Library (University of Michigan), the Division of Rare and Manuscript Collections (Cornell University), the Manuscript Division at the Library of Congress, the Missouri History Museum Library and Research Center, the National Archives (College Park, MD), the Special Collections Research Center (Syracuse University), the United States Army Heritage and Education Center (Carlisle, PA), and the State Historical Society of Missouri (Columbia) assisted me in locating important research material. The Social Sciences and Humanities Research Council of Canada and the University of Western Ontario provided crucial financial support.

Portions of chapter 6 were previously published as "Visiting the Metropole: Muslim Colonial Subjects in the United States, 1904–1927," *Diplomatic History* 42, no. 2 (2018): 204–27, used by permission of Oxford University Press. Portions of chapter 7 were previously published as "The Permeable South: Imperial Interactivities in the Islamic Philippines, 1899–1930s," in *Powering up the Global*, ed. Kristin Hoganson and Jay Sexton, 2020, used by permission of Duke University Press.

Tolerant friends inside and outside of academia buoyed my spirits and gave me perspective when the book threatened to consume everything. Thank you to Tim Compeau, Marilla McCargar, Nic Virtue, Dorotea Gucciardo, Rachael Griffin, and Gregg French for sharing in these joys and miseries with me. I am better at fantasy baseball than Sean Somerton, Robert Leonard Cleaver, P. Ian Quinlan, Mark Dixon, and Dylan Worsell even if I never win championships. Special thanks to the selfless and dignified Paris McCargar-Olivier.

Nijole Kuzmickas did not live to see this book published, but her love informed its composition. A brilliant filmmaker, activist, gourmand, and friend, she provided me with a template for how to be in the world. I carry her memory always. Nijole lives on through Robin Preston, whose fascination with history and sense of adventure are an inspiration. Robert Favetta is an outstanding partner to my mother and among the kindest and most generous people I know. I appreciate his gently provocative sense of humor, culinary talents, and woodpile management skills. Tara Charbonneau and Ralph Sutton have supported me as long as I can recall. My thanks to them and their three children—Aja, John, and Alex—for always welcoming me into their home.

Our strange little dogs, Augie and Lily, saw more of my writing process than any human did. They slept through the writing of each chapter and are staying true to form as I type these words. They are charming, absurd, and couldn't care less whether or not I ever publish again.

My father, Charles Aitkenhead, bequeathed me an obsessive desire to learn and collect, unwittingly jump-starting my life in academia. He uncomplainingly allowed me to steal his books, and nights spent watching British sitcoms on his little television helped shape my comic sensibilities. Dad provided valuable editorial feedback as I wrote early drafts of the book. My mother, Therese Charbonneau, sacrificed years of her life to make sure I became a passable version of a human being. She is the most open-minded, nonjudgmental, and generous person I know. Her constant travels made me consider global issues decades before they became a pillar of my research. Love you, Ma!

This book is dedicated to my partner, Victoria. I am so fortunate to spend my days with someone as insightful and engaged and weird and wonderful as her. V is a voracious reader, tremendous cook, compassionate educator, and all-around amazing person (although the jury is still out on whether that ostrich egg was worth the trip). Her unwavering support made completing *Civilizational Imperatives* possible. She read these pages multiple times, provided equilibrium and laughter during stressful moments, and encouraged activities beyond brooding. Thank you for being my companion and collaborator, V.

Note on Terminology and Transliteration

The term *Moro* as a designation for Muslims in the Philippines originates in Spanish history. The fall of the last Islamic state in Grenada in 1492 occurred mere decades before Magellan reached the Philippines, and memories of the Reconquista resonated among Catholic empire builders. Encountering Islamic populations on the Southeast Asian fringe, Spanish colonials used an act of naming to integrate these groups into their long conflict with North African Muslims. By virtue of their faith, Muslim Malays became "Moros" in the colonial imagination, just as the Christianized natives of the Northern Philippines became "Indios." The term *Moro* simply denoted that an ethnic group had undergone Islamization. An array of competing royal lineages existed in the Southern Philippines, as did differing cultural practices and adaptations of Islam. With some notable exceptions (explored within), Americans adopted these racial-religious taxonomies uncritically. Newspaper and magazine articles emphasized the unitary identity of Muslims, although sustained efforts to map the groups also occurred. Some civilian and military officials on the ground learned to appreciate the differences between Muslim societies in Mindanao and the Sulu Archipelago, yet the notion of "the Moro" remained. This reductionist approach had powerful effects on colonial policy.

I have struggled with the use of *Moro* as shorthand. The term carried negative connotations for many years, but in recent decades Muslim groups have reclaimed it and speak of the Bangsamoro (community or nation of Moro people) struggle. The term *Filipino Muslims* is likewise imperfect in its implicit suggestion that Islamic societies fit neatly into a national identity developed elsewhere in the archipelago. In the following, I use *Moro* and *Muslim* inter-changeably for the sake of flow but wherever possible identify specific ethnic communities. I do not simply use *Moro* where *Tausūg* is applicable, for exam-ple. Nevertheless, I do analyze colonially generated primary source documen-tation where the term is used uncritically. This is most prevalent in the first chapter, which explores how Americans framed Muslim identities in the ar-chipelago. Reducing diversity was a strategy of colonial rule, and I make every attempt to avoid doing so myself. Thirteen Moro groups live in the Southern Philippines: the Badjao, Iranun, Jama Mapun, Kalagan, Kalibugan, Maguin-danao, Maranao, Molbog, Samal, Sangil, Tausūg, and Yakan. The Muslims who inhabit this work hail primarily from the four largest of these: Maguin-danao, Maranao, Tausūg, and Samal (also referred to as the Sama-Bajau). The term *Lumad* is similarly flattening and refers to a diverse collection of indige-nous peoples on Mindanao. These are groups American colonials referred to as "pagans" and in sum represent the animist indigenous peoples of the island. Included in the designation are the B'laan, Manobo, Bukidnon, Subanon, Mandaya, Sangil, Tagabawa, and other groups.

I acknowledge the problems inherent in using the term *Americans* to de-scribe citizens of the United States. I deploy the term for stylistic reasons but recognize that it improperly gives a transcontinental identity to men and women of European descent from limited areas of North America. I use the short-hand *colonials* to describe Euro-American colonizers in the Southern Philip-pines. Here I take my lead from scholars writing on European colonies, par-ticularly the example of the British Empire in India.

In cases where names originate in Arabic, I use the English-language spell-ing most common in the Philippines. This means occasional irregularities: Jamalul Kiram instead of Jamal al-Kiram, for example. I have applied standard transliterations of the many place-names, peoples, official titles, and regional products with Austronesian linguistic origins. In quoted material I have left alternate transliteration in place. There is a small glossary at the end of this book.

While the major island of Mindanao and the islands of the Sulu Archipel-ago are distinct spaces, I use the abbreviated designation *Mindanao-Sulu* when discussing the region itself. This should be read as the Muslim-majority areas of Western Mindanao and the Sulu island chain, and is condensed for read-ability. Those unfamiliar with the geography of the Muslim South should be aware that *Jolo* denotes both the name of the most populous island in the Sulu Archipelago and its largest settlement. When possible, I distinguish between the two by calling the latter *Jolo town* or *the town of Jolo*.

Civilizational Imperatives

Introduction

Other Frontiers

Maj. John Park Finley saw colonial empire as a moral duty. The military officer spent his early career in the Army Signal Service tracking tornadoes along the continental frontier before the U.S. annexation of the Philippine Islands took him across the Pacific. In the new colony, he caught the attention of Leonard Wood, who in 1903 was establishing the Moro Province— a Muslim-majority substate run by U.S. Army officials. Wood appointed Finley as district governor of Zamboanga, a post he would hold for nearly a decade. Possessed with enormous self-regard and a deep sense of mission, Finley administered the Zamboanga Peninsula and island of Basilan with an eye toward cultural transformation. Once fixed on climatological data, the district governor's gaze now turned to his colonial wards: the Moro and Lumad peoples of Western Mindanao.[1] He studied the Subanon "mountain folk" and published his findings, established marketplaces with the goal of civilizing through capital, and led battalions on search-and-destroy missions against Moro holdouts. Public works projects, mandatory labor programs, state-run schools, and legal reforms became priorities. "Colonial work is rough and hard, and results are necessarily slow, yet no work is more intensely interesting because of its creative possibilities," Finley wrote in 1909. "To colonize is to civilize races that need our protection and instruction."[2]

The major returned to the United States in 1912, only revisiting the Philippines briefly the following year in an ill-fated attempt to install an Ottoman sheikh as religious leader of the Moros. Back in North America, Finley became an expert commentator on colonial issues. Journal articles and speaking engagements followed. Islam vexed all the Euro-American empires, Finley argued in the pages of the *Journal of Race Development*: "Italy in Tripoli, Spain in Morocco, France in Algeria, Austria in Herzegovina and Bosnia, England in Egypt, India, Borneo and the Straits Settlements, and the Dutch in the East Indies are in contact with the Mohammedan problem of government." But the United States possessed a providential ability to solve the problem. Doing so meant interfacing with European empires, improving on their models, and reforming the colonized Muslim world in the process. A transoceanic vision of westward development animated Finley's writings. "Our industrial and commercial future is indissolubly linked with the destinies of the thousand millions of souls occupying today the oldest empires of the earth," he declared. National and imperial progress were identical, and their expression in distant colonies was of global significance.[3]

John Finley was one of thousands of Americans who journeyed to the Philippines' Muslim South with fantasies of transformation and national glory. Some, like Leonard Wood, believed colonization widened the "arch of Christian civilization in the Pacific," while others cynically observed that the United States was in Mindanao-Sulu "for the same reason . . . we are in Louisiana, Texas, California, and Oregon—for national aggrandizement."[4] The land and the people of the Southern Philippines became infinitely mutable in colonial narratives. The South held massive commercial and settlement potential but was also a little-understood zone of endless hazard. Native groups presented as ideal vessels for civilizing efforts to some Americans, while others feared they were too mired in unreconstructed primitivism to become modern citizens. Soldiers, settlers, teachers, missionaries, investors, and bureaucrats made Mindanao-Sulu their temporary or permanent home during the American period. They sought and found different things there. Officials built roads, docks, prisons, and courthouses, concerning themselves with the work of modernizing their districts while ensconcing their families in racially segregated sections of Zamboanga. Planters established agricultural operations in the Mindanaoan hinterland, living in degrees of unease among local communities who warily eyed their commercial motives. Soldiers tenuously coexisted with Moro populations and meted out incredible violence when relations broke down. Mindanao-Sulu was at once an imperial showpiece, a capitalist fantasy, and a frontier crucible.

For the multiethnic groups in the Southern Philippines, collectively referred to in this project as Moros and Lumad, American rule provided a disorienting bridge between centuries of independence (punctuated by escalating Spanish incursion) and post-1946 incorporation into the independent Philippines. Like subject populations in other empires, Moros responded to U.S. colonialism in varied ways. Collaboration strengthened certain datus, while others used their opposition to the Americans as a marker of autonomy and strength. At the nonelite level, Moro peasants acquiesced selectively to colonial mandates. The American system demanded Moros adhere to new legal codes, attend secular schoolhouses, embrace state medicine, labor under government direction, surrender firearms, and pay bewildering new taxes. Some groups and individuals engaged in these activities willingly; others signaled noncompliance by moving farther from colonial power centers; still others joined resistance movements led by figures like Datu Ali of Maguindanao and Panglima Hassan of Jolo, engaging in irregular warfare against Americans and Filipinos. After thirty-five years of colonial rule, the Westernized Tausūg Moro Arolas Tulawie observed that the government had killed 70,000—"six each day including Sundays and holidays"—and had not "changed the Moro much." Borrowing a phrase from U.S. president Franklin Roosevelt, he called for a "new deal" for the Southern Philippines.[5]

Colonial Mindanao-Sulu was in constant dialogue with the wider world. From the first, American journalists located the Muslim South relative to other imperial possessions. How could the nation "accomplish such wonders in Mindanao as the British have worked in Ceylon," Frederick Palmer wondered in the pages of Collier's Weekly.[6] Provincial officials journeyed through colonized South and Southeast Asia studying European models; Spanish texts shaped their understandings of Moro groups; they imitated British modes of tropical leisure and sociality and shared similar fears of degeneration and breakdown; and some looked to the Ottoman Empire for alternative means of pacifying colonial wards. American missionaries saw a global threat from Islam, gazing across time and space to link the "Moro problem" to the "Pathan tribes" of the North-West Frontier Province and the Mahdist forces in Khartoum (in British-controlled India and Sudan, respectively).[7] Euro-American businessmen in Zamboanga and white planters in the backcountry envisioned themselves as tropical pioneers completing a settler arc linking North America to the edges of the colonized Pacific. Calls for the "up-building of American empire on the 'Farthest Frontier'" were common in the whites-only clubs of Zamboanga, Jolo, and Davao.[8]

American colonials moved amid peoples enmeshed in their own global networks. Muslims from the Southern Philippines interacted across colonial boundaries with their coreligionists in British North Borneo, Sulawesi, Malaya, and the Dutch East Indies. Groups of pilgrims made the long journey to Mecca, where they accessed forms of spiritual and temporal authority unavailable in the colonized Philippines, while datus invoked Ottoman power in the face of military annihilation. Moro elites also traversed the Pacific to visit the United States, sometimes returning home with unwelcome baggage.

Situating the South

This book tells the story of Americans and Moros in colonial Mindanao and the Sulu Archipelago. It ranges from 1899, when U.S. military forces relieved the Spanish garrison at Zamboanga, to 1941, when Japan invaded the Commonwealth of the Philippines. It also jumps back in time to consider the Spanish legacy in Mindanao-Sulu and American precolonial contacts with the region. These Muslim-majority areas play a minor role in many histories of the American Philippines or are excised entirely. This historiographical absence perpetuates trends originating in American and Christian Filipino colonial imaginaries. The South's position as a colony within a colony, and later as a politically and culturally subordinate space in an emerging nation-state, created the preconditions for its marginalization in the literature on U.S. colonial empire. As a topic of scholarship, the Muslim South is frequently viewed through the prism of U.S. military operations, an undoubtedly valuable area of study (particularly prior to 1914) but a partial one.[9] Not merely a restive outpost existing in relation to colonial and imperial centers in Manila and Washington, Mindanao-Sulu contained its own shifting power structures and supraregional connections.

Colonial rule in the Islamic Philippines was built on the back of a civilizing project that began with idealistic U.S. Army officers at the turn of twentieth century; deepened during the years of the Moro Province (1903–1914) under the leadership of Leonard Wood, Tasker Bliss, and John Pershing; shifted to incorporate Christian Filipinos into governance roles in the Department of Mindanao and Sulu (1914–1920); faltered as Philippine independence was debated in the 1920s and early 1930s; and became an increasingly "national" question in the twilight years of U.S. sovereignty. The civilizational imperatives of the American colonial state arose from a desire to dominate and modernize Mindanao-Sulu and its peoples and were shaped by notions of Islamic recalcitrance, national histories of frontier violence, and fables of environmental malleability and wealth. Programs designed to transform Moro and Lumad populations expanded rapidly into multiple areas of civic and private life, including education, health care, law, labor, settlement, and politics. This disrupted or replaced customary societal structures in Mindanao-Sulu, leading to the rejections of colonial rule discussed above and others. The powers that be in Zamboanga frequently responded to contestation in a manner familiar to students of imperial history: with violence. Rationalizations of force arose from a belief that "warlike" Moros were racially calibrated to respect it. Thus, sporadic massacre served to both eliminate resistance and teach valuable lessons to would-be agitators. Americans lived and labored within these reconfigured landscapes, alternately fetishizing and fearing the spaces they colonized.

U.S. governance in Mindanao-Sulu can be understood in terms of empire and colonialism. Empire operates across diverse spatial and conceptual registers, resisting definitional consensus and providing endless grist for debates on national-imperial overlaps. Intellectual litigation of the U.S. empire question is now decades old and has generated an overwhelming volume of fruitful scholarship exploring extraterritoriality and empire as a way of life.[10] This study heeds Paul Kramer's call to use "the imperial" as a category of analysis.[11] In its classic form, empire involves a polity aggrandizing beyond its commonly held borders. The metropolitan state simultaneously binds and distances subject populations in its new territories through rule by difference, economic extraction, collaborationist hierarchies, and coercion. Imposed governance of disenfranchised majorities is inherently unstable, requiring active maintenance or demographic transformation lest it be compromised and dismantled. Beyond territorially bounded expressions, imperial power manifests itself through the restructuring of global norms by expansionist commercial and cultural regimes and in the truncated sovereignties, persistent exclusions, and codified power differentials within ostensibly levelling national bodies.[12] Colonialism is a specific manifestation of the imperial impulse wherein a state conquers and exercises direct territorial control over a foreign body of people. Under this umbrella are gradations, from frontier settler permanency to indirect rule by a skeleton crew of imported administrators. Colonial empire is typified in the European (and later American) expansion that began in the late fifteenth century and receded in the decades after the Second World War.[13] The dates bounding this project adhere roughly to formal colonialism's apotheosis and the beginning of its rapid decline.

The tangled roots of empire thread themselves through national and global histories. The piecemeal expansions of the United States during the nineteenth century bore all the hallmarks of a continental empire. On the frontiers of the nation, racial logics fueled territorial incursions against neighboring polities, including Mexico and vast numbers of indigenous nations. Colonial annexation and eliminationist violence became routine as Euro-American settlers pushed westward. Many key figures in the establishment of the Moro Province got their start in the so-called Indian Wars of the 1870s–1890s.[14] The progressive dispossessions of the frontier occurred against a backdrop of interimperial transfer. U.S. territory grew rapidly in the wake of the 1803 Louisiana Purchase from France, and subsequent treaties with Spain, Great Britain, Russia, and Mexico expanded the nation's borders further.[15] Filibuster campaigns in Central America, multiyear exploratory ventures (including an 1852 visit to the Sulu Archipelago by the U.S. Exploring Expedition), enclave colonialism in China and Japan, and missionary-capitalist annexation in Hawaii hinted at growing imperial ambitions farther afield.[16] In this light, U.S. sovereignty over Spanish imperial territories after 1898—as well as the subsequent extended occupations of Haiti, Panama, Nicaragua, and the Dominican Republic—can be viewed as an extension rather than an aberration.[17]

Civilizing agendas in the Muslim South were partially born out of the rapid spatial consolidations of the imperial nation-state in the decades preceding overseas expansion. The supposed redemption of the premodern Moro had North American resonances and can be traced backward to debates about racial capacity and assimilation in the post–Civil War United States. Low-status groups presented a set of "problems" and "questions" for Anglo-Saxon elites, who jostled over what (if anything) could be done about indigenous societies, formerly enslaved African Americans, and migrant groups from Asia, Latin America, and Europe.[18] Schools for indigenous youth specialized in acculturating their wards, moving them away from the language, beliefs, and rituals of their ancestors. Elsewhere, the question of the labor potential of ex-slave populations fueled the rise of the industrial education movement. Rule by difference became spatially and legally enshrined in the federally administered reservations of the frontier territories and in the interconnected race regimes of the American South.[19] After 1899, colonial authorities would apply similar strategies to their management of the "Moro problem" in Mindanao-Sulu. Euro-American expertise on questions of race, education, and labor within and beyond the nation's borders coalesced at transnational conferences like those held at Lake Mohonk in upstate New York.

None of which is to say that U.S. power in Mindanao-Sulu was a mere transposition of North American templates onto a Southeast Asian context. When Brig. Gen. John Bates and his men landed on Jolo in mid-1899, they claimed sovereignty over a maritime zone rich with cultural and commercial connections. The British, Dutch, French, and Portuguese empires all maintained territories in Southeast Asia, and the residuum of three centuries of Spanish colonialism cast a long shadow over the Philippines. Despite this, U.S. officials and colonial boosters frequently used the well-worn language of national exceptionalism, heralding the arrival of a new form of republican empire with its own novel version of the civilizing mission: benevolent assimilation. The metrics of civilization and the terminal point of tutelary rule were unclear and remained subjects of debate among American colonials well into the 1930s. Benevolent assimilation's rhetorical novelty and indeterminacy fueled a model of empire that was at once temporary and potentially endless.[20] Behind these public-facing exceptionalist strategies, however, a host of American actors coordinated across imperial boundaries. Many shared John Finley's assessment that they were engaged in "colonial work" and actively sought out European expertise.

Imperial—rather than national—power remained the dominant organizing principle in the rapidly globalizing world of the early twentieth century. Individual empires pursued their own distinct ends but also overlapped with one another, engaging in variable exchanges across distinct geographies. Multidirectional flows of peoples, goods, and ideas through colonized landscapes frustrated the demarcating tendencies of empire. The paradox of high imperialism is that the advances that consolidated metropolitan control across vast distances—steam and rail power, rapid communications networks, border-crossing professional associations and reform movements, commodity and capital flows, multifaceted migrations—also made individual empires more permeable.[21] Locating colonial Mindanao-Sulu within dense webs of transfer complicates two tendencies within the scholarly and popular literatures on the United States: one that denies the imperial character of U.S. power and a softer varietal that insists it was temporary, aberrant, or unique.[22] This is a contemporary debate cast backward over historical actors who had little compunction situating their actions within global traditions of empire. Applying a transimperial lens to these intersections, adaptations, and exchanges problematizes exceptionalist narratives, challenges the colony-metropole dyad, and recognizes global interconnection as an important site for historical analysis.

Ideas imported from other national and imperial frontiers collided with local particularities. As the U.S. Army expanded its control over the Sulu Archipelago and the Mindanao littoral in the opening months of 1900, its agents encountered complex societies that resisted flattening designations of "Moro" or "pagan." The nominal leadership of Sultan Jamalul Kiram concealed shifting Tausūg power structures in Sulu, while on Mindanao datus selectively accepted or rejected tenets of American colonialism. Negotiating colonial rule around Zamboanga was a very different proposition than doing so on the eastern shores of Lake Lanao, which had a limited history of foreign intervention. Farther south, pacified coastal Cotabato gave way to independently minded

Maguindanao communities along the Rio Grande River and in the Liguasan Marsh. Distinctive labor practices, gender relations, approaches to slavery, religious beliefs, and political hierarchies within Muslim and Lumad communities disoriented the ethnocultural templates of white colonials, giving rise to ambitious ethnographic surveys and competing ideas about governance. Mindanao-Sulu's fractious history within the Philippines complicated matters further. Spain's unfinished conquest of the region had not hindered integrationist imaginaries. Despite centuries of Filipino-Moro animosity, northern Christian elites folded the South into their emerging nationalist visions. U.S. colonials fell on both sides of this regional debate: some argued for permanent partition as a means of "protecting" Moros and Lumad from northern predation, while others attempted to incorporate the region into a unified archipelago.[23]

Granular studies of U.S. rule in Mindanao-Sulu first emerged among Filipino social scientists, who parsed the distinct societies of the South and their role within the Philippine nation. Rich in ethnographic detail not found in American battlefield histories, these accounts sometimes also mined history to aid in the unstable project of national integration.[24] In recent decades, Patricio Abinales and others have stressed how strategies of accommodation and resistance to *both* Filipino and American imperatives arose not from the inevitability of integration but from the uncertainty of it. These studies marry thick descriptions of local conditions in the South with wider observations on the Philippine national project before and after independence.[25] North American and European scholars have also begun reintegrating Mindanao-Sulu into the history of the United States in the world. Articles and monographs from the past decade situate the Southern Philippines within structures of imperial historicism, interrogate its place within colonized Muslim Southeast Asia, recognize its connections to the wider history of U.S.-Muslim relations, and critically evaluate its ties to the Middle East.[26]

Located at the intersection of multiple historiographies, this book argues that American power in the Islamic Philippines rested on a transformative vision of colonial rule. Over four decades, U.S. colonials enacted their fantasies of reconfiguration on the peoples and spaces of Mindanao-Sulu, frequently justifying them through prevalent modes of race thinking. The desire to pacify and remake traveled between continental and overseas frontiers, muddling national and imperial histories in the process. It was also informed by circuits of exchange between U.S., European, and Islamic imperial formations, refuting notions that supposed peripheries exist merely in relation to metropolitan centers. Translating these ideas into everyday colonialism was a difficult proposition, and what follows analyzes the contingencies and limitations of governance in unfamiliar cultural terrains. Schismatic applications of power and native responses to them patterned the colonial encounter in Mindanao-Sulu, manifesting in violent excess and negotiated accommodation alike. Beyond the pat narrative of how the Philippines inherited the American Moro problem, this study also presents a portrait of diverse ethnic groups trying to forge spaces for themselves between an ascendant global power and a nation in the making.

Imperial Histories in Mindanao-Sulu

Islam arrived in the Southern Philippines during the fourteenth and fifteenth centuries by way of Arab and Indian trader-missionaries, who spread the faith through economic and cultural networks. Melaka, the Malayan commercial hub and strategic entry point to maritime Southeast Asia, was an initial conversion point. The Melaka Sultanate drove the dissemination of the faith throughout the littoral areas of Java, Sumatra, Borneo, and, eventually, the Southern Philippines. Commercially and militarily dynamic, it fused Hindu-Buddhist court traditions with centralizing Islamic notions of governance. Regional port rulers adopted Islam in part to tap into webs of economic, political, and religious authority that cut across the Indian Ocean world. Interweaving the temporal and the spiritual, Islam provided these leaders with a cohesive framework for governance while simultaneously fusing with local cultural particularities. After gaining traction among elites, the faith spread to the lowland peasantries of coastal Southeast Asia.[27]

The Sulu Archipelago was the first region in the Philippines to undergo Islamization. Fourteen hundred miles from the Strait of Melaka, the nearly nine hundred islands in the Sulu chain stretched between the eastern coast of the Bruneian Empire in North Borneo and Mindanao, the southernmost major Philippine island. During the fourteenth century, the islands were already integrating into the commercial and cultural systems of larger Asian states. Population growth, enlarged trade networks, religio-cultural importations from the Indian subcontinent, and the rise of port cities as administrative and economic centers affected the development of Sulu alongside the arrival of Islam.[28] Makhdum Ibrahim Al-Akhbar, an Arabic trader-missionary, landed at Siminul in 1380. There he encountered peoples in contact with the trading cultures of China, the Malay states, and Siam. Islam became a political force in the Southern Philippines a quarter century later with the appearance of Sayyed Abu Bakr Abirin (also known as Sharif al-Hashim), a Meccan Arab who traveled to Sulu from Brunei. He married Paramisulu, one of the daughters of Raja Baginda, a Sumatran leader whose arrival in the archipelago in 1390 marked the beginning of centralized power there. Abu Bakr assumed leadership after his father-in-law's death, leveraging Baginda's political clout to create a new sultanate. The impact was profound. During thirty years of rule, Abu Bakr built mosques, established a legal code, formalized taxation, and deepened trading relationships with other states. By the late fifteenth century, the Sulu Sultanate was a well-established polity whose power was felt as far north as Luzon.[29]

Spain's colonization of the Philippines occurred in stages throughout the sixteenth century. After Magellan's "discovery" in 1521, the Spanish Crown sent successive military expeditions to conquer the archipelago. One group led by the conquistador Barbosa landed on Mindanao in 1523, only to be slaughtered en masse by natives shortly after arrival.[30] Nevertheless, by the late sixteenth century Spain had progressively eroded the power of Islamic rulers in the Central and Northern Philippines. Miguel Lopez de Legazpi founded a permanent Spanish settlement on Cebu in 1565, and six years later colonial forces overran the Islamic stronghold of Manila. In 1578, Capt. Esteban Rodriguez de Figueroa, a companion of Legazpi, attacked Jolo in an attempt to force the Sulu Sultanate to accept Spanish sovereignty and convert to Roman Catholicism. The people there had "become Moros" by virtue of their conversion to Islam, Governor General Francisco de Sande wrote Figueroa. "You shall order them that there be not among them any more preachers of the sect of Muhammad, since it is evil and that of the Christians alone is good."[31]

Rather than submit to imperial rule and convert to Christianity, the Muslims of the Sulu Archipelago actively resisted Spain. This marked the beginning of three centuries of intermittent conflict between Spanish colonial forces and the peoples of the Southern Philippines. Figueroa became the notional "Governor of Mindanao" in 1596. He launched a campaign along the Rio Grande River in Maguindanao, only to be killed in battle near Tampacan.[32] Like their neighbors in Sulu, the Maguindanao people lived in alternating states of truce and warfare with Spain. Islam had spread there in the mid-fifteenth century, and Sultan Muhammad Kabungsuwan established a ruling dynasty in the sixteenth. It was not until the seventeenth century, however, that Sultan Dipituan Kudarat consolidated the sultanate's regional control.[33] A third center of Islamic culture was located northeast of Maguindanao near Lake Lanao. This was the home of the Maranao people, an inland group who mostly avoided Spain's attentions until the nineteenth century.[34]

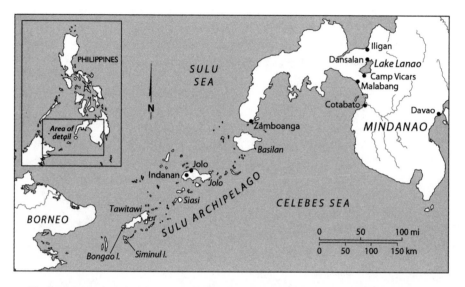

Figure 0.1 Mindanao and the Sulu Archipelago. Muslim populations are concentrated in Western Mindanao near Zamboanga, Lake Lanao, and Cotabato and in the islands of the Sulu chain. (Bill Nelson Cartography)

By the mid-seventeenth century, a discernible pattern emerged in Spanish-Muslim relations. Spain established small coastal outposts on Mindanao, which rose and fell depending on the intensity of conflict. During times of truce, Spanish traders and Jesuit missionaries appeared in the trading ports of Maguindanao, but control over the Muslim South was more the fantasy of administrators in Manila and Madrid than a practical reality. Spanish colonials established the southern colonial capital of Samboangan (later Zamboanga) in 1634, abandoned it in 1662, and only completed it in 1718.[35] Muslim raids on coastal communities and ships plagued the Spanish and Christianized native populations in Luzon and the Visayas. A vigorous slave trade emanated from the Dutch East Indies in the seventeenth and eighteenth centuries. For generations of young men in Mindanao-Sulu, trafficking in humans was a profitable enterprise. Although slavers themselves, Spanish colonials expressed outrage at the actions of the Moro pirates, writing of the indignities committed against Christians and attributing their own successes to divine will.[36]

Communities from North Mindanao to Luzon lived under the specter of violence during the eighteenth century. At times, more than a thousand Moros participated in raids, which occasionally ended in sieges. The community of Tandag, for instance, suffered through a four-month blockade in 1754.

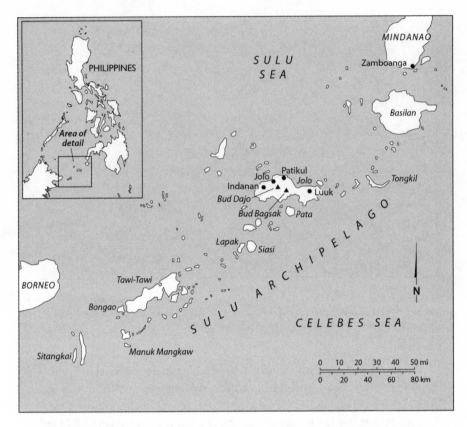

Figure 0.2 The Sulu Archipelago. Jolo is the political and cultural nucleus of the island chain, which stretches between the Zamboanga Peninsula and northeastern Borneo. (Bill Nelson Cartography)

After surrendering, the half-starved survivors became slaves and the raiders looted the town.[37] Moros resented Spain's conversionary zeal, viewed the empire as an economic competitor, and treated Filipinos as a source of profit. Situated amid the heterogeneous trade environment of Southeast Asia, the pirates found ready markets. Slaves not sold elsewhere played a pivotal role in Muslim societies, acting as the "dominant mode of production" in the Sulu Sultanate. In this "open" system of slavery, those captured eventually assimilated into the host society through labor and length of service.[38]

Spain's faltering position in Europe and the peripheral role the Philippines played in its empire benefitted the thriving Muslim societies of Mindanao-Sulu. In 1762, the British East India Company, keen on access to the China trade, occupied Manila and remained in power there for two years. This had limited impact on Sulu, which previously concluded a treaty with the Scottish geographer Alexander Dalrymple, who acted as a representative for the company.[39] In the late eighteenth century, a Spanish blockade of Cotabato reduced the power of the Maguindanao Sultanate, leaving Sulu as the dominant native polity in the Southern Philippines. Patricio Abinales and Donna Amoroso describe the eighteenth century as an impasse, where Mindanao-Sulu "represented a space *inside* the territory claimed by the Spanish that was *outside* the control of the state."[40] This stasis concluded only in the mid-nineteenth century, when technological advances—particularly the advent of military steamships—allowed the Spanish navy to erode the power of the sultanates. The concurrent European imperial marginalization of native polities across Southeast Asia further limited cultural and commercial mobilities.[41]

A series of military encounters with the Spanish between 1850 and 1877 doomed the Sulu Sultanate as an independent actor. Colonial forces repeatedly attacked Jolo, culminating in an 1876 invasion where they captured Jolo town. Spain removed outside threats to its control of Sulu by negotiating a free trade protocol with Great Britain and Germany, who desired unrestricted commercial access to the region. In July 1878, Sultan Jamalul Alam signed a treaty recognizing Spain's sovereignty in Sulu. The situation was unstable. Tausūg warriors—referred to as *juramentados*—routinely attacked Spanish troops garrisoned on Jolo, and the sultan's new residence at Maibun functioned as a site of resistance to foreign rule.[42] The governorship of Juan Arolas increased colonial coercion and deepened Tausūg enmity, as did Spain's installation of a pretender to the throne of Sulu.[43] This approach bore little fruit and was abandoned in 1894, when the Spanish recognized the young Jamalul Kiram II as sultan. Elsewhere, the Chinese-Moro arriviste Datu Piang collaborated with Spain to supplant his mentor, the capricious and unpopular Datu Uto, in Maguindanao. Like Kiram, Piang outlasted Spain by decades.[44] The Lake Lanao region remained problematic for the Spanish until the end. Campaigns directed by Valeriano Weyler, best known for his *reconcentración* policy in Cuba, made limited inroads, and in 1895, Governor General Ramon Blanco sent gunboats to attack Maranao cottas around the lake. English engineers and Chinese coolie laborers built a military road from coastal Iligan to Marawi at the northern end of Lanao. Despite these efforts, when the Spanish departed, the Maranao remained almost entirely unconquered.[45]

Spain ceded the Philippines to the United States through imperial transfer, formally signing over the archipelago in December 1898 at the Treaty of Paris. The United States' colonial inheritance included nominal sovereignty over the

Sulu Archipelago and Mindanao. Spain left behind public works that did not extend far beyond fortified coastal communities, a limited educational system that served some Christian Filipinos but was absent in Muslim areas, fragmented native power structures in states of flux (particularly in Lanao and Sulu), and a long legacy of cultural and military incursion. Preoccupied with matters in Luzon and the Visayas, the U.S. military did not relieve Spanish garrisons in Mindanao-Sulu until the spring of 1899, nearly a year after their arrival in the Philippines. U.S. commanders feared hostilities with the Muslims of the South would open new battlefronts and deplete military resources. With this in mind, they oriented their policies toward détente with Moro leaders in the understanding that conquest could occur once the North was pacified.

In July 1899, Eighth Army Corps commander Elwell S. Otis sent Brig. Gen. John Bates to Sulu and tasked him with negotiating on behalf of the U.S. government.[46] Bates looked to previous Spanish treaties and British native policy in Malaya for inspiration. The resulting agreement with Sultan Kiram—named after Bates—became the basis for U.S.-Tausūg cooperation during the following five years.[47] In Cotabato, military authorities found an ally in Datu Piang, who quickly pledged support for the United States' colonial project.[48] On the Zamboanga Peninsula, the Samal leader Datu Mandi became a key collaborator. Born to poor parents, Mandi fashioned a unique career as an interpreter of dialects for the Spanish on the island of Bongao. He traveled to the 1877 Amsterdam Exposition as a colonial subject and received numerous recognitions of merit from the Spanish government. In the 1880s and 1890s, the datu helped suppress juramentado attacks, supported vaccination campaigns, and provided relief services in the wake of an earthquake. Remaining neutral in the conflict between Filipino nationalists and the Spanish, Mandi recognized the 1899 U.S. arrival as an opportunity. His polyglot talents and ability to effectively mediate between locals and foreigners increased Mandi's value in the new colonial order. The Zamboanga Peninsula under his leadership remained mostly peaceful.[49]

Moro leaders managed the political and social affairs of their people during these first years. Nevertheless, certain cultural practices clashed with the sensibilities of the U.S. officer class. Military governors William A. Kobbé and George W. Davis objected to the persistence of slavery, polygamy, and draconian laws. Successive intelligence-gathering and surveying missions by the U.S. Army caused suspicion among Moros, and in 1901 Jolo became the site of running battles between Tausūg rebels and the Americans.[50] As battles in the North ended, the U.S. military began major military operations in Lanao. Beginning in 1902, Col. Frank Baldwin and Capt. John Pershing led successive punitive expeditions aimed at bringing Maranao datus under U.S. control. The Battle of Bayan, fought in May 1902, marked the first in a series of violent encounters between the U.S. military and Maranao warriors. Characterized by an asymmetry of firepower and resources, the clashes repeatedly ended in disproportionate losses of Moro life. After Bayan, the military governor Adna R. Chaffee wrote to Washington that the "trenches [were] lined with Moro dead," the number of which was "impossible to state." Chaffee thought that violence provided the "only kind of lesson these wild Moros seem to be able to profit by."[51]

Pershing and his men spent the next year stationed at Camp Vicars, a remote outpost at the southern tip of Lake Lanao. There they met with Maranao dignitaries and negotiated the terms of native submission. Cottas at Bacolod, Maciu, and Taraka shared Bayan's fate. Soldiers surveyed the land around Lanao and conducted a census, bringing the region under the surveilling gaze of the colonial state. The connections Pershing cultivated with collaborationist datus progressively marginalized those who looked upon the American presence with skepticism, driving resistance farther into the hinterlands of northern Mindanao. The conquest of the Maranao represented the last major hurdle in the initial consolidation of U.S. military rule in the Muslim South. While anticolonial activities did not cease, no Muslim-majority region remained outside of state control.[52]

Direct rule came with the establishment of the Moro Province in June 1903. Spurred by the 1902 Philippine Bill and Christian Filipino calls to integrate the South into the protonational body, U.S. military officials reoriented themselves toward long-term tutelage and state-building.[53] In September 1903, military officials reorganized the new province, which encompassed the Sulu Archipelago and most of Mindanao, into districts. Each district had its own governor (generally a U.S. military officer) and governing board. Provincial authorities refined the system further in 1904 by subdividing the districts into constituent municipalities and tribal wards. The latter denoted "uncivilized" populations (shorthand for Muslim and Lumad), who would be overseen by hand-selected native leaders with limited legal powers. The ultimate goal was the modernization of "non-Christian" societies.[54]

Districts fell under the supervision of the legislative council of the Moro Province, headed by Governor Leonard Wood. A Harvard-trained physician, Wood developed friendships with powerful political figures in the years preceding the Spanish-American War. He rose to prominence through his regimental command of the First Volunteer Cavalry Regiment—colloquially known as the Rough Riders—in Cuba, serving as military governor there before transferring to the Philippines in 1902. Dismissive of local customs in general and Islam in particular, Wood implemented a series of legislative acts aimed at transforming the region. Drawing on notes gathered during visits to European colonies, Wood and his team created new systems of taxation, made public education mandatory, devised forced-labor schemes, built up regional infrastructure, and enshrined new legal norms.[55]

The abrogation of the Bates Agreement in 1904 and invasiveness of new government initiatives (particularly the cedula poll tax) fueled discontent among Moros. Groups unwilling to submit to state impositions clashed with U.S. military forces. In Cotabato, disagreements over the slavery question and progressive economic marginalization led the Maguindanao royal Datu Ali and his followers to revolt. His insurrection began in early 1904 and lasted until his death in October 1905. U.S. newspapers followed the story, calling Ali "cunning as an Indian" and describing his supporters as "merciless, implacable, and in deadly earnest."[56] On Jolo, the U.S. Army ruthlessly suppressed uprisings. District Governor Hugh Scott led a large force against Panglima Hassan in late 1903, destroying cottas and settlements in the area around Lake Siet. The Americans cornered and killed Hassan in March 1904 near Bud Bagsak.[57] The violence of these early years peaked at Bud Dajo, an extinct volcano southeast of Jolo town. Hundreds of Tausūg peasants, unhappy with taxation and other colonial policies, fortified themselves there and prepared for a confrontation. The resulting battle was more of a massacre, leaving between seven and nine hundred Muslim men, women, and children dead.[58]

Leonard Wood departed the Moro Province in 1906. His successor, Brig. Gen. Tasker Bliss, was a more conciliatory figure. The Bliss years featured initiatives aimed at bringing Muslims into the colonial fold. Authorities toyed with the idea of integrating local educational practices into public schools and also placed greater emphasis on commerce as a civilizing agent. This coincided with a push to populate Mindanao and exploit its bounties. Districts advertised themselves in the northern Philippines as areas of overwhelming natural abundance, where an enterprising settler-capitalist could make his fortune. In Davao, a class of white planters began growing abaca and other agricultural products, a move supported by business elites in Zamboanga but viewed with skepticism by some government officials.[59] Battle weariness and Bliss's more diplomatic approach to governance led to a decrease in violence between 1906 and 1909, although colonial hard-liners worried "official laxity" would allow Muslim depredations to go unpunished. Leonard Wood was critical of Bliss's performance and Governor-General William Cameron Forbes called him a "misfit."[60]

The third and final governor of the Moro Province was John Pershing, who after a meteoric rise through the ranks returned to the Southern Philippines as a brigadier general. His tenure lasted from November 1909 until December 1913, when the South transitioned to civilian rule. Pershing hired more civilian officials, increased public works spending, and pushed for the expansion of state schools. He also oversaw a contentious disarmament campaign, which began in 1911 and sought to eliminate all unlicensed firearms from the province. Notoriously difficult standards for obtaining a weapons permit meant that most Moro guns had to be surrendered. Publicly carrying a barong or kris was also banned. The climax of the campaign occurred in June 1913 at Bud Bagsak on Jolo, where a group of defiant Tausūg stood in opposition to the new laws. Military forces killed nearly five hundred Moros during their attempt to capture the fortification.[61] With major resistance movements neutralized and disarmament completed, Pershing sent recommendations to Luzon that army rule conclude in Mindanao-Sulu. Cotabato was under the firm control of Datu Piang and had had no serious disturbances since Datu Ali's death; antibanditry campaigns had further pacified Lanao between 1908 and 1912; apart from a millenarian uprising by inland Lumad, the Zamboanga Peninsula was entirely stable; and Pershing's actions on Jolo had temporarily ebbed anticolonial struggle there. "General advancement has been made that surpasses in many respects the boasted progress of our more civilized provinces," Pershing bragged to the military commander of the Philippines, J. Franklin Bell.[62]

In Manila, the recently appointed Governor-General Francis Burton Harrison was receptive to Pershing's and Bell's suggestions. An appointee of the new Wilson administration, Harrison shared the Democratic Party's inclination to scale down the American presence in the Philippines. After an inspection tour of the South in 1913, he wrote of the "wonderful progress" made there and advocated U.S. military units be replaced by the Philippine Constabulary (PC).[63] Frank W. Carpenter replaced John Pershing as governor that December. A veteran of the colonial administration in Manila, Carpenter's career had culminated in a posting as executive secretary of the Insular Bureau. Admired by Republicans and Democrats alike, he was, according to Bell, "by long odds better qualified than anyone . . . to assume the important obligations of governor."[64]

The Moro Province officially became the Department of Mindanao and Sulu on July 23, 1914. Although Carpenter had been in office for nearly half a year, the name change and subsequent reorganization marked the terminal point of military rule in the Southern Philippines. Old districts like Cotabato,

Zamboanga, and Lanao became provinces, and Act No. 2408 of the Philippine Commission—colloquially known as the Organic Act—brought extensive administrative reform. The legislation restructured provincial boards and introduced limited democratic structures in an effort to integrate the South. By 1915, Christian-majority provinces were electing their provincial board members through popular vote, although in Muslim regions these appointments were dictated by colonial elites. The municipal district replaced the tribal ward system, and state bureaucracies merged with government departments in Manila. Between 1914 and 1920, tax collection, prisons, public works, education, health care, and the legal system became increasingly harmonized with Luzon and the Visayas. In conception and practice, the Department of Mindanao and Sulu was part of a nation-building exercise.[65]

Reordering Mindanao-Sulu coincided with the larger process of "Filipinization," which saw Americans moved out of government and replaced by Christian Filipinos. The First World War expedited this transition. With increased prospects in the private sector and incentivized retirement packages, many Americans left government service. There remained a strong contingent in Washington and Manila who felt that those who built up the colonial Philippines were being treated unfairly and that Filipinos were unfit for leadership and political independence. Nevertheless, the Jones Law of 1916, which created a fully elected Filipino legislature, further entrenched the shift. By the end of Harrison's tenure in 1921, Filipinos directed nearly all major government bureaus.[66]

Filipinization meant an influx of Christian Filipino bureaucrats in predominantly Muslim areas. This created tensions. Many Moros detested the Filipinos, fearing they heralded the imposition of a monolithic national culture that would dissolve ethnoreligious bonds in Muslim communities. Harrison and Carpenter described the period as one of increasing "good-will and confidence" between Christians and Muslims, but Moro petitions in the 1920s and 1930s contest this reading.[67] Nationalist politicians like Sergio Osmeña attempted to frame the "separation and differences" between Christians and non-Christians as political. The problem, he wrote, was that "non-Christians" viewed Christian Filipinos as aligned with "foreign dominators" and as "anxious to pervert them" through conversion. Willful or not, this was a misreading of Muslim anxieties, which became increasingly centered on notions of the Filipino as "foreign dominator" and not the American.[68]

The Carpenter years marked the end of the Sulu Sultanate as an acknowledged political entity. In March 1915, Carpenter negotiated an updated treaty with Sultan Kiram wherein the ruler forfeited his "pretensions of sovereignty."

The state now recognized Kiram as the "titular spiritual head" of the Muslim faithful in Sulu, a designation that granted him the comparably limited powers of an ecclesiastical authority in the United States. He gave up any right to adjudicate on legal matters, although continued to secretly oversee religious courts.[69] Carpenter's administration also furthered the Moro Province's developmentalist policies, deepened commercial links between the Southern Philippines and Southeast Asia, and expanded lumber and mining operations. Educational staff increased sevenfold between 1913 and 1919, and many new hospitals and dispensaries opened.[70]

With support from Manila politicians, Carpenter began promoting the South as a zone of settlement for landless northerners, incentivizing homesteading through the establishment of agricultural colonies. "Mindanao-Sulu no longer is a frontier attractive only to the adventurous," Carpenter wrote in his 1916 annual report, "but has not progressed to a state warranting the favorable attention of the capitalist and the home seeker."[71] The Jones Law reconstituted the Bureau of Non-Christian Tribes in 1916 to "foster the moral, material, economic, social, and political development" of nonintegrated peoples and territories. Carpenter served as bureau chief from 1918 until his retirement from government service in 1920, when he was replaced by his deputy, the jurist and politician Teofisto Guingona. The Department of Mindanao and Sulu was abolished in February 1920, with ultimate authority over "non-Christian" regions transferring to the bureau.[72]

In 1921, President Warren Harding sent a fact-finding mission led by Leonard Wood and William Cameron Forbes to the Philippines. Acknowledged Anglo-Saxon supremacists, both men questioned Filipino capacity for self-government and eyed Filipinization suspiciously. The report of the Wood-Forbes mission was a compendious accounting of the failures of Democratic appointees and the Filipino political class in the previous eight years. Wood and Forbes called any move toward independence a "distinct step backward in the path of progress" and a "betrayal of the Philippine people." Harding and his cabinet agreed that rapid Filipinization represented a "discreditable neglect" of national duty and subsequently appointed Wood as governor-general of the islands.[73]

Wood's return to the Philippines lasted until his death in 1927. During this time, he was deeply unpopular with pro-independence Filipinos, who found his racial paternalism jarring after the comparatively amiable relations of the Harrison years. In the Muslim South, Moro resistance against education and taxation escalated again. Lanao and Cotabato experienced ongoing disturbances over compulsory public schooling. Scores of Maranao and Maguindanao protesters died in confrontations with Constabulary forces. In the late 1920s, more than twenty schools were burned in Lanao, and public education in the province came to a standstill. The islands of the Sulu Archipelago experienced similar issues, with a revolt breaking out in 1927. Outlaw bands became a concern for the Constabulary across multiple provinces. Faced with an uncertain future, the cultural and political landscape of Mindanao-Sulu resisted stabilization.[74]

Muslim political elites courted both pro- and anti-independence figures among the American and Filipino leaderships. Westernized figures like Gulamu Rasul, Hadji Butu, and Arolas Tulawie advocated for Muslim rights within the government, favoring a continued American presence. In the 1920s and 1930s, Moro groups sent numerous petitions to American political figures in Manila and Washington imploring intervention against Filipino nationalist designs. The petitions warned of strife should the Americans leave, playing into a "myth of ungovernability" that had persisted since the Spanish period.[75] A 1934 plea to Governor-General Frank Murphy from Lanao datus requested that Mindanao-Sulu be separated from any "independent Philippines."[76] These tactics exploited paternalist concerns in the United States, where policy makers believed Moros would only thrive if shielded from Filipino hegemony. Despite these entreaties, many Muslim leaders played both sides during this uncertain period. These vagaries of allegiance, writes Patricio Abinales, "were less the actions of slick operators . . . than of a local elite unsure of its fate."[77]

The question of partition loomed in the 1920s, as it had for American settlers in Mindanao decades earlier.[78] Representative Robert L. Bacon tabled a bill in the U.S. Senate in 1926 that sought to permanently divide Mindanao-Sulu from the remainder of the Philippine Archipelago. Leonard Wood and others supported it, but the bill failed to gain traction stateside. After Wood's sudden death in 1927, the idea of partition receded as the colonial state moved toward an independent Philippines that included the Muslim regions of the South.[79] A major step in this direction was the Tydings-McDuffie Act of 1934, which set terms for independence. A transitional commonwealth period of ten years began with the drafting of a national constitution and the election of the country's first president, Manuel Quezon, in 1935.[80] In Mindanao-Sulu, a younger generation of Muslim leaders trained in colonial schools reconciled themselves to the realities of Filipinization and began identifying as "Muslim Filipinos," using their minority religious identity as a means of promoting their interests within a diffuse political landscape.[81]

In 1936, a parliamentary committee seeking the normalization of Muslim territories abolished the Bureau of Non-Christian Tribes, replacing it with a special commissioner for Mindanao-Sulu. That same year, the death of Sultan Kiram created an opportunity for the government to end all recognition of customary titles.[82] A small but influential group of Americans remained in Mindanao-Sulu after 1935, although almost all white settlers had departed. Instead, the state incentivized Christian settlers from Luzon and the Visayas to venture south, promoting Mindanao as a fertile utopia. Migration began to change the demographics of the region, and large infrastructural projects became the order of the day. Plans for transprovincial highways, hydroelectric dams, airfields, shipping lines, and railroads represented a new connectivity between North and South. Eagerly covered by the Manila press, these developments masked lingering conflicts. Lanao remained a center of antistate activity. When the Constabulary there proved insufficiently able to quell resistance, the Philippine military moved in, using artillery and air power against Maranao cottas. Entrenched patterns of defiance and massacre continued. This tense integration temporarily halted with the Japanese invasion in 1941, which forced Moros, Filipinos, and Americans to contend with a new imperial power.

What Follows

"There is no reason why the Anglo-Saxon settler, that worldwide conqueror of the soil, should not come into this country and 'repair the waste places' and 'cast up a highway' for prosperity," a 1906 editorial in the *Mindanao Herald* declared.[83] The *Herald*'s feverish advocacy for white settlement and rapid economic exploitation of the South drew exploratory committees from Manila, politicians from Washington, and capitalist firms from other Southeast Asian colonies. Yet the paper was only one voice in a crowded colonial landscape. The archival record is populated with prognostications, blueprints, and reservations about how to proceed in Mindanao-Sulu. These competing and coalescing ideas formed the backbone of the civilizing mission, which was always more homogenous in its goals than its methods of application. This variability makes drawing a clean narrative line from John Bates's parlay with the sultan of Sulu in 1899 to the Japanese invasion of Mindanao at the end of 1941 difficult.

This book attends to the history of colonial Mindanao-Sulu through seven interconnected chapters. With the above chronology providing a contextual anchor, each thematic section moves across decades to explore the construction and contestation of imperial modalities. Doing so involves parsing a tremendous amount of documentation. Americans are admittedly the primary denizens of the colonial archives, although wherever possible these chapters incorporate non-Western voices or else identify idiosyncratic moments where colonial agents abandoned mechanistic governmentspeak and revealed complex personal views. The individual and group biographies within humanize otherwise oblique colonial processes, illustrating the calculations and costs of rule. Each chapter takes a critical approach to official histories and makes use of diverse sources. Dime novels, children's radio programs, motion pictures, advertisements, yellow journalism, speeches, personal correspondence, poetry, diary entries, marginalia, captions scrawled on timeworn photographs, fair pamphlets, student journals, petitions, cablegrams, and dinner menus populate these pages, serving as valuable tools of historical reconstruction.

This project addresses a number of crucial questions. How was the category of "Moro" constructed in the U.S. colonial imagination? What did the civilizing mission in Mindanao–Sulu look like when applied to subject groups? How did colonial frontier conflict and prevalent racial concepts inform the practice of state violence and confinement? What anxieties existed among Americans in the Southern Philippines, and how did they reveal themselves? How did Moros appear in the United States, and what forms of cultural exchange occurred between colony and metropole? And finally, what arcs of connectivity existed between the Muslim South and the imperially saturated world of the early twentieth century? The following chapters address these concerns, forming a mutually constitutive tapestry that probes the manifestations of a U.S. colonial state.

Our story begins with ideas, moves into practice, and is textured by connection and exchange. In the nineteenth century, the Southern Philippines appeared in U.S. culture through dubious press accounts, fleeting exploratory contact, and academic texts. The production of racial and territorial knowledge assumed greater importance after 1899, when incoming American soldier-officials scrambled to glean as much information about their new Muslim wards as possible. Chapter 1 explores the ways Americans understood the Muslim South and its inhabitants. The construction of "the Moro" arose from eclectic sources: translated Spanish books, North American frontier expansion, imperial readings of Islam, ethnographic study, and the cultivation of regional expertise. Governors, district administrators, missionaries, and businessmen instrumentalized these ideas in structures they created in the South. Establishing new laws, modernizing Moros through education, introducing Western forms of market capitalism, and inducing sedentism became paramount to the colonial state. Chapters 2 and 3 reveal the complex histories of these programs, which ranged from wide-reaching government initiatives to privately financed missionary endeavors.

Violence permeated the colonial experience. The state imposed its radically transformative agendas under threat of force, using firepower to consolidate rule and punish errant behavior. Moros appeared in official correspondence and newspaper articles as a race habituated to suicidal violence, engendering fear and fury among the colonial soldiery. How military and civilian officials folded massacre and confinement into the pedagogical language of the civilizing mission is the terrain of chapter 4, which parses the violence that accompanied and facilitated colonial modernization schemes. In the midst of these disorientations, American colonials carved out rationalized zones in which to live and labor. In communities like Zamboanga and Dansalan, Moro Province officials engaged in "tropically appropriate" urban planning and reproduced leisure norms found elsewhere in the colonized world. Pervasive environmental and racial anxieties muddied these paradisiac visions, however. Chapter 5 moves amid the Euro-American colonizers of Mindanao-Sulu, traversing the landscapes they built around and within themselves.

The colonized likewise traveled amid foreign landscapes. In the early twentieth century, Moros visited the United States as objects of display, touring aristocrats, and college students. U.S. newspapers followed closely as they met with presidents, performed for midwestern crowds, took in the Manhattan skyline, and embraced collegiate life. Moros also appeared in assorted fictions. Comic operas, children's adventure stories, radio serials, and motion pictures manufactured Muslim colonial subjects, presenting them in varied ways to a curious public. Chapter 6 sifts through these real and imagined visits and considers how empire came home. Beyond colony and metropole, Moros and Americans negotiated an increasingly globalized world. The final chapter considers the role of diverse interactivities in shaping the encounter in Mindanao-Sulu. Despite its portrayal as a colonial backwater, the region maintained its own culturally hybrid character, facilitated by links to maritime Southeast Asia and the wider Muslim world. U.S. actors moved within European colonial circles, gleaning what they could and imparting their own expertise. Some even integrated non-Western empires into their fantasies of transformation. Beyond the obscuring language of American exceptionalism, these multiscalar connections underwrote imperial power in the Southern Philippines.

Chapter 1

Imagining the Moro

Racial and Spatial Fantasies in Mindanao-Sulu

A sense of mission drove American colonials in the Southern Philippines. "Let not the future historian say that the American nation has travelled halfway around the earth in order to degrade and debase a people instead of exalting it," declared Governor Tasker Bliss at the 1907 Zamboanga Fair. He urged the assembled Americans and Europeans to act as "exemplars and mentors of the people among whom you live" and reminded them of their "great power for good and evil."[1] Amid the crowd was a healthy cross-section of the South's Euro-American community, gathered together to celebrate their achievements. Over time, these men and women had developed their own notions of the colonized peoples and territories surrounding them. Such notions are evident in texts from the period and illustrate how Americans attempted to compile a stabilizing archive of racial knowledge. They did so publicly and privately, in published travelogues and periodical articles, in official dispatches and memoranda, in personal letters and journal entries, and in lectures and speeches. Exaltation and debasement, to adopt Bliss's phrasing, coursed through their descriptions, categorizations, and fantasies, underwriting the programs enacted by the colonial regime in Mindanao-Sulu.[2]

This chapter explores the production of racial and territorial knowledge on the Philippines' southern frontier. Through acts of borrowing and creation, Americans composed composite sketches of the natives of the Southern Philippines and the landscapes they inhabited. Their writings varied in form and content. Some texts sensationalized the South, while others attempted rigorous documentation. Authors drew on contemporary tropes about "uncivilized" peoples and "empty" lands, familiarizing themselves with Mindanao-Sulu through their participation in a transimperial economy of ideas.[3] Many of those posted in the Southern Philippines were traveling abroad for the first time. Inscribing peoples and spaces with unitary identities rendered them knowable, lessening fear and alienation.[4] Meshing observation and imagination, Americans became enthusiastic participants in the "racial-cultural mappings and classifications" that powered colonial regimes throughout the globe.[5]

Inert perceptual strategy met colonial praxis in the idea of transformation. Savage peoples could be either civilized or else justifiably eliminated; likewise, native claims to land deemed unoccupied or underutilized could be marginalized in favor of colonial development schemes. U.S. officials mobilized potent imaginative linkages between Muslim Moros and Native Americans as they designed native policy in Mindanao-Sulu. For some, mistakes made on the North American frontier could be redeemed through work among the Moros. Others had bleaker outlooks, believing Muslim and Lumad groups unassimilable.[6] The land itself, especially the vast interior of Mindanao, became a frontier zone of limitless economic and "romantic" potential ready to be rationalized and settled by capable migrants.[7] The result of colonial state-building in far-flung regions, according to evangelizers like Josiah Strong, would be a nation infused with greatness.[8] Although self-identifying as reluctant imperialists, Americans believed their "practical" tendencies and "keenness of intellect" gave them an exceptional ability to understand and reconfigure the peoples and spaces they governed. With these assets in mind, they set about doing so.[9]

Describing Moros

"The Moro" existed as a racial category in the American colonial imagination decades before battalions of the 23rd Infantry landed on Jolo in 1899. British accounts of the Sulu Sea circulated in the United States from the late eighteenth century onward, including Alexander Dalrymple's *An Historical Collection of the Several Voyages and Discoveries in the South Pacific Ocean* and Thomas Forrest's *Voyage to New Guinea and the Moluccas from Balambangan*. Dalrymple enumerated the region's natural resources while Forrest studied the cultures of Sulu and Western Mindanao.[10] Newspaper articles from the antebellum period intermeshed orientalist tropes of fantasy, danger, and wealth in their reporting on the Southern Philippines. Piracy and pearls became defining features of the region in the 1820s. *The American* provided grave reports of the piratical activities of the "Moors . . . from the Sooloo Archipelago and Min-danao," who captured and ransomed Spanish colonials stationed around Zamboanga.[11] Amid the threat, however, were the "famous Sooloo Pearl Banks, celebrated for the fine and large pearls which they produce."[12]

In 1842, the U.S. Exploring Expedition briefly stopped in the Southern Philippines near the end of its four-year, 87,000-mile Pacific journey. Alongside practical goals of securing the safety of U.S. whaling grounds and gaining access to the China trade, the expedition also mapped the foreign peoples it encountered—a task already well under way among American missionaries of the time. The studies compiled by the expedition's mercurial leader Lt. Charles Wilkes and his scientific staff "served as ethnological primers on the world's indigenous cultures" and contained within them a "racial *weltanschauung*" that anticipated future imperial ventures.[13] En route to the Zamboanga Peninsula from Luzon, Wilkes and his men collected Spanish cartographic information about the Sulu Sea and read Dalrymple's accounts of the region from seven decades prior.[14] Sailing through the Mindoro Strait, the crew noticed "telegraphs of rude construction" that warned villages of "the approach of piratical prahus from Sooloo."[15] The expedition first laid anchor at Caldera, a Spanish fortification northeast of the regional capital at Zamboanga, and went ashore to study their surroundings. Here they took in a small sampling of Mindanao's incredible biodiversity and noted that the island's interior was so fearsome—filled with "wild beasts, serpents, and hostile natives"—that the Spanish ventured there rarely and only in numbers.[16]

The squadron spent more time at Jolo, enchanted by the environment but skeptical of the natives. According to the crewmember John Jenkins, the serenity of the island was "destroyed in part by the knowledge that this beautiful archipelago [is] the abode of a cruel and barbarous race of pirates."[17] Writing in the popular physiognomical style, Jenkins, Wilkes, and the philologist Horatio Hale gave descriptions of "tall, thin, and effeminate looking" islanders who had "faces . . . peculiar for length, particularly in the lower jaw and chin, with high cheekbones, sunken lack-lustre eyes, and narrow foreheads." Physical descriptors predictably segued into moral condemnation. The natives had "but few qualities to redeem their treachery, cruelty, and revengeful dispositions."[18] The naturalist Charles Pickering and sailor Joseph G. Clark both wrote of the Malay penchant for acts of suicidal violence.[19] During their stay on Jolo, the expedition engaged in a program of frenzied observation and accumulation. Wilkes compiled a meticulous political and cultural history of the region, detailing fishing habits, sartorial styles, social rituals, religious practices, laws, and the personal hygiene of the islanders. He paid particular attention to piratical activities, including the seasonal fluctuations in raiding, composition of Iranun and Samal raiding parties, and economic relationships between the marauders and the Tausūg elite.[20] The crew's scholars collected flora and fauna, took scientific readings, and bought local manufactures.[21]

On February 5, 1842, Wilkes secured a treaty with the sultan of Sulu guaranteeing the right of safe passage for U.S. vessels in the archipelago, granting favored trading status, offering protections for shipwrecked sailors, and meting out punishment for any subject of the sultan who attacked a U.S. ship. The fleet departed for Singapore shortly thereafter.[22] The expedition's writers provided a collective portrait of Jolo and its inhabitants that mixed curiosity and condescension. Interactions with the Muslim "pirates" were pregnant with threat, and the denigration of their material, moral, and civilizational states contained implicit suggestions of Anglo-Saxon supremacy. These potentially fraught encounters, however, served as useful exercises in expanding American spatial and racial imaginaries. The works published by Wilkes and his crew after returning to the United States spanned twenty-four titles over the next three decades. Until the 1890s, the fifth volume of Wilkes's narrative, Charles Pickering's *The Races of Man and Their Geographical Distribution*, and the crewmember Joseph G. Clark's memoirs remained among the most thorough English-language resources on the Islamic Philippines.

Between the 1840s and 1890s, eclectic accounts of the region surfaced in the United States. Sensationalist news reports sought to link archipelagic piracy to the global threat of Islam; fiction writers published tales of American sailors using the "hot water cure" to defend themselves against "bloodthirsty Sooloos"; and scholars built on the intellectual labors of the expedition.[23] This precolonial accumulation and creation of ethnographic data ensured a nation entering the imperial arena would come "equipped with well-wrought images [of] colonized cultures."[24] Nowhere was this compulsion more evident than in the writings of the University of Michigan zoologist Dean C. Worcester, who would eventually become a towering figure in the colonial administration of the islands. Published on the eve of the Spanish-American War, *The Philippine Islands and Their People* became a guide for curious Americans. Transforming his field notes into modes of racial classification, Worcester assessed the civilizational capacities of the archipelago's various ethnocultural groups. With colonization looming, his expertise and willingness to attack the Spanish Empire publicly became an invaluable asset for the McKinley administration.[25]

Working in the tradition of the German ethnographer Ferdinand Blumentritt, the zoologist-turned-ethnologist attempted to map the peoples of the

Philippines.[26] Despite a scholarly pedigree, Worcester had a flair for the dramatic, describing the "fanatical passions of the fierce Moro warriors" and their depredations against Spanish and Filipino populations. The "Sulu Moro" possessed "inhuman cruelty . . . and [would] cut down a slave merely to try the edge of a new barong." Journeying through Mindanao-Sulu, Worcester blended travel narrative, ethnographic ranking, and editorial commentary under the umbrella of dispassionate academic study. Although praised as such, many of his observations were hardly original. On topics related to the Islamic Philippines, they resembled much of what had come before. The "inhuman cruelty" of the "Sulu Moro" meshed well with the murderous pirates described by Wilkes and other writers, suggesting a common reservoir of derogatory images and assumptions had developed by the late nineteenth century.[27]

These ideas traveled freely across the 1898 divide, deepening as Americans familiarized themselves with their new territories. As he prepared to meet with the sultan of Sulu, John Bates read materials produced by the U.S. Exploring Expedition, translated Spanish texts, and studied British treaties with native leaders in the Malay states.[28] The negotiated conquest of the Islamic Philippines generated significant interest in the United States, where news outlets accentuated the primitive exoticism of the Moros in their descriptions of the Bates Agreement. Piracy, slavery, polygamy, tropical illness, and extreme violence wove their way through the articles, which mixed sober reportage with imaginative fictions. Anna Northend Benjamin, one of the first white women to visit Jolo, warned Americans of the Tausūg penchant for violence in the pages of *Outlook Magazine*. The *Chicago Daily Tribune* disparaged the Muslim's "inborn hatred" of Christians but concluded Bates had secured a fair deal with Sultan Kiram.[29] These accounts from the first months of colonial rule combined the picturesque and the abject.

First impressions were often lasting ones. Many colonials arriving in Mindanao-Sulu had never traveled beyond the continental United States, something especially true among enlisted men. In their writings, soldiers blended pseudoanthropological observation with the sensationalism of the dime novel. Walter Cutter, serving with the 17th Infantry on Jolo in 1901, had a low opinion of the island's inhabitants. The Tausūg Moros were "religious fanatics, and it would be hard to find a more ignorant and filthy set of savages anywhere." Their religion made them "fanatics" of the same stripe as the "Mad Mullah's forces" in the "Soudan" during the 1880s. By invoking Charles Gordon's stand against the Sudanese Mahdi army at Khartoum, the young soldier collapsed time and space to render his new surroundings legible. Facing the Moro at the fringes of empire was in the grand tradition of the colonial army as a bulwark against savagery.[30]

In his memoirs, 6th Cavalry officer Charles Rhodes likewise resorted to essentialized depictions of the environment and peoples of the Sulu Archipelago. The town of Jolo was "fabled in song and story with the glamor of romance and adventure" but also a space where "American soldiers courted death at the hands of crazed fanatics, and fired fruitless shots in mystic darkness at shadowy forms." In his descriptions, the town became an Arabian souk, where datus, "colorful in red fezzes and gold tinsel, rattled jeweled daggers in the face of the American governor."[31] Capt. Matthew F. Steele described the island of Jolo in similarly fantastical terms, noting that it was home to "60,000 of the most hostile, unconquerable, dangerous savages the American army has ever met."[32] In these writings, the Moros were templates for literary savagery, colorful yet exceedingly dangerous barbarians who served as excellent foils to American colonial forces. Influenced by the romantic narrative traditions of European imperialism, soldiers in the Muslim South presented their experiences as vivid oriental tableaus.

For military men, the Moro presented certain complexities. Soldiers spoke with a grudging respect for the fighting prowess and independence of the Muslim peoples of Mindanao-Sulu yet were also exasperated that these same qualities made them resistant to the civilizing prerogatives of the colonial state. Leonard Wood's aide Frank McCoy noted the general unruliness of the Moros, claiming that most were friendly but that in each region existed a handful of datus who "wouldn't obey any orders except for their own." He compared the Moro leadership with the "fierce individualism of chiefs of the highlands of Scotland" and marveled at how the Lake Lanao region alone had an estimated 219 sultans during the military campaigns of 1902–1903.[33] U.S. military officers considered the perceived willfulness of the Moros as both virtue and weakness, depending on the context, and constructed racial typologies in the belief they would aid pacification.

From the signing of the Bates Agreement onward, piracy and the slave trade became touchstones in nearly every Western description of the peoples of Mindanao-Sulu. As Michael Salman has shown, Americans integrated the slavery question—and the role of piracy in facilitating slaving—into broader ideological and religious debates. The United States, less than forty years removed from chattel slavery when it acquired Spain's colonies, sent its agents forth with designs to remap labor and social relations in the Southern Philippines. The colonially generated "Moro" did not have his own constellation of societal structures and primarily existed as a degenerate slaver, pirate, and polygamist. Slavery under the American flag was, to borrow from Salman, an "embarrassment" and one that needed challenging. U.S. military officials, politicians, religious leaders, and moral reformers believed eliminating the twin evils of slavery and piracy (the latter term often used to describe any form of maritime commerce operating outside of colonial regulatory networks) was a national duty and inextricably bound to reforming Islam in Southeast Asia.[34]

Vic Hurley placed special emphasis on the role of piracy in Muslim Malay cultures. His popular history of the Southern Philippines, *The Swish of the Kris*, trafficked in common stereotypes about the Moros yet was not entirely unsympathetic. Although these "bloodthirsty" pirates engaged in wanton "murder and rapine," they also waged a "just war" against "land grabbing aggressors."[35] Sydney Cloman, the first military commander of the Tawi-Tawi island group, claimed he recognized the "ancestral microbe" of piracy in the Moros he governed and devoted a chapter of his memoirs to describing a standoff he had with a local datu who was sheltering a pirate on the island of Siminul.[36] The longtime PC officer John R. White saw the Moros as unwilling to bend to "any form of government that curbed piracy and slavery and operated for the rights of man." Like Cloman and Hurley, White admitted that the Moros practiced a milder form of slavery than what had existed in the American South but noted that resistance to its abolition was a constant. His solution was to channel the "racial emotions" and violent energies of the Moros by enlisting them in the Constabulary. If the spirited nature of the Moro could not be eliminated, it could at least be redirected.[37]

Piracy, slavery, and fanaticism inevitably became entangled in questions surrounding Islam. From its inception, the civilizing mission in the Southern Philippines relied on a Protestant world view that portrayed oriental creeds as antique and degraded. Americans believed Islamic religious practices amplified the savage racial characteristics of the colonized. The act of "going juramentado"—publicly executing nonbelievers in the name of the faith— brought this notion into vivid relief. In popular accounts, the monotheism of Islam simultaneously raised the Moros above their animist neighbors yet also relegated them to a state of retarded civilization. The *Boston Globe* summed up this view, observing "the question of religious fanaticism are here added to those of barbarism, for the Moros, although they are Mahometans, are little better than savages."[38] To some Americans, the Moros were not even properly Islamic, and the religion's syncretic interweaving with preexisting regional practices became evidence of incomplete Islamization.[39] A 1914 government report noted the role of superstition in the local pandita (religious) schools, and the Philippine Scouts officer Charles Ivins estimated that the "veneer of Mohammedanism lays only lightly over a base of animism and superstition."[40] On an expedition to the Mindanao interior, the Constabulary officer Sterling Larrabee commented on local Moro belief in the spiritual qualities of "trees, stones, and wood spirits" and compared them with the Lumad tribes of the region.[41]

Religion implicated Moro groups in broader struggles between the Christian and Muslim worlds. Bishop Charles Brent saw the fight against the "semi-savagery and mad fanaticism" of the Moros in terms of a moral mission, believing the Moros were the inheritors of the worst elements of global Islam. The juramentado was a direct heir to the "fatalism" of the Mahdi army in Sudan (a recurring point of reference, it would seem), and the Islamic world was a "unified and sensitive organ." Through the perfidious influence of "Arab priests" in Mindanao-Sulu, the Moros acquired a deep-seated hatred of the Americans. Brent lobbied the government to restrict all Arab immigration to the Philippines.[42] The missionary-journalist Henry O. Dwight also saw the Moro problem in border-crossing terms. Writing from his American Board of Commissioners for Foreign Missions posting in Constantinople, Dwight cited long passages from the Qur'an on jihad and warned of pan-Islamic revival. The Moros, Dwight wrote, were "imperfect and ignorant Mohammedans," thus making them easier prey for foreign religious teachers. His dark suggestions for counteracting militant Islam in Mindanao-Sulu looked to past instances of colonial violence for instruction. The Americans would have to "strike without conscience . . . literally killing every living thing." Dwight's radical solutions stemmed from the belief that Islamic "fanaticism" could only be met in kind, an outlook that would be adopted to deadly effect by military authorities in later years.[43]

Dueling monotheisms met in comparisons between Moro groups and Christian Filipinos. The latter appeared in colonialist literature as both blessed and burdened by the legacy of Spanish colonialism. The Filipinos had Christianity, but of a Catholic variety looked down on by the American Protestant elite. The same applied to their familiarity with the socioeconomic structures of Western modernity, which had been shaped by outmoded Spanish models. Although savage and premodern, the Moros had no such baggage. Their long-maintained independence from Spain made them, in the eyes of Americans, nobler than the Filipinos. In the Moros "the *conquistadores* met their masters," Vic Hurley wrote.[44] This contrasted with the more typically "oriental" Filipinos, who appeared in American literature as servile and sensuous characters. The journalist Atherton Brownell used music as an entry point for comparison. In the North, the music was "in a minor strain, soft, plaintive, appealing,

and pathetic." In the South, "the major note is struck . . . dominant and thrill-
ing and characteristic of the people."[45] Such comparatives underwrote U.S.
military rule in the Muslim South. During his tenure as governor, John Pershing argued the Filipinos possessed none of the traits necessary to govern the
Moros. "They are in no sense brothers, but are irreconcilable strangers and
enemies in every sense," he wrote. Pershing was unequivocal in his belief that
the Moros, being the stronger of the two peoples, would make quick work of
any Filipino attempt to govern the South.[46]

Moro women elicited varied responses from Americans. The military governor William A. Kobbé wrote in his diary of the "very comely" Maguindanao women of the Cotabato district and the "uncommonly fine looking
native women" he met at a banquet held in Zamboanga.[47] The tendency to
blur ethnographic description with the fetishization of "primitive" sexuality
was evident in a 1900 dispatch from Lanao in the *Atlanta Constitution*. Maranao women assembled alongside the sultan of Mindanao were "basically naked with the exception of one strip of cloth" that the reporter feared "would
slip to the ground."[48] Other accounts aimed to rouse readers in other ways by
depicting Moro women as debased. The newsman Carl Taylor emphasized defeminized barbarism in his accounts of Moro women fighting alongside men,
dubiously suggesting they would "seize their babies and hurl them upon ad-
vancing bayonets" before dying.[49] Writers also denigrated the tendency of
Moro women to chew teeth-staining betel nut and interrogated their clothing choices. Florence Kimball Russel found it difficult to differentiate between
the men and women because both sexes wore similar garb. She disparagingly
noted that the women were "much less attractive than the men, being quite
as unprepossessing in appearance, and lacking the redeeming strength and sym-
metry which gave beauty to the masculine figure."[50]

While sensationalism and generalization dominated public discourse on
the Moros, some U.S. colonials stationed in Mindanao-Sulu did attempt more
sober studies of their wards. Inspired by the work of nineteenth-century ethnologists, these knowledge-production projects rested on the idea that textured study could help channel the energies of subject groups toward colonial
modernity.[51] Intelligence reports, regional histories, translated native texts,
vocabulary guides, and other material all fed into this project of control and
transformation. The push to catalog cultures in Mindanao-Sulu was at its
height during the Moro Province years but did persist afterward through the
individual efforts of missionaries, scholars, schoolteachers, and government
bureaucrats.

Early American expertise on Moro and Lumad populations stemmed largely from one man: Najeeb Mitry Saleeby. A Protestant Lebanese physician and naturalized American citizen, Saleeby traveled to the Philippines as an assistant surgeon in the U.S. Army Volunteers and was posted in Southern Mindanao in mid–1901. Familiar with Islamic culture, fluent in Arabic, and keen to study the Moros, the young doctor increasingly took on the role of an intelligence officer within the military apparatus. In time, Saleeby learned Tausūg and Maguindanao scripts and became conversant in local dialects, allowing him to function as a transcultural intermediary. Released from military service in early 1903, he was appointed assistant to the chief of the Bureau of Non-Christian Tribes in charge of Moro affairs, where he worked alongside the bureau head (and noted anthropologist) David Prescott Barrows cataloging the cultures of the Southern Philippines. This included the assiduous collection of genealogical data and information on native legal structures.[52] Saleeby's most prominent role was as superintendent of schools for the Moro Province between 1903 and 1906, a civilian voice on a legislative council dominated by military men. As superintendent, he argued for a moderate approach to Moro issues that often clashed with the style of direct rule favored by Governor Leonard Wood and his deputies. Although never fully integrated into the Anglo-Saxon world of these military elites, Saleeby was nevertheless recognized as the preeminent expert on the Moros within the colonial regime. His two books on the region and its peoples appeared in 1905 and 1908, each commissioned by governmental agencies involved in ethnological study.[53]

Unlike others, Najeeb Saleeby was uninterested in portraying the Moros through the lens of orientalist threat or titillation. In his 1905 work, *Studies in Moro History, Law, and Religion*, Saleeby translated numerous genealogical manuscripts (*tarsilas*) into English. Alongside the original text, he provided running commentary that considered questions of authorship, dialect, and textual alteration over the centuries. He noted in his translation of the "Genealogy of Maguindanao and the Iranun Datus," for instance, that the reliability of the text varied from manuscript to manuscript but still provided insight into the "nature and tribal characteristics of the datuships and Moro communities."[54] Published three years later, Saleeby's *The History of Sulu* tracked the evolution of an archipelagic sultanate from the pre-Islamic period until the Spanish evacuation in 1899. Written as a primer for Americans interested in their new maritime possessions, the book contained far more narrative than *Studies in Moro History* but was likewise appended with translated letters, reports, protocols, and decrees. Saleeby claimed that being neither "a Sulu . . . [or] a

Spaniard" allowed him to relay history without "prejudice or bias" and "throw light on the actual conditions of life among the Moros."[55] While Saleeby overstated his impartiality, he did offer a sophisticated consideration of the Moros backed by deep research. His writings remained an important resource for American colonials well into the 1930s.[56]

Military authorities responded to Saleeby's 1907 departure by attempting to generate their own expertise. Between that year and 1910, army officers in each district of the Moro Province employed a meticulous intelligence-gathering schematic to evaluate the cultures they governed. J. M. Cullion, a lieutenant with the 2nd Infantry copied out phonetic versions of common Tausūg words, while E. V. Sumner Jr., stationed at Zamboanga, did the same for the Maranao people of the Lake Lanao region.[57] Stanley Koch, an intelligence officer with the 6th Cavalry, compiled information on the Maranao, with a particular focus on sex and sexuality. He observed that masturbation was "often practiced by men and boys" but punished by one hundred lashes from a bejuco stick when discovered. Abortion, infanticide, and the various punishments meted out for "sexual deviance" also appeared in the document, suggesting a fascination with the intimate areas of Muslim life.[58]

The most comprehensive of all these reports came from Edwin L. Smith, an intelligence officer with the 4th Field Artillery. Written in 1908 and focusing on the Tausūg of the Sulu Archipelago, Smith's report was more than one hundred pages in length and impressive in its topical breadth. Genealogies of the Sulu Sultanate appeared alongside detailed descriptions of the games played by Moro children. Smith reproduced the Sulu Code, a set of legal principles, in its entirety, and also gave an extensive political history of the islands. The report provided titles for prominent Tausūg figures and recounted popular superstitions. Numerous drawings and photographs showed how the Tausūg dressed, how they buried their dead, the mechanics of their games, and the designs of their weapons, jewelry, agricultural implements, and housing.[59] As in Koch's report, sexuality and reproductive practices received special attention, including rituals surrounding intercourse, methods for terminating unwanted pregnancies, and punishments for prostitution. Smith listed dozens of social customs, ranging from whom a Tausūg woman could speak with to how often people in Sulu bathed. Although heavy in specifics, the report avoided the condemnatory moralism commonly found in American descriptions of the Moros, presenting the Tausūg and their customs in a straightforward manner.[60]

Several works exploring the languages of the Southern Philippines appeared in print. The military surgeon Ralph Porter compiled a Maguindanao reader

that generated enough interest to be published in Washington.[61] Charles Elliot Winslow, a quartermaster with the 6th Infantry, compiled a Maranao "vocabulary and phrase book." Learning Maranao did not soften Winslow's
opinion of it, however, and he wrote in his introduction that the language was
"a barbarous and incomplete dialect, replete with inconsistencies, absurdities,
and primitive modes of expression."[62] At Zamboanga, Frances E. Bartter assembled a small primer on the Samal dialect, and in Jolo Katharine G. Buffum
did the same for Tausūg.[63] It is important here not to overstate Euro-American
interest in the native cultures surrounding them. While certain military men
and schoolteachers attempted to bridge sociocultural gaps, many white residents of the Muslim South contentedly limited their interactions with Moro
and Lumad groups.

Fifteen years of interaction and a growing corpus of literature did not prevent essentialized notions of the Moro from perpetuating under civilian rule.
Francis Burton Harrison, governor-general of the Philippines between 1914
and 1921, trafficked in many of the same stereotypes, depicting Moros as adversaries of "great personal valor," whose adherence to "Mohammedanism"
rendered them "difficult to deal with." Gendering his understanding of them,
Harrison claimed that Moro men and women were "often indistinguishable"
and repeated the commonly held opinion that the death of women during
the 1906 Bud Dajo massacre arose from an easy confusion between the sexes.[64]
Such stereotypes persisted through the 1920s and 1930s among both Americans and Christian Filipinos. The writings of Sixto Y. Orosa, the district health
officer in Sulu, featured long descriptions of the Tausūg tendency toward piracy and their "fanatical" adherence to Islam.[65] Joseph Ralston Hayden, the
University of Michigan political scientist who became vice-governor of the
Philippines in the 1930s, wrote in the pages of Foreign Affairs that the "Mohammedan and pagan Filipino" of Mindanao-Sulu had "a backward civilization . . . sustained by religious fanaticism, fierce racial pride, and stubborn adherence to ancient custom." That Hayden was a comparatively liberal voice
provides an indication of how steeped Americans were in notions of civilizational capacity.[66]

In 1945, on the eve of Philippine independence, the school official Edward M. Kuder wrote a plea that Americans not pass over "one of earth's little
peoples." The educator, who had fought alongside Moro guerrillas against
the Japanese on Mindanao, reflected on the qualities of the Malay race, the
role of Islam in the Southern Philippines, and how women figured into
Moro societies.[67] Although the language of the civilizing mission had softened over the decades, Kuder's text upheld familiar convictions about the

merits and shortcomings of the Moros. Until the end of the colonial period, American depictions of these groups retained a complex and contradictory quality, alternating, often within the same individual, between curiosity and disgust, pity and fear, embrace and rejection.

Racial Comparatives

In a 1906 *Collier's Weekly* article, the journalist Richard Barry recounted the assassination of the Maguindanaoan leader Datu Ali by U.S. forces. "[Ali's death] marked all but the last phase of that war of extermination which the American race has waged for nearly three centuries against first the red and then the brown race," he wrote, "which has taken our arms from the rock-bound roar of Penobscot across ten thousand miles to the soft lull of the Pacific." Rich with allusion, Barry's text located a centuries-long continuum of colonial warfare, situating battles in the Southern Philippines alongside those fought on the Atlantic littoral during the European conquest of North America. The "dusky" Native Americans who resisted westward expansion were kin to Ali, despite being separated by an ocean. Barry venerated the savage nobility of the datu while simultaneously arguing that his very existence impeded colonial development on Mindanao. His resistance was brave but hopeless: "A royal good fellow that unfortunately got in the way of progress, and had to have a hypodermic injection of gray matter."[68]

Americans in the Southern Philippines would have recognized Barry's narrative flourishes. Frontier reportage on Native American populations brimmed with tales of savagery, futile heroism, and the inevitability of white racial dominance. In a world view predating the republic itself, the "moral development" of indigenous groups came through the adoption of Anglo-Saxon cultural norms and settlement patterns. Once this occurred, the "savage" would be returned from outer darkness, becoming a primitive subject of the state able to appreciate modernity's bounties.[69] The tragic outcomes of this racial idealism are well documented in critical works on the American West and included frontier violence, epidemic illness, coordinated deracination, and mass dislocation. As the U.S. nation spread outward, policy makers justified programs of ethnic cleansing like the Indian Removal Act of 1830 through contrasting explanatory frameworks: the necessary marginalization of cultures scientifically marked for extinction, protective measures to ward off said extinction, or illustrations of divine will and opportunities to save heathen souls.[70] Sites like the Carlisle Indian Industrial School typified ambitious deracination projects, embracing slogans like "Kill the Indian, Save the Man" and utilizing Christian education to remake Native youth into model Americans.[71] Punctuating all of this was "prolonged and brutal fighting" in frontier spaces that allowed "ample opportunity for atrocities directed at a population of 'savages' in which civilians were indistinguishable from combatants." Sporadic colonial massacres, such as that at Wounded Knee in 1890, became the backdrop for U.S. continental expansion in the nineteenth century.[72]

For many white Americans, frontier encounters with Native groups represented the most immediate experience of alien cultures. Newspaper correspondents wrote of the strange repugnance and allure of tribal customs for their audiences back east. Indigenous peoples became paradoxically vilified for their savagery while also idealized as "pure" or "noble" in their freedom from the complex and coercive qualities of modernity. These contradictory impulses—exterminationist, assimilationist, and fetishist—manifested themselves in popular culture, where traveling stage shows and adventure fictions expressed the frontier myth, and in ethnographic kitsch that reduced the indigenous history of the Americas to a series of flattening visual tropes (the tepee, the headdress, the peace pipe, and so on).[73] As Ter Ellingson demonstrates in his study of the discursive construct of the "noble savage," the "negativizing forces of Enlightenment sociocultural evolutionary progressivism and nineteenth-century racism" alongside a "dialectic of vices and virtues" generated a complex of approaches to indigenous Americans that were sentimental and curious yet rooted in an epistemology of violence.[74]

Related attempts to constitute Moro identity did not exist in a vacuum. While Americans built on a transimperial archive of stereotypes and myths about Muslim Malays, they also imported their own cultural baggage from centuries of continental conquest.[75] Many leading military figures in Mindanao-Sulu fought in the Indian Wars of the late nineteenth century, pacifying indigenous populations and ensuring the safety of white settler communities. Governor Leonard Wood served as a surgeon and line officer in the U.S. Cavalry and saw action against Geronimo and the Chiricahua Apaches, while John Pershing participated in campaigns in the American Southwest against the Apaches and in North Dakota against the Sioux. Hugh Scott, the most influential military governor of Sulu, had been a cavalry lieutenant on the frontier and maintained a lifelong interest in Native American lore and sign language.[76] The military posted Frank Carpenter in Wyoming, Montana, and at the Pine Ridge Reservation in South Dakota before his time as the first civilian governor of Mindanao-Sulu. He was at Pine Ridge when the Wounded Knee massacre occurred.[77]

The archival record also contains a wealth of material on low-ranking officers and enlisted men whose careers challenged distinctions between metropole and colony. The trajectory of the military surgeon Charles MacDonald illustrates how personnel developed their skills through intraimperial service. After seven years in the 22nd Regiment of the New York National Guard, MacDonald qualified as a surgeon and served in Puerto Rico at the tail end of the Spanish-American War. From there he transferred to Fort Yates in North Dakota, where life was "of the old-time frontier character, with much riding of the plains and more adjusting of Indian outlaw tangles and efforts to keep them on the Agency Reservation." Moving across the Pacific, MacDonald briefly acted as sanitary inspector in Manila before being sent to Mindanao, where he fought Moros under Leonard Wood. A brief biography described his time there in unpleasant terms, noting numerous combat deaths in his battalion and the ruinous effects of the tropical environment.[78] While he never rose to national prominence, MacDonald was typical in the geographic variability of his service.

Perhaps due to this wealth of personal experience between frontiers, the government reports, letters, personal diaries, and newspaper articles originating in Mindanao-Sulu included frequent comparisons between Moros and Native Americans. En route to Lanao, the army surgeon Charles Hack wondered about the peoples he would encounter. "[The Moros] are said to be something like the Sioux Indians," he wrote. Unsure of the civilizing mission, Hack decried Moro and Filipino "ignorance and superstition," placing it alongside "our lower types of American Indians."[79] Hugh Drum, aide-de-camp to Gen. Frank Baldwin in the Lanao district, made more specific connections in his construction of Moro identity. Moros had "the characteristics of a combination of Malay and Arab and even in some ways the American Navajo Indian," he wrote in his memoirs. As warriors they "resembled the Apache Indian, fleet, courageous with a fatalistic spirit, physically strong and with a confidence resulting from past victories over the Spaniards and Filipino." Drum and Baldwin observed "Indian characteristics and methods in the Moro mode of warfare" as they pushed to pacify Maranao cottas.[80] Military officials translated indigenous resistance movements through the lens of Lakota and Paiute religious practices. Tasker Bliss attributed the 1906 assassination of the Davao governor Edward Bolton by Tagacaolo tribesmen to popular unrest "not unlike . . . the Ghost Dance craze among American Indians."[81] Troubled by millenarian responses to the disorientations of colonial rule, Americans sought familiar antecedents.[82]

Moving beyond racial conflation, government officials in Mindanao-Sulu also maintained contacts with those responsible for shaping indigenous policy in the United States. Hugh Scott not only utilized his previous experience with the Apaches but also corresponded regularly with Francis E. Leupp, the future commissioner of Indian Affairs. The two discussed Geronimo (whom Scott had known) and the Bedonkohe Apaches under his leadership near Fort Sill, Oklahoma.[83] Scott's reputation as an expert on Indian affairs traveled with him to the Philippine frontier, where he was renowned for his close relations with the datus of Jolo. Speaking at a dinner given by the Harmony Club in 1913, Dean Worcester emphasized the importance of Scott's colonial knowledge. "He has had wide experience in dealing with the Indian in our country," Worcester told the guests, "and knew just how to attack the Moro problem."[84]

No one thought more about the linkages between the Moros and Native Americans than John Park Finley. Finley transferred to Mindanao after the Philippine-American War and became the longest-serving district governor in the Moro Province, overseeing the Zamboanga Peninsula and Basilan between 1903 and 1912.[85] He quickly became preoccupied with the civilizational capacities of Moro and Lumad groups. Perhaps taking the advice of David Barrows, Finley dabbled in amateur ethnography, publishing a study of the Subanon people. Like Barrows, the district governor viewed nineteenth-century Indian policy as gravely flawed, deeming it "a century of dishonor" and wondering if the United States would "repeat that dishonor upon a people who worship the same omnipotent God that we do, simply because they fail to salaam in our particular manner."[86] A course correction in Mindanao-Sulu would require "administrative and social engineering policies" that were "more nuanced and tactical . . . than the austere requisites of crude submission."[87]

Finley's outlook crystallized in the pages of the *Journal of Race Development*, where he claimed that developmental failures on the American frontier had resulted from greed and exploitation on the part of settlers. "The lack of true appreciation of the science and art of cooperation," he wrote, "has greatly retarded the industrial and commercial development of our Indian wards in the states, and under similar conditions is experienced as an unreasonable restraint upon a like development of our Indian wards in the Philippines." By studying the continental frontier, colonial administrators in Mindanao-Sulu could avoid "serious errors . . . in conducting the regeneration of our Indian wards in the Southern Philippines." Finley placed subject peoples on the North American and Southeast Asian frontiers within a unified framework, believing that a new approach to colonial uplift would emerge. If managed correctly, the Moros could escape the fate of the Native Americans and become "self-supportive productive agents rather than . . . vagrant parasitic nomads."[88] Emphasizing paternal guidance over violent subjugation, the military official's ideas aligned him with Progressive Era reformers.

John Finley found a natural home for his views at the Lake Mohonk Conference of Friends of the Indian and Other Dependent Peoples. Held at an expansive Victorian castle in upstate New York, the annual meeting featured missionaries, schoolteachers, military officers, businesspeople, academics, and politicians. The Quaker philanthropist Albert K. Smiley founded the conference in 1883 as a means for the architects of Indian policy to discuss topics affecting its implementation.[89] After 1898, the conference expanded to include "other Dependent Peoples." An attendee could visit Mohonk and over a few days listen to Leonard Wood speaking on the Philippines, the associate editor of the *Manila Daily Bulletin* giving his "observations on race contact," the prominent eugenicist Charles B. Davenport reflecting on "good and bad heredity in relation to dependent races," a multidenominational panel discussing missionary work among the Native Americans, and the climactic determinist Ellsworth Huntington exploring the role of environment in colonial administration.[90]

Speakers at Mohonk integrated the American Philippines into a global story of imperial beneficence. Newly returned from Sulu, Hugh Scott told assembled guests that "the United States [has] had a much more altruistic purpose than any other colonizing nation in the Orient and has held consistently to the purpose of governing the Islands in the interest of their inhabitants." The "fearful condition of anarchy" found in Mindanao-Sulu when the Americans arrived was ameliorated by teaching the Moros "the meaning of justice."[91] The missionary bishop Charles Brent praised the similarly "magnificent" work done in British India and the Dutch East Indies.[92] At Mohonk, insights on colonial governance traveled from colony to metropole and vice versa, as well as between the colonial empires. Sharing their experiences from the Philippines, Scott and Brent engaged in dialogue with policy makers responsible for Native American, Puerto Rican, Hawaiian, and other "dependent" populations.

John Finley made his comparisons explicit at Mohonk in 1912. The role of the military in the Southern Philippines was analogous to "that which it has long performed in relation to the Indian tribes in the western part of the United States." As such, a "duty" existed to tutor the "uncivilized of the islands." Authorities in Mindanao-Sulu should follow the lead of the U.S. Congress in their dealings with Native American populations, allowing for "tribal organization and government" under the "wise and firm regulation" of white men, who prevented "barbarous practices and introduced civilized customs." The Moros ought to be raised up through "industrial proselytizing" rather than direct missionary efforts. This faith in the civilizing effects of modern commerce aligned Finley with institutions like the Carlisle Indian Industrial School, which sought to assimilate Native American youth. At the conference, he found an audience receptive to the notion that the fate of these groups rested on their successful acculturation and incorporation into the Western marketplace.

The desire to link Moros and Native Americans persisted into the twilight years of U.S. rule in the Philippines. Filipino politicians and intellectuals in Manila inherited these ideas, placing them in debates over national independence. The journalist José P. Melencio railed against American politicians and writers who used non–Christian populations as justification for continued colonial rule: "It is not fair to predicate Filipino capacity for self-government on the looks, attire, and backwardness of those mountain people. . . . They are to the Philippines what the Indians are to America."[93] In his *Manila Daily Bulletin* column, Juan F. Hilario advocated for a punitive solution to the Moro problem, claiming that their fate would be "the same as [that] of the American Indian"—integration or annihilation.[94] In response, Americans refashioned themselves as guardians of the archipelago's endangered peoples. In a 1933 article entitled "Fighting Moros Are Like Our Indians," the *New York Times* reporter Nicholas Roosevelt warned Muslim populations were under threat from Christian Filipinos. "The Moros are in many respects like the American Indians," Roosevelt wrote. "Fine, upstanding, self-respecting people, courageous unto ferocity, fearless and relentless enemies . . . and yet they face a sad end." With recent history firmly recast, Americans could now act as protectors of these "noble savages."[95]

The Southern Frontier

In 1909, the *Mindanao Herald* celebrated a decade of American rule. A special issue printed for the occasion described Mindanao-Sulu as a space of unexploited potential. "The world is growing older and unexplored lands are becoming fewer each year," wrote the *Herald* editor J. A. Hackett. "The heart of Africa and other interior lands will still hold out their attractive uncertainties to capital, but Mindanao and the Sulu Archipelago lie out in the open." Conjuring visions of the "ancient glory of the spice markets of Mindanao," Hackett urged multifront development, from mineral extraction to the establishment of vast agricultural estates. The entire issue was an advertisement for would-be investors and settlers, promising limitless bounties on the colonial frontier. Situating Mindanao within processes that began with the conquest of the North American Atlantic coast, the *Herald* connected the occupation of the Southern Philippines to centuries of European colonization. As in the American West, the inhabitants of Mindanao-Sulu had forfeited their rights to the soil through underutilization, leaving it free to be "re-made."[96]

The lands of the South became sites of fantasy and comparison—places of economic and human potential left untouched by a Spanish colonial state unable to develop them. The closed continental frontier that Frederick Jackson Turner declared marked the end of "the first period of American history" shifted across the Pacific.[97] Entrepreneurs looking for virgin territories only needed to travel a little farther now.[98] The uncivilized inhabitants of the Southern Philippines posed little problem. Using "primitive and destructive" approaches to agriculture, they had failed to properly exploit the landscapes they inhabited.[99] Muslim and Lumad tribes would either embrace new settlement and labor norms or face violent marginalization. This idea of colonial zones

Figure 1.1 "Mindanao, Moro Country." U.S. colonials recast the large southern island as an exploitable frontier territory. Many understood it relative to individual experiences and national histories of borderlands expansion in North America. (General John J. Pershing Photograph Collection, U-M Library Digital Collections, Philippine Photographs Digital Archive, Special Collections Research Center, University of Michigan)

as tabula rasa or terra nullius ("blank slates" or "nobody's land") was hardly novel, finding its genesis in previous imperial erasures of indigenous polities.[100]

Reshaping the newly colonized spaces of Mindanao-Sulu meant mapping territory. Colonial aggrandizement frequently begins by suppressing preexisting forms of spatial knowledge, replacing them with the panoptic gaze of the modern map and its sharp demarcations.[101] In the Philippines, colonial officials engaged in a sustained campaign of "territorial knowledge construction," purchasing Spanish maps and creating new government bureaus that aimed to rationalize space. The guiding hand of colonial geography, Americans believed, would domesticate the tropical environment and rescue its inhabitants from primitive torpor.[102] From 1899 onward, administrators in the South placed great emphasize on surveying, mapping, and enumerating their surroundings.

Inherited Spanish documents described Moro and Lumad societies incapable of knowing their environment, and American colonials saw the Spanish as only marginally better.[103] The U.S. Army dedicated considerable resources to understanding the South, conducting intelligence-gathering missions throughout the region. A party led by Lt. G. Soulard Turner in the spring of 1903 typified these efforts. Sent from Cotabato, Turner and his men sketched out the physical geography along the coast to Lebak, describing water sources, edible vegetation, forest density, and trail quality. They also compiled data on local Maguindanao and Tiruray villages, taking notes on population figures, local politics, epidemic outbreaks, and the disposition of natives toward the U.S. presence.[104] In Jolo, producing cartographic knowledge was directly tied to the suppression of anticolonial resistance. While fighting against the Tausūg leader Panglima Hassan in 1903, Hugh Scott received orders to send "at least" two hundred men to "resume the topographical survey of the central section of [Jolo]" as soon as hostilities ceased.[105] Back on Mindanao, the need to establish lines of communication necessitated hard surveying trips into the backcountry. Traveling overland on previously unmapped trails, Lt. Roderick Dew and his men faced leeches, blistered feet, and treacherous paths to ascertain whether a telegraph line could be placed between Davao and Fort Pikit.[106]

In Zamboanga, successive provincial governors tapped government agencies to help with "the work of exploring and mapping the area." Tasker Bliss advocated for funds to create a well-funded bureau with a large staff. Collaboration between military authorities and civilian agencies was common. A party that included an army surgeon and an official from the Philippine Bureau of Forestry summited the 9,000-foot Mt. Malindang in 1906, producing "topographical drawings, clinometer sightings, altitudes of peaks, barometric and thermometric readings" and returning with "a botanical collection of 1,000 specimens."[107] In 1907, the Mining Bureau of the Philippine Islands commissioned a geologic reconnaissance led by the geologist Warren Dupre Smith and including a mining engineer and topographer. Under military escort, the men proceeded with "the examination of certain special areas likely to prove of economic interest" in mind, eventually producing a detailed report on their findings. The *Mindanao Herald* celebrated Smith's mission, calling it "invaluable" for potential American prospectors.[108]

Word of Mindanao's bounty filtered back to the United States, and the island became a projection site for troubling metropolitan fantasies. The six-term Alabama senator John Tyler Morgan saw overseas possessions as a dumping ground for African Americans from the Jim Crow South. In 1902, he proposed sending the "easily controlled surplus blacks" to Mindanao, forwarding his plan to Secretary of War Elihu Root, who dutifully passed it along to Adna R. Chaffee, then commander of the Department of the East. According to Morgan, the benefits would be twofold: easing racial tensions on the continent and mitigating domestic opposition to empire by no longer using white troops to maintain colonies.[109] Black regiments served in the Philippine-American War, and some officers commented favorably on the supposed "racial harmony" between African Americans and Filipinos. Morgan played on this sentiment, predicting harmonious race relations between the natives and a permanent black settler class.[110]

Chaffee took Morgan's ideas seriously enough to forward them to Gen. George W. Davis, the military commander of the Southern Philippines. Davis articulated his own vision of African American settlement in the Muslim South, drawing from a wealth of other colonial contexts to do so. The general agreed Mindanao needed settlement, bemoaning its undeveloped state and comparing its potential favorably to the British and Dutch colonies of Southeast Asia. Davis's plan modeled labor contracts on those used by planters in the West Indies and British authorities in Calcutta. Louisiana sugarcane producers could relocate to the Southern Philippines and sign African American men to contracts. These settlers would bring their families and, once their contracts had expired, "would have an opportunity of bettering themselves by engaging in abaca, coffee, cacao and rice culture." He dismissed the idea of using "colored troops" already stationed in the Philippines, deeming them "aristocratic" and incapable of transitioning to tropical agriculture. The nonmilitary black contract laborer or settler, Davis believed, would be ideal.[111]

The construction of black tropicality had long been connected to removal projects in the North American settler imaginary.[112] In the Philippines, African Americans would take up the mantel of archipelagic development, conveniently leaving U.S. soil. Davis explored Spanish, Portuguese, English, French, and Dutch colonial histories in his report, connecting their successes to the effective importation of African slave labor. The same successes could be achieved in the Philippines, he believed. "When Mindanao is thus occupied with industrious immigrants from our southern states, when its sugar lands are in use, its hill and mountain slopes are in abaca, coffee, and cacao . . . then there will be a population of several millions where are now found only the native aborigines and savage Moros."[113] These relocation plans never came to fruition but provide evidence of how socioenvironmental racial agendas contributed to the drive to naturalize settler colonization in the Southern Philippines. The possible migration of African Americans to Mindanao remained under discussion as late as 1909, when the *Mindanao Herald* reported that Booker T. Washington was considering a proposition to bring a "large negro colony" from the United States to develop the resources of the Cotabato Valley.[114]

Much like his predecessors, Frank Carpenter understood Mindanao-Sulu through the prism of future transformation. "This vast territory, greater than many of the kingdoms and republics of Europe and the Americans [is] . . . capable of supporting fifty millions of people," he mused. It contained "the great undeveloped natural resources of the Philippines" that would power national development for decades to come. The island of Mindanao in particular held "practically all first-class agricultural land remaining in the public domain." In a 1914 report, Carpenter described the island in terms of endless possibility: "When the practically uninhabited areas are cultivated at all the soil is rarely plowed or more seriously disturbed than by the point of the sharpened stick or jungle knife with which the seed is planted between the grass roots after the grass itself has been cut closely to the ground by these same knives. With even this very primitive method of planting and practically without subsequent cultivation, rice yields a hundredfold under ordinary climactic conditions."[115]

Cultivating the soil was not without complication. Surveying parties faced opposition from Moro and Lumad villagers, who feared that they portended the appropriation and repurposing of their ancestral domains. Authorities reported widespread resistance and encouraged frontline colonials to use "amicable discussion and demonstrations of 'moral force' to secure acquiescence from native groups."[116] Carpenter became convinced that government schemes such as the so-called rice colonies could convert Moros and Lumad from "nonproductiveness" to "great economic value." Within a generation Mindanao-Sulu "would compare favourably with any producing community in the Orient."[117] These fantasies belied the struggles of spatial and demographic reconfiguration. James Fugate, district governor of Sulu in the 1920s and 1930s, had a more grounded perspective. Armed surveying parties cut down Moro agriculture and planned roads haphazardly, he argued. Such recklessness provoked locals, and the presence of so many firearms invited attacks. Fugate, who sympathized deeply with the Taūsug on Jolo, saw the developmental drive taking on its own frenzied logic—one that did not take into account those already living in supposedly empty lands.[118]

Opening up the Southern Philippines became a prerogative of the entire colonial polity. In the postmilitary period, the Department of Mindanao and Sulu actively advertised itself to "immigrants and capitalists." Its promotional literature boasted an "abundance of work" for migrants from the North and promised opportunities for those seeking to invest in agricultural enterprises.[119] When not reporting sensational stories of Moro banditry, Manila newspapers depicted the South as a place where Filipinos could make a better life and aid national unity by integrating far-flung regions. American-approved Muslim leaders like Sultan Kiram and Datu Piang featured in news stories to illustrate Muslim amenability to the national-colonial agenda.[120] The new departmental provinces (formerly districts) promoted themselves individually. Cotabato declared itself "the paradise of the homeseeker from over-crowded Luzon the Visayas." A 1920 pamphlet touted the province's low population density, claimed any crop would flourish there, and declared the Maguindanao population harmless to settlers. Put under cultivation, the Rio Grande River valley would "prove the granary of the Philippine Islands" and "create a large export trade." The commercial prospects of new labor from the North excited American and Filipino elites, and these early settlement drives anticipated the far-reaching and demographically transformative migrations of the postwar era.[121]

A fixation on remaking Mindanao's "empty" spaces continued well into the commonwealth period. In 1938, the missionary educator Laubach described the island as the "Golden West" of the Philippines, claiming it was "in exactly the same situation that America was in when settlers were flocking toward the western states and taking up homesteads." Laubach spoke with excitement about the massive settlement plans being developed in Manila. "I cannot think of any other colonization project in the world today that is being planned on such a grand scale," he wrote to the contributors to his mission.[122] The enthusiasm of the remaining Americans in Mindanao-Sulu perhaps helped inspire those who saw the islands as a potential homeland for persecuted German Jews. With no entry quotas, and as a territory run by the United States, the Philippines "represented a 'back door' to America" for refugees of Nazi terror. After the failed Evian Conference, Presidents Roosevelt and Quezon both spoke positively of Jewish settlement in the Southern Philippines. In early 1939, the Mindanao Exploration Commission (MEC) assembled to travel to the island and assess its suitability.[123]

The MEC echoed generations of Western visitors in their descriptions of Mindanao. The island's "fertile soils, magnificent scenery, immense virgin forests, and splendid climate" made it ideal for settlement. The sparsely populated interior of Mindanao could be transformed into a space of refuge for German Jews.[124] The MEC's road map faced opposition from Christian Filipinos, who believed they should be given priority before any foreign population. The revolutionary hero Emilio Aguinaldo introduced anti-Semitism into these nativist arguments, explicitly blaming the Jews for their problems in Germany. In Bohol and La Union, municipal councils and settler groups argued Jews were "dangerous" and demanded colonization rights be reserved exclusively for Filipinos. Philip Frieder, the Cincinnati businessman spearheading the plan, tried to assuage these fears by assuring the Manila press that only the most qualified immigrants would relocate to the Philippines, thus avoiding labor competition with other settler groups.[125] Native resistance and "lukewarm support" from the U.S. State Department undermined the MEC's efforts, and the onset of the Second World War crushed the plan altogether.[126]

Americans who fought, administered, taught, traded, and proselytized in the Southern Philippines imagined Moros in myriad ways: as irredeemable premodern leftovers facing an uncertain future; as zealots and fanatics, with penchants for piracy and slaving arising from inchoate adoptions of Islam; as noble savages, whose formidable natural abilities could be productively redirected by colonial uplift programs; or, in later years, as national minorities in need of protection from Filipino predation. Americans conjured Moros (and, to a lesser extent, Lumads) as they saw fit, and their portrayal was often contradictory. Moros were barely cognizant of being Muslims yet under the sway of dangerous foreign clerics who preached pan-Islamic revival; they possessed an admirable martial spirit but faced extinction if they held out against civilization's mandates; their "struggle to preserve [their] race" against Filipino demographic encroachment deserved support, yet they also needed to integrate into the Philippine national body; they managed their land well or hardly at all.[127] A select number of Americans could differentiate between diverse Muslim and Lumad ethnic kinship networks, although many adopted the habit of viewing them as monolithic religio-cultural entities. Spurred by precolonial contact and European writings, "Mohammedans" and "pagans" developed as durable categories in the nineteenth-century American imagination and remained so after conquest. Serious study of the peoples of the Southern Philippines did exist within this representational matrix but was frequently tinted with the racial assumptions of the day.

When imagining the Moro, American colonials looked back across the Pacific to their own nation's imperial expansions on the continental frontier. Many who served in Mindanao-Sulu previously fought and administered Native American groups, and after 1898 their experiences were exportable colonial expertise. The North American frontier and its peoples swiftly became a reference point for the Southern Philippines even among those without a background in military governance. Officials like John Finley believed the nation's "Mohammedan wards" presented a fresh opportunity to build on the successes and failures of nineteenth-century Indian policy using rigorously modern colonial methods. When met with opposition, Americans could likewise draw from histories of frontier violence and dispossession, which provided coercive solutions where incentive faltered.[128] Prevalent Anglo-Saxon concepts about indigenous racial capacity easily transferred to the Muslim South, where Muslims and Lumads lacked the familiar cultural touchstones of Christianized Filipinos. Hardly idle comparison, the Moro-as-Indian framing represented an intraimperial discursive current that captured the imaginations of U.S. officials and guided policy in the Philippines.

Like its peoples, the environments of Mindanao-Sulu presented threats and opportunities. The Spanish had been unable to administer the "empty" spaces of the Southern Philippines, and the natives were untutored in Western modes of spatial rationalization. Harnessing tropical fecundity and mineral wealth—first through cartographic reconnaissance and later through agricultural colonization projects—became a primary focus of the U.S. colonial state. Spurred by the potential of the land, U.S. and Filipino administrators pursued multiple developmental avenues, entertaining the notion of importing diverse settler populations and seeking inspiration from European colonies. Initial forays into colonizing the South began in the American period but resonated into the postwar era when mass migration led to settler naturalization on Mindanao. From the beginning of military rule until independence, U.S. colonials viewed Mindanao-Sulu as a place of *possibility*. Their perceptions embedded themselves in ambitious plans to create a new Muslim South.

Chapter 2

Courtrooms, Clinics, and Colonies

Remaking the Southern Philippines

Civilizing fantasies became civilizational imperatives through a spectrum of state-building projects aimed at refashioning the Southern Philippines. Little could be salvaged from the past, and Muslim and Lumad groups needed to be guided away from objectionable tradition toward material productivity by instruction, force, or some combination of each. Governor Tasker Bliss gave the clearest expression of this mind-set in 1909, when he described precolonial life in the region: "In general the people were living in a state of bondage to their feudal lord, suffering from all the diseases that man in a tropical clime is heir to, and living in rude, squalid nipa huts . . . Such a thing as public institutions were unknown among [the Moros]. No roads or docks were ever built to promote intercourse and further trade, no schools or other public institutions to disseminate knowledge."[1] By reducing the heterogeneous cultures of the South into a single debased scape, Bliss gave rhetorical justification to the erasure of tradition resulting from a new status quo. The precolonial Moro was a pirate, slaver, polygamist, gambler, thief, religious fanatic, and murderer who was averse to productive labor, disinclined to sanitary living, and indifferent to the public good. What, then, was worth preserving? The Moros, too, fierce to be dominated by the indolent Spanish yet unable to progress independently, could be redeemed only through the guidance of Americans and, later, their Filipino protégés.

To civilize meant one had access to civilization. In the Progressive Era United States, this denoted Anglo-Saxon modernity, which fused the ethics of mid-Atlantic Protestantism with a prevailing faith in the redemptive capacities of commerce and technology. This outlook germinated in the tenements of U.S. cities and along the nation's settler borderlands. Locating haves and have-nots within a civilizational continuum and creating road maps for tutelage became a means of delineating cultural power. Well before the U.S. fleet landed in the Philippines, government bodies and metropolitan reformers targeted out-groups (the urban and rural poor, African Americans, indigenous peoples, Latino/as) under the auspices of the civilizing mission. Many of the actors in the following—Charles Brent, Caroline Spencer, Hugh Scott, Leonard Wood, Frank Laubach, John Finley—moved between colony and metropole, applying similar metrics of civilization to foreign and domestic spaces.[2]

Those working to reshape the Southern Philippines also tapped into the global logics of imperialism. American colonials readily participated in interimperial conversations about uplift in places likes Lake Mohonk, but also farther afield. Questions of racial progress, hygiene and sanitation, colonial agricultural and settlement, education, and law stretched well beyond the metropole-colony binary into transnational and transimperial dialogues on conquest and culture.[3] In their Asian colonies, British, Dutch, and French officials struggled with educating the natives in ways that minimized protonationalist movements. Elsewhere in Asia and Africa, empires experimented with agricultural settlement programs as tools of pacification and profit.[4] Throughout the Global South, colonial elites confronted medical issues and grappled with how to administer justice in environments characterized by vast power differentials.[5] While they brought much from home, civilizing programs in Mindanao-Sulu also drew from and contributed to multidirectional circuits of imperial knowledge.

The following explores how the civilizing mission was practiced in the colonized spaces of Mindanao-Sulu. If the Moros were, like Native Americans in the prior century, uncivilized peoples who failed to utilize their land, how could this be corrected? The ways Americans in the Southern Philippines answered this question informs subsequent sections. The colonial mind standardized notions of progress and modernity, mapping gradients of civilization across time and space. Inhabitants of the Muslim South, lagging somewhere behind the Christians of the North, could be partially or fully civilized only through the replication of American models. The clearest expression of this idea manifested in the institutions established in Mindanao-Sulu.[6] The areas of focus here represent core concerns of the U.S. colonial state. Replacing customary law, tutoring Moros in the basics of market capitalism, encouraging permanent settlement, and educating Muslim youth to be diligent laborers preoccupied Americans (and later Filipinos) for decades. All of these endeavors arose from utopian notions of what vigorous stewardship could draw out of the nation's Islamic wards. "The United States government guarantees to you protection from enemies without your borders, and assures you peace within," Governor Frank Carpenter told the assembled crowd at his 1914 inauguration. "It brings to you the greatest good that can be given to any people; opportunity to use your *krises* to harvest golden grain, to build towns where *cottas* have been, to make the trails through the forests of your mountains and valleys the highways of commerce and all that makes the civilization of today."[7] As happened elsewhere, grand intentions collided with a host of local conditions, complicating the idealistic programs of colonial actors.

Competing Systems of Justice

Governor Tasker Bliss thought little of Moro legal structures. "If anything was found that even a loose and superficial writer could call law, it rested upon no commonly accepted authority even among people of the same section," he wrote in 1907. The average Muslim had a "notion of government [that was] a dim reflection of theocracy as interpreted by the prophet and reinterpreted by ignorant, corrupt, and superstitious local teachers." Bliss marveled at Moro applications of justice and complained of the tenacity with which they clung to "corrupt and degraded" manifestations of Islam. Instituting secular law was delicate work, and Bliss believed it could only be accomplished if the Moros were brought up to the standard of "the civilized Mohammedan of India or the civilized Hindoo." Bliss's goal was the codification of "sensible and humane" laws, representing a "civilized" interpretation of Islam. He acknowledged that even this would be "repugnant to Western ideas" but believed it preferable to what then existed in Mindanao-Sulu.[8]

Efforts to bring the Muslim South under a unified legal framework began in 1904 with the passing of Act No. 39 of the Legislative Council of the Moro Province. The act provided for the organization of the five provincial districts into municipalities and tribal wards. Regional hubs like Zamboanga, Iligan, Cotabato, and Jolo became municipalities, while the small indigenous communities of the hinterlands were folded into the tribal wards. Fifty-one of these tribal wards existed: eighteen in Cotabato, thirteen in Lanao, nine in Sulu, six in Davao, and five in Zamboanga. Moro Province secretary George Langhorne described their purpose as transitional. Colonial authorities would control non-Christian settlements through collaborating native leaders, and these populations, slowly introduced to the benefits of modern governance, would in time decide to become "full citizens of a municipality."[9]

Tribal Ward No. 1, not far from Zamboanga, had a model farm, a jail, a market, a rest house, a hospital, and an administrative building. All of this was designed to nudge Moros and Lumad toward modernity, albeit in an incremental way that lessened opposition. The tribal court made some concessions to customary practices. Datus and panditas still adjudicated criminal and civil matters, levying fines to bolster their personal income and acting as representatives of the district governor in their ward. Moro headmen would in turn appoint their own deputies to serve as local police officers. The tribal ward courts tried civil and criminal cases between non-Christians (with the exception of first-degree murder), while municipal courts handled attacks on American and Filipinos. Over time, colonial officials planned to decrease the powers of the wards to make way for modern governance.[10] The system was flawed. The courts' reliance on the very men whose revenue stream and political clout they hoped to eventually abolish meant cases often went unreported. Traditional modes of settling disputes remained common. Tasker Bliss complained that the only way the tribal ward court system could be enforced was if every part of the country had a strong garrison, although this would have undermined the administrative rationale of the program. Bliss recommended giving limited legal powers back to native leaders, including the right to collect fines in certain cases (rather than having them go to the provincial treasury), and establishing small native courts for judging nonviolent crimes.[11]

While the transitional justice of the tribal ward courts was tedious for colonials, those assigned to oversee the process believed it was indispensable to the civilizing project. In Lanao, District Governor John McAuley Palmer oversaw courts at Marawi, Iligan, Camp Vicars, and Malabang. Problems often sprung from the unstable labor market around the lake, which Palmer attributed to a slackening of traditional authority. The labor pool, mainly young and unmarried men, was increasingly mobile as the power of local datus waned. These itinerant laborers moved between communities looking for the best pay, disrupted local rhythms, and were unresponsive to threats from the datus. The related rise in property crimes and thefts, unwittingly facilitated by the tribal ward system's remapping of economic and social relations, bore itself out in the courts. In 1906, tribal ward courts convicted Maranao Moros for theft, bootlegging, assault, resisting arrest, and trespass. During the same year, eight Maranao men were convicted of slave trading, with a further six cases awaiting trial.[12]

Sulu presented its own unique challenges for lawmakers. Communities of various sizes dotted the nearly nine hundred islands, and maintaining a consistent governmental presence in all of them was impossible. Successive district governors experimented with traveling justices of the court, who made regularly scheduled trips to outlying islands. On islands with permanent PC stations, the commanding officer often served in this capacity. Transferred from Lanao to the remote outpost of Cagayan de Sulu in 1911, Sterling Larrabee took on the combined role of head policeman and judge for the island. He worked to gain the population's trust and met with chiefs to discuss disarmament. Writing to his parents, Larrabee described his role: "The power of the Tribal Ward Court justices has lately been increased so that in criminal cases, I can imprison a man for 20 years. I cannot give a death sentence, however." New to the job, Larrabee had only tried four cases when he wrote the letter. The most serious of these involved a rape, where the perpetrator was sentenced to three months' jail time. "I am practically a king here," he said of his role, "and so like it very much!"[13]

American military leaders remained skeptical of datu authority yet reluctantly understood that attempts to enforce the Philippine legal code and strip these rulers of their powers had the potential to create violent unrest. Writing in 1913, John Pershing illustrated the tension between co-opting datus and rejecting customary practices outright:

> Naturally, the majority of datus have always been opposed to our criminal code, not only because it really punishes crime, but more especially because it removes the administration of justice from the arbitrary control of the mercenary datus and places it in the hands of a disinterested judiciary. As our criminal code replaces the Moro code the power of the datu is gradually being superseded. However, the unsettled condition of society produced by their low standards still remains and the Mohammedan sanction of their immoral practices still exists . . . Their system can never be successfully used as a basis of municipal organization, since government by datus accustomed to arbitrary action is inconsistent with enlightened consideration for personal rights. To attempt to restore datu rule would be to go backward a hundred years.[14]

Pershing's dismissal of Islam-inspired Moro legal traditions arose from his belief that pre-American cultural survivals needed to be eliminated if civilization were to flourish. Other officials had more moderate views. Gen. J. Franklin Bell believed the limited accommodation of "Moro customs" would ensure the peaceful continuance of state rule.[15] The abolishment of the tribal ward courts in 1915 mooted this line of thinking. Their replacements, the justice of the peace courts, functioned in a similar capacity and included new provisos about taking local practices into consideration.

Traditional methods of settling legal disputes persisted. The Tausūg of the Sulu Archipelago avoided secular channels, relying instead on older sources of authority. The Sulu Code, a series of articles combining customary and Qur'anic laws, dictated outcomes for transgressors. The code, transcribed in 1878 in the wake of the Spanish Treaty of Peace and updated in 1902, was a sophisticated document and covered a wide range of offenses. The murderer of a free man, for instance, was required to pay blood money as restitution to the victim's family, and if the murderers were unknown or hidden, an entire village would be culpable. The code imposed fines for marriage by abduction, and any woman who committed adultery became a "slave to her husband." The 1902 update detailed punishments for theft, murder, adultery, opprobrium, false claims, unlawful exactions, debt, and unjust decisions. To not adhere to the articles of the code, according to local rulers, was akin to swearing falsely on the Qur'an itself. Representing centuries of legal practice in the islands, the Sulu Code was a compelling alternative to the alien court structures of the colonial state.[16]

Following the abrogation of the Bates Agreement in 1904, American military authorities expected Sultan Kiram and his datus to accept their reduced status as arbiters of disputes. This progressive erosion of the datuship generated violent resistance and perpetuated shadow legal structures like the religious (agama) courts. The Carpenter Agreement of 1915 attempted to solve the issue by having Kiram foreswear any claim to legal authority and accept his position as a mere spiritual and symbolic figurehead. The sultan agreed to cease operation of the agama courts and the collection of fines and taxes from his subjects. In effect, the agreement enshrined the separation of church and state in Sulu and forced the sultan to recognize U.S. sovereignty and "the attributes of sovereign government that are exercised elsewhere in American territory and dependencies, including the adjudication by government courts . . . of all civil and criminal causes falling within the laws and orders of the Government."[17] Governor-General Francis Burton claimed the agreement was a victory for the United States and marked the "extension of the peaceful functions of the Government" through the region.[18]

The Sulu Code survived the Carpenter Agreement. Through the 1920s and 1930s, colonial officials still struggled with the issue of the agama courts. Although legal matters were the domain of the government, the operation of ecclesiastical courts by Kiram and his followers continually probed the limits

Figure 2.1 Governor Frank W. Carpenter and Sultan Jamalul Kiram together in Zamboanga, c. 1915. Carpenter was the first and only civilian governor of the Department of Mindanao and Sulu, which replaced the Moro Province after the U.S. Army's departure in 1914. Kiram was the Tausūg leader U.S. military forces negotiated with in 1899 and held his position until his death in 1936, albeit in politically reduced circumstances. ("Islam in Mindanao & Sulu," Nonlinearhistorynut's Blog, https://nonlinearhistorynut.files.wordpress.com/2010/08/carpenter-with-sultan001.jpg)

of what could be acceptably adjudicated outside state institutions. Some re-gional governors tolerated the agama courts, but the Bureau of Non-Christian Tribes viewed the arrangement as unsatisfactory. Bureau chiefs in Manila feared Kiram and other leaders were punishing residents for taking their issues to the government and bankrolling themselves through a covert system of fines. A report received by Vice-Governor J. R. Hayden claimed the courts had "re-tarded the political progress of the people." The Tausūg, it claimed, were "trained in the belief that they can bring before the agama court even those cases covered by laws and regulations. Its effect upon the people is that the Government Court to their own thinking is not the only court where they can bring their cases for settlement or seek redress."[19] Kiram and his coterie denied running a parallel legal system, arguing they were acting entirely within the purview of the 1915 agreement and only overseeing matters of a religious nature. Evidence suggests this was likely untrue and that Tausūg leaders played a double game. For their part, Americans and Filipinos failed to recognize that spiritual and legal authority were interwoven in the Islamic world view. Representatives of the state accused the agama courts of being a simple extortion racket, but these courts did provide social and religious functions—especially in areas where government presence was slight or nonexistent. Addressing disputes through traditional avenues allowed the average Tausūg to resolve their issues through culturally familiar processes rather than taking them outside of the community.

Gulamu Rasul, a justice of the peace and staunch modernizer in Sulu, reported that by 1931 there were approximately thirty agama courts in the archipelago. These courts generated ₱3,000 per month, of which between ₱1,000 and ₱1,500 went directly to Sultan Kiram. Rasul despised the courts and accused the sultan's "ignorant and superstitious" agents of working against the interests of the people. He bemoaned the resurgence of the courts in the 1920s, arguing that coexisting legal structures were one of the "great stumbling blocks to progress in the region." Aggrieved parties bounced back and forth between government and agama courts, racking up fines in the process. "Conditions here are like an open sore," Rasul wrote.[20] A 1934 government memorandum was more measured in its analysis, claiming that the agama courts gained prestige from the sluggish response of the state. The conflicting systems created violent confrontations. Offenders who paid fines in the religious courts would become incensed when they discovered there was a government warrant for their arrest. This led to confrontations with the Constabulary and ensuing loss of life. Strengthening the justice system in Sulu, the memorandum argued, would make the agama courts less appealing and reduce these scenarios.[21]

In 1934, Governor Frank Murphy appealed directly to Sultan Kiram, demanding he "refrain from infringing upon the rights of the civil authorities" in Sulu. The governor ordered Kiram, who had complained that Governor James Fugate and others were impinging on his religious rights, to participate in a conference with other leading figures on Jolo to reestablish boundaries between state and spiritual authority.[22] The death of the sultan in 1936 temporarily solved the problem of the agama courts. A succession struggle ensued that monopolized the energies of the Tausūg elite. The recently established Philippine Commonwealth used Kiram's passing to further delegitimize the sultanate. Attempts to displace or remove native modes of mediating disputes and replace them with a Western-facing legal apparatus persisted through the entire colonial period. At times they were successful, but Americans and Filipinos also overestimated the appeal of imported concepts of justice in spaces with long-established legal traditions. The assumption that customary legal norms in Mindanao-Sulu could be overhauled within a generation was one of the more glaring examples of colonial hubris and something that would haunt the postcolonial Philippine state.[23]

"The Moro Does Not Take Naturally to Cleanliness"

"I don't think there is anything that we have on hand more important than to develop the Filipino physically," Secretary of War William Howard Taft declared in a 1907 missive to Dean Worcester. Taft's letter placed education, physical development, and modern hygienic practices—"an evangel of decent, healthful living"—at the center of the civilizing mission. Worcester was then secretary of the interior and thus responsible for the Department of Sanitation and other health-oriented bureaus. Alongside tropical-medicine experts like Victor Heiser and Paul Freer, Worcester helped define a moral approach to medicine within the colonial state. This approach relied heavily on racialized discourse that located native redemption in the adoption of modern medical advances, from proper personal hygiene to vaccination. Civilization meant clean, healthy bodies.[24]

Military officers in the Southern Philippines recognized the importance of medical infrastructure in cementing colonial rule. In 1900, Gen. William Kobbé and Maj. James Pettit worked to establish better sanitary conditions in Zamboanga. This was partially to protect American troops from real and perceived environmental threats but also tied to state-building.[25] In Jolo, Hugh Scott corresponded with the "sanitary engineer" George Barbour, who provided guidelines for combatting infectious diseases.[26] The district governor's concerns were not without merit. A cholera epidemic in Sulu killed five thousand people in 1902. Cholera also hit several areas around Lake Lanao the same year, a situation exacerbated by warfare between Maranao datus and the U.S. Army. Cotabato suffered an outbreak in 1903, and Davao underwent quarantine in 1905. Fearful of contagion, Leonard Wood refused to eat any food given to him by natives during inspection tours apart from the yolks of hard-boiled eggs.[27]

Funding issues plagued government health programs during these early years. The provincial treasury ran on a limited budget, and efforts to establish a health board in 1905 faltered due to limited personnel and resources. Although Manila claimed it wanted the South integrated into colonywide health strategies, the Legislative Council of the Moro Province had the "sense" that finances did not exist to support "such an elaborate organization." Instead, the council recommended officials already serving in other capacities be given the added task of staffing provincial health boards and hired medical doctors as part-time consultants.[28] The health of enlisted men proved a more easily addressed issue. During his first year as governor, Tasker Bliss focused mainly on ameliorating health conditions in military encampments. Destroying mosquito-breeding sites near outposts and treating sexually transmitted infections was a more achievable goal than constructing a functioning public health infrastructure.[29]

Private initiatives outpaced government ones in some districts. The Episcopal bishop Charles Brent opened a hospital in Zamboanga focused on Moro patients. Believing that Moro children "lived in huddled fashion in one or two-room shacks where filth and vermin abound," he outlined a plan to first cure them of tropical ailments and then educate them toward conversion (or at minimum to "emulate Christian conduct, citizenship and virtue"). Brent argued that medicine was a powerful avenue to approach Moro adults, "without whose confidence we shall never be allowed to handle the children."[30] The Episcopal Church financed and oversaw the Zamboanga operation. It often lacked funds but remained steadfast in its aim of attracting Muslim patients. The contract surgeon C. H. Halliday directed the hospital during the First World War. Moros came to the facility voluntarily but, perhaps suspecting its secondary missionary motives, were in the minority. During the second half of 1918, Muslims represented only 38 of the 421 in-patient treatments and only 11 percent the following year, but used the hospital's dispensaries and in-home services more frequently.[31]

Dispensaries helped government health agendas gain traction toward the end of military rule. These small outposts provided basic medicines, limited treatments, and information designed to impress natives of the state's "high motives." By 1913, thirty-seven dispensaries existed throughout the Moro Province, supplied by regional hospitals in Zamboanga and Jolo. Programs to promote health and hygiene extended beyond these modest facilities. Moro Province health officials distributed literature to expectant mothers aimed at "reducing the high rate of infant mortality." Native midwives received training in the "most recent sanitation and birthing practices." In provincial schools, district health officers lectured on how to treat and prevent communicable diseases. Reports detailed the sanitary conditions of school buildings, the effects of light and heat on educational conditions, and the "relation between health and intellectual progress" among the students.

Daily collection and disposal of human waste became standard in larger communities. On Jolo, residents used a special refuse pail designed by the Bureau of Health in Manila. Officials deemed the town the "cleanest and most sanitary" in the Philippines. This regime of medical and sanitary surveillance had disciplinary foundations. "The Moro does not take naturally to cleanliness, but it must be thrust upon him," declared John Pershing. "Recourse to arrest and even imprisonment is often necessary to enforce sanitary rules among the uncivilized population." The government began actively tracking, capturing, and deporting lepers, who after identification were quarantined at the San Ramon Penal Farm en route to the Culion Leper Colony. Martial measures also extended to the general population. An outbreak of the parasitic infection surra among horses in Zamboanga and local refusal to abide by quarantine caused the military to place guards in the affected districts and forbid the movement of animals.[32]

Medical work continued in the Department of Mindanao and Sulu after 1914, with Governor Frank Carpenter boasting of "popular acceptance and appreciation of hospital facilities." Dispensaries and traveling health care specialists remained primary nodes of "amicable contact and control" in the Mindanaoan interior.[33] The services met with only limited resistance, mostly around enforced sanitary regulations, and were generally better received than educational policies. Like his military predecessors, Carpenter viewed health and hygiene as integral to colonial success, although his ability to mobilize the state was limited by "meagre financial resources." Despite this, the Carpenter years saw improvements in the medical infrastructure of Mindanao-Sulu, with new hospitals opening in Cotabato and Dansalan.[34]

Poor resource allocation hindered public health programs during the interwar era. In 1921, newly elected President Warren Harding sent a fact-finding mission led by Leonard Wood and William Cameron Forbes to assess the effects of Filipinization. The group was critical of Governor-General Francis Burton Harrison's regime, dismissing development in the archipelago between 1913 and 1921. Wood and Forbes compiled a forthright report on real shortcomings in the colonial state. Citing statistics from the Philippine Health Service, they observed that cases of preventable diseases like typhoid, malaria, and tuberculosis were rising and that shortages of trained doctors, nurses, and sanitary personnel aggravated this. "Outside of the largest towns," the report stated, "hospitals are so few and far between that they are a negligible quantity." The Wood-Forbes mission deemed care for the mentally ill to be at a "medieval" level and noted that there were only around 930 nurses in a nation of 10.5 million people.[35]

Wood and Forbes had a political agenda, taking conscious aim at what they viewed as a native takeover of the colonial bureaucracy. Despite this, some of their claims are borne out in less partial reports from Mindanao-Sulu. On Jolo, vaccination campaigns progressed incrementally, and poor medical surveying led to an agricultural colony being established in a heavily malarial area (448 cases out of a population of 1,831). Sanitary conditions at markets around Mindanao had improved, but officials still complained that in places like Parang food was regularly displayed on the ground.[36] A 1933 report on schools in Sulu called the lack of medicine there "pathetic." Students regularly suffered from skin diseases and often only received medical attention if their teachers had first-aid training or the district supervisor visited the village.[37] George Dunham, a health advisor to the governor-general, observed all of these issues, lamenting the difficulties of providing services in the remote islands of the Sulu Archipelago. He saw training more female public nurses as a potential solution. Echoing Carpenter, Dunham wrote that "good public health work could be made a very effective means of promoting the acceptance of government by the Moro people."[38]

Public health work moved slowly in late-colonial Lanao. Christian Filipinos comprised the vast majority of doctors and nurses in the region. Maranao communities often viewed them as foreign interlopers and were reticent to visit their clinics. The early 1930s saw successive campaigns against cholera, intestinal parasites, and malaria around the lake. The last of these faltered from a quinine shortage. Officials complained that a policy of "attraction" slowed the implementation of public health programs but admitted that pursuing them by "force of law" had backfired. In 1933, the district health officer for Lanao reported that the Maranao were "intolerant and conservative in their mode of living" and as such slow to adopt the latest medical-sanitary technologies or allow children to be vaccinated. Illness was common. Maranao children had high incidences of measles and pneumonia. Among the broader population, water contamination and a lack of proper sewage systems increased the spread of infectious disease.[39]

Frank Laubach viewed health and morality in interactive terms. Living on the northern edge of Lake Lanao, he fixated on its "filthy condition." Dansalan locals had no toilets and used the lake, contaminating it in the process. Bathing in nearby water created further issues in the form of parasitic ailments. Mirroring missionaries and officials elsewhere in the Philippines, Laubach became fixated on issues of excrement and hygiene.[40] He cajoled datus to enforce sanitation and published letters from public health officials in his newspaper. "More sanitary toilets should be constructed throughout the provinces," Laubach associate Juan Fernando declared in the pages of the Lanao Progress.[41] Youth attending Laubach's school began taking local doctors and nurses back to their communities to explain the "laws of health," and Laubach arranged for a nurse from the Nestlé and Anglo-Swiss Condensed Milk Company to demonstrate "how to use the various kinds of canned milk" to fifty nursing Maranao mothers.[42]

Laubach's activities created health panics, such as one arising in 1933 over a proposed dance hall in Dansalan. After town counselors voted to grant a cabaret license to the business, Laubach and his allies rallied against it. The desire for a dance hall represented the adoption of Western culture stripped of ethics and a "misunderstanding of what a high civilization is." Laubach's Maranao associate Hadji Pambaya used venereal disease as a scare tactic, claiming that "half the girls" who visited the cabarets were "immoral" and spread "diseases of vice." Pambaya informed the municipal council and local panditas that the business would attract prostitutes, and an epidemic of sexually transmitted infections would follow. Laubach himself warned followers of an unspecified venereal infection that was "the most killing disease on earth" and would be introduced by the dance hall. Tapping into fears of difference and aberration, Laubach claimed a "woman dressed like a man" that trafficked young girls was one of the principal backers behind the establishment. Receptive to tropes of the diseased and sexually licentious female corrupting weak men, socially conservative Maranao rallied around Laubach. The pandita bankrolling the project withdrew, and the missionary expressed relief that the "evil thing" was banished.[43]

Colonial dialogues folded public health measures, personal morality, and education into a larger narrative of an unclean, premodern past juxtaposed with a rigorously sanitized present.[44] For Frank McCoy, the years prior to American arrival were ones of cholera and plague outbreaks, "roaming lepers," malnutrition, and a complete absence of sanitary infrastructure. Writing in 1925, he argued that the U.S. colonial state had changed this, suppressing plague, smallpox, cholera, malaria, and dysentery and introducing "respected and enforced" public health guidelines.[45] By the early 1930s, each province in the Southern Philippines had at least one hospital under the supervision of the Philippine Health Service. Zamboanga had three Health Service hospitals, one supervised by the Bureau of Prisons, one military hospital, two private hospitals, and twenty dispensaries scattered around the peninsula. The Sulu Archipelago had a lone hospital but nineteen dispensaries throughout its islands. As small as some of these facilities were, the above numbers represented an impressive expansion of medical services and modern medicines into areas previously unreached. The unpleasant grammar of colonial medicine persisted well into the 1930s but was mitigated by some beneficial outcomes: the construction of small clinics in rural areas, increased access to medicine, declining mortality from preventable disease, and the dissemination of useful health information.[46]

Marketing Civilization

In June 1904, the Legislative Council passed into law Act No. 55, which bore the lengthy title: "An Act Appropriating the Sum of One Thousand Eight Hundred and Fifty Pesos, Philippine Currency, or so Much Thereof as may be Necessary, for the Construction in the Municipality of Zamboanga of a Public Market for the Especial Use of the Moro and Other Non-Christian Inhabitants of the District of Zamboanga, and Providing for the Administration Thereof."[47] This piece of legislation marked the founding of what became known as the Moro Exchange, an experiment in the salutary effects of commerce on Moro and Lumad groups. Ideologically aligned with the industrial-educational projects discussed in chapter 3, the Moro Exchange system represented the victory of the modern marketplace over the stifling dictates of native traditionalism. When combined with access to vocational training, the Moro Exchanges would free the peasantry of Mindanao-Sulu from the oppressive yoke of the datuship and the exploitation of the Chinese merchant. Market participation, according to Michael Hawkins, introduced Moros to the "universal narrative of progress from which they had been excluded for thousands of years."[48]

The first Moro Exchange opened at Zamboanga in September 1904. John Park Finley supervised the operation and used his position as district governor to evangelize for it. As regional capital and commercial hub, Zamboanga was a natural test site that officials could closely monitor. Visiting the marketplace two months after its inauguration, William Cameron Forbes observed thousands of visitors "delighted to find they can get good prices."[49] Vendors were housed in a tall thatched-roofed structure, open at either end and lined with stalls. Finley organized the building into separate departments. Fishermen had forty stalls and displayed their daily catch, small farmers and foragers hawked "jungle produce," and local artisans peddled brass work. A small restaurant staffed by Samal women and children sold prepared foods, and vendors could spend the night at the adjacent lodging house. A wooden stockade surrounded the complex, which also had its own security officers. Visiting the exchange, the journalist Atherton Brownell called it an "absolute revelation" for the Moros and praised its "civilizing influence."[50]

The exchange system operated through an executive board under Finley's direction. Moro leaders from the Zamboanga Peninsula and nearby island of Basilan served as board officers, including Datu Mandi, Datu Hadji Nuno, and Datu Pedro Cuevas. They convened regularly to discuss organizational matters and settle operational disputes.[51] Finley believed that if the Moros and Lumad were to be civilized, they needed simultaneous discipline and protection. The U.S. military presence provided the former, while the latter was strictly enforced by regulatory controls meant to safeguard non-Christians against "exploitation in the sale of their property, products of their labor, and in purchase of such supplies as may be needful for them." Here Finley had in mind the injurious debt relationships Samal Moros often had with Chinese merchants, whose prominence in Southeast Asian trade networks allowed them to dominate commerce in Moro communities. To remedy this, the governor created strict guidelines that fixed rates for market licenses, forbade bartering within the exchanges, prevented the undervaluation of native labor, provided funds for the construction of new buildings, and assigned a series of superintendents and supervisory agents to carry out his directives.[52]

In 1905, Secretary of War Taft visited Zamboanga and toured the Moro Exchange there. His delegation bought local manufactures and delighted in the civilizing effects the marketplace had on the Moros.[53] The Samal had "quickly learned the law of supply and demand," doubling their prices when Taft and his congressional travel companions arrived.[54] Buoyed by these initial successes, Finley became convinced the Moro Exchange could be utilized across the Moro Province. He put this to the test when a revolt broke out on Basilan in 1907. The imposition of new taxes became a rallying point there for the religious leader Salip Agil and his followers. After Moros killed two American lumbermen and a Chinese merchant, Finley led a force of six hundred U.S. Army and PC troops to confront Agil, capturing him and killing a number of his followers. To quell unrest, the Americans established exchange outposts at the rancherias of Bojelebung, Amaluy, Cambingbing, Guiong, LuMut, Malusu, Lunpinigan, Lamitan, Panigayan, and Lahi Lahi. The new markets acted as primary means of government contact in these tiny settlements, and Finley made the dubious claim that they had been opened at the express request of the Yakan Moros who inhabited Basilan's interior. "Prosperity, peace and contentment reigns among these thousands of picturesque savages," he wrote. "The Moro Exchange is the industrial and commercial school that opens a hopeful future to these benighted people, once the ignorant and downtrodden slaves of a Mohammedan satrap."[55]

The system grew on the Mindanaoan mainland as well. By 1908, twenty-five exchanges dotted the Zamboanga Peninsula, and business was brisk. Sales totaled ₱795,768.00 in 1906–1907 and ₱573,875.05 in 1907–1908, up from ₱102,747.66 in 1905. Although lower prices for hemp and copra deflated profits, the markets offered a diverse range of products. Fish comprised the largest share of sales at ₱134,319.00, with Moro-run restaurants coming a distant second at ₱31,848.26. Eggs, copra, chickens, rice, cattle, and fruits also sold well.[56] The central location at Zamboanga expanded to ten buildings, with "cattle sheds, [a] tool house, wood and lumber yards, chicken pens, goat pens, latrines, dormitory, and water supply." The number of Exchanges rose to thirty-two by 1911, although sales never again reached the heights of 1907. Finley attributed this to global market fluctuations and a decreased demand for hemp and forest products.[57]

In 1911, Atherton Brownell returned to Zamboanga to check on the markets. Slumping sales mattered little, he thought, and the salutary experiments in colonial capitalism taking place "could not be estimated entirely in dollars and cents." It was their "moral effect" that stood out. A picture in Brownell's subsequent article showing the vendor stalls at Zamboanga was captioned "The Market of Civilization," and the writer praised Finley for channeling the skills of Moro tradespeople toward economic productivity. Moros now understood property rights, and murder had ceased in a place where human life was once "valued at six spittoons."[58] To Finley, marketplace civilization represented a "righteous colonial policy." Righteousness meant respecting the customs of the "subjugated . . . or protected" peoples who bought and sold at the markets—so long as they were not "repugnant to the requirements of human good."[59] Colonial reports contained no indication of how Moros and Lumad experienced the markets beyond declarative statements of progress.

Despite Finley's promotional efforts, opposition to the Moro Exchange system grew within government ranks. Governor John Pershing personally disliked Finley and removed him from office in April 1912. The district governor's subsequent contacts with the Ottoman Empire and continuing interference in the politics of Mindanao-Sulu cast further suspicion on him. In 1912, Pershing undertook a full investigation of the exchange system. His findings ran contrary to Finley's relentless propagandizing. "The people of Zamboanga district are decidedly opposed to the continuation or reestablishment of Moro markets or Moro Exchanges as they were formerly conducted," wrote Pershing. District Governor George A. Helfert, who had replaced Finley, believed the exchange system had no appreciable benefit, bringing "hardship on the farmer" and driving isolated groups farther inland. Operational details uncovered by the investigation painted a grim picture. Exchange agents "compelled" Moros and Lumad from the countryside to take their products to specific markets, even if demand was limited and prospective buyers lacking. The exchanges also levied a fee of 1 percent on all items sold. Charles R. Morales, head of the provincial Industrial Office, claimed the institutions were "very unpopular" among the natives.[60]

Portions of this negative assessment undoubtedly arose from Finley's ignominious exit, although the swift dissolution of the exchange system after 1913 suggests it was genuinely disliked. Convinced of his own virtue, the district governor enacted a scheme that became coercive and unresponsive to local conditions. Yet even as the Moro Exchanges were dismantled, Finley promoted them in the United States. In September 1912, he had Leonard Wood, an early supporter of his work, pass along observations on the industrial transformation of the Moros to President Taft. His report credited the exchanges for a staggering array of colonial advances: instilling a sense of civic duty among the Moros, opening schools, completed public works projects, greater dialogue between native communities, falling crime rates, adoptions of new agricultural practices, successful disarmament campaigns, and a new receptivity to "sanitary methods of living."[61]

Not content to simply petition political leaders, Finley also took to the pages of Stateside periodicals. In the *North American Review*, he contrasted the religious proselytism of the Spanish with his own commercial-industrial proselytism. Faith in the markets, not God, was key to successful native policy. Finley lashed out against the transition to civilian rule, believing that indefinite military control provided the necessary conditions to remake Mindanao-Sulu. Perhaps unaware that his grand project was being dismantled, the former governor provided his clearest statement of purpose: "The Moro Exchange System has become an active agent for wakening the commercial spirit of the uncivilized tribes of the Philippines, has become a powerful instrument for peace and unity among Moros and Pagans, and is serving the public by materially aiding in the collection of public revenues, and thus providing the general progress of the community."[62] Despite his exile, John Finley's vision for the peoples of Mindanao-Sulu remained the purest articulation of the missionary capitalist spirit that drove many colonials in the region. The concept of redemption and transformation through commerce did not simply vanish when the Moro Exchanges did in 1913. Rather, industrial and agricultural education remained a linchpin in efforts to develop Muslim and Lumad populations, particularly in regional schools.

Model Colonies

Civilization also meant settlement. Writing to Tasker Bliss in early 1908, John McAuley Palmer outlined plans for a model agricultural colony at the northern end of Lake Lanao. Although his military tour was over and he had returned to Fort Douglas in Utah, the former district governor still harbored designs for the Maranao Moros of the district. Fifty families would live in the proposed colony, each with a forty-acre homestead. The plan required an initial outlay of government funds, but the colonists would quickly become self-subsisting as they raised the crops required to feed themselves. Authorities would allot certain minimums for export crops like coffee, cacao, and tobacco, which the families would use to pay their debts and, over time, turn a profit. Palmer provided estimates for resource costs and a chart with projected monetary returns. He hoped officials in other districts would be inspired by the model's success and attempt to replicate it. The "greatest advantages of the colonies would be political," and settler successes would serve as "an object lesson to other Moros."[63]

The provincial leadership in Zamboanga proved a receptive audience, sharing Palmer's belief that the development and domestication of space was crucial to colonial success. The experimental farms and agricultural colonies represented the final stage of a model oriented toward creating small landholdings. With fields to oversee and produce to sell, the Moros and Lumad of the Southern Philippines would render previously "useless" territory productive. In the process, they would tie their own fates to the success or failure of state objectives, lessening the likelihood of violent revolt. This was the ideal, at least. Unlocking the bounty of the South required a population well beyond what existed—a problem that could be potentially solved by importing settlers.

Under Leonard Wood, the colonial government initially attempted to populate the Moro Province with Anglo-Saxon migrants. Inspired by frontier expansion in North America, white men and women sought to create "a new West in Mindanao." They did so by establishing plantations throughout the province's districts, concentrating most heavily around Davao. Supporters at the *Mindanao Herald* and among Zamboanga's white elite believed Euro-American settlement would naturalize colonial rule, unlock environmental wealth, and uplift the native.[64] In the Moro Province, government officials often transitioned into plantation work after their service ended. Luther R. Stevens, onetime governor of Lanao and a colonel in the Philippine Constabulary, became a manager of a 60,000-hectare coconut plantation at Malabang.[65] Others came to Mindanao to make their fortune, often with mixed results.

Arriving in the twilight years of settlement, the writer Vic Hurley eked out a miserable existence on a remote plantation upcountry from Zamboanga.[66] As previously shown, insufficient white migration led to a number of abortive plans to bring other populations—African Americans, Greeks, Italians, and Armenians—to Mindanao.[67] After the dissolution of the Moro Province in 1914, white settler colonization ebbed. In Davao, the planter heartland, Japanese and Filipino firms steadily replaced American and European ones.[68]

Although Mindanao-Sulu never transformed into "a white man's country" as some hoped it would, the desire to populate the South did not vanish. Tasker Bliss always believed Moros and Lumad would be the main cultivators of the soil. "The white man will never come here in such numbers as to make even a beginning of ousting the native from his occupation of the soil," he declared in 1907. Bliss and John Finley encouraged "non-Christians" to embrace the homestead provisions of the Philippine public land act, which allowed for the settlement on sixteen-hectare tracts. Through regulation and development, the vast spaces claimed as public land would give way to private ownership.[69] After the dissolution of the Moro Province, Frank Carpenter's administration continued emphasizing settlement as a means of redeeming the South. This sentiment grew as the colonial administrative class underwent Filipinization. In 1913, the Philippine Commission passed two acts (2254 and 2280) designating specific areas in Cotabato and Lanao for settlement. Filipino and American legislators collaborated to create these settler projects, known as the "rice colonies," and established mechanisms—called the Rice Colonization and Plantation Fund and the Moro Colonization and Plantation Fund, respectively—to finance them.[70]

The rice colonies would feature both Filipino and Moro communities, albeit partly segregated from one another for security reasons. Authorities established the first of these in the Rio Grande River valley, about fifty-five miles upstream from Cotabato. Two settlements began simultaneously, one for the Christians and one for Maguindanao Moros, with the latter group being placed near the local leader Datu Piang's homestead at his request.[71] The government vetted individual settlers for suitability and transferred an additional five PC companies to Mindanao to assist in the "protection and regulation of the colonies." The model colonies were to be a "practical school of agriculture," where instructors guided settlers from land selection to cultivation to the harvesting and marketing of their products. The operation had multigenerational aims, with the children of colonists attending local schools focused exclusively on training future farmers.[72]

The small colonies in Cotabato had a dual purpose: to help ease population pressures in the North and to draw the "partially nomadic inhabitants" of the South into sedentist modes of living. Planners hoped that over time the two groups would blend "into a homogenous whole." Agricultural colonies became the forge upon which formerly landless and culturally suspect groups could be recast into ideal colonial citizens: landowning, economically productive, and politically quiescent. In 1914, Frank Carpenter observed that Christian and Muslim colonists had begun to trade with one another, attend each other's festivals, and compete in field sports. Carpenter hoped this would lead the Maguindanao Moros to "consciously emulate the higher type of civilization" and the "constant and diligent directed labor . . . [of their] more civilized Christian fellow colonist."[73] As in the Moro Exchanges, proselytism occurred in the field and the marketplace rather than at the pulpit. Carpenter was careful to discourage active religious missionary work in the colonies, correctly surmising the Moros would greet conversionary overtures with hostility.[74]

Christian settlers initially came from Cebu. Male colonists had to be married and willing to bring their families with them and signed contracts pledging a minimum five-year residency. The government helped pay off their personal debts and advanced an interest-free loan to cover travel expenses to Mindanao. On arriving in Cotabato, the colonist received basic tools for survival, building materials, a carabao, and a plow. He kept the proceeds from his first-year crop yields, after which the government took 35 percent of the income derived from agricultural products until his debt amortization ended. Colonists received expert advice on land management practices, recent advances in agricultural science, product marketing, and establishing public infrastructure. Moros came from nearby communities and were individually selected by local datus and panditas. They received only eight hectares of land, as opposed to the sixteen Christian colonists were provided. In 1914, forty Moro families lived on the colony near Dulawan, although a further fifteen hundred sought integration into the program. "Had I the necessary funds with which to pay for surveys, and purchase work cattle and implements," Carpenter wrote to Dean Worcester, "I could place more than ninety-five percent of the Mohammedans and pagans of the Cotabato District on homesteads in the most fertile and easily cultivated portions of the district within the next twelve months." The colonization scheme would contribute to the "general betterment and civilization" of the Moros, Carpenter claimed, and within a generation they would "compare favorably with any producing community in the Islands of the Orient."[75]

Despite Carpenter's expansive designs, life in the remote colonies was far from ideal. The headquarters of Cotabato Agricultural Colony No. 1 was a solidly built two-story structure, but all the homes of the colonists were rudimentary nipa-thatched huts of one or two rooms. Mainly built along river flats, where there was easily cleared wild grass but little forest, these buildings were prone to damage from flooding. Colonists relied on the irregular visits of government steamers for supplies and lived isolated existences in a foreign environment.[76] A share tenancy system and reliance on purchasing supplies from the state led some critics of the program to argue that colonists were trapped in endless cycles of debt peonage. Limiting land sales and prohibiting individual merchants from operating in the colonies, they claimed, stifled private investment. Carpenter responded indignantly, citing the well-established predations of American and Chinese traders. If allowed to grow, the colonies would be more beneficial than any other tenancy system in Asia "or in fact anywhere in the United States." In time, the governor emphatically declared, the "so-called 'Moro Problem' would not be one of public order, but of securing markets for our produce."[77]

Dean Worcester, who had resigned as secretary of the interior in 1913 and established a coconut plantation in North Mindanao, openly questioned the feasibility of the rice colonies. A bitter critic of Filipinization and Philippine independence, he believed that the settlements could only succeed under direct U.S. supervision. Trafficking in racist stereotypes, Worcester informed Carpenter that the Filipinos would never pay their debts and would mismanage the land to the point of collapse. Entertaining dark thoughts, he argued there was also the possibility that "some Moro fanatic will break loose in one of your colonies some day and chop up the population." The agricultural colonies were doomed to failure because they put too much faith in the Filipino. "This is a white man's job and it will take a mighty good white man to do it," Worcester wrote. At the end of his letter, Worcester invoked the British imperial experience, telling Carpenter he had the opportunity to be "a second Rajali Brooke" of Sarawak if he managed the region properly.[78]

The program faced less sensational problems than duplicitous Filipinos or homicidal Moros. Contrary to expectation, the Maguindanaos did not clamor to leave their homes for the uncertainties of colony life. Settled among kin and embedded in their own economic networks, most were unwilling to uproot their families and live under the strict dictates of state administrators. In 1914, the colonies had 774 families, and in 1915 this grew to 940 families. More than half the residents in 1915 (2,682) were Moros, while the rest were Christians. During the following five years, the colonies suffered a variety of misfortunes. As the program wound down, the Cotabato Valley experienced massive flooding that destroyed much of the colonists' crops. Other misfortunes followed, including drought, earthquakes, smallpox, rinderpest, locusts, and influenza. In 1919, the number of families (943) remained nearly unchanged from five years earlier, contradicting projections that the colonies would expand rapidly.[79]

Government settlement programs fizzled, but independent settlers from Cebu and other islands in the North continued arriving, a trend that only increased as more Filipinos replaced Americans in the colonial bureaucracy. Moro groups responded to this development warily or with alarm. Datu Piang, once an enthusiastic supporter of settlement, became disillusioned. In 1927, he wrote a series of entreaties to President Calvin Coolidge. The Americans, Piang asserted, had created a system wherein Moros fell victim to the predominantly Filipino leadership in Mindanao-Sulu. Moro homes were "violated," their altars "desecrated"; entire families were "wiped out," and "bribery fraud, [and] chicanery" had "marked the whole period." Moro lands had been "parceled out and granted to Filipinos" through colonization, and places of worship converted into "pig walls or grog shops." The anti-Filipino vitriol of Piang's letter veered into outright race hatred in places but also evinced the sense of alarm and fear Moros felt toward migration. Piang correctly diagnosed the system as rigged. Filipinos dominated state administration and law enforcement in the 1920s and 1930s. They aided incoming Christian settlers and often viewed Muslim populations as threats to be marginalized.[80]

Government reports from the 1930s illustrate how the idea of settlement transitioned naturally into broader designs for Philippine nationhood. The Bureau of Lands worked alongside the Bureau of Non-Christian Tribes to make colonization as frictionless as possible. "Homeseekers" from the North entered into tenancy agreements with the government similar to the ones provided to the Cotabato settlers. A small loan covered travel and start-up costs, and new arrivals could expect a tract of land and agricultural guidance once in Mindanao. A committee established to examine infrastructure in the South recommended Moros and Lumad, whose territories settlers encroached on, be moved onto reservations.[81] A report compiled by the agricultural specialist Inocencio Elayda and director of prisons Paulino Santos was even more proscriptive. Convinced of the "need [for] Christian immigrants from the north to balance [Mindanao's] Non-Christian population," Elayda and Santos sketched out plans for correcting the mistakes of the past, which had included poor surveying and an underutilization of natural resources. With suitable colonists and sound planning, the colonization of the South could expand rapidly.[82] American ideas about the salutary and instructive effects of settlement on "non-Christians" remained. Echoing Frank Carpenter's words from two decades earlier, the Bureau of Non-Christian Tribes head Teofisto Guingona declared that the settlement of Mindanao-Sulu was a "great factor in the solution of the so-called Moro Problem."[83]

In March 1936, President Manuel Quezon toured the "fertile unexplored lands" of the Cotabato Valley and urged Christians and non-Christians alike to "take advantage of the opportunity being offered by the government."[84] That same year, the subdivision of territory in Cotabato, Lanao, and Davao created over eight thousand new vacant lots. Secretary of Lands José P. Dans encouraged settlers from Cebu and Bohol to move south.[85] The Bureau of Lands drafted plans to settle six thousand families along the district boundary between Cotabato and Davao, facilitated by a massive expansion of roads stretching from Misamis in the north to the Davao Penal Colony in the south and passing through Bukidnon, Lanao, and Cotabato. Long-term goals included building railroads, harnessing waterfalls for power generation, and incentivizing agricultural, industrial, and mining concerns to exploit the island's resources. "The present administration expects to see Mindanao fully developed and wealth-producing by the end of the Commonwealth transition period," reported the *Manila Tribune*.[86]

As in previous generations, Maranao, Samal, Maguindanao, and Lumad groups living in the vicinity of new settlements had little interest in uprooting their lives. Despite this, the rapid influx of northern migrants caused some Moros to apply for homesteads, fearing that "public lands in Mindanao [were] rapidly failing into Christian hands."[87] Muslim and Lumad residents could not combat the sheer scale of migration planned. Officials in Manila saw Mindanao as a demographic steam valve that could mitigate issues of overcrowding and resource allocation. In 1937, Secretary of Agriculture and Commerce Eulogio Rodriguez declared that the social problems in Japan, Italy, and Germany arose from a lack of space. The same could not be said of the Philippines: "We have excess lands and manpower and force to develop these lands. . . . We need strong pioneering spirit, strong will and the national-spirited decision to develop our country, to move from place to place, to spread out and occupy our own agricultural lands a patrimony which God has given us as a gift." Mimicking North American frontier rhetoric, Rodriguez conjured a divinely constituted Philippines to drive internal colonization.[88]

An orientation toward settlement and transformation during the American period prefaced the vast migrations that engulfed Mindanao after the Second World War. Although the early agricultural colonies floundered, a reorganized settlement plan under the Interisland Migration Division of the Bureau of Labor, which operated from 1919 until 1939, managed to attract nearly 35,000 colonists by the mid-1930s. More significant, the aggressive marketing of Mindanao in the press, first by Americans and later Filipinos, intensified independent migration to the South. During the entire colonial period, Mindanao was "considerably above the national average in population growth" and experienced "sizeable in-migration."[89] Demographics shifted accordingly. Cotabato provides a good example of what this looked like in terms of numbers. In the 1903 census, Muslims accounted for 113,875 residents out of 125,875 in the district. By 1939, Cotabato's population had risen to 298,935, out of which 162,996 were Muslims and 70,493 Lumad, indicating tens of thousands of new Christian settlers.[90] In Lanao, a province considered comparatively hostile to settlement, a net migration of 163,990 people occurred between 1903 and 1939. The numbers were even more significant in Christian-majority areas like Davao, where indigenous populations were displaced more easily than Moros elsewhere.[91]

The colonization of the South never fostered the integrationist harmony U.S. colonial officials believed it would, but exaggerated settler success stories peddled in the North did convince many Filipinos, particularly from the Visayas, that Mindanao was an ideal space for personal reinvention and financial gain. Alongside real population pressures and wealth disparities in the North, this generated migratory momentum. What Patricio Abinales calls "the most massive movement of Filipinos in the history of the nation" occurred between 1946 and 1960. At 7.4 percent, Mindanao's annual growth rate significantly outpaced the rest of the Philippines, and by 1960 its population reached over 5 million.[92] At this time, one quarter of the island's residents—some 1.2 million people—reported being born elsewhere, and a further 365,798 residents had moved between provinces within Mindanao. U.S. colonialism created a lasting legacy of settlement and commercial development in the Southern Philippines—one that bore itself out five decades after U.S. military administrators had begun promoting the region as an empty space of infinite potential.[93]

Chapter 3

Civilizational Imperatives

Building Colonial Classrooms

Americans encountered diverse educational practices in the Southern Philippines. Farther north, Catholic religious orders had overseen a process of acculturation in line with Spanish colonial objectives. Difficulties conquering the Muslim South led Spain to concentrate its resources there on military and political subjugation rather than cultural initiatives. As such, the conditions necessary to develop and operate school systems only existed in a few areas of Mindanao. Nineteenth-century Spanish census records from Muslim areas show either zero enrollment in colonial schools or, as was the case in Zamboanga and Cotabato in 1866, enrollment hovering as low as 4 to 5 percent of eligible youth.[1] Limited colonization meant preexisting native educational structures operated with minimal interference.

Prior to 1899, education came primarily in the form of the pandita school, so named after the religious figure in the community who administrated it.[2] Here, local youth learned the Arabic alphabet, studied the Qur'an and other Islamic texts, and gained insight into the complex genealogies anchoring their kinship networks. Teachers instructed them on general issues of comportment, such as the proper way to greet an elder and the rituals that accompanied prayer.[3] The pandita schools provided a road map for living within one's family, community, ethnic group, and Islam itself. Although the form and content of the schools varied between Moro groups, all focused on what Jeffrey Ayala Milligan describes as "cultural reproduction through the socialization of Muslim youth into the traditions and values of Muslim Filipino ethnic communities."[4]

Such were the structures Americans attempted to displace after arriving in Mindanao-Sulu.

U.S. military authorities identified education as a civilizational linchpin. Negotiating with Sultan Kiram in 1899, John Bates received directives from Manila to emphasize the benefits of new educational forms to the Tausūg leader. Instructing "the rising generation of Moros in industrial and mechanical pursuits through the medium of schools" took precedence. Authorities would assign select Americans to "impart constant valuable information" among the Tausūg through practical instruction.[5] During his time on Jolo, Bates also studied regional colonial histories, noting in his reports that the British in Malaya curbed piracy and slavery through the establishment of industrial schools.[6]

Public Schools in the South

Between 1899 and 1903, public schools in Mindanao-Sulu operated in an ad hoc fashion. Although technically run by the Department of Public Instruction in Manila, their character and resources varied greatly by community. Church-run schools remained standard in places like Zamboanga, while elsewhere smaller pandita schoolhouses predominated. When the U.S. military took charge of public education, they faced resistance from both Christian and Muslim religious figures. Governor William Kobbé adopted a carrot-and-stick approach to the problem. He disciplined a Catholic priest who sermonized against educational secularization but also made it publicly known that a preexisting Spanish law allowed for religion to be taught in public schools.[7] In rural districts, military officers and their families provided coverage. At Malabang, the 23rd Infantry chaplain J. H. Sutherland established a school attended by forty pupils. A mother of a regimental lieutenant, Mrs. White, volunteered her services as a teacher alongside the chaplain. The two worked on a voluntary basis in a rented building but forwarded requests to Zamboanga "begging that a school-house be built, that it be furnished with modern fixtures and that a teacher be sent [there] to direct the work along systematic lines." Stephen Fuqua, an intelligence officer in the community, believed the military's "moral right" to occupy rested on its ability to educate the Moros. Nevertheless, efforts remained limited.[8]

The establishment of the Moro Province in 1903 created the political conditions necessary to organize and operate schools. That year, Governor Wood and the province's Legislative Council passed an act providing for "the establishment and maintenance of a public school system." The doctor and Moro specialist Najeeb Saleeby became the province's first superintendent of schools. A proponent of intercultural education, he enacted a number of ambitious programs aimed at acculturating Muslims through mediums they understood. Under Saleeby's watch, translation dictionaries appeared, and pandita schools were tolerated. This elastic approach to colonial education displeased certain members of the government, who wanted secular English-language instruction prioritized, but was pragmatic enough to gain some native support.[9] By the end of Wood's governorship in 1906, the school system had progressed enough that the provincial council legislated disciplinary power over students, including "reasonable corporal punishment." Act No. 167 of the Legislative Council made school attendance compulsory for all children between the ages of seven and thirteen. Parents failing to comply with the law faced fines between three and thirty pesos. In passing the act, Wood and his council created a source of lasting tension between Moro groups and the government.[10]

The newly appointed governor Tasker Bliss described the objectives of the public schools in a 1907 speech. The province would teach children "not only the knowledge which comes from books but the knowledge which comes from training in industrial and agricultural schools." A laboring Moro was better than an educated one. Bliss's educational vision built on economic plans for the province. Colonial capital would establish mines, plantations, and logging operations, and the roads of the province would soon throng "with an industrious population bringing this wealth to the market." Accomplishing this required not only white leadership but also a pliant and well-trained native labor force. Here the emphasis on industrial education—basic vocational training—dovetailed with broader developmental agendas for the region. Allied with endeavors like John Finley's Moro Exchanges, a practically oriented education curriculum would civilize Moros through the gospel of work. Bliss admitted that at the time "perhaps one tenth" of the estimated thirty thousand eligible children in the province attended state schools but was confident numbers would soar once natives realized the "value of the free gift" the government offered.[11]

Training began in the first grade, where children learned "sticklaying, slat-plaiting, paper-folding, block-building," and other skills. They advanced to weaving hats and mats in the second grade. Gender segregation began in the third, with boys instructed to work with rattan and girls focusing on needlework. Upper-year boys received one hour of instruction in carpentry each day. The curriculum allowed a degree of flexibility. Alongside basic arithmetic and literacy lessons, teachers could incorporate materials and activities suitable to the individual locality. Budget-conscious officials directed schools to produce "salable" goods in their classrooms. Although industrial education was unfamiliar to many American and Filipino teachers, the provincial superintendent made strides to create a uniform curriculum through "rigid inspections." By 1907, the province operated fifty-eight schools. Of these, fifty-five were primary, two were strictly industrial, and the final was the provincial high school at Zamboanga. The teaching staff was comprised of twenty-one Americans, fifty-six Filipinos, and nine Moros. The majority taught in English, with two Filipinos giving lessons in Spanish and four Moros in local dialects.[12]

Big plans obscured difficult realities. With provincial resources earmarked for maintaining order and building transportation infrastructure, authorities frequently underfunded education. Schools in rural areas lacked connectivity with Zamboanga and were difficult to get to. Training a suitable number of native teachers who could connect with students linguistically and culturally remained a struggle. Most importantly, the major groups targeted for education—Tausūg, Maranao, Maguindanao, and Samal Moros—distrusted state plans for their children. While government schools did not overtly push religious conversion (as some Muslims feared), they did act as tools of deculturation. Education in public schools meant forgoing the customary cultural knowledge provided by a pandita in favor of colonially mandated values. As such, some communities looked on the schoolteacher with suspicion, and the job came with certain risks. American, Filipino, and Moro teachers became targets for violence. Arolas Tulawie, later a prominent political figure in Sulu, requested the government provide him with a revolver to wear while he taught. An early adopter of Western fashions, Tulawie could not properly fit a barong into his suit jacket.[13]

The rough enforcement of Act No. 167 by U.S. Army and PC officers also stoked discontent. A lack of clarity among state security agencies about how far to push the directive made matters worse. Writing Tasker Bliss from Jolo, Col. E. Z. Steever asked for better instructions, unsure whether he should be using his discretion or imposing the act "notwithstanding whatever opposition may arise."[14] Primary schools at Parang, Maibun, and Bongao closed due to "dangerous conditions," and a planned school for the children of Moro elites never advanced past the planning stage. Saleeby's successor Charles Cameron found this frustrating. In 1909, he wrote a letter to David Prescott Barrows complaining that other officials in the Moro Province were discrediting native teachers without providing any alternative to them. Further issues arose from constant turnovers in military personnel, which made developing long-term relationships with local leaders difficult and dampened support for industrial education initiatives.[15]

These difficulties bore out in the numbers. Between 1903 and 1907, total enrollment in public schools for the Moro Province jumped from 2,114 to 5,394 students (although average daily attendance was only 2,968). Of these, 4,414 were Filipinos, 793 Moros, 165 Lumad, and 22 Americans. Charles Cameron attributed Filipino participation in the school system to their "greater natural friendliness" and tendency to concentrate around American garrisons along the coastlines of Mindanao. Enrollment remained low in Muslim communities. The 793 Moro students in Mindanao-Sulu came from a pool of over 50,000 eligible to attend school. Cameron blamed impermanent settlements and "ancient migratory habits" for Moro reticence, arguing that only industrial development and sedentism could remedy the issue.[16] By 1913, total enrollment in provincial schools reached 7,568 pupils (with an average daily attendance of 4,535). This broke down to 5,111 Filipinos, 1,825 Moros, 525 Lumad, and 100 or so Chinese, American, and Spanish students. The annual report from that

Figure 3.1 Maguindanao students at a school for Moro girls in Cotabato, c. 1910s. Established and operated by Anna Dworak, wife of District Governor Edward Dworak, the institution met with some suspicion in socially conservative Moro communities. Although no overt proselytizing was permitted in the school, Governor John Pershing boasted that the "lived" Christianity of the teachers influenced students. (Edward Bowditch Papers, No. 4292, Division of Rare and Manuscript Collections, Cornell University Library)

year boasted of a 47 percent increase in Moro students, although this still only represented a fraction of school-age Muslim children in the province.[17]

Disagreements within the Moro Province establishment hindered cohesive policy formation. Najeeb Saleeby promoted the idea of carefully managed datuships, wherein Americans co-opted instead of bypassed native political and religious leaders.[18] These ideas deeply influenced Charles Cameron, who donated "books and materials to Islamic schools" and encouraged them to "modernize their techniques."[19] Troubled by low literacy rates among the Moros, Saleeby and Cameron published and distributed Tausūg and Maranao primers that utilized Arabic script.[20] This desire to see native cultural institutions meld with the colonial state never came to fruition. Leonard Wood and other military men pushed for pandita schools to be "superseded" by public ones "as fast as funds will permit and competent teachers can be found." Governor John Pershing thought tolerating religious instructors was dangerous and argued that the "occult inspiration" of Islam had caused problems in the past. Only the "civilizing forces" of the colonial school system could create conditions of "social evolution."[21] Moros allowed to teach in public schools were invariably those who had trained at the Zamboanga Provincial Normal School, where a "heterogeneous mass" of Filipino and Moro teachers were "welded into greater homogeneity" under American supervision.[22]

An emphasis on vocational training—agricultural in the interior, marine resources on the coast—continued during the Carpenter years, and in larger towns some students received advanced instruction in wood- and ironworking. Carpenter inherited his predecessor's skepticism toward customary teaching practices, dismissively noting an "inclination to mysticism and pretense to magic" among the panditas. The school system also received an influx of teachers during this time, the majority of whom were Christian Filipinos. In Zamboanga, the Episcopal Church and Christian and Missionary Alliance ran independent schools. Enrollment numbers grew provincewide, although in 1914 an estimated 107,000 school-age children did not receive primary education.[23] Establishing schools in isolated areas remained delicate work. Southeast of Cotabato, the supervising teacher James McCall visited the community of Maganoy to negotiate with its leader, Datu Ampatuan. The datu, advanced in age and religiously conservative, expressed his skepticism to McCall that mandatory schooling in the community could work. For many Moros and Lumad in the hinterlands, government presence was limited to the coercive Philippine Constabulary. This created a lack of trust that filtered into interactions with civilian representatives like McCall, who returned to Cotabato without much to show for his efforts.[24]

One method of shaping Moro youth involved giving them scholarships to study outside their home communities. In 1914, the Department of Mindanao and Sulu distributed twenty-eight scholarships to Moro boys. The young scholars relocated to Zamboanga, where they trained as teachers under the "immediate observation and influence of department officers." That same year, a number of Moro students received scholarships to attend schools in Manila. This included the Training School for Nurses, the Philippine School of Arts and Trades, the Philippine General Hospital Training School for Nurses, the School of Commerce, and the Philippine Normal School. Those selected were often the children of Moro elites, such as Tarhata Kiram, the niece of the sultan of Sulu.[25] When administration of Moro lands transferred to the Bureau of Non-Christian Tribes in 1920, a host of official scholarships solidified this educational patronage model.[26]

Documents from the 1930s illustrate the challenges student pensionados faced. Poor communication between the far-flung islands of the Sulu Archipelago and Manila created instances where young men and women arrived in Manila falsely believing they had scholarships. Sustaining funds for scholarships were limited, and strict quotas enacted.[27] In the capital, students often lived in poverty. Some petitioned high officials for financial aid. Gowa Mohammad, who had been singled out by Governor-General Frank Murphy on a visit to Zamboanga, wrote directly to Vice-Governor J. R. Hayden for assistance. Enrolled at the Columbian Institute to study "Police and Detective Science," the young Moro worked menial jobs to cover his tuition and matriculation fees. Mohammad begged Hayden to help with his costs and save him from "committing suicide," telling the vice-governor he had "strong faith and confidence" in him as a "great sympathizer of the Moro people." Hayden replied tersely that all available funds for scholarships had been exhausted for the year.[28]

Filipino administrators and Westernized Moros inherited American ideas about the role of the public school system. The bureau chief Teofisto Guingona believed the government had "a moral duty and obligation to give instruction to the Mohammedan people." Guingona wrote to the Tausūg educator and politician Arolas Tulawie that education was the "basis of the greatness of peoples" and led to "enlightenment."[29] Yet for all the high-minded talk, education remained in a state of flux as Filipinization progressed. In the mid-1920s, a spate of school burnings around Lanao dropped attendance to new lows. Officials attempted to correct this by filling teaching positions with qualified Maranao candidates, but children stayed at home. At Tamparan, a community on Lake Lanao's east coast, student performance was so poor and attendance so irregular that officials began fining parents. The move fueled antigovernment sentiment, and attacks on teachers continued.[30] In Sulu, a wave of opposition to public schooling crested in the 1920s. Arolas Tulawie wrote against the "Filipinization of education" and feared Filipino teachers would erode the customs and values of the Tausūg people.[31] Governor James Fugate complained of unsympathetic Christian teaching staff and the long classes small children from rural districts had to attend.[32]

Qualified teachers remained in short supply. In 1931, only 1 percent of teachers in Sulu had any sort of professional training, although this number rose to 8 percent the following year. Even with the jump, Sulu's quality of education ranked sixth from the bottom in the entire Philippines. Superintendent of Public Instruction K. W. Chapman pushed to have Muslim boys sent to the Zamboanga Normal School for advanced vocational instruction. Authorities encouraged Muslim women to be trained as schoolteachers, which was unpopular among socially conservative communities.[33] Chapman's replacement, Edward Kuder, became convinced that Muslims were being unfairly targeted by Christian-dominated entities like the Philippine Constabulary. He aimed to remedy these predations by educating a class of Moros who could assert themselves in the language of Western governance. They would identify themselves as part of the Filipino national body yet maintain distinct ethnoreligious identities. "The Commonwealth was preparing [the students] to fit harmoniously into the world," Kuder recalled in a postwar article, "when the Japanese pestilence swept across."[34]

Reports from Mindanao-Sulu in the mid-1930s show constant struggle. Kuder and his subordinates faced the same roadblocks as their predecessors: meager funding, poor attendance figures, resistance to secular schools, and a lack of coverage in remote areas.[35] The small number of Muslim youth who received advanced education often found that there were no openings for them in white-collar positions, leading Teofisto Guingona to declare that "intellectual unemployment" could only be remedied if young Moros "make up their minds that while there is dignity of labor in an office there is as much dignity of labor in the field." A racially tinged development plan for the Southern Philippines urged the government to place emphasis on vocational education so that Moros could be "trained for the household industries to which they are naturally inclined."[36] Three decades after Tasker Bliss had trumpeted the benefits of industrial training, government officials encouraged Muslims to follow a similar route and transform themselves into farmers, fishermen, and laborers. In doing so, they would support state power but have little say otherwise.

Missionary Education in Sulu

The long legacy of Spanish Christianization in the Philippines drew American ecumenical bodies to the archipelago.[37] Although Catholicism reigned, Protestant missionaries arrived in 1898 determined to convert Filipinos. A comity agreement signed that year demarcated territory for each denomination. Baptists had "rights" to the Western Visayas, while the Congregationalists claimed most of Mindanao. These men and women hoped to win over "savage" tribes to Christ, combat Catholic corruption, and push colonial authorities to confront moral issues like prostitution, human trafficking, and narcotics use. Missionaries came from pro- and anti-imperialist camps, although all embraced some type of reform agenda. Well-placed religious figures in the Philippines held substantial clout and often had the ability to influence colonial policy.[38]

Although ostensibly independent, Western missionaries in Mindanao-Sulu nevertheless received substantial support through state channels. Most stationed in Muslim areas understood spreading the gospel of Christ through conventional proselytizing would not work. Spanish efforts to convert the Moros to Catholicism had been greeted with stiff resistance, leaving some American missionaries to wonder whether the Moros should be "left to their own society and devices."[39] Spanish histories of the Philippines railed against Muslims, claiming they were "so obstinate to God's grace, that it is impossible to convert them to Christianity."[40] Cognizant of Islam's resilience, American missionaries tried spreading Christianity through indirect means. This idea—"Christian religion expressed in work"—coincided with prevalent ideas about industrial education. "The school, the hospital, [and] the playground" became pulpits in missionary endeavors. In Mindanao-Sulu, half a million Muslims could be "reached, inspired, [and] empowered" by Protestant outreach "as nowhere else."[41] For district governors, short on funds and hard-pressed to achieve civilizing goals, missionary willingness to fund schools and medical dispensaries made them welcome visitors.

The village of Indanan on the island of Jolo was home to one of these religious initiatives. The prominent Episcopal bishop Charles Henry Brent and the Rhode Island socialite Caroline Spencer operated a missionary school, medical station, and small printing press there. Brent was the most influential foreign religious figure in the Philippines. A Canadian who emigrated to the United States after ordination, he spent time ministering to impoverished congregations in Boston and became prominent enough to be considered for dean at the Union Theological Seminary in New York City. Instead of staying in

North America, Brent accepted a position as missionary bishop to the Philippines in 1902. His ability to cultivate friendships with powerful political figures like Theodore Roosevelt and William Howard Taft served him well in the new colony.[42] Brent's early overseas projects included a school at Baguio for the sons and daughters of the colonial elite, missionary work among the Bontoc Igorots, and advocacy for international drug laws.[43] Hagiographic accounts of the bishop's labors praised him as a "great social force" who "represented the Twentieth Century."[44] Brent turned his attention to the southern islands during his second decade in the Philippines.

In 1913, as the Moro Province transitioned to the Department of Mindanao and Sulu, Caroline Spencer sailed for Jolo. Born Caroline Berryman, she lived a moneyed coastal life between New York City and Newport, Rhode Island. After her husband's death in 1912, Spencer embarked on a world tour. On her stop in the Philippines, she became "intensely interested in the work Bishop Brent [was] . . . doing among the heathen tribes" and committed to returning to teach the Moros. Reporting on her decision, the *New York Times* fixated on the dangers the socialite missionary faced among the Tausūg. Spencer insisted otherwise. "The Moros of Jolo have so far come into contact with hardly any other Americans than soldiers," she told the paper. "We are going to try to show that Americans possess other traits than an ability to fight."[45] Accompanied by her friend Virginia Young, Spencer traveled to Jolo by way of England, Singapore, and Zamboanga. "We are not going to attempt to force Christianity down the throats of the people," she told the *Times* before her departure, "but we want to teach the Moros some of the principles of right living."[46]

In Zamboanga, Bishop Brent parlayed his connections with Governor-General Forbes and John Pershing to lay groundwork for his new school.[47] Spencer received little fanfare when she arrived in Jolo, however. Rumors circulated that juramentados planned to kill the missionary, and members of the officer class felt her presence generated needless tension with local groups. Fawning profiles written later in Spencer's life described her mesmeric effect on the Tausūg, although she more likely ingratiated herself by establishing a medical dispensary where villagers went for health complaints and vaccinations.[48] Under the supervision of the U.S. Army Medical Corps, the site served several hundred people each month. Spencer became friendly enough with locals that she began traveling the island freely, often attending weddings and birth ceremonies.[49]

Brent and Spencer established the school at Indanan on the site of an old U.S. military camp.[50] Located near a market and a Constabulary station, the school eventually sprawled across sixty-eight acres. A ceremony in January 1916 marked its official opening. Dignitaries like Frank Carpenter and Hadji Butu attended the event, which included games and a tree-planting ceremony. The Willard Straight Agricultural School for Moro Boys (later the Bishop Brent Moro School) focused on training Tausūg youth in the industrial and agricultural arts in the hope they would become, in Brent's words, "a higher type of Moro." Initial enrollment was just over thirty students but eventually grew to more than one hundred. J. W. Light, supervisor for the Department of Public Instruction in Sulu, saw the school as an important component in turning Southeast Asian Muslims into producers. "I have studied intensely the Sulu phase of the Moro problem for two years and I think the Moro Agricultural School has before it the greatest possibilities for development that I know of in the Orient," he wrote to Caroline Spencer. He noted that Sulu's close connections with Borneo meant the institution could expand and "develop into a college that will be looked upon with yearning hearts by the youth of the Malay Mohammedan World."[51]

Photographs from the period show a modest two-story building with long porches where the students slept. Indoors one found classrooms, offices, and even a bowling alley. Students grew a variety of crops year-round on the grounds and had facilities to process rice and corn. Press photographs displayed baseball games with captions like "The Moro Boys Love Our American Games."[52] By the early 1920s, the school had expanded to seventy-five acres with plans to reach five hundred. Each male student learned farming, building, and road maintenance, while females were taught basketwork and housekeeping. The Moro Education Fund (MEF), a nonprofit body that oversaw the school, argued that these activities represented "a powerful influence against insurrections among the Moros." Press reports glowed. The *New York Times Magazine* published an article comprised mainly of John Pershing's praise for the school, and the academic Eleanor Crosby Kemp deemed the experiment to be "anthropologically sound" in its teaching of English, arithmetic, and hygienic living.[53]

Brent and Spencer's plans for an all-girls institution met with reticence among the Tausūg. A charitable fund for the proposed school managed to raise $37,000 in 1924, $5,000 of which came from the prominent New York City philanthropist Mary Williamson Averell.[54] A girls' dormitory on Jolo staffed by Filipino teachers operated for several years but was opposed by Moro leaders, who believed Moro girls there were being taught to "marry Filipinos or else become prostitutes." The Tausūg teacher and politician Arolas Tulawie worried girls educated at the dormitory would turn away from their own people and customs.[55] The latter concern had its merits. An Episcopalian report from the late 1930s mentioned Moro girls in Zamboanga schools being "won over to Christianity by constant association with it." The missionary writer Claude Pickens observed that "girls from Basilan and the Sulu Archipelago have passed through the school and caught the Christian spirit."[56] Spencer had the famed architect Whitney Warren draw up plans for a girls' school in the 1920s, but the project faltered.[57]

During its first decade, the school operated under the supervision of the educational director James R. Fugate, whose remarkably varied career in the colonial Philippines spanned three decades. After a brief stint at the University of Michigan, Fugate traveled to the archipelago as a sergeant with the California volunteers. He eventually became governor of Siquijor, a small island in the Central Visayas. In 1916, Bishop Brent and Caroline Spencer asked Fugate to relocate to Jolo.[58] By all accounts energetic and efficient, Fugate ran day-to-day operations at Indanan. Spencer spent long stretches as the overall authority at the institution but was away frequently, and Brent's primary role involved generating revenue in the United States. Fugate's views on the Moros were more liberal than those of his patrons. He believed integrating local cultural practices into colonial educational and governance structures (rather than bypassing them) would lead to long-term successes.

Alongside agricultural and industrial activities, Fugate helped Brent establish the Sulu Press (also referred to as the Moro Press). The bishop saw literacy as key to bringing the Moros onside and disagreed with former officials like Najeeb Saleeby who worked with "hopelessly corrupt" local leaders. He ordered a small printing press from Baguio and Arabic typeface from Beirut, establishing the operation on school grounds. Billed as "the only Moro type in the world" and praised by Frank Carpenter as beneficial to the "material . . . [and] spiritual welfare of the Mohammedans of the region," the Sulu Press became a signal feature of missionary endeavors on Jolo.[59] Under Fugate's supervision, the chief product of the press was a small newspaper called *The Student Weekly* (later *The Moro Outlook*). The *Weekly* provided students an opportunity to hone their English skills but also operated as a subtle outlet for proselytism. In March 1925, for example, it ran an article extolling the virtues of "Christian motherhood," claiming childbearing was "close to the sufferings of Christ."[60] The paper cataloged births and deaths, recorded local color, and listed school events. Occasionally, it ventured into more serious topics, such as state violence. In 1926, the *Weekly* reported on a judicial inquiry into the death of a local man who had been shot in the back by the Constabulary.[61]

Despite its biases, the newspaper represented the only venue where Moro voices were regularly published.

The school suffered setbacks in the mid-1920s. Fugate grew exasperated with the constant demands placed on him. His interactions with Spencer were strained, and the operation faced financial issues. The Sulu Press shuttered as a result, and Fugate sent fevered letters to Brent condemning donor pressure to expand and requesting more aid. The bishop promised to send out "1000 appeals" for funds and expressed anxiety over Fugate's welfare.[62] Overworked and in the midst of collapse, the educational director resigned in 1926. In a scathing missive to Brent the following year, he excoriated the bishop for failing to appreciate his mental, physical, and financial sacrifices and for standing by while Spencer and others planned to have him "humiliatingly eliminated." Fugate speculated that if he had "belonged to the hierarchy" with his "address gilding the Social Registry of Manhattan," his contributions would have been better appreciated. Ending his relationship with Brent, Spencer, and the school, Fugate once again sought work with the colonial government and in 1928 was appointed district governor of Sulu.[63]

As Fugate implied, wealthy patronage networks did keep the Moro School afloat. Before his death in 1929, Charles Brent expressed to friends that he wished the school to be his legacy. In the 1930s, the Moro Educational Foundation (MEF) parlayed Brent's social connections into a series of fund-raisers for Indanan. The most lavish of these was a memorial dinner in 1939 held at New York's Waldorf Astoria hotel. The lawyer and politician George Wharton Pepper hosted, and the event featured speeches from William Cameron Forbes, Frank McCoy, the writer Katharine Mayo, and John Pershing (who could not attend but had his speech read for him). Forbes delivered the longest address, situating Brent's school at the forefront of the civilizing mission in the islands. The work at Indanan taught "the Christian spirit rather than the tenets of the Christian Church" to a people "recently redeemed from savagery." Forbes praised the work of Caroline Spencer and James Fugate, whose murder in the late 1930s on Mindanao made him "one of the many martyrs to the great cause of pacification and betterment of these people."[64]

A series of testimonials from prominent Americans was attached to the evening's proceedings and read like an index of colonial officialdom in the Philippines. Leonard Wood, Dean Worcester, Elihu Root, Najeeb Saleeby, Herbert Hoover, Warren G. Harding, William Taft, Frank Murphy, Dwight Davis, J. R. Hayden, Frank W. Carpenter, Henry Stimson, and J. G. Harbord all made appearances.[65] For these men, the work Brent and Spencer performed on Jolo was a corollary of their own efforts among the Moros. Brent himself would have agreed, having compared the hardships of missionary work to those faced by the "founders of empire" in his writings.[66] The proceedings featured a separate set of testimonials from the school's students. Juli Samsialam wrote of all the different vegetables planted in the school gardens, the smallpox vaccinations given to the community, the track-and-field meetings, and the popularity of baseball among the boys. Another student, Ahmaraja Dadjiliul, described a movie screening put on by the new headmaster that nearly one thousand people attended.[67]

The mythologizing of Brent and the elite support the school received did not solve its financial woes. Fugate's replacement, Leo Meyette, traveled the United States in the 1930s promoting Indanan. At Columbia University he described the successes of the school in "changing the fierce Moro pirates into business men, mechanics, and policemen." Former students became teachers, government administrators, and farmers, Meyette told the audience.[68] Despite these apparent successes, setbacks plagued the Indanan school. Donations decreased as patrons felt the impact of the Great Depression, and a powerful typhoon in the spring of 1932 destroyed the main building. The school struggled to rebuild and shuttered for a time but reopened in the mid-1930s under the direction of W. Carr Cooper.[69]

By the early 1940s, school trustees were searching for ways to ensure its continued operation without wholesale reliance on donations. William Cameron Forbes cabled President Manuel Quezon in late 1940 requesting a government allowance. He further appealed to Secretary of War Henry L. Stimson to press for the Bishop Brent Moro School to be merged with the public school system but in a manner where it retained "its character as a memorial to Bishop Brent." Forbes admitted that MEF funds were exhausted and assured Stimson that the school was "purely non-sectarian" (unlike other church schools).[70] In January 1941, the head of Philippine affairs at the State Department, Richard R. Ely, informed Stimson that the Filipinos were not amenable to Forbes's requests. If the school were to become a publicly funded entity it would only retain its name and nothing else. Ely advised the trustees not to "trade their birthright for a very doubtful mess of pottage," although the matter resolved itself in unspectacular fashion when the Japanese occupied Jolo later in the year. After the war, the Philippine government took over the school, and Ely's prediction bore itself out.[71]

Frank Laubach and the Maranao

Cautious missionary efforts also took place on Mindanao. Following the Spanish-American War, Christian and Missionary Alliance members set up operations in non-Muslim areas of the island's north coast and around Zamboanga. In predominantly Islamic regions missionary work could be dangerous, and government agencies were reluctant to sanction it. The presence of foreign religious groups created rumors of forced conversions, stoked support for antigovernment preachers, and otherwise complicated already tenuous state-building efforts. The district of Lanao had many of these issues. The relationship between local Maranao communities and the Philippine Constabulary was particularly strained in the 1910s–1920s. Datus and outlaw leaders tested government power by engaging in running battles with the Constabulary. Cycles of state and antistate violence punctuated life in Lanao.[72]

Undeterred by these obstacles, Frank C. Laubach settled in Lanao in December 1929. The Congregationalist missionary's interest in Mindanao began decades prior during his college years. The son of a dentist from Benton, Pennsylvania, Laubach studied sociology at Princeton before attending the Union Theological Seminary. There he explored the question of the Islamic Philippines, composing a paper titled "Problems in Religious Education on the Island of Mindanao." Laubach's student writings lacked the sophistication or empathy of his later work, and he determined the United States "must either abandon [the Moros] entirely . . . or enter upon a war of extermination." He argued the Moros would share the same lamentable fate as the Native Americans after contact with European settlers.[73] After completing doctoral work at Columbia University in 1915, Laubach was ordained as a Congregationalist minister and departed with his wife for the Philippines. He initially worked with Christians in Cagayan de Oro, before moving to Manila in the 1920s to teach and publish.[74] Laubach visited Lanao most summers, and his thoughts often returned there while in the colonial capital. This initially manifested in plans to Christianize first the Southern Philippines and then the entire Islamic world, a militant position that stood in stark contrast to his views in ensuing decades.[75]

The provincial government in Lanao began considering new avenues for educating the Maranao people at the end of the 1920s. Violence was ebbing in the region, and the government offered Laubach property at a reduced rate. In 1929, he left his wife and son in Baguio and traveled to Dansalan to open a school.[76] There Laubach's views on Islam softened. He quickly became friendly with Maranao datus, read the Qur'an with an "unprejudiced mind" to understand Muhammad, and reflected critically on how vices ascribed solely to Islam also prevailed in the United States. Christians and Muslims, he came to believe, had been misled about one another. In the midst of personal experiments with intercessory prayer, Laubach realized the Islamic concept of submission to God's will was entirely compatible with his own religious outlook.[77]

Open-minded discussion with local Maranao contributed to Laubach's spiritual transformation, allowing for a more inclusive understanding of how an individual could perform religious service. His drive to dismantle Muslim and Lumad societies ebbed, and, over time, he even became concerned about the impact of colonial incursions into Maranao culture. "I fear that the Moros as a separate civilization will be almost a forgotten thing," he wrote his father in 1930. "One can see the inroads of civilization in the adoption of western clothes, in the breaking down of customs, and in the advent of the public school." Laubach saw the school system as an "intellectual steamroller," which would ultimately cause more harm than "fanatical Spanish priests" had. He struggled with the commonly held notion that the civilizing project was fundamentally virtuous and worried that "something worse" might replace what the Moros already had.[78] During a decade in Lanao, Laubach would both reject and embrace tropes of the colonial missionary.[79]

The proposed school was to be a hub of learning for the entire region—an ever-expanding space where Laubach's developmental desires for the Maranao could find expression. What began as a single schoolhouse in 1930 was four years later a complex of nine buildings spread over sixteen hectares of land. Beyond classrooms, this included a nursing station that coordinated with the public hospital in Dansalan, a church and recreation center, dormitories for students, a library with thousands of books and periodicals from around the world, and ten hectares of fields dedicated to nurseries and experimental crops, ranging from soybeans to durian to California orange trees. With the assistance of his Columbia-educated assistant Donato Galia, Laubach took it upon himself to transform Lanao.[80]

Underpinning the entire operation was the missionary's fervent belief that literacy could help the Maranao people avoid cultural and demographic elimination as the Southern Philippines integrated into the emerging Philippine nation-state. Literacy in Lanao was limited to panditas and other elites. Laubach estimated around one in every five hundred people in the region could read Arabic script. Although Najeeb Saleeby and Charles Cameron experimented with Arabic in their own literary efforts, the colonial government had increasingly moved toward English-language instruction in the intervening decades.[81] Laubach decided both Arabic and English were undesirable and instead decided to transliterate the Maranao language using the Roman alphabet. To do so, he compiled regional dictionaries and then phonetically translated the words with them. Laubach identified three of these words as containing every consonant in the alphabet but containing each only once. These were *Malabanga* (or Malabang, a town in the area), *karatasa* (paper), and *paganada* (to learn). Together, they represented "key" words in the local dialect. Laubach named his method after this idea: the Lanao key system.[82]

Staff at the newly christened Maranao Folk School used a series of charts to teach locals. Advocates of the method claimed beginners learned to read and write their language—as phonetically interpreted by Laubach's system—within an hour. Convinced of the revolutionary character of his method, Laubach began training men and women to spread it to outlying areas of Lanao. The school paid these teachers ten dollars per month for their efforts. Proponents of the key system contended that the literacy rate in Lanao, which stood at 3 percent in the early 1930s, could rise to 80 percent by decade's close. Laubach believed the work represented the only way for the Moros to "catch up with the rest of world."[83]

While many Moros praised Laubach for his ceaseless campaigns, others saw a subtle conversion agenda at play. These concerns had some merit. Laubach was looking to transform the Maranao, although the religious dimensions of his goals were sometimes opaque. The Maranao Folk School recognized this public unease, releasing a peculiar public statement in 1932. In it, local datus that supported the school argued that "infidel" Christian Filipinos had spread the conversion rumors. Rather than a means of Christianization, the literacy drives were actually a means of combatting cultural incursion. "We inform [the Filipinos] that we are Islams [sic] as we were born by our Islam [sic] parents," the notice read. "We do not want them to have the least idea that we have been converted to Christianity: no, not even unto death! We have willingly joined Dr. Laubach in his work for it is beneficial to us all." The school's success rested on its legitimacy among the Maranao, and its advocates feared any depiction as a fifth column for Filipino hegemony would halt the work being done in Lanao.[84]

Frank Laubach also faced pushback from officials, who viewed his methods as at odds with public education. The Bureau of Education in Manila aggressively promoted English-language learning (and, toward the end of the decade, Tagalog) as a means of creating a unified Philippine culture, yet Laubach openly advocated Maranao as the primary conduit for literacy. Lanao governor J. J. Heffington noted the issue in reports, believing that the Moros would not have "access to the literature of the country" if they only studied the Maranao vernacular. "For some reason the tried and established method of teaching people to read by the regular use of the Roman alphabet . . . fails to appeal to him," Heffington complained, "and he prefers to use his own system which may, to the malformed, appear more spectacular."[85] Visiting Lanao in 1935, the University of Michigan botanist H. H. Bartlett noted a litany of errors in the school's original Maranao dictionary, although admitted subsequent editions were more reliable. Laubach himself conceded his methods were unique and that "sticklers for orthodoxy" would find fault with them.[86]

The Maranao Folk School published a small newspaper to spread its message, the *Lanao Progress*. Laubach purchased a printing press from Cagayan de Oro in 1930, and by 1933 the paper was appearing biweekly. English and Maranao versions of each story appeared side by side, the latter transliterated phonetically into the Roman alphabet as per the key system. The paper was eight to twelve pages long and featured a mix of local, national, and international topics. The local material ranged from regional boosterism to lurid coverage of the latest criminal outrages. The *Progress* was also a pulpit for social messaging, encouraging its Maranao readership to abstain from gambling and drinking.[87] Staff culled national and international news from the twenty-five newspapers and periodicals the school subscribed to. Subscribers could read about Russo-Japanese relations or Italian colonial empire in North Africa. The paper published instructive stories from elsewhere in the Islamic world about female professionals and suffrage activists.[88] Laubach also encouraged Dansalan locals to write opinion pieces, on topics ranging from "despotism" to slavery.[89] When not preoccupied with culturally refashioning the Maranao, the *Progress* occasionally veered into the bizarre, publishing accounts of shark-octopus battles and speculating that murders could be solved "by developing the last picture taken on the eye of a dead person."[90]

The school also actively collected, translated, and printed Moro oral histories and myths. The first of these, "An Odyssey from Lanao," appeared in the periodical *Philippine Public Schools* in late 1930. Composed in epic verse, it followed the mythical Moro warrior-prince Bantugan as he traversed temporal and spiritual realms and warred with the Spanish.[91] The press published other stories in pamphlet form, such as "The Lanao Belief about the Hereafter" and "The Story of the Vagrant Boy." H. H. Bartlett received a copy of Laubach's translation of the Bantugan myth, now referred to as the *Darangen* epic. At first he believed Laubach guilty of "literary faking" but later changed his mind, declaring the missionary had "done the cause of Philippine ethnology and literature a very great service."[92] The oral traditions of the Maranao fascinated

Laubach, and his efforts to compile them arose from a genuine preservationist instinct. Yet missionary impulses remained, and alongside his work on the epics he also published the New Testament in Maranao.[93]

Frank Laubach's programs expanded outward from Lanao in the mid-1930s, assuming global dimensions. He promoted his literacy techniques in the United States, and the *Boston Globe* wrote of how the "alphabet [was] taming Moros."[94] In 1934, Laubach began a letter-writing campaign, promoting his techniques to missionaries, officials, academics, and native leaders around the world. This included leading colonial educators like Arthur Mayhew, who edited the journal *Oversea Education*, and Samuel T. Moyer, an American missionary in India. Elaine Swenson at the Language Research Institute at New York University recommended Laubach get in contact with Ernest Boas, son of the famed anthropologist Franz.[95] In Dansalan, a large map of the world hung in the middle of the schoolroom. On it, silk threads connected Mindanao to other points on the globe the school had corresponded with.[96] Laubach began teaching the key system in other regions of the Philippines, before embarking on a world tour in 1935. The missionary and his family first visited India for several months and from there traveled to the Middle East. Laubach's son Robert wrote letters to the *Progress* updating readers on the journey, and in the Dansalan classroom, a blue line on the world map tracked the family's progress. Although he returned to Lanao in 1936, Frank Laubach's attentions increasingly turned outward.[97]

The missionary grappled with the idea of converting Muslims during his final years in Mindanao. He wondered in the pages of *The Muslim World* how Christian practices could be married to Islamic ones: "Should we make our church look like a mosque, have a large drum to call people to prayer, invite *panditas* and *imams* to share the service with us, have a place for washing their feet and hands before entering the church, and perhaps even use prayer rugs instead of chairs?" Lanao was a "laboratory" for new approaches to proselytism, although in Laubach's accounts to other missionaries his work was depicted as a conventional conduit for Christianity.[98] The *Progress* contained articles describing the deeds of Christ, and Laubach led a small church service in Maranao for a handful of converts.[99] Practicing a quieter form of cultural imperialism, Laubach oriented his efforts toward simultaneously protecting and transforming Islamic colonial subjects. A subtle and perceptive missionary, he was a missionary nonetheless and retained conversion as the ultimate signifier of success.

The work in Lanao continued until 1941. Laubach established a new high school and teacher's college, while his son Robert ran a group called the Society for English-Speaking Youth.[100] Laubach became increasingly convinced that educating the Maranao was the only means to avoid cultural collapse. His writings in these final years focused on the fate of the Moros in an independent Philippines. Migration from the northern islands had accelerated, and integration seemed inevitable. A fork in the road lay ahead. Either "responsible young Moros" would "remake their Province," or the "whole Moro race" would be "wiped out by Filipinos."[101] Laubach was not present to witness the struggles of the Maranao postindependence. A brief trip outside of Mindanao in October 1941 became permanent after the Japanese invasion. The missionary turned his attentions elsewhere, dedicating the remainder of his life to spreading his literacy method to other parts of the globe.[102]

In 1932, the former governor-general Henry L. Stimson reflected on prior successes as he advocated for continued U.S. rule in the Philippines. "Under enlightened leadership we framed our policy along no selfish lines of colonial domination, but from the beginning undertook the courageous experiment of trying to establish among an Oriental people the practices of Western economic and social development and principles of political democracy," he wrote. Although Europeans had "scoffed" at American plans, time had proven them correct. As Stimson saw it, the Philippines in the 1930s represented "an islet of growing Western development and thought surrounded by an ocean of Orientalism." Its people were now "interpreters of American idealism to the Far East," and the archipelago a durable paean to U.S. civilizational largesse.[103]

Many colonials shared Stimson's triumphant vision. In Mindanao-Sulu, a colonially generated and interconnected set of racial, political, religious, and economic impulses drove fantasies of transformation. These civilizational imperatives—establishing new systems of law, health care, education, settlement, and commerce—stemmed from a conviction that Western modes of living demanded replication among the peoples of the Islamic Philippines. They remained remarkably consistent throughout the U.S. colonial period, although methods for achieving them shifted. While the number of Americans in the South decreased after 1914, those remaining occupied important positions and dictated policy, particularly in law enforcement and education. The Filipinos replacing outgoing Americans often took similarly proactive approaches to "civilizing" Muslim and Lumad groups. Elites like Teofisto Guingona viewed Moro areas as a puzzle to be solved in much the same way Leonard Wood, Tasker Bliss, or Frank Carpenter had. As such, the so-called "Moro Problem" remained a social and political factor in the politics of the Philippines well after the Americans departed.

Over forty years, the colonial state managed to Westernize a small number of Muslim subjects. These men and women eschewed traditional customs, instead clothing themselves in American-style suits and dresses, speaking and writing fluent English, and advocating secular schooling for Muslim children. Many originated from elite families like that of Datu Piang in Cotabato or Sultan Jamalul Kiram on Jolo. Yet even the elect could be skeptical of the civilizing mission. Arolas Tulawie worked to modernize Sulu's institutions yet blamed colonial rule for the "deplorable condition[s]" there. A functional form of local leadership—the datuship—had been replaced by inconsistent colonial policies implemented with little regard for the needs of distinct communities. Further, the abolition of slavery had presaged a new sort of "wage slavery" that was little better. Writing in 1933, Tulawie prophesized that a hundred years hence the Muslims of the Southern Philippines would remain in a similarly disenfranchised state.[104]

Stimson and Tulawie presented competing visions of the civilizing mission in the Philippines, diverging wildly in their conclusions but each suggesting that deep veins of cultural and racial supremacism ran through it. Tensions between sites of authority (the administrator and the datu) hindered efforts to transform the Moros and their lands, as did financial shortages and competing power centers within the colonial state. Americans and Filipinos experimented with an array of programs aimed at furthering their civilizational imperatives. When these faltered, state and nonstate actors sometimes responded with calculated adjustments to their approaches. Just as often, however, their frustrations fed into the violent dynamics that plagued colonial rule.

Chapter 4

Corrective Violence

On Fear, Massacre, and Punishment

In August 1923, the Philippine Constabulary confronted a group of Maranao near Lake Lanao. The Moro resented their exclusion from regional politics, threatening to destroy communications infrastructure and burn schoolhouses if the exclusionary practices continued. Recalling his own experiences leading the Moro Province two decades prior, Governor-General Leonard Wood took special interest in the uprising. He blamed Islam—rather than local conditions—for the problems in Lanao. Trips to Mecca had radicalized the Maranao, Wood believed, and caused them to attack Americans and Filipinos on their return. Islamic militancy and the incapacity of Moro moderates to temper the group's behaviors meant punitive solutions were required. "I believe the opportune time has come to cut short their fanatical activities by means of force," Wood declared. "If we postpone action until later, we will have to kill a larger number than now." Colonial forces mobilized, and in the ensuing battle fifty Maranao warriors and three members of the Constabulary died.[1]

The confrontation in Lanao typified long-established patterns of violence between Moros and the colonial state. Defying government directives exposed Muslim populations to removal, torture, or death. Superior organization, resources, tactics, and technology ensured battles were one-sided affairs, with government security forces suffering minimal casualties. During military rule and beyond, provincial officials read resistance as evidence of religious fanaticism or racial incapacity. Wood's belief that slaughter prevented further slaughter reflected a peculiar twist of colonial logic found elsewhere in the literature. The overwhelming force used in pacification campaigns against the Moros obliterated indigenous power centers and warned would-be antagonists of the high costs attached to defying the colonial status quo. State violence in Mindanao-Sulu was an exercise in correcting those Moros unwilling to collaborate in the transformation process designed for them by Americans, Filipinos, and their own elites.

The use of violence by colonial security organs in the Philippines did not occur in isolation but rather shared spatial, material, and ideological features with other colonized zones. This "family resemblance" led Americans down familiar avenues. The frustrations of the colonial frontier—poor logistical support, environmental obstacles, and irregular enemy tactics—increased the likelihood of asymmetrical slaughter.[2] Military and civilian officials devised rhetorical strategies to justify these controversial practices. The idea of corrective violence finds its closest conceptual parallel in Michael Vann's exploration of the "pedagogic execution" in French Indochina. The violent spectacle of the guillotined criminal was an "effective way of communicating the colonial order of things" and a "pedagogical tool to discipline the colonial subject who might consider an act of rebellion."[3] Racialized violence was also a feature of American rule in other parts of the Philippines.[4] Violence safeguarded or even promoted civilizational transformation where dialogue failed, officials believed. American colonials emphasized violence as a mode of communication with the martial Moro character. Force, not diplomacy, was a language the Moro understood. As such, sporadic slaughter served its own function in the larger quest to refashion the Southern Philippines and its inhabitants.

The penal system in the Muslim South augmented this violent reconstruction. Within the region's detention facilities, prisoners learned to become model citizens of a distinctly colonial mold. Surveillance and labor in the South's prisons functioned in a totalizing capacity, "mingling ceaselessly the art of rectifying and the right to punish." Provincial officials envisioned a disciplinary superstructure that would correct errant Moro behaviors while simultaneously operating as a self-supporting "apparatus of production."[5] Fantasies of panoptic control and reformation, however, often faltered before the dismal realities of prison conditions. In his own study of colonial prisons, Peter Zinoman observes that the "pervasive circulation of disciplinary processes throughout the social body" was often undermined by failures of administration within the colonial carceral system.[6] Corruption and prisoner abuse meant that wide-scale reform frequently remained aspirational. Beyond this, the ambitious penological goals of American colonials ran up against the banal limitations of government resource allocation to remote spaces.[7]

Fears of the Moro ability to unleash their own spectacular displays of force provided rationales for state coercion. The violence of the Moro juramentado warrior, a term used to describe Muslims that challenged colonial rule through ritualized religious suicide attacks, pervaded American accounts of the South.[8] Coined by the Spanish, it was an elastic concept and imprecise enough to survive successive administrative shifts in Mindanao-Sulu. Structural continuities between military and civilian governance meant that the threat assessments of the early 1900s resurfaced for decades to come. Between 1913 and 1930, seven of fifteen provincial governors in Mindanao-Sulu were PC officers, many with prior experience in the Moro Province. Accepting official claims of a post-1913 "normalization" of the Philippines involves overlooking conceptual continuities and ongoing cycles of violence. Liberally applied force remained a key governmental tool across the 1914 divide, and exploring these histories of fear, confinement, and punishment is crucial to understanding the American period.

Fixating on Juramentados

A double homicide shook the small island of Tabawan in 1934. According to reports, a Moro named Asnol, wracked with grief over the death of his wife, had decided to forfeit his own life. Due to Islamic prohibitions against suicide, he would accomplish this by "going juramentado"—or "running amuck"—in the neighboring community of Laum, where the Bureau of Education ran a small school. The teachers at Laum were Christian Filipinos, and Asnol suspected them of imposing alien customs on Moro children. Dying in the act of killing these cultural infiltrators would uphold Muslim dignity. Asnol approached the school armed with a bolo and ambushed two teachers, Felipe Collante and Ruperto Rosos, before being shot dead by a retired instructor named Ignacio Aguilar. The bodies of Collante and Rosos underwent medical examination on Jolo. Photographs show arms nearly severed and heads marked by deep lacerations. The superintendent of schools K. W. Chapman observed that the injuries were "not exceptional but simply an average cause after an amuck has finished with his victim." Writing to his superiors in Manila, Chapman pushed authorities to take a harder line in Sulu. "When a man in Borneo runs amuck," he wrote, "[his] whole village is held responsible. The British promptly burn the whole village. The Dutch cut off the head of the offender and place it on a pole in the market." Violent reprisals would pacify the Moros, who respected governance "tempered with the kind of justice they understand."[9]

Chapman's brutal retributory fantasies had a deep history. The specter of the juramentado (or amuck) provided Americans and Filipinos with one of their most durable fears, becoming shorthand for Islamic threat in Mindanao-Sulu. The Americans inherited the term *juramentado*—"one who has taken an oath"—from the Spanish. It described a form of ritual suicide enacted against illegitimate sources of authority. During Spain's occupation of Jolo in the late nineteenth century, the Tausūg people called the practice *parang sabil* ("war in the path of God") and used it to denote "an individual decision and action, sanctioned and even encouraged by the *panditas* as a form of resistance against the Spanish."[10] In this private act of jihad, the juramentado performed a series of ritualized practices before the attack, including purification ceremonies to prepare himself for death. As American colonial control tightened after 1899, individual acts of violence by *mujahid* (the person intent on "going juramentado") became more common than group resistance.[11]

Spanish experiences—real and apocryphal—informed American perceptions of the Muslim capacity for violence. One Jesuit history spoke of juramentados as those who decided to "vanquish or die rushing against the enemy's forces, no matter how strong they may be without ever drawing back, till they fall dead."[12] In letters to his mother, Frank McCoy relayed tales of Gen. Juan Arolas, the Spanish governor of Jolo in the 1880s. In McCoy's telling, Arolas ended the practice of juramentado by shelling the sultan's capital at Maibun. When the sultan complained, Arolas replied, "The gunboat is running amuck, the Captain is juramentado. What control have I over such?" The idea that Muslims only understood the language of violence proved seductive, and the story became part of the colonial folklore of the Southern Philippines. Later chroniclers used the same sequence of events but attributed the disciplinary lesson to Leonard Wood or John Pershing.[13] The Samal Moro leader Datu Mandi established his bona fides with the Americans by relating how the Spanish awarded him a medal of merit for assisting in the killing of a juramentado in 1895.[14] Shortly after the U.S. military landed on Jolo in 1899, Sultan Jamalul Kiram II tried to curry favor by issuing a public letter urging the people of Sulu not to engage in the practice as they had with the Spanish.[15]

The story in which the sultan had no control over the juramentados contained some truth, and ritual suicides continued. The "old Arolas regulations" at the gates of Jolo remained in place. Every person passing into the walled town first surrendered their weapons. Despite this precaution, juramentados occasionally slipped through. This occurred three separate times in 1903. The Moro attackers concealed their weapons inside bamboo or baskets of fruit, and once past the guards "they ran amuck, cutting and slashing at everybody in sight" until shot dead.[16] Although Americans suspected coordinated resistance, evidence suggests Moro leaders were being truthful when they claimed the attacks took place without communal foreknowledge. Besides perhaps receiving a blessing from his parents or a local pandita, the juramentado's intentions were not widely known until he struck. The frenzied, unpredictable acts engendered violent state responses. "A juramentado [should] be hanged along with the pandita who gave him his oath, the barber who shaved his head and anointed him, the person who made his white robe for him, and anybody who should know of his vow without sending warning to the Americans," declared John Bates.[17]

U.S. colonials struggled with what the phenomenon *meant* and how to best describe it. The *Mindanao Herald* suggested the practice was a holdover from Spanish times and a remnant of the jihad waged during that period. Quoting Esteban Rodriguez de Figueroa, a sixteenth-century military officer who traveled to Sulu to exact tribute from the sultan, the paper declared that early iterations of jihad against foreign occupiers were genuine as they responded to a direct threat to Islam. Acting as unlikely interpreter of Qur'anic doctrine, the *Herald* deemed pre-1878 juramentados as legitimate actors because the sultan of Sulu sanctioned them. After the 1878 treaty, ritual suicide in combat became delegitimized because it was no longer "an act of war performed thru the cooperation of large bodies of men actuated by religious motives." The holy warrior became "little different" from those "running amuck" in Malaysia, which could be explained away through personal grievance and racial madness. Although reflective in its treatment of Spanish-Muslim relations, the paper made no attempt to understand the role of the juramentado during the American period, calling them merely "pseudo-juramentado." To the editors of the *Herald*, the rational actors fighting colonial rule became madmen unworthy of notice after 1878 and a threat to colonial order after 1899.[18]

Like most Americans, John Pershing interpreted running amuck as something other than an act of protest against colonial rule. The Moro could not "in any sense be called true believers," and therefore the religious implications of the practice were also nullified. Pershing blamed the social order of Moro communities for fomenting the attacks. The "degrading slavery of concubinage and polygamy" allowed wealthy Moro men to accumulate wives while those without money or power were constantly outbid on dowries. Denied a partner, the discouraged Moro male took it on himself to become a juramentado and attack Christians. Although Pershing acknowledged that running

When Moros Run Amuck.

FANATIC JURAMENTADO CUTS DOWN ALL THE CHRISTIANS HE CAN REACH IN RELIGIOUS FRENZY.

[New York Post.]

MORO outlaws will no longer be able to defy the United States Government, and Moro raids will no longer offer hope of battle to the peace-worn soldiers in Luzon, for orders have gone out that all the Moros in Mindanao and Jolo—better known as Sulu—be disarmed.

The expedition which Major General John J. Pershing, commanding the Department of Mindanao, sent to carry out this order, has not found the Moros meekly ready to lay down their arms. Already 42 outlaws, according to the press dispatches, have died fighting, and the latest report by cable from Manila last Wednesday, says that 600 more have made a last stand on the peak of Bud Dajo, an extinct volcano in the center of the Island of Jolo.

What can a Christian nation do when it comes up against a race which be-self, and his relatives have a celebration when the news of his death reaches them. They always insist that just as night is coming, on they see him riding by on a white horse, bound for the abode of the blessed.".

In the time of the Spanish occupation of Jolo most careful precautions were taken against juramentados. By the side of the path that led from the country to the gate a little white slab marked the dead line. In a small building about 50 yards from the gate a guard of four privates, under a Sergeant, kept their guns loaded and their bayonets fixed.

As soon as the guard saw a Moro approaching along this path they would shout, "Moro armado!" and that would bring the rest of the soldiers out from the gate at a double quick, with rifles leveled. Supported thus from the rear the outside guard advanced to search the intruder. Even then they were not willing to trust him—the privates stopped 10 paces off and covered him with their guns also, while the Sergeant advanced and relieved him of his arms. These were not returned to him until he left the town.

Figure 4.1 U.S. newspapers relished sensational tales of Moro violence, frequently lingering on the spectacle of the juramentado warrior. Sensational accounts of the Muslim South made for good copy and reassured the American public that punitive measures against the Muslims of the Southern Philippines were justified. This article (originally run in the *New York Post* and reprinted in the *Washington Post*) described conditions on Jolo in 1912 during John Pershing's disarmament campaign, framing the initiative as a response to Moro fanaticism. ("When Moros Run Amuck," *Washington Post*, January 14, 1912, ProQuest Historical Newspapers, https://www-lib-uwo-ca .proxy1.lib.uwo.ca/cgi-bin/ezpauthn.cgi?url=http://search.proquest.com.proxy1.lib.uwo.ca /docview/145130486?accountid=15115)

amuck could be an act of war against enemies, he saw its principal cause as unequal social relations. "A code which recognizes plurality and authorizes concubinage," he wrote, "cannot prevail against civilized standards of morality." In this reading, the links between juramentados and polygamy meant that suicidal attacks were an internal problem and could be fixed through overhauling Moro culture.[19]

Other writers ascribed blame to mental health issues or malign foreign influences. Sources from Jolo in the 1920s and 1930s describe Moros being "treated for insanity" and possessing brooding minds. The act of violence by-passed religious prohibitions on suicide, and once the individual was determined to die, it was immaterial whom he killed.[20] The muckraking journalist Charles Edward Russell took this line of thinking further in his racialized descriptions of the "strange fits and starts" of the Moro mind. Russell compared the Moro to a carabao that "after years of plodding patience, may be seized all of a sudden with temporary madness," suggesting the only way to alter these animalistic qualities was through civic education.[21] Some blamed the presence of Arab imams in the Southern Philippines, who preached "death and destruction for Christians" to the locals and interpreted the Qur'an to the Moros "in such a way that the Moro feels it often his duty to kill as many Christians as possible." While there is no evidence that Muslim clerics incited violence, the idea of a pan-Islamic threat to colonial order persisted.[22]

U.S. newspapers also focused on Islam, portraying the juramentado as the ultimate expression of religious fanaticism. That an American soldier or civilian could be slain at any moment by a frenzied Moro in a state of divine ecstasy made for good copy, and most pieces on the region made some mention of the practice. In 1912, the *Washington Post* described the murder of Lt. Walter H. Rodney, killed in Jolo town by a "fanatic, dashing down the street, slashing right and left with his bolo."[23] The press delighted in military responses to the juramentado threat, particularly when Americans weaponized Islam against the Moros. The *New York Times* reported on Col. W. H. Wallace's novel approach to punishing the families and communities of those who ran amuck on Jolo. Wallace began burying pigs in the graves of juramentados to discourage other Tausūg from engaging in the activity. Military officers believed the Islamic admonition against pork would lead young men to fear contamination after death. Wallace described the interment, done before a large crowd, with some relish, noting that "news of the form of punishment adopted soon spread" and that "the method had a wholesome effect" in establishing order on the island.[24] Col. Alexander Rogers repeated this method some years later in an even more gruesome fashion. Authorities laid dead juramentados out in village marketplaces and placed slaughtered pigs on top of them.[25] Americans reveled in their ability to tap into native fears of ritual pollution, and these stories of "tough" approaches to an Islamic threat have had troubling afterlives in the twenty-first century.[26]

It is difficult to overstate the presence of the juramentado in the American colonial psyche. Western observers recounted incidents in lurid detail, oftentimes emphasizing the sheer unpredictability of the attackers. Constabulary officer John R. White told the story of two Yakan Moros from Basilan who traveled by sea to the market at Taluksangay, north of Zamboanga, to sell unprocessed cocoa pods. Their boat capsized in a storm en route, and their goods were lost. Washing up on shore, they decided to run amuck in the nearest Christian town: "Slash, cut, slice, a child's head here, a woman's arm there, and in as many seconds as it has taken words to tell, the peaceful village became a place of massacre and wailing." Eventually the Filipino townsfolk overwhelmed the two men and strung their dismembered bodies in the village square. In another of White's anecdotes, a Tausūg ran amuck after his friends had made fun of his hiccups. Such was the market for juramentado stories that dubious ones received notice. A Moro, it seemed, degenerated into a murderous frenzy at the slightest provocation—something American audiences were eager to read about.[27]

Distinctions between juramentado and amuck shifted over time. White claimed his stories were garden-variety cases of Moros running amuck, which he saw as an innate Malay characteristic. He likened the violent outbursts to "spontaneous combustion," where a hitherto law-abiding citizen suddenly transformed into a "dancing, frenzied, fiend rushing frantically about to slay, blindly, and indiscriminately." The proper juramentado, on the other hand, was an "amuck with religious and other frills" who worked himself into a state of religious frenzy before attacking.[28] Vic Hurley distinguished between the two practices, arguing that to run amuck was "prevalent among all Eastern peoples" but lacked religious significance. Hurley believed that of all the Muslims in the world, only the Moros practiced the private form of "constructive self-destruction" known as juramentado. In his history of the Moros, he spent considerable time cataloging a litany of religiously inspired attacks, claiming the juramentado period spanned from 1509 until 1913.[29] Many accounts, however, did not make any distinction between amuck and juramentado. The teacher William B. Freer described the amuck and juramentado interchangeably, while others saw the latter as a Spanish designation for a practice common among all Malay groups in Southeast Asia.[30]

No reliable figures exist concerning juramentado attacks, but the term's conceptual malleability and loose application suggest a statistically limited phenomenon. At times, there was disagreement as to whether the juramentado even existed, with some describing them as near-invincible avatars of Muslim rage, and others claiming the attacks no longer took place. The specter of the amuck appeared in even the most routine murders, or not at all. Juramentado became shorthand for a series of fearsome and awe-inspiring Moro traits, making heroes of the Americans who dared serve in Mindanao-Sulu and preemptively legitimating state violence. Consensus on the meanings of Moro violence proved elusive, with religious fanaticism, mental illness, racial traits, and honor all ascribed or disavowed as explanatory factors. Confident in the beneficence of the civilizing mission, colonial officials frequently interpreted antistate violence as an expression of something broken within the Moro cultures they governed.[31]

More likely, Moro suicide attacks continued after coordinated resistance to colonial rule ended due to feelings of defeat and dispossession. If the Moro could not meet the foreign occupier—American or Filipino—on equal military footing, he could at least express his displeasure with colonial rule by dying in spectacular fashion. The cultural disorientations detailed in the previous chapter created ruptures in Muslim societies.[32] Innovations of empire "undermine[d] customary beliefs, institutions, and patterns of human interaction so rapidly that viable replacements often cannot be developed quickly enough to cushion the perilous transition to a new order."[33] In Mindanao-Sulu, civilizational imperatives supplanted the institution of the datuship, rearranged Moro commercial practices, and secularized education and law. In this dizzying atmosphere of reconfiguration, violent resistance became more likely. While the larger attempt to remake Moros cannot account for the granularities of each instance of amuck—the petty jealousies, the grief, the outrage—it does speak to the linkages between violence and destabilized societies. Regardless of how they chose to interpret the phenomenon, white colonials shared a belief that the pervasive Moro threat could only be contained and corrected if met with force. Paranoia about juramentados, as well as indignation at the supposed ingratitude of the Moros, fueled colonial violence.

Resistance and Massacre

Gen. Adna R. Chaffee believed strategically applied violence would control the Moros. "We must not fail duty which demands application of Mosaic law, 'An eye for an eye', when dealing with savages who know no other way of obtaining redress for wrong," he wrote in 1902. Fearing Mindanao-Sulu would remain in its underdeveloped state, he encouraged his officers to "press into [Moro] settlements in friendly spirit [rather] than stand barred out at their gates and lose their respect."[34] The language and practice of force quickly became a prerequisite for successful civilizing projects. After the collapse of the First Philippine Republic, U.S. military forces in Mindanao-Sulu increasingly carried out punitive measures. Early confrontations occurred around the southern shore of Lake Lanao. Lacking unifying leaders and riven with internecine conflicts, the Maranao Moros presented manifold challenges to colonial rule. A series of military expeditions in 1902 and 1903 demonstrated the power of the U.S. military to unconquered Muslims. The first of these occurred in May 1902. Col. Frank Baldwin led a force of twelve hundred men against Moro cottas at Bayan and Pandapatan. Two days of bloody fighting left between four and five hundred Moros dead, with American losses of only eleven killed and forty-two wounded. In a terse postbattle cablegram, General Chaffee declared that "Bayan caused much astonishment; was extremely necessary wholesome lesson, which don't think will have to be repeated."[35]

The "wholesome lesson" of Bayan repeated itself in patterns that stretched to Philippine independence and beyond. A template swiftly emerged: first, "obstinate" Moros rejected one or more core tenets of the colonial state (education, taxation, disarmament, trade controls, secular courts); second, Americans engaged in limited negotiations with oppositional datus; third, antistate Moros retreated to a remote fortification or engaged in loosely organized banditry against state agents; fourth, the state used military and paramilitary groups to overwhelm local resistance, leading to asymmetrical casualty rates; fifth, the government and media declared the targeted group had been reformed through force. The results of the Lanao campaigns generated predictable news stories: "Victorious American commander attacks the recalcitrants of Mindanao, losing not a single man in advance."[36] In the wake of the Battle of Bacolod in early April 1903, the *Chicago Evening Post* reported that native defeat would "lead all Moros to acknowledge American sovereignty."[37]

This did not happen, and the pacification of the Maranao in Lanao came to be regarded as something of a high point thanks to John Pershing's keen politicking among the datus and sultans of the region. In following years, Americans instigated a host of violent confrontations aimed at eliminating anticolonial resistance. Antipiracy and antibanditry campaigns, search-and-destroy expeditions, and large-scale military assaults all concluded in similarly lopsided fashions. Cyclical violence embedded itself into state-citizenry relations, setting ominous precedents for the postcolonial Philippines. While the most publicized of these incidents occurred under military rule, resistance and massacre continued well past the 1914 divide, becoming characteristic of the region as colonial and national governance merged.

Moro leaders displeased with colonial directives gathered followers and took to the jungles in opposition. Panglima Hassan of Jolo urged other datus to arm themselves against the occupiers and harassed U.S. military outposts on the island. District Governor Hugh Scott led repeated expeditions into the interior in pursuit of Hassan. "Wherever we met resistance," he wrote home, "we killed them and burned the houses." American forces tracked Hassan to Bud Bagsak in March 1904 and shot him dead.[38] In the Cotabato region, Datu Ali, the sultan of Buyuan, became a symbol of opposition. Initially amenable to the Americans, Ali bristled at antislavery measures, economic constraints, and a rescinded offer to participate in the 1904 St. Louis World's Fair. The Moro aristocrat split with Datu Piang, the main U.S. ally in Cotabato, and exploited growing anticolonial sentiment among the Maguindanao to galvanize his supporters. Governor Leonard Wood and his deputies inflamed the situation with their inability to negotiate between Moro power centers in the region.[39]

An initial battle at Ali's cotta at Sirinaya left over one hundred Moros dead and gave way to running fights between the datu's men and the army. Unconventional warfare suited the Moros well, lessening the advantages of superior American firepower. Using environmental knowledge to their benefit, Ali's followers struck colonial patrols quickly and then retreated. These guerrilla tactics frustrated the government, which adopted punitive concentration policies for Moro communities in areas suspected of harboring or supplying Datu Ali. Shoot-on-sight orders targeted any Moro male acting suspiciously. Buildings outside of designated concentration zones were burned, as were crops. Difficulties differentiating hostiles and civilians produced indiscriminate applications of force. Even Vic Hurley, no great opponent of the colonial presence, admitted "there was some criticism directed at this engagement due to the numbers of women and children killed by the artillery and rifle fire of the American troops." All told, as many as 20,000 Moro villagers suffered relocation in 1904–1905.[40]

Frustrated by their inability to locate Ali and cognizant of the human and material costs of endless conflict, Wood and his coterie briefly opened backchannel negotiations with the datu. Najeeb Saleeby acted as intermediary, securing an agreement from Ali to cease hostilities. This was not the unconditional surrender the military authorities desired, and in October 1905 a tracking party led by Wood's deputy Frank McCoy trekked overland from Davao to Buluan, catching the datu unawares and shooting him dead on the porch of a hideout.[41] Ali became a folk hero among the Maguindanao following his death. Unlike Datu Piang, a self-made leader of mixed Chinese-Maguindanao parentage, Ali's genealogy linked him to centuries of regional rulers. This fact provided fertile ground for mythologizing. Rumors spread that the datu still lived, the stories gaining enough traction that they were printed in colonial newspapers. The Moro Province reluctantly opened an investigation into the matter. Ali remained a hero in Cotabato for decades following his death. In 1914, his son and nephews participated in antistate activities there.[42]

The violence of the early Moro Province years culminated in March 1906 at Bud Dajo, an extinct volcano five miles from the town of Jolo. The incident began with protest. Hundreds of Tausūg Moros fortified themselves in the extinct volcanic crater at the summit of Bud Dajo in opposition to the unpopular cedula head tax, a perennial source of friction between Joloanos and the colonial government. The issue had led to violence in the previous two years, including a massacre where 226 Moros died in a single afternoon.[43] In an effort to avoid a recurrence, Hugh Scott conducted meetings with the Dajo group to explain the cedula and reassure them that it did not interfere with the "tenets of the Mohammedan religion."[44] Officials co-opted local elites to collect the tax from their followers, but widespread allegations of corruption during the process further alienated peasant groups. Armed incidents over the issue occurred in late 1905 and early 1906.[45]

Scott's departure for medical treatment in the United States suited Leonard Wood. Having already assured superiors in Manila and Washington that the Moros were nearly pacified, the provincial governor desired expedient resolutions over protracted negotiations. The secretary of the Moro Province, George Langhorne, put it bluntly: the Dajo Moros would "have to be exterminated."[46] James Reeves, heading military operations on Jolo, concurred. An attack party that included U.S. soldiers from the 6th and 19th Infantry, the 4th Cavalry, and the 28th Artillery, American sailors, and Philippine Constabulary troops gathered under the leadership of Col. Joseph W. Duncan and prepared for an assault on Dajo.

Embarking from the Schuck family homestead near Jolo town, Duncan and his troops marched toward the mountain, destroying "suspicious" food supplies and structures en route. Fighting broke out on March 6, and the troops faced resistance on the slopes of Dajo. They reached the summit the following day. Massacre followed. Using Krag-Jorgenson rifles and Colt automatics, the soldiers cut down a mixed group of Tausūg men, women, and children. Capt. Edward P. Lawton, commander of one of the three attacking columns, noted the "desperate resistance" of the Moros, who were "shot down in their tracks with terrible slaughter, so that their cotta and lip of the crater were soon piled up with the dead, several bodies deep." Lawton then sent detachments into the mouth of the crater "to burn the shacks and destroy all Moros who might be alive there." On March 8, the Americans captured the final Moro cotta. Inside they found a "mass of bodies piled up." Duncan and Wood ordered the destruction of all remaining fortifications on the mountain.[47]

Estimates of the dead at Bud Dajo varied. Maj. Omar Bundy, who led one of the attack columns, spoke with Moro interpreters who claimed "about 1000 Moros were living in the crater, and that of this number nearly all were killed."[48] Official army estimates placed the figure at around six hundred, while historians have suggested between seven and nine hundred. Twenty-one members of the attacking force—Americans and their Moro allies—died and seventy-three were wounded.[49] In his concluding remarks, Joseph Duncan lamented that "some women and children" were "inadvertently killed." He described medical attention given to an injured Tausūg woman who came down the mountain with her child, using it as evidence of the war party's humane intentions. "It is not believed that a woman or child was intentionally killed by anyone," Duncan reported, "even though in many instances the women are said to have fought like demons." The American soldiers represented a "superior type of manhood" and would "never willingly lift an avenging hand against woman or child." Duncan held Moro men responsible for the deaths.[50]

The government of the Moro Province stage-managed information about the slaughter. Newspaper reports in the wake of Dajo included long quotations from Leonard Wood's official report to the War Department. It framed the massacre as the regrettable product of fierce Moro resistance to colonial progress. Using familiar racial descriptors, Wood claimed the problem arose from the martial Moro's habit of fighting to the death rather than retreating as the Christians of the North did.[51] An array of explanations emerged for the high casualty figures. Most blamed the Moros themselves: Tausūg warriors forced women and children to stay, using them as human shields in battle; Moro men feared if they died, their wives would remarry, and thus insisted they stay with them; civilian deaths occurred only due to "preliminary shelling at distance," and no killing occurred "except such as was indispensable to end an intolerable situation."[52] Females became both victims and combatants. Hugh Scott declared they fought "as hard as the man," and Leonard Wood saw them as a "bold and active party in the action."[53] This transgression, according to Michael Hawkins, "violated a reciprocal relationship between femininity and chivalry" in the minds of military leaders.[54]

In the United States, Bud Dajo became shorthand for the excesses of imperialism. The massacre represented the violent corruption of American ideals, critics leveled at the Roosevelt administration. The social reformer Reverend Charles Parkhurst railed against Roosevelt's letter of congratulations to Wood in the wake of Dajo, claiming it was composed "in the presence . . . of mangled men, torn women, armless and headless children" and evinced the "heartlessness and greed of unregenerate nationality." *The Nation* called Moro policy "an aimless drifting along, with occasional bloody successes," and Democratic politicians condemned the violence as "wanton butchery."[55] The most vociferous opposition came from the Anti-Imperialist League, which had formed in 1898 to oppose the acquisition of Spain's territories. The league president Moorfield Storey questioned the official narrative of Dajo and used cross-colonial comparison to shape public opinion. "Suppose we had heard that the British had dealt thus with a Boer Force, that the Turks had so attacked and slaughtered Armenians, that colored men had so massacred white men, or even that 600 song birds had been slaughtered for their plumage, would not our papers have been filled with protests and expressions of horror?" Storey's indictment reached its peak when he declared that "the spirit which slaughters brown men in Jolo is the spirit which lynches black men in the South."[56]

Opponent of empire and Anti-Imperialist League member Mark Twain had his own thoughts about what transpired in the crater. Comparing casualty statistics at Bud Dajo to those of the Civil War, the writer acidly observed that the massacre was "incomparably the greatest victory . . . achieved by the Christian soldiers of the United States." Twain tore into U.S. military forces, calling them "uniformed assassins" and claiming they "dishonored" the flag. He also accused Leonard Wood of using contradictory cablegrams as a smokescreen for murder. Twain's outrage never appeared in print during his lifetime but captured a mood of public dismay over the slaughter on the mountain and subsequent cover-ups. Dajo confirmed the worst fears of anti-imperialists: unchecked by domestic oversight, U.S. colonial governance had taken on the coercive characteristics of its European neighbors.[57]

Back in Zamboanga, Leonard Wood publicly maintained journalists had sensationalized the events at Dajo. The term "fake news" appeared in rebuttals.[58] Behind the scenes, however, the provincial government scrambled to contain the scandal—and photographs of the massacre, in particular. In May 1906, Secretary of Public Instruction W. Morgan Shuster relayed claims to Wood that a schoolteacher named Miller had a troubling photograph in his possession. It showed "a half-naked female corpse, with a gash in the breast . . . lying near the bodies of several infants. American soldiers are standing near, gazing at them, and due to light and shade the female corpse looks like that of a white woman." If released, the image would damage the credibility of military rule in Mindanao-Sulu and could potentially hurt Republican electoral prospects that autumn. The Moro woman's Caucasian appearance presented

Figure 4.2 U.S. soldiers pose with the bodies of dead Tausūg Moros at the summit of Bud Dajo in March 1906. In the background are destroyed nipa-roofed dwellings. A Tausūg woman and child, survivors of the massacre, crouch in the upper left corner among the military men. The photograph made its way from Jolo back to the United States months later, where it stoked moral outrage over military conduct in Southeast Asia. (National Archives photo no. 111-SC-83648)

further complications in a nation where many weighed tragedy relative to race. Shuster suggested attempting to destroy the photograph on Miller's return to the Philippines.[59]

Taken after the frenzied killing on the afternoon of March 7, the photograph shows Capt. A. M. Wetherill and his men standing above a trench lined with Tausūg corpses. Many of the Americans pose as if for a formal portrait, but their faces are serious and some wear haunted, battle-weary expressions. In the foreground, heaps of undifferentiated bodies blend into one another, although the faces of dead children are identifiable. Most striking is the aforementioned "female corpse" in the center of the shot. Her right breast is exposed, and she appears to have been struck in the neck with a bullet or a bayonet. Against her stomach is a dead infant with a bullet wound through its cheek. A second photograph of the atrocity—labeled "Six Weeks after the Battle of Dajo"—shows a group of American soldiers posing by a trench, this time as tourists at the battle site. Skulls of the dead, which had swiftly decomposed in the tropical climate, line a tree trunk running over the trench. The unease of the first photograph is not present here. In under two months, Bud Dajo was transformed into imperial kitsch—a site for visiting, photographing, and describing in letters home.[60]

Bud Dajo retreated from the public eye within a matter of weeks. Official narratives proved durable, with military leaders and their political allies continuing to frame the violence as an unpleasant necessity. Optics aside, they argued, the Tausūg in the crater represented a threat to colonial order, and their elimination served as a cautionary tale to future transgressors. A second massacre at Bud Dajo was narrowly avoided in 1911. In 1913, a similarly lopsided conflagration at nearby Bud Bagsak saw between four and five hundred Moros killed by the Americans, who tested the efficacy of Colt .45 revolvers and Winchester shotguns on their enemies.[61]

Piracy, banditry, and other limited types of revolt provided long-lasting rationales for using military force against the Moros. This was evident in the attention colonial authorities paid the Moro pirate Jikiri. A Samal from the island of Patian, Jikiri began his outlaw career hijacking the small Chinese merchant vintas that plied their trade between Basilan and Jolo. Exploiting a power vacuum following the death of the Basilan strongman Datu Kalun, Jikiri acquired a small fleet of purloined ships and grew his following. In December 1907, his group attacked an American logging encampment on Basilan, killing three men. The ensuing uproar in Zamboanga resulted in John Finley leading a military expedition to scour the island. U.S. Army and Philippine Constabulary units destroyed native rancherias and captured Salip Agil, a local ally of Jikiri. The following month a separate search-and-destroy mission landed on Jolo and Patian to locate the pirate band.[62]

Jikiri avoided the colonial dragnet and remained at large in Sulu. His group attacked Maibun, capital of the Sulu Sultanate, in March 1908, killing Chinese shop owners and burning houses. Large groups of Moro collaborators hunted Jikiri across the Jolo countryside. He escaped and struck Chinese merchants on Parang and Kabingaan, before returning to Jolo, where his followers killed Pvt. Albert L. Burleigh, a U.S. soldier serving as a schoolteacher.[63] Ranging from Basilan to British North Borneo, the mobile outlaw group attacked a PC outpost at Siasi, British colonial outposts near Sandakan, and a series of pearling vessels. The story of the manhunt for Jikiri featured on the front page of the New York Times, and his successes avoiding capture raised his status with other Moros.[64] Directing operations against Jikiri, Capt. Charles Rhodes wrote in his diary of a growing suspicion that the pirate benefitted from covert local support. Changes to maritime regulations had stripped wealth from leading Tausūg families, perhaps generating tacit support for an outlaw who struck primarily against the Euro-American and Chinese business concerns profiting from the restructuring of Moroland.[65]

In July 1909, government forces tracked Jikiri to Patian. His band barricaded themselves in a mountainside cave, which American troops fired artillery rounds into. After the barrage, Jikiri and his followers emerged and were met with "a storm of shot . . . so fierce that everyone was killed." Jikiri's head was "shot to pieces at a distance of four feet." Afterward, Governor-General William Cameron Forbes trekked to the scene of the slaughter and sketched it in his notebook.[66] Like Datu Ali, Jikiri remained a source of fascination for both Americans and Moros after his death. The *Atlanta Constitution* emphasized his piratical ways and described the relish he took in killing white men, and the *Washington Post* compared him to continental frontier bandits in his "reckless audacity and defiance."[67] The cave on Patian became a minor pilgrimage site for decades to come. In 1931, a Moro named Islani Sapal recounted how his Boy Scout troop visited the spot where the "famous old outlaw of former years" met his end.[68]

The departure of the U.S. military at the end of 1913 did not end asymmetrical warfare in Mindanao-Sulu. The Philippine Constabulary inherited many long-running conflicts with aggrieved groups. Rapid Filipinization, new Christian settlers, and continuing drives to extend state authority kept tensions high. PC reports from the period detailed patterns of resistance and massacre. Outlaw bands in Sulu, Cotabato, and Lanao mixed social protest with economic opportunism, committing "an unusually large number of murders and robberies" in the early 1920s. The cedula tax, which had sparked events leading to the Bud Dajo massacre, continued to fuel anticolonial sentiment, as did compulsory education. A typical encounter occurred in 1921, when the Maranao leader Datu Amai Binanning and his followers barricaded themselves in a cotta to protest state schools. Constabulary forces attacked the fortification, killing the datu and several others.[69]

In 1920, on the small island of Pata, opposition to public education led to tragedy. Native police began visiting the homes of those who refused to send their children to the new schoolhouses. In the village of Sapa-Malaom, the community leader Hatib Sihaban transformed his residence into a small cotta to protest, and supporters began adding their own adjoining structures. Negotiations between the Moros and the governor of Sulu, P. D. Rogers, broke down in November of that year. In early December a policeman named Adjalani died at Sihaban's cotta under murky circumstances. The day after the murder, a PC detachment led by Lt. Pastor Soriano arrived in Sapa-Malaom to confront Sihaban. Soriano's report of what followed was grim. Constabulary forces faced determined resistance. Women refused to leave and threatened Soriano and his men with spears. When talks broke down, the Constabulary opened fire on the cotta, killing fourteen men, eleven women, and eight children. Ten other Moros suffered injuries and had to be transported to Jolo for treatment. Soriano's unit recovered six kris, eight barongs, five bolos and an assortment of spears from the cotta, but no firearms.[70] In the only public account of the events, Charles Edward Russell parroted Soriano's narrative and framed the massacre as unavoidable. Sihaban's followers had "run amuck," and the outcome was predictable. "Civilization is more efficient in taming devils than making angels," Russell wrote.[71]

Soriano's superior Lt. Col. John Tharp exonerated the group's actions on Pata, determining that reasoning with the Moros was "entirely out of the question."[72] The PC leadership in Manila was not as sanguine. An investigation revealed petty precipitating factors: the murdered Moro policeman had been having an affair with Hatib Sihaban's wife. Future Constabulary head C. E. Nathorst was livid. "The mere fact that [Soriano] knowingly attacked 15 defenceless men with 29 soldiers and 3 officers armed with rifles condemns him," he wrote to the Mindanao-Sulu commander Ole Waloe. "Please send us a report and show the real cause for this unwarranted killing."[73] The events on Pata generated grave questions within the PC command structure. Nathorst continued pressing Ole Waloe about a culture of massacre in the South. In September 1921, he questioned the practice among Constabulary officers to "eliminate any Moro who causes trouble."[74] Much of this came out of the schooling question. Nathorst reminded Waloe that both the school superintendent for Mindanao-Sulu and head of the Bureau of Non-Christian Tribes opposed enforced attendance and named several officers known for using wanton violence against Muslim populations. "The killing of a Moro in that part of the country," he reflected, "is evidently of no consequence and all in a day's work."[75]

Institutional soul-searching did not stop similar incidents from reoccurring on Pata. In March 1923, a Moro named Akbara openly opposed the cedula tax, establishment of schools, and new government land surveys. His followers confronted a PC detachment led by Lt. Leon Angeles and were fired on. Twenty-five Moros died without a Constabulary casualty. That May, Hatib Sihaban reappeared in support of Akbara. His group rushed PC officers, who shot dead twenty-three of them. Ten days later, another encounter ended with forty-five more deaths, none of them among the PC. A local government official killed Akbara shortly thereafter, and Hatib Sihaban surrendered to authorities.[76] Constabulary reports provided peculiar explanations for the violence on Pata. One blamed wage labor for allowing peasants to compete with datus for the romantic attentions of Moro women. More likely, community leaders used antigovernment campaigns to galvanize eroding support.[77]

The 1920s was a fraught decade in Lanao. Schoolhouses shuttered, antigovernment groups killed teachers, and Constabulary installations came under attack. Nineteen buildings burned in 1924 alone. Under U.S. military supervision, PC hydroplanes bombed Maranao cottas, and troops shelled them with mountain guns and Stokes mortars. State and antistate violence kept the region destabilized and facilitated the emergence of new outlaw bands. The most prominent of these was led by a Maranao named Dimakaling, an alternately venerated and reviled character in Lanao. Although wanted for murder as early as 1925, Dimakaling did not catch the provincial government's attention until several years later.[78] Early attempts to detain him were disorganized affairs, with one ending in the death of two soldiers and a Moro guide. The American governor of Lanao, J. J. Heffington, initially dismissed the threat, citing the group's lack of firearms. Doubting the government's commitment to pursuing Dimakaling, datus around Lake Lanao provided him with refuge.[79]

Roving from village to village, Dimakaling soon became a regular fixture in the fledging Lanao press. He ransacked farms and robbed merchants near Malabang, proving a nuisance to authorities but little more.[80] This changed after an incident at the Lumbatan Agricultural School. Located south of Lake Lanao, the school used modern industry and farming practices as a template for educating Maranao youth. An American teacher named Clayton Douglas supervised the operation and lived on its grounds with his family, but the remainder of the staff and students were natives. Dimakaling and his followers raided the school in May 1934, killing two of Douglas's servants. Douglas himself confronted the outlaws but was chased off by rifle fire. The attack mobilized Americans and Filipinos, who now viewed the band as a threat to regional order.[81] The education superintendent, Edward Kuder, worried that Dimakaling was gaining sympathy among the Maranao by advertising himself as a defender of local autonomy.[82]

Philippine Constabulary units carried out multiple raids against suspected hideouts of Dimakaling and his compatriots during the summer of 1934. The bandit leader was wounded during one but managed to escape, leaving behind his trousers and a belt with eighty-six rounds of ammunition.[83] Governor Heffington railed against the deference local Maranao leaders paid the outlaw. Many of these leaders felt trapped between the demands of foreign rulers and the depredations of a local desperado. Muti Kurut of Saguiaran was once briefly in the same room as Dimakaling but feared for his own safety too much to kill or capture him. Kurut claimed Dimakaling's web of informants in the region was vast and that Moros would not make any effort to capture him unless the man who brought him down was handsomely rewarded. The outlaw loomed large in the imaginations of the Maranao people and rivaled authorities in terms of his intelligence network and ability to mete out punishment to those who defied him. Rumors circulated that the only way to join Dimakaling's inner circle was to kill a Christian in front of witnesses. The murders at Lumbatan became gang initiation practices in the colonial imaginary.[84]

Further attacks drew the attention of government officials in Manila. Vice-Governor J. R. Hayden visited the region in September 1935 accompanied by the botanist Harley Harris Bartlett, who wrote in his diaries: "Dimakaling has committed numerous murders, defies the authority of the Government, and appears to have some of the local datus on his side, for they have refused now for some months to give any information about local affairs."[85] Despite the silence, the Constabulary tracked Dimakaling to Kapai, northeast of Dansalan, in November 1935. The *Philippines Free Press* reveled in the details of how "Lanao's No. 1 outlaw" had been "riddled by a dozen Constabulary bullets" as he attempted to escape. In the wake of his death, Dimakaling inspired a discussion of the social factors that garnered him support. Many Maranao believed PC officers planted evidence, made unwarranted arrests, and killed with impunity. Beyond this, Moros chafed at government infringements on their personal rights, including arbitrary search and seizures and high fines for families who did not send their children to state schools. Dimakaling framed his actions, some of which were no doubt inspired by personal gain, as a response to these indignities.[86] Like other outlaws of the period, he achieved a mythical status following his death. In his idealized form, Dimakaling served important symbolic functions, representing the resistance of a rural society to alien cultural mandates.[87]

Beyond Lanao, colonizer-colonized relations remained tense through the 1930s. Frequent attacks on officials, especially teachers, occurred in the Sulu Archipelago. On the island of Sitangkai, near the coast of Borneo, an amuck murdered a Filipino teacher named Sofronio Aquino. The incident ended in a shootout between locals and the Constabulary, which left three Moros and two Constabulary soldiers dead.[88] The aforementioned case of Asnol on Tabawan was one of several incidents between Moros and educators in Sulu during the summer of 1934, and the following years saw no cessation in attacks.[89] The Manila press routinely reported on outrages committed by Moros in the most sensational language possible: babies used as human shields, cottas stormed by the Constabulary, love affairs ending in massacre, resistance to military service resulting in murder.[90] While coordinated antistate resistance did not remerge until the postindependence period, small groups of Moros—like those led by Hatib Sihaban and Dimakaling—continued to present challenges to the state. Muslims who refused to integrate into the burgeoning Philippine nation faced often-lethal punishment. The small but frequent armed encounters that replaced Bud Dajo–style massacres in the 1920s and 1930s ensured colonial rule did not end quietly.

Colonial Discipline

The colonial carceral system in Mindanao-Sulu evolved over time. In the first years of military rule, Moro leaders determined punishments for small crimes. Citizens reported transgressions to their local datu; if the datu had sufficient resources and local support, he handled the issue himself; if he did not, he contacted the American district governor and allowed the U.S. military to address the matter.[91] In Zamboanga, Brig. Gen. William Kobbé delegated Moro affairs to the local Samal strongman Datu Mandi, leaving the general free to focus on the ongoing Filipino insurgency. Mandi was a source of "good order," and Kobbé allowed the datu's power to expand.[92] U.S. approaches shifted as the colonial state consolidated control after 1903. U.S. Army officers became increasingly involved with nonpolitical crimes. Stationed with the 23rd Infantry at Malabang, Lt. Stephen Fuqua headed Moro affairs and developed what he called a "broad and elastic policy" toward criminality. A case involving the rape of a young Maguindanao woman was turned over to Muslim panditas for adjudication, and Fuqua believed the resulting punishment "produced satisfaction to all parties." In other cases, the army directly intervened. The 15th Cavalry pursued a group of Moros who had murdered a man and wounded a woman near the mouth of the Marga River, albeit without result. Lacking express directives, junior officers responsible for administering justice in remote areas had to forge their own hybrid approaches.[93]

American colonials worried that official laxity encouraged native crime. Moro noncooperation with investigations presented further problems.[94] The provincial government saw the expansion of the carceral system as a potential solution but wanted to accomplish this without undue financial strain. In 1904, Leonard Wood and William Cameron Forbes, then commissioner of commerce and police, settled on a plan to take one thousand inmates from Luzon to work on road building in Mindanao. These Filipino prisoners would provide the bedrock for the Muslim South's carceral future, modeling convict labor practices for incoming Moros and Lumad. The inmates arrived in March 1905, and Wood announced he was confident the Moro Province could "handle them all right and work them profitably."[95] If run correctly, the new system would pay for itself. At the same time, the U.S. Army and Philippine Constabulary increased coordination to present a united front to Moro leaders, who had hitherto been "independent of all authority."[96] Putting prisoners to work around Camp Overton, Wood enshrined the reform-through-labor approach that would become a key feature of colonial prisons in the South.

In 1906, the Legislative Council of the Moro Province enacted a compulsory labor program for all able-bodied prisoners. This measure occurred alongside a broader push to tie Moro men to state construction projects. A similar act required any male inhabitant of the province to "labor on the public highways, bridges, wharves or trails for five days of nine hours every calendar year." Those who refused had to either compensate the government for missed labor or face confinement.[97] Using prisoners on these public works projects, Moro Province officials were able to maintain higher carceral rates while defraying costs. This freed the army and PC to expand their arrest powers, further weakening the datuship as an institution. Authorities tied these developments to the civilizing mission. Imprisoned Moros would be exposed to novel technologies and disciplinary techniques and after their sentences could reintegrate into free society as sedentary producers. The construction of the capitol building at Zamboanga seemed proof of this. Moro prisoners learned how to lay stones, plaster walls, and use an American-made concrete block machine.[98]

Nowhere was the meeting of labor, technology, and discipline more evident than at San Ramon. The Spanish established the penal colony, located fifteen miles north of Zamboanga, in 1870, naming it after the patron saint of Governor-General Ramon Blanco. It was a place for *deportados*, northern prisoners serving long sentences. Those deemed "socially undesirable" by the Spanish colonial state "for reasons of political persuasion, criminal intention, or moral laxity" found themselves exiled to this southern detention center.[99] Prisoners toiled on the colony's plantations, but high rates of disease, insect infestations, crop failure, and corrupt administrators ensured that San Ramon never turned a profit. Its isolation made it "far more effective as a prison than as an economic venture."[100] As in the other remote penal settlements dotting the colonized world, environment became as much of a jailer as the guards.

Nationalist forces destroyed San Ramon and released its prisoners during the Spanish-American War, and afterward the U.S. military grew hemp and other agricultural products there. In 1900, a visiting American journalist observed that the colony's fields could be used to enrich the colonial state.[101] Following the establishment of the Moro Province, the provincial council member George Langhorne advocated San Ramon serve tutelary functions, teaching Muslims and Christians to work alongside one another and "cultivate the soil in a scientific manner."[102] In late 1905, the Philippine Commission approved the site's repurposing as an experimental farm.[103] District officials shipped products north to pay for the operation, and seeds and cuttings were sent south to Davao to encourage white settlers there to diversify their plantations. Crop experiments took place in the mountains behind the property, with workers studying the effects of altitude. Farm employees grew coffee, vegetables, cinnamon, and lemon and rubber trees.[104] San Ramon also served instructive purposes. Moro leaders visited the farm, including Sultan Jamalul Kiram and other Tausūg dignitaries. The men showed interest in the "modern plows, cultivators, and barrows," Tasker Bliss happily reported."[105]

San Ramon only remained an experimental farm for three years. In 1908, the province built a small annex to the provincial prison at the old penal colony. Two years hence, authorities decided the jail in Zamboanga was "not well situated" and drafted plans to move the entire operation to the farm.[106] By 1913, San Ramon's reversion to its original function was complete. Photographs from the period show a series of modern single-story buildings, constructed in the tropical style with gently sloping roofs and large open windows. Each white bunkhouse held 108 prisoners. Surrounded by concrete walls with iron grills, the prison grounds also housed storehouses, kitchens, workshops, and an administrative office. The women's ward had its own small hospital, outdoor bake oven, dining room, and work areas. Inmates mingled in an interior yard amid tall palms, some wearing prison stripes but most dressed in civilian clothes. They spent their work hours harvesting coconuts, foraging crops, and raising carabao, with the ultimate goal of making the institution self-supporting.[107] Bandolerismo (130), robbery (130), and assassination (113) accounted for the majority of inmate crimes, and Tausūg Moros represented the largest population group (191), followed by Maranao (117).[108] Dr. W. H. Dade, a former prison official from Kentucky, headed the facility, and a company of Philippine Scouts guarded it.[109]

The government advertised San Ramon as a unique example of colonial penology, built to facilitate prisoner health through "free circulation of air" and "plenty of sunshine."[110] Frank Carpenter declared the prison merited "classification as an educational center rather than a penitentiary."[111] Books touted miraculous stories of inmate reform. Charles Edward Russell told readers of a Tausūg Moro, imprisoned for murder, whose "obedient, industrious, willing" character made him a favorite of Dade. Allowed to fish freely so long as he returned to San Ramon each evening, the Moro encountered a capsized PC boat and helped rescue its crew. Governor Carpenter pardoned the man in an emotional ceremony. The tale was triumphal, a carceral redemption narrative for American audiences. The Tausūg convict, once primitive and murderous, became heroic under a transformative regimen of directed labor and moral instruction.[112] The plaudits continued through the 1920s and 1930s. The inmate population was 80 percent Muslim and viewed as "students."[113] After visiting San Ramon in 1926, J. R. Hayden wrote home that it was a "generation ahead" of similar facilities in the United States.[114] Frank Laubach declared the facility had the "finest record of cured inmates" in the world, which he put down to the civilizational programs in place. While American prisoners were "abnormal" and "morally defective," Moros committed crimes due to childlike notions of law and order. San Ramon provided them with an opportunity to "catch up with [the] new . . . age of law."[115]

This same mixture of idealism and racial paternalism spawned a second penal colony amid the plantations of Davao. The director of prisons, Paulino Santos, chose model inmates from San Ramon and Bilibid Prison to populate the Davao Penal Colony, which opened in 1931. Expanding on the San Ramon model, authorities referred to their charges as "colonists" and encouraged them to establish some homesteads. Agronomists, rice culture specialists, and mechanical engineers from the Bureau of Plant Industry lent expertise to colonists, helping them grow crops and raise animals.[116] The operation grew from four hundred to one thousand colonists in its first five years. Santos bragged that escape attempts were unheard of and that the institution was run at minimal costs.[117]

The official narratives of reform presented by Santos and others obscured the corruption, partiality, and violence plaguing detention practices in Mindanao-Sulu. In the 1921 Wood-Forbes mission report, Assistant Judge Advocate General L. P. Johnson reported that penal facilities at Bilibid, San Ramon, and Iwahig suffered from "political influence." American and Christian Filipino inmates used influential friends and ready access to money to receive special treatment from the poorly trained and underpaid prison employees. Such was the case with José I. Baluyot, a Luzon politico who received a life sentence in 1918 for murdering the governor of Bataan.[118] Transferred to San Ramon in 1921, Baluyot lived in a house with his family. Officials granted him two servants, made him a trustee, and did not require that he spend any time within prison walls. When the Wood-Forbes group visited San Ramon, Baluyot feigned illness so he would not be required to line up with other inmates, a ruse facilitated by the prison surgeon.[119]

Johnson's report also highlighted troubling discrepancies in how crimes were prosecuted in the South. Criminal Case No. 2671, which appeared before the justice of the peace at Jolo, involved Filipinos caught gambling illegally. The arrested men each received a fifteen-peso fine. A week later, Moros caught playing a lower-stakes game called *igud* were levied fifty-peso fines, despite igud not being listed on the antigambling ordinances. Additionally, Moros could also face dual punishments for petty crimes, appearing first before a justice of the peace and then again in the Court of the First Instance. Officials on Jolo explained the harsher treatment as a regrettable byproduct of trying to correct Moro behaviors, but the problem extended to more serious cases. In one instance, a Filipino tried to swindle a Tausūg peasant out of four hundred pesos for a fake land survey. Despite sufficient evidence for conviction, the local Christian fiscal judge exonerated the pseudosurveyor.[120] Similar issues persisted in the 1930s, with Moro prisoners in Sulu facing sentencing delays and neglect due to administrative torpor.[121]

Constabulary abuses against Muslim prisoners occurred frequently. Johnson described a "vicious situation" where young and inexperienced PC officers received deputy governor positions, which included power over policing and the judiciary. "Inclined to use force rather than discretion," these officers fostered an atmosphere of recrimination between local governments and Moro populations, contributing to the violence discussed in the previous section. After the first Pata massacre, Johnson visited the island. There he encountered several imprisoned Moros. The PC guard book had no entries for their arrests, suggesting detention on unclear or false grounds.[122]

In Lanao, the death of a Constabulary prisoner brought intra-administrative conflicts to a head. According to PC reports, a Moro named Bogalong and another prisoner had attempted to escape. Shackled together, the two fell down a flight of stairs, killing Bogalong and grievously injuring the other man. The education superintendent Edward Kuder suspected the official story was cover for an extrajudicial execution, pushing the provincial governor J. J. Heffington and the Bureau of Non-Christian Tribes to investigate further.[123] Kuder argued that violence was embedded in processes of arrest and detention because of structural deficits within the PC itself and requested enrollment of more Muslims at the PC academy in Baguio. He pointed to Cotabato, where a Maguindanao majority had "no representative" in the Constabulary. Outsiders maintained law and order in most areas of the Southern Philippines. A Maguindanao candidate, Samaon Afday, struggled to gain entrance to the academy and was eventually sidelined in favor of Christian Filipino candidates from elite schools in the North.[124] Heffington and Joseph Hayden suspected Kuder of encouraging Moros to file unfounded grievances against the Constabulary, but ongoing disciplinary investigations within the organization suggest real merit to the educator's claims of abuse.[125] Arbitrary detentions, harsher legal penalties for Moros, and intermittent massacres by the PC dulled the supposedly rehabilitative effects of colonial discipline and ensured resistance to the state persisted.

Between 1899 and 1942, colonial officials and the press routinely declared the end of disorder in the South. Reluctant U.S. imperialists and their Filipino allies, the narrative ran, used carrot-and-stick approaches to correct the Moro of his "bestial exhibitions of religious frenzy," bringing closure to a centuries-long war. Incentivized modernity and demonstrative violence functioned in tandem, correcting criminal or aberrant native customs and leading to rapid advances in settlement, commercial growth, and education.[126] While the dream of a Muslim South under permanent U.S. sovereignty gave way to the integrationist realities of Philippine nationhood, the Filipino inheritors of the colonial mantle proved no less willing to adopt similar approaches to the region, often through the Constabulary and courts system.[127]

Conventional histories date the end of the so-called Moro War to 1913–1914, when John Pershing handed power to Frank Carpenter and the Moro Province dissolved. This periodization was created by the departure of the U.S. military, an act precipitated as much by U.S. domestic politics as the success of pacification. Resistance to colonial rule had not vanished by the time Pershing left and did not vanish afterward, instead shifting in quality and scale. For each report claiming banditry had been eliminated was another indicating campaigns against outlaws were at all-time highs.[128] Resistance became diffuse in the post–Moro Province years, with the lines between criminal and folk hero often blurred. Likewise, the tactics of the Philippine Constabulary brought into question separations between law enforcement and military assault. Using the 1913 slaughter at Bud Bagsak as an end point of coordinated rebellion suggests later conflicts be understood as mere police actions. This interpretation fails on two fronts. First, it ignores the fragmented nature of resistance to colonial rule prior to 1913. There was no all-encompassing revolt during this time. Different Muslim and Lumad groups fought their own battles against the Americans for diverse reasons. Second, it assumes military power neatly resolved the ongoing traumas of colonially governed societies in transition. A more useful view might be to understand the U.S. military and government law enforcement agencies as enmeshed in dynamics of violent reciprocity with local populations—ones that mutated over time but retained core features: alienation, resistance, and massacre.

The colonial state failed in its pedagogic goals, and ambient violence prevailed. State authority in Mindanao–Sulu was frequently coercive or else absent, creating environments characterized by predation. Murder and reprisal became commonplace. Habituated to ill treatment from security forces and unrepresented by regional politicians, Moros vested legitimacy in figures who flouted the status quo. The willingness of datus to protect outlaws confirmed the stereotypes of Muslim recalcitrance shared by Americans and Filipinos, perpetuating cyclical violence.[129] In the Southern Philippines, Americans killed Muslims, Muslims killed Americans, Filipinos killed Muslims, Muslims killed Filipinos, and nearly everyone preyed on isolated Lumad communities. While evidence suggests native actors suffered disproportionate casualties at the hands of armed colonials, we should be careful to avoid a simplistic victim–perpetrator binary, instead considering how the colonial encounter itself explains the persistence of these violent encounters.

The late 1930s saw repeated military expeditions in Mindanao. The Philippine Army subjected Maranao cottas to sustained bombardment. Ground forces shelled fortifications while warplanes strafed them. This went through the month of Ramadan, leading Frank Laubach to fear that the Maranao would believe the government was purposely attacking Islam. Some of those fighting against the Filipinos were young Maranao men who had recently completed their half year of mandatory military training. Laubach complained that the army was actively working against the interests of peace in Lanao. Each time they killed an outlaw, "his relatives [became] angry. . . . The result is that instead of a dozen outlaws which might have been found at the beginning of the campaign, there are now nearly one hundred." This grim reflection on how counterinsurgency operations radicalized civilian populations could be read backward through the entire colonial period. It also darkly predicted the violence that would ravage the South in the decades following independence.[130]

Chapter 5

Tropical Idylls

Maintaining Colonial Spaces and Bodies

"The Far East prior to World War II was definitely a white man's heaven," the military officer Charles Ivins recalled. "[He] had a raft of servants, lived like a lord of the manor, and demanded and usually got the servile deference of the native." Serving with the Philippine Scouts in Zamboanga during the early 1930s, Ivins's days brimmed with revelry. Perusing his unpublished memoirs, one could be forgiven for believing the late colonial period in Mindanao-Sulu consisted mainly of alcohol-soaked comic vignettes. Ivins provides an entry point into as yet unexplored dimensions of colonial life in the region. When they were not storming cottas or dreaming of racial reform, Americans struggled with how to live amid unfamiliar and unyielding landscapes. How they accomplished this—or failed to—reveals much about the colonial encounter.[1]

Surveying these lived experiences means slipping between contextual realms, where measurements of threat and safety varied dramatically. White colonials mastered the imagined chaos of native spaces through the built environment. The planned community, the clubhouse veranda, the golf course, and the steamship deck allowed Americans in the Southern Philippines to sip their favorite whiskeys, indulge in sport, and swap the latest news in relative comfort. Beyond these spaces lay the sensory overload of the indigenous marketplace, the perilous fecundity of the overgrown jungle, and the threat of the invisible—whether it be attack by juramentado or tropical pathogen. These dichotomized zones—boundaries between colonial order and native chaos—required regulation lest transgression occur. If administrators and military personnel fixated on reforming native minds and bodies in their official lives, in their private time they gave considerably more attention to their own. For many, balancing pleasure and caution took on an obsessive quality, fueled by nebulous and inexact formulations of how an Anglo-Saxon should conduct themselves in the tropics.[2]

The orientalist trope of the Other is intimately linked to the construction of self.[3] Americans living in Mindanao-Sulu keenly internalized this observation, defining themselves against the Moro, Lumad, and Filipino masses that vastly outnumbered them. Concerns about uplifting the benighted races of the Philippine Archipelago doubled as motivating factors for American strategies of differentiation. Social rituals surrounding food and drink, compulsive photographing and collecting, and the construction of culturally and climactically "appropriate" domiciles all attest to this fact. In these sections, Moros and their communities appear spectral. This is by design and speaks to their relative absence in accounts of life in white enclaves like Zamboanga. Serving as domestics, porters, and guides, Moros played ephemeral roles in accounts of social outings—exiting the story as quickly as they entered, usually after providing the writer with some instance of local "color." Only in tales of transformation and reform did Moros take center stage. By barring the natives from participating in their personal lives, American colonials tacitly recognized the intimate sphere as an area where power relations were more readily compromised. By banishing white colonials who freely intermingled with native women, they openly acknowledged it.[4]

The drive to create colonial spaces and distinct leisure cultures was not uniquely American; nor was the fetishization and fear of tropical liminality. Urban planning, climactic determinism, and tropical medicine have all figured heavily into studies of European imperialism. The following examines the pleasures and anxieties of American colonials as they negotiated landscapes pregnant with hazard. The writings of Charles Ivins and others contain vivid depictions of how schismatic notions of the tropics and their inhabitants shaped colonial rule. White colonials built real and imaginary enclosures that served dissonant ends: protection and instruction. Rooted in fears of collapse, the social environment of Mindanao-Sulu also laid bare the tension between the integrationist claims of the tutelary colonial state and the continued operation of racially exclusionist structures.[5]

Structure and Space

Writing for *Outlook* magazine, the journalist and playwright Atherton Brownell fawned over Zamboanga as a "model of cleanliness and tropical picturesqueness." Colonial homes with manicured lawns lined the "well made" streets, afforded shade by tropical foliage. Absent was the refuse and roaming animals of the native sections. Near the seawall, the whites-only Army and Navy Club looked out onto the islands of the Basilan Strait. The warm climate had a "distinctly genial touch." The provincial capital was a safe—and perhaps even desirable—place for Americans to settle. Spatial rationalization had dissolved omnipresent threats, leaving behind paradisiacal landscapes well suited for temperate Anglo-Saxons. Colonial boosters promoted this image to U.S. audiences eager to know their nation's new territories.[6]

Empire builders in Mindanao-Sulu looked to preestablished discourses on tropical architecture, sanitation, and urban planning for inspiration. The nineteenth century had witnessed a massive expansion of European colonies in tropical regions of Asia and Africa. Administrators in these spaces interwove prevalent understandings of race, disease, and climate as they consolidated control. Metropolitan alarm at the squalor of industrial urbanization spurred European city planners, architects, police officials, and ethnologists to theorize on the environmental origins of societal decay. The miasmic theory of disease transmission held that the noxious city airs were vectors for contagion, the fruits of which manifested in the racialized bodies of slum dwellers. These ideas flowed to the colonies, where they entered debates on "tropical-temperate distinctions." Imperiled white bodies, unacclimated and besieged by the native and his sweltering primeval landscapes, required safeguards. Built environments provided them.[7]

In the postemancipation United States, race theorists tropicalized black populations and argued for their expulsion to the islands of the Caribbean and coasts of West Africa. Settler colonial prerogatives in the western and southern reaches of the imperial nation-state ensured similar programs of identification and dislocation targeted Native American and Hispanic groups. By the late nineteenth century, the rapid growth of industrial cities on the Atlantic seaboard gave rise to familiar discussions about "healthful" environments and their relation to race.[8] When the nation acquired its Pacific empire in 1898, an array of architectural and medical specialists ventured forth to explore how the Philippines could be made safe for white colonials—and how European models could be improved upon. Americans overhauled sanitation in Manila and constructed tropically "appropriate" buildings across the archipelago. In mountainous Northern Luzon, authorities cleared highland forest to create the resort town of Baguio, which became the summer capital of the colonial Philippines. Partially planned by the famed architect Daniel Burnham, Baguio took its inspiration from the hill stations dotting British India.[9] Much like these sites, it was designed to help dissipated colonials recover from the climactic and cultural challenges found at lower altitudes.

The "imperial pastoral" of Baguio allowed Americans to enact cultural rituals amid a scrupulously engineered and sanitized landscape. In its marketplaces, municipal buildings, private homes, golf greens, and mountain highways, the "government reservation" promoted a vision of colonial rule stripped of its unruly and contradictory elements.[10] Burnham's plans for Baguio expressed a larger desire to familiarize foreign spaces by reproducing Anglo-Saxon upper-class domestic norms within them. Amid a primitive Philippine environment marred by imperfect Spanish remnants, the designers and administrators of Baguio looked to the centrally planned communities of the U.S. heartland for inspiration. Burnham imported templates for reform from American cities, anticipating colonial fixations on urban ills like poor sanitation and inadequate ventilation. Local native groups involved in the construction of Baguio became showpieces for boosters. Coercive labor and the overhaul of indigenous terrain became evidence of American beneficence. Far from the fetid, overcrowded slums of Manila, Baguio stood as a vision of what could be: a literally and figuratively elevated landscape where tropical degeneration gave way to colonial modernity.[11]

Moro Province officials shared many of the same preoccupations, although municipalities in the South received fewer resources than imperial vanity projects like Baguio. To compensate for Mindanao-Sulu's peripheral status, administrators there built on what already existed. Zamboanga received the most fastidious maintenance. In early spring 1899, the U.S. military arrived there and discovered that fighting between the Spanish and Filipino insurrectos had ravaged the town. Shortly after, a large fire spread through central Zamboanga, destroying or damaging many buildings. This presented an opportunity to reshape the community.[12] In the following years, a range of municipal buildings underwent renovations. Repaired city wharves allowed for maritime commerce to expand, and enlarged provincial jails housed the growing convict population. After 1903, the Legislative Council of the Moro Province began building new roads and structures of a "substantial and lasting character." Authorities encouraged local Moros and Filipinos to participate in public improvements, integrating them into voluntary and enforced labor programs.[13]

Construction continued through 1906, including additions to the town army barracks.[14]

Zamboanga became the jewel of the South. The *Boston Globe* reporter Frank G. Carpenter described the town in idyllic terms, claiming it appeared "more like a botanical garden with the accompaniment of midway plaisance than an everyday American garrison." Along the water, the "stiff sea breeze" blew through the bright, high-ceilinged Spanish buildings, where Americans dreamed of ways to transform the community into the colony's maritime capital.[15] This involved spatially and socially segregating different groups, a practice initiated by Spain. Samal Moros lived on the margins of Zamboanga, while Chinese and Filipinos interacted with Euro-American residents in matters of commerce or acted as domestic servants. Although Governor Tasker Bliss described the town as "entirely cosmopolitan in character," rigid racial demarcations dictated interaction between white and nonwhite residents.[16] Beyond the military-administrative class, Zamboanga had an eclectic European and North American population. A list compiled during the final years of the Moro Province includes engineers, missionaries, bookkeepers, teachers, bartenders, veterinarians, dentists, numerous small business owners, and someone identified simply as a "capitalist." The document also noted interracial couples in the community, providing a window into the latent anxieties of the colonial state.[17]

The hub of colonial power in Mindanao-Sulu and its major population center, Zamboanga advertised itself as a commercial dynamo in the making. Bliss excitedly reported on the "energy" driving American, European, and Chinese capital in the region. Promotional literature declared the community "the Key to the Orient" and boasted of its leadership in agricultural and industrial development. Zamboanga was on all regional trade routes and could be easily integrated into networks servicing Australia, China, the Dutch East Indies, and Singapore. Extensive plantations, cattle ranches, coal deposits, and logging sites surrounded the town, which served as an access point to Mindanao's untapped interior. Booster hyperbole also emphasized Zamboanga's visual appeal. It was "without question the most attractive little city in the Philippines," where well-tended tropical nature surrounded "well-paved" streets and "beautifully arranged" parks. Looking to attract business, tourists, and settlers, the city self-promoted as an ideal colonial space: modern, hygienic, and economically connected.[18]

The town remained an enclave of Euro-American power into the 1930s. Charles Ivins wrote of the airy two-story frame houses he and his fellow Scouts officers lived in. Purpose built for the tropics, the homes mimicked European colonial spaces with large wraparound verandas.[19] A spacious main building connected via breezeway to a servant quarters and kitchen. Maintaining standards in Zamboanga meant not only living in spaces designed for Westerners but also differentiating oneself from the natives through domestic management. In the Ivins household, this job fell to Charles's wife, Vivian, whose "experience . . . running a home in Puerto Rico" made "this tropical stuff . . . old hat to her." Vivian directed a staff of servants in attempts to stave off filth, returning from the commissary "laden with soaps, scouring powder, waxes and cleaners of all types."[20]

With Zamboanga as the cosmopolitan capital of the South, Jolo was the frontier town, exhilarating in its proximity to Moro life. Surrounded by the azure waters of the Sulu Sea, the trading hub welcomed new arrivals at its quarter-mile pier, which stretched out from the harbor. Chinese merchants' two-story frame houses ran along the pier, connected by boardwalks. Tausūg residents lived closer to shore, many of them in homes built on stilts over the water.[21] A white sand beach gave way to the walled town of Jolo, built and fortified by the Spanish in the late nineteenth century. Americans adopted their colonial predecessors' policy of controlling native entry into the enclosure, keeping the center of the community racially segregated. A wide palm-lined boulevard—named Arolas Avenue after the famed Spanish general—ran through the center of the walled town. The young soldier Walter Cutter described Jolo as the "garden spot of the Philippines," complimenting its "Moorish" architecture and coral-lined streets. Nature intruded pleasantly through the scent of ylang-ylang and the caged tropical birds in local parks. Pumps brought fresh mountain water, and an ice plant ensured cool libations for colonials.[22]

Assessments of life beyond the walls coalesced around the notion of difference. Some visitors presented native life through orientalist tableaux, full of "gay and picturesque" costumes and exotic trading goods.[23] Others had less complimentary impressions, describing their experiences in terms of visual and olfactory assault. Walter Cutter wrote with disdain about nearby Tausūg settlements, comparing the Moros unfavorably to Christian Filipinos.[24] Three decades hence, Charles Ivins's impressions were similar. "The whole town reeked of sweat, garbage and filth," he recalled in his memoirs.[25] Using sensory perceptions and notions of the unclean to assess civilizational fitness was common practice in the liminal communities of Mindanao-Sulu. Cotabato, Malabang, Davao, Pikit, and other towns where Americans regularly encountered Muslim populations underwent similar appraisals. Far from the white zones of Zamboanga, these settlements found themselves romanticized and denigrated. Colonial sentimentalism sought out the authentic and undisturbed but was tempered by the chauvinist instinct to place native spaces outside the bounds of civilization.

The town of Dansalan represented an attempt to build something entirely new, unanchored from Spanish or Moro pasts. In 1906, the Legislative Council of the Moro Province decided a centrally planned community would aid in enacting social policy among the Maranao of Lanao. Spain's inability to maintain a reliable foothold among the "Lake Moros" had left the region largely autonomous, which frustrated the centralizing tendencies of American colonials. Tasker Bliss announced that "creating" Dansalan (it had sporadically served as a Spanish outpost for centuries and was close to permanent Maranao communities) was necessary to tame the region. The chosen site lay at the northern edge of Lake Lanao, about twenty-five miles inland from coastal Iligan. Dansalan sat across the Agus River from the U.S. Army garrison at Camp Keithley and the Maranao settlement of Marawi. Looking to continental antecedents, Bliss announced the project represented the "first and only instance in the Philippine Islands of the establishment of an orderly and well-regulated community after the manner followed by the Anglo-Saxon settlers of the United States."[26]

Planners drew up ways to populate the new town. Marawi was filled with Maranao "squatters," and Moro homes ringed Camp Keithley, leading to transfer programs. Although Bliss initially balked at claims of Maranao communal ownership in the area, he eventually conceded that paying off local datus to move their people to Dansalan was preferable to bloodshed. Once the Maranao were settled, Japanese, Chinese, and Filipino migrants could be introduced, followed by Americans of "sturdy old stock" to supervise the community and turn it into an engine of economic growth.[27] Dealing with Maranao leaders fell to District Governor John McAuley Palmer. Throughout 1907, he commissioned land surveys, partitioned lots, subsidized white businesses that hired Moros, and oversaw the removal of noncompliant residents in Marawi.[28] Meanwhile, town planners drafted municipal bylaws, debating issues like licensed saloons. Bliss himself worried about the effects of easy access to alcohol for soldiers stationed near Dansalan and its potential to strain relations with abstemious Moros. Authorities eventually created a special liquor zone with prohibitively high licensing fees to address the matter.[29]

Much like John Finley in Zamboanga, Palmer was excited about the ways market capitalism could civilize the new Muslim residents of Dansalan. He wrote prominent white merchants in Iligan, urging them to establish businesses at the lake and promising the "industrial capacity" of the Maranao would mean profit for all. Target areas for development included fabric production, brass work, and the nascent coffee trade. Dansalan was a place for people to "make money," Palmer told the Iligan businessman Martin Geary.[30] Meanwhile, authorities experimented with agricultural colonies outside of Dansalan that ran on enforced labor. While admitting the idea was "startling to Americans," Palmer insisted it was necessary "in dealing with people like the Moros" and cited evidence from other colonized regions in Islamic Southeast Asia.[31] The governor imagined the colonies having a domino effect, organically multiplying as other Moros began to adopt Western modes of production. In the lake district of the future, villagers grew and harvested agricultural products and sold them to traveling Moro middlemen, who brought their goods to white commercial enterprises in Dansalan.[32]

The planned community grew at a modest but steady rate. A bridge was built across the Agus River, and Dansalan received the trappings of a permanent town: schools, markets, a jail, and a government building. The small hospital and dispensary there treated around seventy patients per day.[33] By the 1920s, the community was a fixed presence, playing host to missionaries, businesspeople, and other members of colonial society. Visiting in 1926, Joseph Hayden met with local datus, dined with the governor, and shot nine holes of "poor" golf on a course overlooking the lake.[34] As in Zamboanga or Jolo, white colonials remained mostly within the confines of the town and socialized among themselves. Adventures into the Lanao hinterland were rare, and visitors had mixed views on the area. The journalist S. S. Schier enjoyed the culture, climate, and scenery of Lanao, describing Dansalan as the "Mecca of Moroland" and predicting tourist development.[35] Charles Ivins was less enthused, remarking the town would not win a "contest for municipal achievement" and condemning the "war-like" Maranao.[36] Dansalan remained more like Jolo than Zamboanga—an imperial outpost in an unstable region. The grand social experiments planned by John McAuley Palmer and others were contested by the Maranao, many of whom chose to remain in remote villages where the state held little sway. Dansalan was renamed Marawi following independence, growing into the largest city in the province of Lanao del Sur.[37]

Sociality and Leisure

White elites placed great importance on learning to live comfortably in the Muslim South. Colonials organized sports teams, drank at the Zamboanga golf and country club, threw parties, took photographs, attended the cinema, organized parades, trekked across the Mindanaoan interior, and sailed the Sulu Sea. While many Americans remained in the Southern Philippines only the length of a tour of duty, others found ways of extending their stay or settled permanently. Some developed sentimental attachments to life in the tropics. When Leonard Wood visited his old governor's residence in Zamboanga near the end of his life, nostalgic tears "[streamed] down his cheeks," and he was wistful about his tenure in the Moro Province. When not engaged in administration and warfare, Wood had played tennis with his children, took "grand picnics" in the hills above Zamboanga, and paddled through Mangrove swamps. The "free and independent" life afforded white colonials marked their impressions of the places they governed.[38]

Zamboanga was the hub of colonial sociality under U.S. rule. Club life dominated leisure time for many in the military-administrative class during the early 1900s. The whites-only Army and Navy Club had a broad covered gallery that extended out over the water and was equipped with "every kind of cane or bamboo lazy chair and lounge known to this tropical climate." On Saturday evenings, officers brought their wives to drink, dance, and socialize.[39] The club also hosted visiting dignitaries. In 1905, Secretary of War William Howard Taft and his coterie spent a night there. As they dined outside, a parade of two hundred native vessels passed before them on the waterfront: a romanticized spectacle of primitive peoples in their "natural" state safely consumed within the confines of the segregated club.[40]

The Zamboanga Overseas Club, a civilian analog to the Army and Navy Club, was a raucous watering hole in the 1920s and 1930s. In Zamboanga to secure the photograph collection of Dean Worcester, the anthropologist Charles Eugen Guthe spent his free time drinking until the early hours of the morning at the club. His diary paints an image of near-constant drunken revelry among club members.[41] The Zamboanga Golf and Country Club was also popular. Charles Ivins passed afternoons in the clubhouse drinking with resident business figures, including the manager of the Chartered Bank of India, Australia, and China. Ivins peppered his memoirs with comic vignettes of playing golf amid the varied local fauna and holding drunken contests. After comparing the "relative merits" of various scotch whiskeys, the idle colonials would race their cars back into town for amusement.[42] Problematic alcohol consumption had marked colonial life from the earliest days of the Moro Province. Attending a military banquet in 1903, Maud Huntley Jenks observed officers drinking themselves into unconsciousness. "The drinking is terrible over here," she wrote in a letter home, "as it is in the tropics wherever the white man has gone in any numbers—whether American, British, Dutch."[43]

Outside the clubs, colonial families took pains to establish domestic spaces for themselves that replicated (insofar as possible) the pleasures of home. They achieved this by using local labor, employing Filipino cooks, houseboys, and laundrywomen. Officers' wives often managed a staff, and dull floors or untidy living quarters signaled a white woman did not know how to "run her servants."[44] This reliance on domestics freed up time for leisurely lunches, bridge games, walks, and cocktail hours. Special societies like the Military Order of the Kris, which borrowed its name from the famed Moro weapon, held holiday celebrations with minstrel shows, field sports, and horse racing.[45] The presence of important American families like the Worcesters ensured continuity in the social rituals practiced in Zamboanga. In the 1930s, consensus held that Dean Worcester's widow set the standard for colonial hauteur in the southern capital.[46]

Despite access to tropical foodstuffs, Americans desired staples from home. Most goods arrived from Manila, which meant personnel in the South often settled for picked-over remainders. As such, celebratory meals would feature closely guarded specialty food items. Walter Cutter recorded the entire menu of his 1901 Thanksgiving meal in Jolo. "Under the fierce rays of the tropical sun, with swarthy Mohammedans looking curiously on, it seemed a strange setting for the old New England holiday," he wrote in his diary. Cutter bested this account in his description of Christmas dinner the following month.[47] The officer class received even more extensive celebratory meals. At a 23rd Infantry celebration in 1909, attendees feasted on caviar, Illana Bay crabs, and beef fillet with mushroom sauce. The evening concluded with crème de menthe, cigars, and songs skewering colonial life on Jolo.[48]

Beyond comfort and familiarity, culinary habits demonstrated "cultural affiliation" in the Southern Philippines.[49] What food was consumed and how it was consumed served an important function in maintaining hierarchies of difference. Charles Ivins noticed this when he visited the Goodyear rubber plantation at Kabsalan. Despite arriving in the middle of the night, he was met by two Moro laborers, who pushed him on a flat car along a narrow-gauge railway for two miles over a "pestilential" swamp. When he reached the plantation manager's house in the early hours of the morning, Ivins received drinks and a large dinner—prepared for the Americans by the native cooks and houseboys. "[The Filipino] likes to make people happy," Ivins wrote in his memoirs. For men like Ivins and the writer Vic Hurley, who was working at Kabsalan, maintaining civilized rituals in the midst of the Mindanao wilderness cemented their status as bearers of superior culture. Meals took on totemic significance.[50]

Publications like the *Mindanao Herald* promoted community among white colonials. A weekly broadsheet, the *Herald* relayed the latest developments around the Moro Province in the early 1900s. Its small team of writers covered military campaigns against Moro groups, announced the establishment of new American plantations, critiqued the government in Manila for neglecting the South, advocated for pro-settler legislation, and relayed news from European colonies. The *Herald*'s editor J. A. Hackett was a former U.S. Army intelligence operative who unapologetically advocated for long-term annexation of the South. Surveying the burgeoning white settler culture in regions like Davao, Hackett and his staff saw a future for Moroland that melded North American frontier expansionism with the tropical plantation economics of Hawaii. Zamboanga's burgeoning white community and the provincial government's ambitious plans to transform Mindanao-Sulu showed evidence of the need for settler permanency. Although founded a scant four years after the U.S. military arrived in the South, the *Herald* presented a vision of naturalized colonial rule to its readership. A planter or investor thumbing through its pages in 1907 or 1908 could be forgiven for believing Zamboanga had been under U.S. control for decades.[51]

Military men stationed outside Zamboanga created their own newspapers and bulletins. Published in Parang, the *Twenty-Third Infantry Lantaka* relayed baseball scores, poked fun at military culture, and notified soldiers of upcoming social functions. Serious matters like the depredations of the Moro pirate Jikiri became sources of levity. An entirely satirical spin-off of the *Lantaka* called the *Twenty-Third Infantry Bolo* enumerated the sexual experiences of local army officers in Japan (claiming one had written a book titled *Geisha Girls I Have Known*) and acidly described the medical threats posed by the environment.[52] The *Jolo Howler* provided a similar outlet for men stationed in Sulu, skewering military life in the tropics. It denigrated Tausūg culture mercilessly in poems like "The Belle of Jolo," where each quatrain began with a saccharine romantic sentiment and ended by disparaging Moro women: "There's a beautiful Sulu belle, / with a queenly, shapely head; / There's a mystic spell in her eyes gazelle— / And her teeth are betel-red," or "Her nose is gently retroussé / And mayhap, slightly flat; / I've often thought that it once caught / A swinging baseball bat."[53] Elsewhere in the *Howler*, articles ridiculed the Chinese penchant for fireworks, advertised fake businesses on Jolo, and covered native dress in the style of haute couture fashion reports from Europe.[54]

Many lyrical compositions from Mindanao-Sulu filtered back to the United States. In 1911, the soldier and journalist Damon Runyon published a song about the supposed penchant of Moro females to fight alongside the men titled

"The Ladies in the Trenches: A Soldier Song of the Sulu Isles; or, If a Lady's Wearing Pantaloons." Another ditty described the hunt for Datu Ali amid the jungles of Cotabato: "Oh, sing a song of hikers, / On Dato Ali's trail, / On straight tips from old Piang / Who ought to be in jail. / Three commands of dough-boys / And one of horseless horse, / Through mud and slime; / Through filth and grime; / We wend our way perforce." Other tunes mixed sentimentality with racialized humor in their description of Moro "romances," "queens," "chiefs," and "nights." Songs about Moros provided a glancing introduction to the nation's Pacific frontier for many Americans. The soldiers who wrote them used racial difference to interpret their experiences and add humor to lives punctuated by the performance of violence.[55]

Sport provided another avenue for maintaining colonial social structures. By participating in physical contests unfamiliar to the natives, Americans distinguished themselves as bearers of civilization. White colonials used hunting, polo, sport fishing, and baseball as a means of re-creating a distant homeland.[56] During inspection trips to the Southern Philippines in 1909–1910, Governor-General William Cameron Forbes mixed government business with sporting activities. Using Moro guides, Forbes and his entourage repeatedly visited Lake Liguasan in the Cotabato district to hunt ducks. On their second trip, the group bagged 475 ducks and afterward visited with Datu Enoch near Lake Buluan. The detour conjured wistful memories for the governor-general, who wrote of the "varying degrees of hominess" he felt in Mindanao. The island's interior did not offer the luxuries of life in Manila but instead provided an "authentic" vision of life on the imperial fringe.[57]

Baseball was a leisure activity for colonials and also a means to inculcate natives into Western team sports.[58] When not engaged in pacification campaigns, military regiments regularly organized teams and played against one another. Newspapers like the *Lantaka* gave detailed accountings of recent games, noting standout offensive and defensive plays. In Lanao, N. M. Green headed the regimental team and organized matches for them in Jolo, Malabang, Parang, Iloilo, and Manila.[59] Commanders like John Pershing and Matthew Steele often served as umpires.[60] Military clubs also played against Filipino and Moro teams, and Filipino and Moro teams against one another. The widespread adoption of baseball and basketball in the Philippine Islands meant there was no shortage of native participants. Visayan regimental teams traveled to Zamboanga to play the Americans there. The *Twenty-Third Infantry Lantaka* wrote of the "natural aptitude" of the Filipinos for the "great American game." An annual July Fourth match in Zamboanga pitted the local Filipino team against the Moros.[61] Decades on, similar contests continued between Moro and Filipino companies of the Philippine Scouts.[62] Writing in the pages of *National Geographic*, Dean Worcester called baseball "one of the really important things" Americans had introduced to the "Non-Christian Peoples" of the Philippines.[63]

The desire to know Mindanao-Sulu spurred informal adventuring. Mastering the territory beyond town boundaries involved pitting oneself against untamed nature and the unpredictable native. The American presence in the archipelago coincided with the last great era of exploration, and the intrepid adventurer of Victorian imagination still held considerable appeal. Newspapers avidly covered doomed expeditions and feats of mountaineering well into the interwar era. Added to this was the Rooseveltian ideal of "strenuous" living, resulting in a class of American men and women in Mindanao-Sulu who viewed sojourning in the wilds as a mark of strength. Traveling across Lanao with her husband as they secured the human exhibits for the St. Louis World's Fair, Maud Huntley Jenks boasted of "[probing] the wilds where no white woman has ever been before" in letters to her mother.[64] Betty Hurley, wife of Vic, similarly led treks into the jungle surrounding the Goodyear plantation at Kabsalan and avidly fished for barracuda along the coast of the Zamboanga Peninsula.[65]

Government bodies encouraged journeys into the unknown from the outset. Under the direction of the anthropologist David Prescott Barrows, the Bureau of Non-Christian Tribes sent specific directives to its volunteer fieldworkers throughout the Philippine Archipelago. The bureau encouraged nonspecialists to study the natives in numerous ways, including taking anthropometric measurements, administering extensive questionnaires, and compiling local vocabularies in rural areas. Mapping the "racial pathology," "racial psychology," and "criminal anthropology" of the Philippines arose from the desire to control colonized peoples, but the main thrust of the document—that the amateur observer could serve as an agent of imperial knowledge production—dovetailed with the activities of white men and women who sought out remote areas. Barrows issued his directives in 1901, and their spirit remained evident for years afterward in the hiking trips, river tours, and mountaineering practiced by colonials in Mindanao-Sulu.[66]

Cataloging the natural environment and collecting Moro manufactures were staples of backcountry exploring. Posted on the southern shore of Lake Lanao, the army surgeon Charles Hack spent his idle time studying local flora and fauna. It was "strange to think of the United States having territory that is yet unexplored," he wrote in his journal. Near the Mataling River, he recorded descriptions of plant life and marveled at being so close to the "heart

of nature." The surgeon also purchased an array of items from the Maranao
Moros in the area, including fifteen krises, seven agungs, a lantaka, three spears,
a betel nut box, a coat of mail, a brass helmet, and some sarongs. He eventually shipped his collection back to the United States, and it was donated to the
Museum of Natural History in New York City after his death.[67] William Cameron Forbes also amassed Moro weapons on his trips to the South, Seymour

Figure 5.1 Americans posted in Mindanao-Sulu collected the material culture of the peoples
they fought and governed. This was especially true of weaponry. The collection of barongs, bolos,
and kris pictured above belonged to a U.S. Army officer stationed on the island of Bongao in the
Sulu Archipelago, c. 1901. (Robert Lee Bullard Papers, 1881–1955, box 10, Library of Congress,
Manuscript Division)

Howell searched for "desirable brass work" in Zamboanga, and J. R. Hayden located fine silks on Jolo.[68] Here, the enthusiasms of the amateur ethnographer coalesced with the commodification of Moro cultures, which were admired for their oriental exoticism in the United States. Business-minded residents, Muslim and American alike, soon realized the demand for such items and produced them at greater rates.[69]

Photography was a related means of exploring the Southern Philippines. By the early twentieth century, technological advances had removed barriers to owning a camera and turned photography into a popular hobby. Those intent on compiling environmental and ethnocultural data through the medium became increasingly able to do so. Dean Worcester spearheaded the trend in the Philippines, transforming his interest in anthropology into a sprawling visual archive of life in the archipelago.[70] Other colonials taking photographs in the Muslim South did not have the resources, access, or archival inclinations of Worcester, yet what pictures they did take were telling. Images often depicted idealized versions of the tropical environment while conveying a sense of "exemplary and disciplined" colonial societies.[71] Photographs from Mindanao-Sulu also highlighted the innate foreignness of indigenous peoples and the landscapes they inhabited.

The Constabulary officer Sterling Larrabee regularly included photographs in his letters home. A missive in 1912 included a variety of pictures taken during his time on expedition in remote areas of the Lanao district. A casual shot of "Lt. Johnson frying some carabao liver" is appended with the offhand comment: "We shot the carabao along with two Moros that morning." Another photograph shows the officer Guy Fort with two Moro *capitazes*. The Moros stand with their hands on their hips as Captain Fort observes them. "Fort speaks the Malanao dialect like a native," Larrabee explained to his parents.[72] In his personal scrapbook, the young lieutenant paired newspaper articles about skirmishes he participated in with the photographs. A report from the *New York Herald* about a battle between Constabulary soldiers and Moro outlaws featured alongside shots of Moros at rest and work.[73] Larrabee also dabbled in formal ethnographic portraiture. An August 1911 letter included two pictures— one of a Moro sergeant named Malaco and another of a Maranao boy called Bwasa. Each subject is isolated from his surroundings by a white sheet hung behind him. They are similarly captured: full body, hands to side, staring directly into the camera.[74]

Staged group portraits in the collection of Robert Lee Bullard include nearly every important Moro leader in the region. A fastidious caption writer, Bullard recorded not only the names of the Muslim dignitaries but also the roles of their retainers. He took informal photographs of Moro weaponry, Americans on patrol and at rest, colonial architecture, and even Moro women bathing. Frank McCoy, who returned to the Philippines in 1921 with the Wood-Forbes mission, likewise photographed exposed natives.[75] Photographs of nude or seminude Moros took their lead from magazines like *National Geographic*, which dictated that images of nudity did not constitute moral transgression if taken for dispassionate scholarly purposes. Anthropologists and eugenicists of the period promoted "scientifically managed" photography of naked nonwhite peoples as a means of revealing racial-civilizational truths. Neither Bullard nor McCoy took their photos for academic purposes but rather had internalized the dominant modes of visually cataloging foreign bodies and applied them to their own photography.[76]

Dissipation and Breakdown

Americans in Mindanao-Sulu went to great lengths to manage their environment, uphold domestic standards, and replicate the popular leisure activities they enjoyed in the United States. The South provided space to express one's adventurous spirit by studying plant life, "discovering" the trackless wilderness, and collecting indigenous manufactures. Yet pervasive fears rested near the surface. How might the environment have deleterious effects on the white body and psyche? Likewise, what impact did social or sexual intercourse with natives have? Anxieties about what was alternately referred to as tropical neurasthenia, colonial breakdown, or "Philippinitis" coursed through colonial life. Bucolic conditions in the white areas of Zamboanga masked the serious work of maintaining racial boundaries, the transgression of which could undermine the colonial state.[77]

Nonspecific explanations for colonial breakdown ranged from a "failure of character" to psychosexual disorder. Writers argued white men were at risk from a combination heat, alcohol, and the licentious native, and medical officials in Mindanao-Sulu speculated on the climactic, emotional, and psychosexual dimensions of this nebulous disorder. Imagined linkages between breakdown and depleted manliness made many colonials reticent to seek treatment.[78] Fears of tropical neurasthenia and related forms of breakdown circulated through the British Empire, where colonial administrators used the diagnosis to control their officials, discarding those deemed unfit to serve. Breakdown cast in bold relief the epistemic uncertainties and "helplessness" of empire builders arising from environmental unfamiliarity, cultural dislocation, and a fear of encirclement.[79] Americans anchored their understandings of collapse in these transimperial ideas, writing reports that situated colonial life in the Philippines amid other empires. The secretary of the Moro Province, George Langhorne, considered the impact of climate on the British in Malaya and the Dutch in Java. Service there was "severe" but not a deterrent to governance. He believed Americans could "do good work where any other white race can." Fastidious living and diligent labor would combat the "demoralizing effects of the Philippine climate."[80]

Others did not share Langhorne's optimism. The army surgeon Charles Hack was initially impressed by the ready availability of fruits and vegetables on Mindanao, the quality of the rubber market there, and Moro fluency in English and remained pragmatically upbeat even when posted to remote Camp Vicars. "Life is rough and hard here; we have no pleasures except those we make ourselves. We sleep with our clothes on . . . but I do not care so much," he wrote in June 1902.[81] But the difficult environment, poor-quality food, and Hack's racial paranoia began to erode his bonhomie. At the end of the month, he transferred to an even more remote post near Mataling Falls, where he began to suspect nearby Maranao communities. "They (being Mohammedan) have no regard for human life. . . . It seems that no Malay can be trusted, whether Moro, Filipino, or whatever," he fulminated. The surgeon blamed "politics in the States" for the army's unwillingness to move with force against the Moros. He began dreading roll call each morning, and by September racist screeds about the Maranao punctuated his daily diary entries.[82]

Charles Hack believed his deterioration arose from an unhealthful climate and a remove from civilization. "Nearly six months without . . . being in a house," he complained. There was no access to "music, theatres, clubs . . . or church," and he felt "nothing short of lazy." Hack self-diagnosed his condition as Philippinitis, which sapped his resolve to engage in common pastimes. He observed similar effects among fellow soldiers in Lanao. "I trust when we return to the States any energy we may have once had will return," he wrote.[83] Hack's writings represented a creeping unease about ambient threats. Fear of boredom and inertia mingled with a fear of pathogens. During the Philippine-American War, epidemic diseases ravaged the islands.[84] The *Manila Times* described soldiers in Lanao being plagued by ill health and malnourishment. Forced to double as road laborers because the Moros "did not have the heart" to participate in their own betterment, U.S. troops succumbed to cholera, smallpox, and "fevers of the most malignant type." Constant rainfall, flooding, and humid conditions created grim scenes: soldiers wasting away from dysentery and corpses suspended from trees "on account of the lack of dry earth in which to bury them."[85]

Regimental newspapers openly discussed forms of emotional and physical collapse. The *Twenty-Third Infantry Lantaka* was comically philosophical in its descriptions of Philippinitis. "There is no theory to account for it and no practice to fit it. It is like a wicked flea: the moment a man discovers that he has it, he has it not," the paper concluded. "There is neither subjective nor objective consciousness of a Philippinitic state. It is fortuitous, sporadic, imminent, and may be figured on as closely as where the lightning will strike or what turn a balky mule will take next."[86] The evasive "Philippinitic" state, thought to afflict most white bodies in the tropics, differed from the sober diagnosis of neurasthenia. The paper lamented the departure of a Lieutenant Pepper, stationed in Parang: "He has been afflicted with neurasthenia for some time, and it is sincerely hoped that the trip and home atmosphere will return him to health." When breakdown reached a critical stage—manifesting in suicide attempts, substance use disorders, or psychotic episodes—it ceased being the existentially absurd Philippinitis and was medicalized as neurasthenia.[87]

Inspectors studied military stations in the South, noting climactic conditions, sanitation, access to potable water, and supply reliability.[88] J. Franklin Bell, commander of the Philippines Division in the waning years of the military period, explored the effects of isolation and environment on American servicemen in Mindanao-Sulu, highlighting the successes of the Moro Province in providing adequate facilities for military men and their families. Zamboanga featured "every comfort and convenience," while Camp Keithley was exceeded only by Baguio in the "healthfulness" of its climate. Augur Barracks in Jolo received mild criticism, but Bell mainly blamed individual moral failure for instances of breakdown. Soldiers who did not have "sufficient determination . . . to maintain a proper regimen" were more likely to deteriorate; only those who craved the "fleshpots of society" would suffer in Mindanao-Sulu. Bell implicated substance abuse, sexual immorality, and personal weakness in his conception of breakdown, suggesting tropical dissipation was a litmus test for personal character.[89]

Civilian rule did not assuage fears about the state of the occidental body. Governor Frank Carpenter's service in the Philippines was punctuated by repeated breakdowns and a "progressive invalidism."[90] Governor-General Francis Burton Harrison attributed Carpenter's ill health to his ceaseless work ethic and "continued residence for so long a time in tropics," implying white ability to labor in the Philippines was finite.[91] Long after returning to the United

States, Carpenter lobbied the U.S. Congress for dispensation to receive a military pension on account of the length of his service and his ailments. In 1937, the Senate granted him an annuity amounting to $1,800 per annum, in recognition that he was "broken in health" from service in the Philippines.[92] The governor of Sulu James Fugate also attributed his failing health to life in the tropics. Recurrent stomach troubles and throat issues limited him to a single meal per day.[93] The botanist H. H. Bartlett met Fugate in 1935 and described him as being "in bad health . . . and hanging on by grim determination."[94] Fugate's correspondence from the time was marked by a stoic fatalism: the lone colonial administrator fighting for civilization amid native indifference and a pathogenic environment.[95]

Civilizational and sexual degeneration provided rich fodder for Charles Ivins, who believed tropical life eroded a "white man's character." Constabulary officers he met at Camp Keithley were mired in vice, abusing alcohol and sleeping with native women, while the Moros there assimilated Western "thought and science." To Ivins, Moro contact with U.S. culture could only improve their well-being, while prolonged existence in Mindanao-Sulu did the opposite to white men.[96] Americans who violated racial boundaries and entered into affairs with Moro or Filipino women found themselves on the margins of colonial society. Living in remote communities with multiracial families, these men adopted the mantle of "Sunshiners." Ivins classed them as something other than white or American, noting their penchant for cheap gin, "dull vacant eyes," and aversion to personal hygiene. Their amours resulted in a "fair sprinkling of young mestizos" in the Southern Philippines. Lost to the tropical sun, these problematic men became ridiculous savages rather than fellow countrymen.[97] Alongside racial cautionary tales, Ivins presented the Sunshiners as a source of sexual titillation. In lusty prose, he described an ex-soldier who had married several native women. Each time the man visited the Zamboanga commissary, he offered Ivins—with a "broad wink"—the sexual services of his daughters. The Mindanao-Sulu of Ivins's tales was a sensuous and debased scape where a man could indulge himself in temporal delights at the cost of his racial fitness.[98]

The writer Vic Hurley depicted the Muslim South as a crucible of frontier manliness and afforded the Sunshiners grudging respect. He saw the Southern Philippines as a land of untold riches. With enough resolve, the white pioneer could adapt to the alien environment and reap its bounties. Hurley arrived in Zamboanga in the mid-1920s after an NCAA track career at the University of Oregon, eager to grow coconuts and belladonna for profit.[99] Surveying the human landscape in the colonial capital, he sneered at the provincial elites who confined themselves to "drinking parties and bridge games" and then bragged of "tropic service" on returning to the United States. The Sunshiners and their isolation fascinated the young writer, who marveled at how they forsook the "ways of the white men." Tending their small, isolated plots of land, these outcasts had integrated themselves into the tropics without effete Western pleasures like golf, whiskey, and shaded verandas.[100]

"Manly virtues provided the mettle of empire," Robert Aldrich writes of French masculinity in the colonies.[101] As with the French colonial man so with the American one. With a business partner, Vic Hurley acquired an isolated plot of land in southern Cotabato hoping to get rich and prove his grit. His plan soon unraveled. Living in a small shack at the edge of the jungle, the would-be plantation tycoon dreamed of wealth while experiencing the opposite. Clearing the land was hard, and crop yields were small. The resident fauna plagued Hurley, who had numerous run-ins with giant centipedes, wild boar, pythons, and crocodiles. He fretted about living in the "unsettled and dangerous" interior and grew paranoid about the local Moros.[102] His mental and physical equilibrium deteriorated. Some nights he brought his kerosene lamp outside into the darkness and fired his pistol in the direction of animal eyes reflecting back at him from the brush. The well-armed Hurley feared the Moros, who occasionally made trading visits to his property, would kill him for his guns, but it was malaria that finally undid him. Alone in his shack with a pistol by his side, Hurley spent his final days in Cotabato in feverish delirium waiting for his long-since-departed partner to collect him.[103] "This is my reward for going to impossible places where no white man should be," he wrote. "I *cannot* stand up to the bush in Mindanao. It is sapping me and I am becoming more afraid every day."[104] Abandoning the plantation, Hurley nevertheless remained in Mindanao until the 1930s. A review of his memoirs was titled "No Place for a White Man."[105]

Solving or overcoming tropical threat involved porous and shifting solutions. Americans living and laboring in the Southern Philippines developed an explanatory spectrum to address issues ranging from ennui to utter collapse. Even in comic accounts of Philippinitis lingered an anxious undercurrent acknowledging the harsh realities of serving on the colonial frontier. What all accounts shared was a sense that Americans moved within an environment actively hostile to them in every sense: through a lack of modern amenities, through the relentless tropical heat, through the strange and dangerous wildlife, and through transgressive contact with inferior races. Those failing to monitor their personal hygiene, alcohol consumption, or contact with the natives faced degeneration and, in the most extreme cases, became Sunshiners eking out a marginal existence along the Mindanao littoral. The threat to the American mind and body posed by the environment was not just an individual concern but also illustrated what Alison Bashford calls the "simultaneous imperatives of individual contact and political administration" in the colonies.[106] U.S. Army commanders like J. Franklin Bell spent considerable time pondering the relationship between personal breakdown and military security. Even after direct military rule concluded, the stresses of tropical life, real and imagined, continued to plague U.S. colonials.

Charles Ivins and his wife, Vivian, left Zamboanga in 1934. "Firm friends" with the Euro-American establishment in town and operators of the outlying plantations alike, the couple celebrated their final night in the colonial capital with "toasts, handshakes, kisses, laughter and tears." Standing at the rail of the S. S. *Mayon*, Charles and Vivian listened as a military band on the pier below played them off to "The Monkeys Have No Tails in Zamboanga," a popular racially charged song that Ivins adapted as the title of his memoirs. The Scouts officer recalled his time in Mindanao-Sulu as a colonial idyll, filled with socializing, drinking, larger-than-life characters, and not much actual work. In many ways, his stories played out like South Seas tales of Fiji or Hawaii, with the natives acting as color for the larger tale of white bonhomie and leisure. "Back in those halcyon days," he wrote, "all white men were brothers." Nevertheless, Ivins believed "teeming" Asian populations presented a threat to isolated white communities (or, in the case of Australia, countries). Maintaining a "white man's heaven" involved cultivating local collaborators, which Ivins contributed to in the Philippine Scouts, and taking a firm hand against native transgression. Tropical leisure was earned. From the deck of the *Mayon*, the Ivinses waved to their friends as the "pier became smaller and smaller" and "Zamboanga dropped below the horizon into the sea of pleasant, wistful memories."[107]

Colonials experienced Mindanao-Sulu as a series of bifurcations. It appealed to their romantic notions of a tropical paradise yet also teemed with uncontrolled filth and pestilence. It was ripe for exploration but incredibly dangerous. The Moros were fascinating and "picturesque" and also practitioners of a degraded and violent form of Islam. Native bodies required close scrutiny but also needed to be kept at a distance. Indigenous manufactures were sought-after collectors' items yet symbolized profound barbarism. The landscape allured and repulsed in near equal measure. To combat threats of breakdown and deracination in the "sensuous" tropics, American colonials fashioned spaces for themselves that borrowed from European colonial models and attempted to reorder native communities to make them more amenable to Anglo-Saxon existence.[108] In their leisure time, they published small newspapers, golfed, and drank liberally within their enclosures—whether club, barrack, or home. When they ventured beyond these protected zones, the natural environment (which, to colonials, included the natives) provided an opportunity to demonstrate an adventuring spirit, participate in the colonial impulse to "discover," show a familiarity with native cultures through collection, or photograph the surroundings. These pursuits rested on unstable ground, however. Fears of moral degeneration, racially transgressive contact, and physical breakdown infused U.S. colonialism in Mindanao-Sulu with a permanently anxious quality.

Chapter 6

Moros in America

Visiting the Metropole in Fact and Fiction

In the summer of 1904, a married couple from rural Maine made the long journey to the Louisiana Purchase Exposition in St. Louis. After several days of sight-seeing, Bob and Becky visited the Philippine Reservation. Built with ample funding from the Insular Government in Manila and spread across forty-seven acres, the sprawling exhibit was a paean to the moral and commercial triumphs of empire. Visiting the faux-natural villages of "uncivilized" Moros and Igorots, Bob gazed on the peoples before him and declared the United States could not "civilize 'em in three centuries or more."[1] His mind changed when he saw native members of the Philippine Scouts and Philippine Constabulary marching under the American flag to "The Battle Hymn of the Republic." Overcome by patriotic sentiment, the New Englanders declared the nation should "scatter the influence of Christianity, [and] build up and disseminate the fruits of civilization where cruelty, ignorance and superstition exist."[2]

This Damascene moment was imagined. Bob and Becky were two provincial characters in a vernacular dime novel about the St. Louis World's Fair. Published in 1904 to capitalize on the fair's popularity, *Uncle Bob and Aunt Becky's Strange Adventures at the World's Great Exposition* wrestled with the presentation of empire. How should overseas colonies appear to a skeptical metropolitan public, and how could cultural producers appropriately portray the nation's foreign subjects? The Moro villages in St. Louis were an entry point into the U.S. public consciousness, although not the only place the Muslims of Mindanao-Sulu appeared. Moros arrived in the United States as carnival display objects but also as visiting dignitaries and students eager for the freedoms of college life. Journalists covered these tutelary journeys but often undercut their own messages by highlighting the innate otherness of the nation's colonial wards. In certain instances, Moros themselves complicated clean narratives of imperial citizenship. Beyond Bob and Becky, the fictions produced about the Southern Philippines included comic operas, juvenile adventure stories, radio serials, and movies. They, too, portrayed a colonized landscape in which Moros were lesser than Filipinos yet possessed of martial bravery and potentially redeemable if provided guidance.

Muslim colonial subjects surfaced in U.S. cultural discourse in myriad ways. U.S. administrators, politicians, and fair planners adopted the late-Victorian penchant for importing and displaying nonwhite peoples as a form of public spectacle. Organizers of the St. Louis World's Fair utilized what Bernard Cohn describes as the "museological modality" of empire to create a "monumental record" of Muslim civilization in the Southern Philippines.[3] This historicizing of difference allowed organizers, through living and nonliving exhibits alike, to promote Social Darwinian fables about prehistory, evolution, and the positive moral implications of empire.[4] Beyond the Philippine Reservation, public reactions to elite Moro visitors like the sultan of Sulu revealed the "double vision" of U.S. colonial discourse, which was marked by the "repetitious slippage of difference and desire."[5] As we shall see, ideological superstructures of racialized power both cautiously encouraged *and* delimited colonial mimicry.

Moros on Display

The Samal and Maranao Moros who made the long trip from Mindanao to Missouri lived within the Philippine Reservation, which organizers designed as a grand tribute to the morally edifying qualities of colonial empire. The othered bodies of colonized peoples had long been a staple in the royal courts, traveling circus shows, and museums of Europe, although the art of human display arguably did not reach its zenith until the latter half of the nineteenth century. During this period, national competition and colonial aggrandizement gave rise to international expositions. At these showcases, spectators judged colonized peoples against symbols of Euro-American progress and "evolutionary time" turned global.[6] The fairs allowed Euro-American states to create a didactic vision of colonial empire. Western modernity rescued benighted races and empires profited enormously in the process, the story went.

The human zoos of London, Paris, and Berlin developed alongside a growing fascination with the products of "primitive" civilizations. "New forms of
expertise associated with evolutionary forms of natural history and ethnology,"
writes Tony Bennett, "sought to arrange a different kind of show through the
studied manipulation of bones, skulls, teeth, carcasses, fossils and artifacts, representing what were believed to be the dead or dying customs and practices of
colonized peoples."[7] In this "necrology practiced on the living," Eurocentric
notions of racial advancement or torpor comingled with the colonial imagination to produce ethnographic spectacle.[8] For the sober-minded anthropologists and ethnologists who legitimized these manufactured scenes, nonwhite
peoples and their cultural products were windows onto a vanishing past and
validated totalizing notions of progress. For the ticket seller and the general
public, they were titillating demonstrations of exoticism that reinscribed collectively held racial-hierarchical beliefs.[9]

The intricately plotted ethnographic showcase that the Samal and Maranao
found themselves amidst in St. Louis had links not only to European colonial
ethnography but also a series of U.S. fairs held in the decade prior. The Anthropology Building and living exhibits of the 1893 World's Columbian Exposition in Chicago promoted powerful evolutionary messages, encouraging
fairgoers to consider Anglo-Saxon "physical and cultural achievements" against
the detritus of conquered Native American peoples. The racial logics of the
frontier blended with consumerist fantasies in implications that chosen Native
groups who adopted signifiers of civilization—from the bespoke suit to the
sewing machine—could perhaps escape extinction.[10] At the 1898 Trans-
Mississippi and International Exposition in Omaha, the recent U.S. victory
over the Spanish in Cuba and the Philippines suffused the proceedings with
an air of imperial triumphalism. The most popular attraction at the fair was
the Indian Congress, a meeting place for and showcase of indigenous peoples
"self-consciously modeled after colonial exhibits at recent European world's
fairs."[11] At Buffalo's 1901 Pan-American Exposition, "living ethnological displays" of Native Americans served as celebrations of hemispheric dominance.[12]
The Filipino Village there anticipated the 1904 Philippine Reservation, with
press reports calling the site a "representation of actual life in this most interesting new possession of the United States"—actual life in this case involved
daily performances by village residents and a guard of U.S. soldiers "to give a
military glamor to the scene."[13] Fair organizers in St. Louis drew from these
antecedents and designed their performative spaces to highlight similar bina-
ries of assimilation and abjection.

Plans for the Philippine Reservation began as the Pan-American Exposition ended in 1901, when the civil governor of the Philippines, William Howard Taft, sent an official communiqué to the Louisiana Purchase Exposition Company (LPEC) expressing interest in securing "a suitable exhibition of the resources of the Philippines." The War Department authorized Taft to set aside funds to defray expenses for the Philippine exhibit. Although fighting was ongoing throughout the archipelago, U.S. officials and collaborating Filipino elites looked ahead to 1904 as a chance to make the case for empire. Even at this early stage, the LPEC secretary Charles Monroe Reeves projected that the exhibit would be thirty to forty acres in size.[14] In the summer of 1902, Taft hired W. P. Wilson, director of the Philadelphia Commercial Museum, as head of the newly formed Philippine Exposition Board (PEB). The Philippine Commission gave the PEB impressive powers, placing at its disposal an array of government bureaus and transportation networks. Meanwhile, board members urged colonial officials to form committees to secure collections for the PEB that "would illustrate the habits, customs, and life of the people."[15]

In the Muslim South, the sizeable job of creating a representational record of Moro civilization fell upon two men: Albert Ernest Jenks and Gustavo Niederlein. Jenks collected the living exhibits for the exposition. A Michigan-born academic whose expertise in anthropology was self-taught, he came to the Philippines via his work with the Bureau of American Ethnology. Initially serving with the Bureau of Non-Christian Tribes, Jenks soon became head of the islands' Ethnological Survey.[16] Niederlein, a globetrotting German botanist, perennial exposition participant, and Wilson's deputy in Philadelphia was in charge of the nonliving items. Authorities in Manila gave both men carte blanche to scour the archipelago for material, human and otherwise, as part of the vast ethnological initiative. A pamphlet printed by the PEB and distributed throughout the Philippines provided colonials with detailed instructions about selecting, preparing, and shipping their items. Each department at the fair gave specific descriptions of the "tribal and racial" items it desired. Niederlein carried with him a letter from Governor Taft instructing all bureaus, governors, and provincial officials to extend him "every assistance in your power in the very important task [of] preparing exhibits for the Philippine part of the St. Louis Exposition."[17]

Albert Jenks began assembling living participants in November 1902. He secured a small contingent of Samal Moros in Zamboanga, who agreed to travel to St. Louis under the supervision of an American expatriate named Frederick Lewis.[18] Jenks and his wife, Maud, found a second group of Muslim participants during a journey they took to the Lanao district.[19] The trip was fraught and nearly failed on multiple occasions. Simple matters of money delayed the work, as authorizing wire transfers proved difficult and Jenks was reticent to carry large amounts of cash.[20] Gustavo Niederlein made hundreds of stops the following year on his collection tour of the Philippines. He arrived in the Sulu Archipelago in October 1903, disembarking on the island of Jolo. With the aid of a European merchant named S. A. Korczki, Niederlein meticulously cataloged and purchased the material culture of the Tausūg Moros. He made further stops at Basilan, Zamboanga, Lake Lanao, and Cotabato, venturing up the Rio Grande to secure "valuable collections." The botanist-turned-ethnographer returned to the United States with a trove of weapons, household items, clothes, and natural products.[21]

Although he visited the Philippines briefly in May 1903, W. P. Wilson spent the majority of his time preparing the grounds of the Philippine Reservation in St. Louis. The exhibit was located in the southwest corner of the exposition and accessed by three bridges crossing over Lake Arrowhead, the artificial body of water bounding it on two sides.[22] The largest of the bridges deposited spectators into a miniature replica of Manila's walled city. Further along, the central plaza featured buildings devoted to education, forestry, mining, agriculture, wild game, and ethnology. The "non-Christian" groups of the archipelago lived along the shore of Lake Arrowhead and in the forest surrounding the central plaza. Fair planners categorized and displayed the peoples of the Philippines based on their perceived level of civilization, with the Muslims of Mindanao falling somewhere between the "prehistoric" Negritos and refined Visayans.[23]

The Samal and Maranao participants departed Mindanao in late 1903. Accompanied by the manager, Frederick Lewis, the Samal group consisted of nineteen men, eleven women, five boys, and five girls. They traveled north from Zamboanga to Manila, partaking in test exhibitions in the capital. Organizers claimed the stopover gave them "an opportunity of seeing their first city of any size, and [to become] accustomed to the ways of modern civilization." Thirty-eight Maranao Moros and their manager C. H. Wax soon joined the others in Manila, and together they crossed the Pacific.[24] In St. Louis, the two groups resided along the northern section of Lake Arrowhead. Organizers modeled the Samal village on buildings from Magay, the Muslim sector of Zamboanga, and went to great lengths to maintain realism. The Samal built their own dwellings from a combination of nipa, rattan, and bamboo, and with no nails. LPEC president David Francis boasted they constructed their homes "in accordance with their own peculiar style of architecture." The village included several small residences, a theater for public performances, and an

Figure 6.1 A scene from the Moro village at the 1904 Louisiana Purchase Exposition in
St. Louis. The Samal and Maranao Moros brought to the United States performed "traditional"
pastimes for American audiences each day. They lived in thatched-roof houses built on stilts over
water and traversed the artificial lake in vintas. (Crop of b&w film copy negative of photographic
print on stereo card, Underwood & Underwood, c. 1904. St. Louis, Louisiana Purchase
Exposition, 1904 image group, Library of Congress, Prints and Photographs Division)

administrative building housing ethnographic curiosities. Organizers covered
the shores of Lake Arrowhead with gravel to mimic the sandy beaches of
the Southern Philippines. A planned second village for Maranao never came
to fruition, and the living exhibit opened to the public in June 1904.[25]

As employees and objects of display, the Moros had robust schedules. The
village theater staged hourly performances featuring men beating agungs and
doing a shield and spear dance called the "Moro-Moro." In the mornings, Samal boys raced canoes, rode the "chutes" (waterslides), or dove into Lake
Arrowhead for coins thrown by spectators. Moro women wove items that were

later sold in the central plaza.[26] When not at the theater, the men engaged in "their native industries and occupations," which meant fishing and pearl diving in the lake. Samal and Maranao youth attended the model schoolhouse run by Pilar Zamora, a Christian Filipino instructor brought from the elite Government Normal School in Manila. Teachers instructed Muslim students separately because of their perceived unruliness, although press coverage depicted the school as a practical illustration of how modern pedagogical techniques redeemed backward peoples.[27] Visitors even watched the Moros eat their meals, bringing the must mundane daily rituals under the surveilling eye of the crowd. The final report of the PEB boasted that the Samal and Maranao groups followed a diet similar to what they ate on Mindanao and that the Moros had "no complaints."[28]

The materials collected by American colonials and assembled by Gustavo Niederlein were housed in the Ethnology Building, located just off the central plaza. While the products of Christian Filipinos featured in a variety of buildings (horticulture, agriculture, industry, forestry), the manufactures of "savage" and "semi-savage" peoples appeared in a single location—presented as evidence of stunted historical and racial development. The Ethnology Building included items from thirty separate groups. From the Samal Moros were household utensils, clothing, ornaments, musical instruments, and hunting implements, while the Tausūg contributed looms, brass armor, betel nut boxes, bedding, saddles, and cannon.[29] The Philippine Constabulary, whose numbers included nine Muslims identifiable by their specially designed fez, displayed a collection of Moro weaponry. Promotional literature declared that the lantakas, bolos, kris, and other objects of war told "a varied and interesting story of the peculiarly misdirected . . . struggle against America."[30]

Newspaper reporters routinely covered the villages, often including a liberal dose of racial commentary in their reporting. The *Pittsburgh Dispatch*'s Martha Root claimed the Moros "were not bred so dull they cannot learn" but "so far . . . have been immune from the epidemic called civilization." Drawing on stock phraseology, Root described the Samal and Maranao as the "fiercest of all tribes" and called their village a "primitive Atlantic City, where the inhabitants practically live in the water."[31] William E. Curtis, former head of the Latin American Department at the 1893 World's Columbian Exposition, saw the Moros as remarkable athletic specimens and superior to the Christian Filipinos. They were an "interesting problem for [the] ethnologists and sociologists," he thought, telling readers that the exhibit was "an object lesson for the information and edification of the American people" and "accurate and quite true to life."[32] The *Washington Post* observed that Christian Filipinos refused to mix with the Moros in the reservation's playgrounds, but American children did, illustrating the contrast between "democratic America" and the "Filipino caste system."[33] Echoing exposition managers, press accounts presented the Moros as prehistoric relics, martially impressive specimens, and human clay waiting to be shaped by colonial institutions.[34]

Organizers mapped the benefits of empire in the human displays. From the first, the exhibit was meant to have a "moral effect." Speaking in 1902, Governor-General Taft believed native participation in the fair would help complete "pacification" and encourage residents of the Philippine Islands to "improve their condition."[35] The head of the Department of Anthropology, W. J. McGee, had a similarly righteous outlook. "The primary motives of expositions are commercial and intellectual," he wrote, "yet the time would seem ripe for introducing a moral motive."[36] Bestowing upon LPEC endeavors the veil of academic legitimacy, McGee's racial cartography located U.S. bourgeois culture at the apogee of human development. With this guiding notion, he collapsed continental expansion, Native American removal, and overseas empire into a single moral-racialist scape.[37] McGee believed members of the public could easily follow "the course of human progress . . . in a general way from the ethnic and cultural types assembled on the grounds under the Department of Anthropology, in the Philippine display, and in some of the attractions on The Pike."[38]

Departing from station six of the intramural railway, sightseers would head north, stopping to view "primitive" tools and art in the Ethnology Building before continuing through the living displays of the anthropology exhibit. The Ainu of Japan, Patagonian tribespeople, and Cocopah from Mexico stood in supposed contrast to Native Americans, who had been made "by American methods . . . into civilized workers."[39] Didactic before-and-after displays drove home the moralistic message.[40] The commissioner for Indian Affairs, Francis E. Leupp, toured the grounds and praised the contrast between the "savage, dirty, ignorant, and forlorn . . . old Indian" and the "government pupil trained to fit a place in the world of to-day." Crossing over Lake Arrowhead, he saw similar dichotomies in the redeemed overseas subjects of the reservation. The work of racial reform on the continental and Pacific frontiers was not so different.[41]

In late November, a week before the fair closed, President Theodore Roosevelt toured the Philippine Reservation. He watched members of the Constabulary perform drills, studied the collections at the Ethnology Building, and met with the Moros. The Samal leader Datu Facundo symbolically surrendered his bolo to the president, claiming he no longer had use for it.[42] All told, the Moro village brought in $40,624.37 from sales and admissions, a higher take than the Visayan or Negrito villages but well below the $137,147.92 made by the Igorots. For all their moralism, the displays existed primarily as moneymaking ventures.[43] Numerous Moro manufactures earned official plaudits, and Facundo received a gold medal for the quality of his participation. Two Muslims died from beriberi in St. Louis, while another expired from heat exhaustion after a prolonged theatrical display.[44] Nevertheless, supporters of overseas expansion saw the reservation as an unmitigated triumph. "Without doubt it is the best colonial exhibit ever brought together," gushed William E. Curtis in the *Chicago Record-Herald*.[45] Enthusiasm aside, the colonial state's return on investment proved meagre; disposing of collected materials and promotional items was problematic; and a museum based on the exhibit in Manila, originally intended to be permanent, closed swiftly.[46]

Shaping the array of racial tropes into a unified message proved difficult for American actors in both metropole and colony. The head of publicity for the PEB, Herbert Stone, gave the official line of fair organizers, declaring that the fair would educate the public on the "real conditions" of the Philippines and teach them "just what is meant by the 'White Man's Burden'."[47] Antiimperialists, meanwhile, presented the reservation as a cautionary tale about bringing primitive peoples into the national fold.[48] The 1904 World's Fair did not resolve disagreements over civilizational progress nor the "sense that colonists and colonized were separated by an unbridgeable gap."[49] In the Southern Philippines, questions over the human displays took on more pragmatic dimensions, with military authorities worrying that the presentation of "semicivilized" peoples would hinder modernization efforts.[50]

Metropolitan Sojourns

A series of visits beyond the midway deepened the U.S. public's notion of the Moros as imperial wards. Press fixations on the ability of Moros to absorb U.S. culture threw into stark relief the frictions and contradictions of colonial mimicry. Colonial encounters inevitably featured elements of cultural impersonation, wherein colonized subjects adopted the "customs and norms" of the colonial overseer without being able to "fully emulate . . . 'whiteness'."[51] Implicit in these "performative identity strategies" are not only representations of domination and submission but also subversive suggestions about the contingency of racial, cultural, and gendered hierarchies.[52] In his analysis of the American Philippines, Warwick Anderson has deployed mimicry to describe the development of public health regimes, so frequently unsettled by the native "imitator of hygiene" and the precarious racial certainties of dislocated colonial officials. "An awareness of mimicry," he writes, "might also inadvertently challenge the boundaries of citizenship in the colony."[53] What of imitation in metropolitan settings? As shown, the fairgrounds were spaces of anthropological moralism and imperial race mapping. Within them, Muslims could be picaresque savages, recipients of colonial beneficence, or some combination of each. There was, in other words, an in-built circumscription in their presentation by others and presentation of self. American writers produced reckonings of how visiting Moros absorbed, mimicked, or rejected the material and intellectual markers of "civilization" only after they left the shores of Lake Arrowhead.

A chaperoned trip from St. Louis to Washington marked the first encounters outside the fairgrounds. On August 7, 1904, the manager of the Moro village Frederick Lewis received a telegram from the White House extending an invitation to Datu Facundo and some of his followers to visit President Roosevelt in Washington. The three Moros and four Igorots chosen for the journey intended to tell the president of "the appreciation which their people [felt] for the changes from their old system to the present form of government, inaugurated by the United States."[54] Those publicizing the visit emphasized links between the Moros and conquered Native American populations. Insular Bureau chief Clarence R. Edwards called the visitors "about on a par . . . with some of the Indians in this country. . . . They are as much objects of interest in Manila as they are in America." He extended this comparison, claiming that the Moro and Igorot tribesmen imagined Roosevelt as their "Great White Father."[55]

Facundo and his companions traveled overnight and arrived in Washington on the morning of August 9. Crowds massed at the train station and outside their Third Street hotel. The *Washington Post* followed the arrival closely, paying special attention to the group's sartorial choices. Spectators hoping to behold exotic fashions from the Mindanaoan littoral and Cordilleran mountainside were disappointed to see the Moros and Igorots mostly clothed. In adopting occidental styles of dress, the visitors "took away from the day . . . one-half of the interest and all of its picturesque character." The traditionally garbed Moro was "as alluring as a new toy and as entertaining as a pet monkey" yet in Western clothes had "a hobo appearance that no amount of stage setting [could] redeem." The paper was similarly disappointed that Datu Facundo insisted on wearing shoes during the visit, sneering that neither "the Moro nor the Igorrote foot [was] made for the ordinary shoe of civilization."[56] Here we see in miniature the imperial "nostalgia" Michael Hawkins explores in his study: the urge to foment cultural reproduction running up against the urge to witness "untamed" Moros escape the "regulating gaze of modernity."[57] A sense of disenchantment colored the accounts. After years of sensational reports from the Southern Philippines and the theatricality of St. Louis, the dull mimicry of the suits landed with an unceremonious thud. "A shoe of moderate length, almost six inches wide at the toe and tapering almost to a point at the back of the heel would be the style for these most recent wards of the nation," the *Post* recommended.[58]

Accompanied by white "mentors" to prevent any "social faux pas," the group toured the War Department, the Naval Yards, and the Treasury Department. At the last of these, the Igorot chief Antonio expressed his new hybrid identity by giving a rendition of "My Country, 'Tis of Thee" for an assembled crowd of seven hundred. At the War Department Facundo declared any resistance against the colonial state in the Philippines to be hopeless. The United States had "more guns in the navy than there were Moro warriors in the Island of Mindanao," he informed onlookers.[59] At the White House, Facundo swore fealty to President Roosevelt, who told his visitors through a translator of the American people's wish to aid them in their development. Parallels to depictions of Native Americans again appeared in the *Washington Post*'s account of Facundo's conversation with Roosevelt, written in the literary style of pidgin English later referred to as "Tontospeak": "Tell great white Chief that me know big chief who fight Americans," Facundo reportedly said. "Me go back home and get head chief. This stop little chiefs. Me go right now." Roosevelt replied that he appreciated the offer but that U.S. troops in Mindanao were "entirely able to master the rebellious chief" themselves.[60]

Roosevelt maintained an active interest in his colonial subjects, entertaining Datu Sansaluna at the White House in 1907. Son of Datu Ali, who had been killed by U.S. bullets two years before, the young noble came to the United States under the auspices of the Jamestown Exposition in Norfolk, Virginia. The press portrayed Sansaluna as a transitional figure whose modern aspirations were tempered by his martial race origins. Seeking a college education in the metropole, reserving rooms at the New Willard Hotel, and traveling with his own private secretary, Sansaluna was in some ways a revised version of Facundo. The *Washington Evening Star* noted his royal lineage and was impressed when he gifted Roosevelt a double-edged kris belonging to Datu Ali that had been ceremonially passed down within the Maguindanao Sultanate for centuries.[61] Notions of oriental otherness remained present, however. The actions and colorful dress of the "Moro Prince" signified difference. The *Post* reported Sansaluna had nearly killed a Christian Filipino guide at the exposition for claiming the Maguindanao royal had five wives. Sansaluna himself observed that it was "bad enough to be stared at by the crowds without being pointed out as the husband of five women," illustrating the gaps between metropolitan fascination with polygamous Muslims and Sansaluna's own longing to pass as Westernized.[62]

During the grand tour of the United States by Sultan Jamalul Kiram II, colonial mimetic desire and embedded concepts of Asian-Islamic otherness coalesced further. Kiram had long been the public face of the Islamic Philippines. He was the first Muslim leader U.S. forces negotiated with in 1899, satirical plays about his life had been staged in New York City, and his "harem" endlessly fascinated the news-reading public.[63] Ruling from his modest residence at Maibun on Jolo, Kiram had limited power, ever lessened by colonial governors and the machinations of local Tausūg datus. His letters from the period show a leader constantly concerned about his legitimacy.[64] American officials frequently dismissed Kiram's character and abilities. J. Franklin Bell described the Tausūg leader as a "weakling—mentally, morally and physically" and compared him unfavorably to other Moro political figures.[65] Despite many challenges to his status, Kiram managed to remain politically active until his death in 1936.

The sultan arrived in New York City aboard the ocean liner *St. Louis* on September 24, 1910. The former military governor of Sulu Hugh Scott greeted him at the docks. Accompanying Kiram was a small coterie that included Hadji Mohammad, Panglima Mulian, Hadji Tahib, Salip Maydano, and Hadji Gulamu Rasul. Coverage of the group's arrival emphasized the mystique, grandeur, and subversive sexuality of an Asiatic potentate abroad. The *Los Angeles Times* speculated (incorrectly) that the sultan was bringing hundreds of thousands of dollars in pearls and intended to pay upward of $25,000 for a "choice Southern California girl" to add to his harem. The newspaper further reported (also incorrectly) that Kiram's lustful nature had led him to proposition Alice Roosevelt with marriage during her visit to the Philippines, offering the president "a large price for his daughter."[66] Rumors of the "famous pearls" abounded, with the *Boston Daily Globe* claiming their worth at $500,000 and predicting that the Treasury Department would deal with the matter harshly if they were declared at customs.[67] When questioned by Hugh Scott on the matter, Kiram claimed he had sold pearls worth $100,000 during his stay in England and had none remaining with him.[68]

Questions of hidden treasure and sexual licentiousness vanished during Kiram's multicity tour, replaced by an instructive tale about colonial subjecthood and cultural osmosis. The *New York Times* relished how awed Kiram's group were by the metropolis. Traveling to the Astor Hotel, the Tausūg dignitaries "hardly said a word. . . . They simply looked and marvelled at the wonderful sight." Viewing the city from the top of the Times Building, they "could not find words to express their delight." Passing Wallack's Theatre, where George Ade's satire about Kiram had had its run, the sultan regretted not witnessing "what he looked like on stage."[69] The party taxied around Manhattan and Brooklyn, visiting Central Park, the Bowery, and Grant's Tomb. In Chicago, the industrial frenzy of the meatpacking district, recently immortalized in Upton Sinclair's *The Jungle*, also impressed Kiram. Amid the noise and stink, the sultan inquired as to whether he was allowed to slaughter an animal and mulled over importing new abattoir techniques to Jolo.[70]

Clothing was yet again a means by which to "absorb distant cultures into familiar frameworks."[71] The *Chicago Daily Tribune* reported that the sultan had "fell prey" to an unscrupulous merchant who had sold him ill-fitting pants in New York City. The problem was apparently corrected when Kiram visited a Chicago clothier and purchased a seven-dollar pair of trousers that were "cut off right and hung straight."[72] Other outlets claimed Kiram was "doubtful about civilization's sartorial mandates," with a winking suggestion that a wild and unclothed Malay tribesman still lurked beneath the domesticated facade. As Philippa Levine has shown, the "containment" represented in shifts from "undress to dress"—from traditional to modern garb—signified success across the colonized world. This compulsion ran up against the desire of the colonizer to see "natural" versions of the colonized other, a longing satisfied in the visual immediacy of strange clothing and partial or complete nakedness.[73] Kiram's portrayal suggested that even the apt pupil of civilization never strayed far from fairground inscriptions of difference.

The tour involved what had become a customary visit to the White House, where Kiram briefly met with President Taft and congratulated "the government of a great people" for doing "all possible to make him happy."[74] While in Washington, Kiram declared his mission in the United States was to "learn of the world for my people." Playing to the imperial pride of the American audience, the sultan claimed he wanted to tell the Tausūg "fully of the nation of which they [had] become a part."[75] The U.S. press remarked on the visit with characteristic racial condescension, observing that it was the first time the "fiercest fighting strain" of Malays had seen "civilization." The *Washington Post* was impressed that "there was not a sign of the uncouth, of the bizarre, of the savage" about the Moros.[76] A reporter for the *Christian Science Monitor* was more explicit about the moral effects of colonial rule on the Moros. Once returned to Sulu, the article contended, the sultan could educate his people on the benefits of Western technology and encourage participation in industrial education. Soon automobiles, "talking machines," and agricultural equipment would span the island chain. Kiram and his companions left the continental United States in early October, departing from San Francisco en route to Honolulu, Manila, and, finally, Jolo.[77]

The colonial fantasy of the Moro's journey from jungle primitive to modern subject reached its apex in the figure of Princess Tarhata Kiram. A niece of the sultan, she was born on Jolo in 1904 shortly following the establishment of the Moro Province. Provincial administrators identified her at a young age as the type of Muslim woman the state wanted to nurture. The lowly status of women in the Islamic Philippines was a cause célèbre for many Americans. The colonial imagination held that the average Moro woman lived in a pitifully immiserated state brought on by the rapacious polygamy of community patriarchs. Governor John Pershing blamed this "degrading" social slavery for the worst social ills in the region.[78] Plural marriage upset the Victorian sensibilities of American colonials, who believed the issue could only be addressed through educating Moro girls. To this end, the Moro Province opened the Cotabato Girls School in 1913 and a female-only dormitory school on Jolo in 1916. Young Muslim women who learned "personal cleanliness, housekeeping, cooking, embroidery, and English" could potentially reproduce North American gender norms in Mindanao-Sulu. These women would still serve in a subordinate domestic role, but multiple marriages would cease, and Mindanao-Sulu would inch closer to civilization.[79] Pershing boasted that the teenage girls at the Cotabato school flourished under the "elevating moral influence of the American Christian woman."[80]

Although Sulu society remained male dominated, Moro Province officials recognized the influential role played by women from elite families. This was evident in the deference paid to the sultan's mother Inchy Jamela. In 1914, ten-year-old Tarhata Kiram was sent to the exclusive Normal School in Manila to receive "training in domestic science and other appropriate branches." Civilian leaders in the Department of Mindanao and Sulu used scholarships as a way to reshape the region.[81] Governor Frank W. Carpenter hoped that bringing Moro girls into contact with the dominant Christian culture of the North would help assimilate them into acceptable "beliefs, standards and ideals" and advance a unified Filipino national identity.[82] This educational patronage model became further embedded when control of Muslim issues passed to the Bureau of Non-Christian Tribes in 1920.[83]

Following her graduation from the Normal School, the Bureau of Insular Affairs encouraged Tarhata Kiram to enroll in a U.S. postsecondary institution. She chose the University of Illinois at Urbana-Champaign, becoming the first woman from the Islamic Philippines to attend school in the United States. Educating promising students from colonized populations shaped future leaders, a practice already common in European empires.[84] For Kiram, Illinois was to be a sort of finishing school for a process begun in Manila, completing the transition from "Moro" to "Muslim Filipino." By absorbing the culture of the Christian North and the United States, Kiram would be a faithful national subject within a larger colonial community. This was the idealized outlook, at least. Tarhata Kiram did represent a new sort of Moro citizen—tolerant to Christian Filipinos and an enthusiastic consumer of Euro-American culture— but not without complications.

Still a teenager, Kiram arrived in Illinois at the end of August 1919 accompanied by her friend and roommate Carmen Aguinaldo, daughter of the revolutionary leader Emilio Aguinaldo.[85] The *Washington Herald* claimed Kiram came to the country hoping to "acquire as much as possible of American training and ideas" and that she had chosen a Midwest college because it would allow her a "greater opportunity to mingle with and meet everyday Americans."[86] Her time at the University of Illinois was busy. She began her studies in the School of Music but soon switched to the College of Liberal Arts and Sciences, where she took courses in history, economics, political science, and trigonometry. Kiram adopted a Western style of dress, owning numerous skirts, dresses, and fur coats. She kept her hair in a bob, as per the style of the time, and was light-heartedly called the "one and only Sulu flapper" by her peers. Her campus social schedule was full of dances and parties, not unlike any other well-heeled American college student.[87]

Keenly aware of American stereotypes of Moros, Kiram joked with her friends about going juramentado, a practice that still found traction in newspaper accounts of Mindanao-Sulu in the 1920s.[88] Amid a liberal campus setting, the Sulu princess took up smoking, kept abreast of the latest fashions, and dated American men. The press delighted in portraying her as a lapsed Muslim, whose love of Western culture led her to decry the "silly Moslem custom" of praying toward Mecca and embrace the condescending nickname "Hattie the Head-Hunter."[89] These depictions played into the long-standing (and contradictory) belief among empire boosters that Moro religious fanaticism covered up an imperfect grasp of Islam.[90] By this logic, Kiram's experiences showed how easily the Moro character was transformed by American cultural influences.

Tarhata Kiram returned to the Sulu Archipelago after five years in the Midwest, depicted by the press as a colonial success story and evidence that two decades of U.S. stewardship could "redeem" a backward people. This narrative did not hold long, destabilized in the wake of an anticolonial revolt three years later. In 1926, Kiram became the fourth wife of Datu Tahil, son of the famed Datu Jokanain and one of the leading figures at the Battle of Bud Bagsak in 1913. Following Bagsak, Tahil made peace with the government and for a time served as third member of the Sulu provincial board. But after being outmaneuvered by a rival, he turned against state taxation policies and built a fortification at Patikul, east of Jolo town.[91] Governor Carl Moore directed the Philippine Constabulary to confront the rebels. Knowing that Tarhata Kiram was inside with her husband, the PC troops did not approach the cotta. A tense standoff lasted several days, only ending once word filtered back that Kiram had escaped the fortification via a tunnel. On January 27, 1927, thirty-five of Tahil's followers died in a brief but intense firefight with the Constabulary. Tahil was taken into PC custody soon after, while Tarhata Kiram was arrested and charged with sedition on February 4.[92]

Reaction in the United States to the princess's perceived betrayal was swift. The *Atlanta Constitution* declared that she had backslid into savagery "despite the best efforts of the University of Illinois and other agencies of American culture to send her back to the Philippines thoroughly and incurably Americanized," suggesting that any accumulated civilizational cachet had been replaced by defeminized barbarism. Media organs described this reversion in physical terms, with clothing as an anchor point. The *Los Angeles Times*'s Elizabeth Walker visited Kiram during her period of house arrest and described how the princess had replaced her "fashionable foreign clothes" with a traditional sarong. She had also filed her teeth and grown her hair out, leading Walker to describe her as a "slatternly creature in native garb" who "scandalized [her] sophisticated American neighbors."[93] Subsequent reports gave further shape to a cautionary tale about the limits of assimilation.[94] The dissenting voice was Kiram's friend Margaret C. Stoll, who wrote a letter of support to the *Chicago Daily Tribune*. Yet even this was tempered by racial assumptions. "[Kiram] is a cultured, refined, and keen-witted woman, who, against the odds of century-old oriental customs, is struggling to maintain her thoroughly occidental ideas," Stoll wrote, still framing the issue as a question of mimicry.[95]

Tarhata Kiram responded to condemnation with a measured editorial. Published in the *Los Angeles Times*, the piece explained the revolt as a byproduct of unjust power dynamics in Sulu. Governor Carl Moore, Kiram wrote, was not only the chief executive in the region but also acted as superintendent of schools and justice of the peace, thereby usurping "the prerogative of other officials, who are being converted into mere pawns on the chessboard." Kiram characterized her defiance to this as a direct result of her U.S. education, where she was taught that the "true essence of free government is that all powers should not be vested in one man." She mused that it was the "experience of all colonial governments that the most troublesome elements in a subjugated country belong to the educated class, particularly those educated abroad. It is axiomatic that you cannot make a slave of a man after educating him."[96] The sanguine response showed a complex understanding of the paradoxes inherent in relationships between colonial officials, Western education, and colonized elites. Eager to produce model subjects, supporters of overseas rule were also swift to rule out the possibility of doing so when met with resistance. In an interview following her arrest, Kiram showed a continued interest in the United States, inquiring about the outcome of the Leopold and Loeb murder case and asking after friends in Illinois. She explained her return to traditional Tausūg garb as a pragmatic means of becoming "a power" among her people, with an ultimate goal of protecting them against Filipino hegemony.[97]

Subjects and Sidekicks

Regrettably missed by its titular character, George Ade's comic opera *The Sultan of Sulu* opened in Chicago in March 1902. Before fixing his gaze on the Southern Philippines, the Indiana-born writer had established his reputation penning vernacular fables for midwestern newspapers. Ade was famed for his keen understanding of the American character and, like his contemporary Mark Twain, made extensive use of regional slang.[98] A staunch anti-imperialist, Ade critiqued benevolent assimilation in print, imbuing in his Filipino characters a plainspoken common sense that cut through the grandiose rhetoric of empire.[99] His visit to the Philippines in 1900 coincided with a decision to focus on writing for the stage. In Manila, Ade met with reporters who had traveled to the Sulu Archipelago and was intrigued by their stories of Kiram's "pretentious court, extensive harem, and [disagreements] with certain provisos of the American constitution." He wrote the play over the next two years, keeping current with developments in Sulu. Its 1902 debut marked the first of many times Moros surfaced in American popular culture over the next four decades.[100]

Despite being set on Jolo, Ade's satire did not include much detail about the Tausūg Moros. Although an owner of slaves and dedicated polygamist, the "Ki-Ram" of Ade's imagination is a mostly harmless figure. The play's dramatic tension arises from the arrival of the Americans, under the leadership of a John Bates stand-in named Col. Jefferson Budd, who introduces the sultan to democratic rule and then uses it to strip him of his wives and imprison him for failure to pay alimony. The Kiram figure, dressed in a clown costume, plays a Malay variant of the rural naïf in one of Ade's midwestern fables, constantly duped yet possessed with a charming ability to see through the blithe hypocrisies of his persecutors (if not his own). Ade's songs take aim at the dissonant relationship between military conquest and benevolent assimilation. In one, a group of American soldiers sing: "We want to assimilate, if we can, / Our brother who is brown; / We love our dusky fellow-man / And we hate to hunt him down / So, when we perforate his frame, / We want him to be good / We shoot at him to make him tame, / If he'd but understood."[101] Shortly thereafter, Colonel Budd asks Ki-Ram if he "consents" to the "benevolent plan" of educating the "neglected race" of Moros. The sultan, ringed by bayonets, does.[102]

Ade's play was for many Americans the primary cultural product associated with the region. It moved to New York City in December 1902 and was staged 192 times during its inaugural run, making it Ade's first major theatrical success. George Barbour, a friend of the governor of Sulu Hugh Scott, wrote to him to say that he had seen the play three times and "liked it very much." He was surprised when Scott was assigned to Jolo, never thinking he would "have the pleasure of an acquaintance with the Sultan himself of that strange and very interesting part of our common country." Barbour encouraged Scott in his new role as governor, marveling that he was now a real-life Col. Jefferson Budd.[103] Scott's associate perhaps missed the point of Ade's satire. If Ki-Ram and his subjects were orientalist tropes, the self-righteous Americans, secure in the knowledge that civilization blossomed at gunpoint, were occidental ones. Although the play emphasized Tausūg otherness, it was comparatively mild when placed alongside later depictions of Moros.[104]

Offstage, Moros came to the United States in children's literature and radio serials. Imperial adventure tales were already a staple in the English-speaking world of the early twentieth century. Works by Rudyard Kipling, a famous proponent of the United States' colonial mission, and Hugh Lofting typified the trend. Colonized lands were places of fantasy, where a child's imagination

Figure 6.2 A poster for George Ade's comic opera *The Sultan of Sulu* showing a whitened Sultan "Ki-Ram" surrounded by women from his harem. The image plays to the U.S. public's fascination with polygamy, which alongside piracy and slavery contributed to orientalist constructions of "the Moro." The tag line speaks to this fixation and also another theme of the play: the sultan's transformation from Muslim despot to Western-style "Governor." (Strobridge Lithographing Company, 1902, Theater Posters, ST-0232, Public Library of Cincinnati and Hamilton County)

could run wild, and zones of moral inscription, where civilizational values proved their mettle against the chaos of precolonial cultures. "Empire and exploitation," writes M. Daphne Kutzer, "[lent] themselves to sensationalism, to exoticism, to ceremony, to jargon and lingo and secret societies, all of which have an appeal for children."[105] In the United States, works like Burtis M. Little's *Francisco the Filipino* harnessed this exoticism and used it for instructive ends. Learning the utility of English and witnessing the reorganization of his homeland, Francisco revealed the moral and commercial possibilities of colonial rule to American and Filipino youth.[106]

Like the untamed spaces of British India or colonial Africa, the Southern Philippines became a backdrop for articulations of civilization and savagery.

Florence Partello Stuart's *The Adventures of Piang the Moro Jungle Boy* relied on colonial sources for its fictionalized depiction of Muslim life on Mindanao. The author spent time in Mindanao during the Moro Province years and credited Dean Worcester with providing information about the "origin and development of the Moro." Certain tales in the collection were "actual incidents of Dean Worcester's travels," illustrating direct connections between U.S. officials and the production of colonial fantasy.[107] Published in 1917, the book aimed to remedy metropolitan public indifference toward the Philippines. The former governor of Zamboanga John Finley provided the jacket blurb, praising Stuart for accurately depicting "the Malayan Moro youth." Drawing on materials from the War Department, her access to Worcester and Finley, and her own experiences in Mindanao, Stuart presented the Piang stories as lightly fictionalized accounts of the lives of "loyal" Muslims. The *New York Times* praised the book as being "full of information about the customs, beliefs, and way of living of the Moros."[108]

Piang's adventures provided a simplistic portrait of Maguindanao Moro civilization in the Cotabato region and highlighted the ameliorating impact of colonial governance on Mindanao.[109] Although Stuart claimed in the preface that Piang was a real Moro boy, she likely borrowed his name from Datu Piang, the primary Moro leader in Cotabato during the American period. The text is littered with fictionalized versions of real colonial actors, including Finley, Leonard Wood, John Pershing, Datu Mandi, Datu Enoch, Jikiri, Datu Ali, and the insurrecto Vincente Alvarez. Piang's journey to become hero of his tribe plays out as a crude bildungsroman, with the eponymous character acting as sidekick to a local datu, struggling against the natural elements, and besting his rival, a mestizo bully named Sicto. American military forces arrive in Piang's village during a time of famine, bringing supplies to ease Moro suffering and banishing native suspicions in the process."[110]

Piang travels to Lanao, where he aids "General Bushing" in the Lanao district and becomes a companion to Lieutenant Lewis, a young American military officer. The two hunt pirates together on the island of Basilan. Piang is shamed by the presence of juramentado warriors there, whom he describes as riding into the afterlife on a "shadowy white horse taller than a carabao." Lewis chides the boy for believing "fairy tales" now that he is a "good American." Colonial officials confront the issue by tricking a local sultan into believing one of their gunboats has gone juramentado, the mythologized tale now seeping out into fiction. Oblivious to modern technology and mired in superstition, the Moros relent.[111] Elsewhere in Piang's adventure, the "boy hero" visits a *bichara* held by "Governor Findy," where he marvels at U.S. carnival treats like popcorn and pink lemonade. Piang also witnesses the benefits of the Moro Exchange system, which Stuart notes has brought the "light of freedom and peace" to "misguided savages."[112]

Army operations in the Southern Philippines likewise inspired H. Irving Hancock's novel *Uncle Sam's Boys in the Philippines; or, Following the Flag against the Moros*. A great advocate of the war preparedness movement, Hancock glorified militarism in his boys' adventure series. *Following the Flag* is set in the fictional town of Bantoc, likely named after Bontoc in Mountain Province but modeled on Zamboanga in the novel. The young men of B Company in the 24th Infantry fight Moros who have burned down a colonial schoolhouse and desecrated its U.S. flag.[113] B Company uses superior weapons technology to protect American plantation owners under threat from local datus, mowing down "dense brown ranks" of Moros with their Gatling gun.[114] At one point, two American soldiers infiltrate the encampment of the hostile Datu Hakkut by "playing goo-goo"—covering themselves with dirt and speaking gibberish to the guards (who assume it is local dialect). Crude minstrelsy segues into a battle scene that culminates with Company B flinging the body of the defeated Moro leader over his fort ramparts. The novel closes with vulgar patriotic fervor and racial denigration. The U.S. flag is raised above the captured cotta, and Moro prisoners are "forced to pay it humble reverence" and crawl out of the fort on their hands and knees. National honor is thus restored.[115]

On the radio, Jack Armstrong—"the all-American boy"—also visited Mindanao. Accompanied by his friends and industrialist uncle, Jack's weekly adventures married juvenile adventures with accelerating consumer culture. Underwritten by General Mills and vetted by a child psychologist, each episode promoted athleticism, personal hygiene, and American ingenuity.[116] Buoyed by a regular diet of Wheaties, Jack and his gang battled Moros in the early 1940s, searching the Southern Philippines for a missing professor and a cache of uranium-235. Jack's Uncle Jim warns the young sojourner that the civilization they see in Zamboanga is tenuous: "You wouldn't think so to look at this orderly town. . . . On the surface everything is peaceful, but look at that range of hills beyond the parade grounds. They are only a few miles away, and yet once you get on the other side of them you're in a wild and savage country." In the world of Jack Armstrong, the impact of a decades-long colonial presence has been limited; Zamboanga remains an imperiled outpost amid an unredeemed land.[117]

Narrative convention ensures Jack and his band are traveling in the "wild and savage country" beyond the colonial capital by the next episode. Hostile Moros threaten the young Americans, who trick them with the latest technology.

The radio serial dichotomizes Muslims as either violent and deceptive or dull witted and faithful. Civilizational redemption is not on offer as Jack's group battles numerous Moro and Lumad "tribes" using their innate resourcefulness and new wonders like the autogyro. "Piratical" plans are thwarted, gun smugglers defeated, captives rescued, and uranium recovered.[118] *Jack Armstrong* introduced a generation of American youth to bygone days of triumphal conquest in the Islamic Philippines, which had increasingly vacated the national consciousness in the decades following Filipinization. With Uncle Jim's heroic service in the Moro Province connecting the narrative to an earlier time, the young protagonists traverse Mindanao and reinscribe national mastery on a vanishing Pacific domain.

Fictions produced for an adult audience carried many of the same themes found in boys' adventure stories and radio dramas. In the spring of 1939, the movie production company United Artists erected a replica Philippine village across six acres of their lot in Los Angeles. It featured a seven-hundred-foot tropical lagoon.[119] This was the set for *The Real Glory*, the only movie ever made about the "Moro Rebellion." Produced by Samuel Goldwyn and directed by Henry Hathaway, best known for his westerns and *The Lives of a Bengal Lancer*, the film starred Gary Cooper, David Niven, and Reginald Owen as PC officers besieged by Moros in a remote outpost.[120] *The Real Glory* premiered in September 1939 to limited fanfare and was rereleased in 1942 to capitalize on war-driven public interest in Southeast Asia. Fearful that the movie was stigmatizing Moros as they aided in guerrilla operations against the Japanese, the Motion Picture Division of the Office of War Information had it pulled from theaters.[121]

The Real Glory leads with a dedication to the men of the Philippine Constabulary, whose "unfailing courage" had "made possible the great Philippine Commonwealth."[122] The film is set in 1906 at the fictional Fort Mysang in Northern Mindanao and portrays a Tagalog community in mortal danger from the predations of a Moro datu named Alipang and his followers. The U.S. Army has departed, leaving only the Constabulary to ward off the threat (something that did not actually occur until years later). Alipang's monomaniacal desire to kill and enslave Christians borders on the absurd, with Filipinos and Americans in the film initially helpless before the Moro bolos. When successive Constabulary commanders at Mysang are assassinated by juramentados, Dr. Canavan, played by Cooper, decides to attack what he views as the root of the problem: the Filipino fear of the Moro. Canavan locates Moro weakness within Islam itself. After being told by the local Filipino priest that Moros dread ritual pollution, the doctor captures a would-be juramentado and parades him before the Filipinos. The Moro screams in terror as he is placed into a pigskin. "Look at him, your brave Moro, your terrible Moro," Canavan implores the villagers, "begging for help, scared out of his skin because of the skin of a dead pig." Buoyed by the spectacle, the invigorated Filipinos are shown hitting and bayonetting dummies of the Moro warriors they once cowered before.[123]

Mysang is a stand-in for the larger colonial project. The village, declares the PC commander, is a "test" of the ability of Americans to train self-sufficient Filipinos. Canavan overcomes numerous threats. Alipang dams the local water supply, leading to an outbreak of cholera, and a fellow Constabulary officer is buried up to his neck by Moros and left to the jungle ants. The commander responds to these challenges by deploying sanitary technologies and, in the latter case, meeting the Moro threat with force. *The Real Glory*'s violent denouement sees Americans and Filipinos destroy Alipang's war party with Gatling guns and Krag-Jørganson rifles. In a symbolic final confrontation, Yamo, the detachment's Filipino lieutenant, confronts the Moro leader, beating Alipang to death with the butt of his Krag and casting his lifeless body into the nearby river. Afterward, as Canavan leaves for Manila, the newly empowered Filipinos of the Constabulary stand at attention, and the villagers throw garlands of flowers at the departing Americans.[124]

The film functions as tutelary fantasy, reimagining the legacy of U.S. colonialism from the vantage of its final years. Moros are relegated to the role of primitive, despotic villains, with the exception of a young Moro boy named Miguel who plays a sidekick role to Canavan. Miguel shines Canavan's boots, laughs when a fellow Muslim is threatened with pigskin, and dispenses observations in pidgin sentences like "Moro no afraid of things he can see, only afraid of things he can't see."[125] The PC men reward Miguel's fidelity by Americanizing his name. "Mike" is last seen dressed in a Western-style suit on Canavan's boat to Manila, his Muslim identity overcome and discarded. The U.S. press praised Hathaway's film and Cooper's one-man encapsulation of colonial dynamism, in particular. As war raged with the Japanese, the movie provided domestic audiences with a redemptive vision of "American sagacity and scientific heroism" in Southeast Asia. Decades removed from Ade's operatic critique of benevolent assimilation, *The Real Glory* recast Moros as impediments bested by civilizational grit.[126]

The Samal and Maranao Moros displayed in St. Louis vanished from the historical record after departing the fair. Most returned to homes along the Mindanao littoral and the small villages dotting Lake Lanao, where they spent lives under U.S. or Christian Filipino rule. Their documentary remains are spectral, comprising fleeting mentions in the U.S. press and the odd souvenir photograph from the exposition.[127] With the exception of Datu Facundo, the fair participants were not from the elite families whose children were targeted for acculturation. Unsurprisingly, it is easier to track the Kirams, neither of whom ever returned to the United States. The sultan died in 1936, a long-serving but increasingly irrelevant figure in a sultanate whose real power vanished under U.S. sovereignty. The succession struggle after his death provided an opportunity for the Philippine Commonwealth government to withdraw recognition from the sultanate entirely, completing a process that began decades earlier with the abrogation of the Bates Agreement.[128]

The short-lived rebellion of 1927 sidelined Princess Tarhata Kiram briefly, but by the early 1930s she was politically active again, advocating for the return of territories in British North Borneo to the Sulu Sultanate. She later became a special agent for the Bureau of Non-Christian Tribes, leading raids against outlaws and completing her return to the colonial fold.[129] Kiram remained active in public life until her death in 1979, in many ways typifying a younger generation of Islamic elites born into colonialism who gradually came to imagine themselves as "Muslim Filipinos." In her later years, Tarhata Kiram acted as a consultant on Islamic affairs to the Philippine government, married twice more, and even composed some music. Five years after her death, she was officially commemorated when her portrait appeared on a three-peso stamp.[130]

The U.S. public grappled with questions of presentation and interpretation as they negotiated empire. The constructed morality of tutelage ran up against the imagined barbarity of subject groups. American writers used Moro figures, real and imagined, for their own ends. Datu Facundo became a clueless primitive paying tribute to the "great white chief" Roosevelt, while Sultan Kiram possessed mysterious oriental riches and sought U.S. technology for his people. Piang the Moro Jungle Boy was a resourceful young ally for the U.S. military, but the Moros in *The Real Glory* were violent impediments to progress. The majority of material produced about Moros in the United States supported their continued status as colonial wards, but instances of subversion existed. George Ade's comic opera *The Sultan of Sulu* skewered the pretensions and contradictions of the civilizing mission, and Tarhata Kiram used the pages of the *Los Angeles Times* to confront detractors who accused her of betraying her patrons. These examples, sometimes buried beneath validations of empire, indicate that the racial and cultural logics driving colonial rule did not pass through public discourse unchallenged.

Like many other groups—Filipinos, Haitians, Puerto Ricans, Native Americans, Pacific Islanders, deterritorialized laborers—the peoples of the Islamic Philippines existed in a liminal space skirting the boundaries of subjecthood and citizenship. In the early twentieth century, U.S. citizens grappled with many of the same issues faced by other colonial powers, feeling the push and pull of integrationist and rejectionist desires. If the nation never developed as extensive or long-lived an imperial community as the British or French, it still took steps to simultaneously bind and distance its subjects through familiar racialized metrics. Participating in this transimperial dialogue, Americans drew from common indexes of civility: extravagant anthropological displays, fixations on how subject populations dressed, convictions about the benefits of occidental education, and discussions about the limits of benevolent assimilation.[131] Moro visitors became shorthand for a type of civilizational beneficence developed between the fairgrounds of Europe and the conquests of the American West—the racially suspect but martially proud savage guided through firm but fair means toward a brighter future. The proclamations of fair organizers like David R. Francis—who touted the "moral and educational benefits" of display—and reactions of spectators present a contradictory portrait. Transformational agendas competed with the mournful desire to maintain Moros in their "natural" state and skepticism about their capacity for change, revealing the tensions of life within the permeable borders of a nascent imperial community.

Chapter 7

Imperial Interactivities

Mindanao-Sulu in a Connected World

"Example is contagious," José Rizal asserted in an 1890 piece for *La Solaridad*. "Perhaps the great American Republic, which has interest in the Pacific and does not share in the spoils of Africa may some day think of ultramarine possessions."[1] Rizal's prediction manifested itself less than a decade later, when the United States took possession of the Philippines from Spain. This was a period of rapid Euro-American territorial expansion, where imperial formations simultaneously competed with and drew from one another. Example *was* contagious and extended to shared governance strategies, modes of violence, extractive agendas, and inclusionary and exclusionary cultural codes. In Mindanao-Sulu, U.S. colonials interacted with other imperial powers and encountered preexisting connections that stretched between and through localities, colonies, regions, and empires. These dense relational networks shaped how Americans, Moros, and Filipinos positioned themselves relative to one another. Although conceptualized as a colonial remote, a "last place" on the fringes of empire, the Muslim South was in constant conversation with the wider world.[2]

Many of these connections have surfaced in other chapters. We see them in the colonial penchant for exhibiting racially othered bodies, through a faith in the mediating power of massacre, in the conjuring of Moro identity relative to prevalent concepts of race, through the labors of transnationally oriented missionary reformers, and in the latent anxieties of white men in the tropics. A cacophony of peoples, ideas, products, and practices informed U.S. colonialism in the Southern Philippines. Situating it amid these wide-ranging encounters means eschewing methodological nationalism. This does not deny U.S. empire its own particularities but rather stipulates a reading of the colonial encounter that incorporates multiple layers of reciprocal connection involving "outside" actors.[3] Examining these cross-pollinations—and their adaptations, hybridities, and rejections—allows for a richer conceptualization of the period that bypasses national-exceptionalist and colonial-exceptionalist models.

This chapter analyzes diverse instances of overlap and exchange involving American, European, Southeast Asian Muslim, Filipino, Chinese, Arab, and Ottoman Turkish actors. Transimperial flows shaped the Southern Philippines before, during, and after U.S. rule. They operated well beyond traditional power centers in Washington and Manila, giving a mongrel character to the colonial encounter. PC officials in Sulu conducted operations with security forces in British North Borneo and Dutch Sulawesi; devout Moros networked with Muslims in Singapore, India, and the Middle East en route to Mecca; Moro Province overseers traveled through the colonized zones of South and Southeast Asia seeking guidance from seasoned European colonials; culturally hybrid individuals and families served as interlocutors between foreign rulers and native communities; and Americans interfaced with Ottomans in attempts to "modernize" Islam in the archipelago. Undergirding these stories are individual biographies that render the transimperial less oblique, reveal the permeability of borders, and highlight the complexities of cultural transfer.[4] Looking beyond the metropole-colony binary reveals how imperial power developed between colonies and through the assertion of local identities against broader prerogatives of control and reconfiguration.[5] The frontiers of empire were heterogeneous spaces connected to and reshaped by the "uneven pulses" of global integration—an observation that complicates and textures the history of the Southern Philippines under U.S. rule.[6]

Affinities and Transfers

The many borrowings of the U.S. colonial state in the Islamic Philippines began with ethnographic and environmental knowledge acquired from Spain. During the Spanish-American War, American politicians, military leaders, and press outlets portrayed their adversaries as morally debased—the products of a sensuous Latinate culture at odds with the virile masculinity and political progressivism of the U.S. republic. If Spanish colonials were corrupted by their links to missionary Catholicism, American empire builders believed their Protestant sensibilities and nation's expanding power elevated them. Spain was an old empire and failing in its twin duties of uplifting subjects and profiting in the process. Inefficient and arbitrarily cruel to their wards, the Spanish lacked the dynamism required to manage their overseas possessions.[7] The United States would correct these issues, introducing rationalized colonial governance to spaces where tyranny and chaos prevailed. Underdeveloped peoples and lands would rise out of neglected squalor via unique forms of capitalist state-building perfected in the U.S. metropole.[8]

This was a pristine ideal rather than a functional reality. The practical challenges of managing a colonial possession drove Americans to analyze Spanish antecedents, undercutting their own bellicose positioning. Military brass and civilian bureaucrats pored over Jesuit scientific research as they reorganized the Philippine Meteorological Service, recognizing the significant accomplishments of the religious order at their Manila observatory. Economic experts studied Spanish monetary policies to reduce the frictions of colonial transition. Spanish elites across the archipelago provided intelligence on the Filipino *ilustrado* class and helped the U.S. authorities establish surveillance networks.[9] While public pronouncements continued to emphasize the "religious despotism and greed" of the centuries-old colonial state, Americans in the Philippines were quietly learning from their predecessors.[10] This extended to the southern islands, where military personnel desperate to orient themselves in unfamiliar environments consumed whatever material was available.

Spanish-language texts and their translations became key reference points for U.S. military officers. The Jesuit priest Francisco Baranera's *Compendio de la Historia de Filipinas* appeared in English a decade prior to the U.S. occupation. It included long descriptions of the islands' physical landscapes, instructions on crop growing, detailed explanations of Spanish military organization and education policy, and information on commercial operations.[11] New arrivals could consult Baranera's work and find out, for instance, that Jolo was "a pretty town with clean and shady streets" located on an island whose vegetation resembled that of Mindanao.[12] Spanish writers also taught Americans how to approach their new Muslim wards, warning that Moros were "very cunning characters" who had "souls habituated towards crime" and were possessed by a "ferocious barbarism."[13] Many American soldiers adopted these crude ethnographic portraits in their own writings.[14] Pvt. Walter Cutter, the amateur reporter who sent missives about Mindanao-Sulu back to the United States, carried with him a copy of Baranera's text, and translated Spanish documents are likewise found in the personal papers of John Pershing. The collection of translated texts compiled by Emma Blair and James Alexander

Robinson was a monumental testament to the interest in Spain's experiences in Southeast Asia. *The Philippine Islands 1493–1898* spanned fifty-five volumes and served as the standard resource for Americans seeking historical information about the archipelago.[15]

Spain's legacy shaped how U.S. Army officers negotiated with Moro leaders. In the lead-up to their 1899 agreement, Brig. Gen. John Bates and Sultan Jamalul Kiram II both relied on treaties Tausūg royals had made with the Spanish in previous decades. Bates and his staff paid close attention to how Spanish negotiators handled issues ranging from the treatment of missionaries, to trade and taxation, to native colonial salaries, to the purchase and sale of firearms. The Spanish had promised not to interfere with local religio-cultural practices in their 1851 treaty with the Sulu Sultanate.[16] In his interviews with Tausūg datus, Bates declared that the United States would honor the spirit of these agreements. He responded to protests by sharply reminding the Tausūg leadership that the United States "whipped the Spanish, drove them out and took their place, and . . . got all the rights Spain had." Taking a carrot-and-stick approach, Bates assured Kiram that the Americans would show the Tausūg the same "dignity" the British did for the "great many Mohammedans" living in their colonial possessions.[17] The military governor of the Philippines, Elwell S. Otis, did not mince words in his directives to Bates in the summer of 1899. "The kingly prerogatives of Spain . . . have descended to the United States," he wrote in a missive to Jolo. The Moros were "entitled to enjoy identical privileges" to those maintained under the Spanish until "abridged or modified by future agreement."[18] Strategies of colonial comparison worked, and the so-called Bates Agreement that followed was in many ways a successor document to the 1851 and 1878 Spanish ones, providing for U.S. sovereignty over the Sulu Archipelago but leaving the internal affairs of the islands to the Moros.

Spanish experiences fighting and governing Muslims informed American ideas on the South. During his wanderings through Jolo, Walter Cutter reflected on the memorial tablets marking spots where "Moros had butchered Spanish soldiers in times past." The massacres proved to the young soldier that American precautions were "well taken."[19] With the looming threat of native violence ever present in American minds, authorities in Mindanao-Sulu tasked the Spanish Jesuit priest Pio Pi with providing a breakdown of Moro character. Using his decades of experience in Mindanao as evidence of his authority, Pi laid out a plan for dominating and assimilating Muslim groups into colonial modernity. Published as an appendix in the military commander of the Philippines Gen. George W. Davis's 1902 annual report, the Jesuit's meticulous directives identified the Moros as an "obstacle to civilization" and proffered

solutions.[20] Integrating Spanish expertise into their colonial management strategies softened American views of their predecessors. John Finley peppered his
writings and speeches with stories from Spain's colonial history in the Philippines, while J. R. Hayden studied Spanish rule in Sulu to see where the United
States could improve.[21]

As the animosities of 1898 ebbed, Spanish military and religious figures became valued sources of useable knowledge. They shared with the Americans a
belief in Moro threat and a Christian colonial desire to reform "infidel" populations. Their texts circulated widely in Mindanao-Sulu, and the Spanish priests
and planters who remained after the imperial transfers of 1898–1899 actively
contributed to the new regime. Many American military men began to roman-
ticize Spain's legacy. Frank McCoy believed that relinquishing their colonial
possessions had allowed the Spanish to "live the modern life" and "retake [their]
brilliant place in the world."[22] The governor of the Moro Province Tasker Bliss
went further in a 1907 speech, praising the "intelligence and experience" of
three centuries of Spanish rule in the Southern Philippines. The buildings,
roads, and other public projects left behind by Spain demonstrated the "skill" of
their colonizers, while the "heroic labors" of the religious orders spread Christian influences "into the most remote regions of the province."[23]

The Iberian legacy also lingered among the Moros. The Samal leader Datu
Mandi, an early and staunch U.S. ally, served Spain as an interpreter on the
island of Bongao during the 1890s, while Datu Piang had leveraged Spanish
support in his quest for preeminence among the Maguindanao people. Arolas
Tulawie, a key figure in the cultural battles waged between traditionalists and
modernizers during the 1920s–1930s, took his name from the Spanish military leader Juan Arolas, claiming the general was "respected and loved . . .
because he was great and respected our religious rights." Nevertheless, Tulawie
linked the weakness of the Spanish to the Christian Filipino arrivals in these
decades. "A Moro despises weakness," he wrote to the Bureau of Non-
Christian Tribes head Teofisto Guingona in 1920, pointing out that the Spanish military had never been able to fully govern Mindanao-Sulu.[24] Datu Piang
also used this logic in his later years, believing that Spain's incomplete conquest meant that the Treaty of Paris did not extend to the Southern Philippines. The Moros deserved a separate deal.[25]

Despite its utility, American colonials saw Spanish colonialism as a dead
end. By the late nineteenth century, Spain's overseas possessions were leftovers
from an earlier epoch of conquest. Religious orders, a key component of Spanish rule in the Philippines, provided American colonials with valuable infor-

mation on the islands yet also functioned in a conversionary spirit. This was at odds with the colonial world of the early twentieth century, which melded soul-saving missions with "scientific" evaluations of racial capacity. Redemption was no longer just a matter of Christianization but also involved full-spectrum reform. A Moro could retain his Muslim faith so long as he readily participated in a white-led market economy, sent his children to state-operated schools, and adhered to secular law. Moro Province leaders believed in the mitigating power of Christianity and welcomed missionary groups into the South but increasingly understood success in Mindanao-Sulu in developmental terms. Neighboring European colonies in Southeast Asia, particularly those of the British and Dutch, provided templates for accomplishing this task.

At its peak, the British Empire claimed sovereignty over a quarter of the world's population. The preeminent engine in the first era of globalization, it alternately inspired American colonials and convinced them that their ascendant nation could improve on British legacies. Sharing a common language, imperial boosters on both sides of the Atlantic swapped ideas in newspapers, traveled together on steam liners, intermarried, conducted transoceanic commerce, and circulated in a growing international conference scene. In a rapidly connecting world, the perception of shared cultural inheritances led many Americans to look to the British as they designed their own colonial futures. Mutual critiques existed but were often overridden by a conjoined sense of Anglo-Saxon moral mission.[26] In the Philippines, American elites joined British trade networks that linked the islands with the global economy. They modeled their racially exclusive clubs and associations on those the British had already established. Meanwhile, Protestant moral reformers from Britain and the United States used the Philippines as staging grounds for their battles against the twin scourges of prostitution and opium.[27]

American colonials en route to or from the Philippines frequently stopped in Britain and its possessions. The missionary bishop of the Philippines Charles Henry Brent traveled to Cairo to visit the famed Lord Cromer in 1905. The Episcopal clergyman wrote to Leonard Wood's aide in Zamboanga that the Moro Province "was in the mouth of everyone he met in Cairo" and praised Cromer as a "statesman of no ordinary caliber."[28] His enthusiasm for the British project in North Africa did not dim with time. Years later he gave speeches in Mindanao and Lake Mohonk, where he placed Cromer alongside Gen. Charles Gordon and the British foreign secretary Lord Palmerston as an example of upstanding imperial stewardship. The Americans could take inspiration from such men, he believed.[29] Governor-General W. Cameron Forbes, a

Boston Brahmin who "consciously modelled himself on British officials," met repeatedly with Cromer.[30] During a 1909 meeting, the two discussed agriculture, the Philippines' "unused" land, and systems of taxation. Cromer furnished Forbes with Foreign Office reports and put the American in contact with other old hands in the colonial bureaucracy. Following the meeting, Forbes traveled to Egypt, eager to see how an Islamic state was managed by a Western power. Using the contacts Cromer provided, the incoming governor-general examined irrigation plans, weighed the merits of fellahin wage labor schemes, and visited Port Said to see the waterworks there. The trip also provided an excuse for cultural tourism. Forbes climbed the Great Pyramid, attempted to acquire an Arab stallion for polo (to no avail), and reflected on the *Rubaiyat of Omar Khayyam* in his idle time. He returned to the Philippines by way of the Indian Ocean and five months hence was putting his impressions of the Muslim world to work on an inspection tour of the Moro Province.[31]

Affinities for European empire directly affected the character of rule in Mindanao-Sulu. Leonard Wood undertook multiple overseas fact-finding trips to help sharpen his understanding of colonial governance. In the late summer and autumn of 1902, Wood and his aide Frank McCoy traveled to London to meet with Prime Minister Arthur Balfour, King Edward VII, and Lord Kitchener, then commander in chief of the Indian army. The two moved on to Germany, where they had an audience with Kaiser Wilhelm II and observed German military maneuvers.[32] The trip served as preamble for a larger tour the following year. Wood, McCoy, and Hugh Scott, each crucial in the early administration of the Southern Philippines, first toured Egypt and India. Mimicking his European counterparts, McCoy wrote that the "only decent, clean people east of Suez are the native Christians and the British native soldiers." Anticipating later U.S. political opposition to independence for the Philippines, he declared that civilizing India would be "a question of centuries."[33]

The party's ten-day stop in the Dutch East Indies provided guidelines for ruling Southeast Asian Muslims. The civil service there was "such as we should build up for our colonies," and the colonial army was likewise impressive. The only lapse in interimperial harmony came when Wood physically threw an insolent Dutch official out of a train carriage the group was traveling in.[34] The men enjoyed similarly positive experiences in Singapore and Hong Kong, and McCoy's letters home from the Muslim South illustrate how thoroughly his time in other colonies influenced his thinking on issues like the juramentado.[35] Toward the end of his Philippines service, McCoy again toured the Dutch East Indies and also did intelligence work for the military in southern China.[36] Wood sent other officers on trips around Southeast Asia. "One of the first

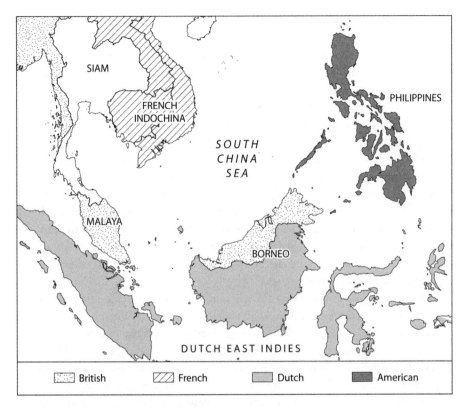

Figure 7.1 Colonial empires ruled much of Southeast Asia in the early twentieth century. White colonials in the Southern Philippines were in frequent contact with their European neighbors in British Borneo and Malaya, French Indochina, and the Dutch East Indies. Muslim groups in Mindanao-Sulu likewise maintained ties to their co-religionists in the region. (Bill Nelson Cartography)

things" George Langhorne did was travel throughout Borneo, Java, and the Malayan Peninsula: "On that trip we went into all sorts of details with local governments and brought back a number of things in the way of plans for houses [and] ways of running things." Whatever "good" returned from the trip was "put into effect" in the Moro Province, including early blueprints for what would become the Moro Exchange system.[37]

The military officers governing the Moro Province maintained an active interest in all things European. Tasker Bliss had a fondness for British military history and spent his spare time writing letters on the topic to his wife.[38] Leonard Wood kept abreast of developments in India through his correspondence with the journalist Richard Barry, who informed the governor that Lord Kitchener's eyes had "brightened" when the Moro Province was discussed.[39] These affinities took on practical forms. Lord Cromer's "proper recognition and protection of the rights of the fellahin producing class" inspired John Finley's commercial proselytism among the Moros and Lumad.[40] The district governor of Lanao John McAuley Palmer looked to the Dutch East Indies as he built up the area around Dansalan in 1908, experimenting with enforced labor programs imported from Java. Palmer added a progressive twist on the Dutch model—the Maranao would "only labor for his own interest"—that allowed Americans to avoid the label of slavery while turning natives into sedentary agriculturalists. The idea of forced labor would be "rather startling to Americans," Palmer admitted to Tasker Bliss, but "its necessity in dealing with people like the Moros must be apparent to anyone who has had occasion to study them or similar peoples in Malaysia." Palmer advocated a punishment and reward system similar to "the method employed by the Dutch to secure the loyalty of the native chiefs on Java."[41]

Developments in the Moro Province mirrored colonywide initiatives to learn from European neighbors in Southeast Asia. In 1902, the military commander of the Philippines Gen. George Davis studied the composition of armies in Java, Sumatra, and the Straits Settlements, finding that the Dutch and British relied mainly on native soldiers, while also maintaining a European officer class in these Muslim-majority states. Davis recommended Christian Filipinos and Moros be utilized to defray costs but that a permanent American officer class would ensure long-term success.[42] After outbreaks of beriberi and cholera on Mindanao, Davis dispatched army medical officers to India and the Dutch East Indies, where they visited hospitals, examined the diets of European colonials, and studied rates of infection with the aim of curbing epidemics in the Philippines.[43] A decade later, Governor-General Francis Burton Harrison was similarly preoccupied with neighboring colonies, studying the British handling of the "Mohammedan religion" and Dutch war against the Aceh Sultanate. Writing to U.S. secretary of war Lindley Garrison, he compared the Moros to the Beja warriors who fought against the British in Sudan.[44]

Colonial know-how also circulated through the Muslim South by way of low- and mid-ranking personnel whose careers straddled different empires. Multidirectional flows of expert knowledge allowed observation and experience to be "compared, tested, confirmed, and connected together" by institutions and individuals. Most evident in academia and government administration, these tendencies were also present in other occupations. Soldiers, nurses, engineers, teachers, merchants, and missionaries moved between colonized spaces, participating in transimperial exchanges and deepening linkages between U.S. possessions and the globe.[45] The career of Oscar Preuss in Mindanao-Sulu illuminates this phenomenon. Born in Germany, he enlisted at a young age with the Hussars and then transferred to German East Africa where he led a company of Askaris. After a short stint with the Austrian army, Preuss signed up with the German Expeditionary Force and fought in the Boxer Rebellion. He subsequently returned to Africa, where he fought with the Boers against the British. After traveling to the United States by way of South America, Preuss enlisted with the 3rd Cavalry and saw three years' service in the Philippines. Still only twenty-five years old, he joined the Philippine Constabulary immediately after his discharge.[46]

Serving as a lieutenant, Preuss brought a wealth of martial knowledge from his varied colonial career. He became a traveling expert on the elimination of banditry, earning a notoriously brutal reputation during his time in Lanao, Jolo, and Dapitan. Vic Hurley later wrote that Preuss was "the most ruthless Moro killer of them all." Brought before a PC tribunal in Manila and accused of personally killing 250 Moros, Preuss responded: "The report is in error, Colonel. I place the total at 265."[47] Regardless of whether Hurley exaggerated this exchange, Preuss's predilection for violence was widely acknowledged in Mindanao-Sulu. PC reports described his unit engaging in acts of wanton cruelty, including shaving off the ends of bullets to create dumdums that could "[blow] a hole in a man as large as a bucket."[48] Perennially restless, Preuss took leave of the Philippines in 1911 to serve for three months in the American gendarmerie in Iran under the direction of W. Morgan Shuster, another old Philippines hand. The soldier of fortune returned to Germany in time for the First World War.[49]

The Constabulary in Mindanao-Sulu was filled with other similarly transient characters. John R. White, famous for his role at Bud Dajo and his sensationalist memoir *Bullets and Bolos*, was born in England and began his military career when he abandoned school to join the Greek army and fight the Ottomans. After a stint in the Klondike during the Gold Rush, he enlisted in the U.S. Army and spent over a decade in the Philippines. Ole Waloe, PC commander in Mindanao-Sulu during the First World War, migrated from Norway to the United States, where he joined the military and fought in frontier campaigns against Sitting Bull and the Lakota. His infantry service brought him to the Philippines, where he became a key figure in the Constabulary.[50] Expertise also traveled out of the U.S. colonies. Oscar Preuss's protégé, a young blue blood named Sterling Larrabee, left the organization in

1913 and leveraged a meeting with Winston Churchill, then First Lord of the Admiralty, into an appointment with the Mediterranean Expeditionary Force. He spent two years in the Middle Eastern theater before being transferred to the Royal Field Artillery and fighting at the Somme and Vimy Ridge.[51]

The desirability of military expertise created a cross-border market for soldiers, but this was not the only avenue for professional mobility. Engineers moved freely between empires, often finding work on expansive public projects. Their technical accomplishments gave physical form to the civilizing mission, creating developmental metrics against which peoples could be ranked.[52] The colonial government in Mindanao-Sulu was eager to attract such specialists. A junior engineer in the Moro Province named Manly typified the acquisition and use of engineering knowledge across colonized zones. Trained at the Indiana College of Agricultural and Mechanical Arts, the young engineer worked in Mexico, Central and South America, and the Antipodes. Using his professional skills to finance travel, Manly reached Mindanao and served under Frank McCoy, helping the provincial official design roads, bridges, docks, and the provincial headquarters. After a year there, Manly moved to Canton and then to Burma, where he worked for Standard Oil at the headwaters of the Irawaddy River. In the last letter McCoy received from Manly, the engineer was proposing to travel to Mombosa in colonial Kenya to assist in the construction of a railway line over the Nile. The Moro Province was a mere stop in a transimperial life.[53]

Harnessing knowledge across imperial borders continued into the waning years of U.S. colonial rule. Governor Dwight F. Davis's extensive 1931 inspection tour stopped in various parts of French Indochina, Siam, British Malaya, and the Dutch East Indies. Promoted as an opportunity for an "interchange of ideas," the trip saw Davis map out broad comparisons between the Philippines and other colonies. He did so by observing the operation of these regimes in minute detail, visiting "banks, post offices, scientific plants, hospitals, air services, roads, experimental stations, estates and farms . . . schools, museums . . . palm oil factories, tin mines, automobile factories, [and] opium plants."[54] A confidential memorandum sent back to Washington after Davis's return described the physical conditions, role of the native elite, lives of the native peasantry, governmental systems, and commercial conditions of the European colonies, measuring them relative to U.S. accomplishments in the Philippines. The document paid particular attention to relations between ruler and ruled in Muslim-majority Malaya and the Dutch East Indies. Even as Filipino autonomy grew and Mindanao-Sulu became increasingly integrated into the embryonic nation-state, U.S. officials maintained their long-standing habit of looking to other empires for guidance, perspective, and expertise.[55]

Intermediaries and Border Crossings

Durable flows of cultural and economic exchange gave Mindanao-Sulu a permeable quality of its own, predating American rule and shaping the colonial state in unexpected ways. For centuries, the Sulu and Maguindanao Sultanates proved resilient in maintaining their positions as small but dynamic polities in island Southeast Asia. Ethnically subdivided yet linked through Islam and vigorous maritime commerce, the region's inhabitants chafed at the consolidation of Euro-American colonialism in the late nineteenth century.[56] This supraregional fluidity ran counter to U.S. boundary-making initiatives that sought to monopolize and harness outside transmissions and entanglements. Faced with a host of obstacles to their demarcating agendas, colonial authorities looked toward hybridic interlocutors and ad hoc imperial coordination to shore up control of Mindanao-Sulu. The platonic ideal for imperial exchange remained studious, rigorously applied adaptations of European expertise. But in practice, negotiating rule in porous spaces often meant pragmatic concessions to a region with its own entrenched linkages.

Zamboanga maintained a diverse character throughout the colonial period and was home to a variety of peoples: Spanish planters; Christian Filipino descendants of deportados exiled from the North; creole Zamboanguenos, who claimed both Filipino and Spanish identities; a Chinese merchant class; and, on the perimeters of the settlement, Samal Moros. Under U.S. rule, military officers and their families represented the upper strata of colonial society, establishing racially segregated clubs, entertaining visiting dignitaries from other empires, and having their domestic needs met by native servants.[57] The white population also included small business owners, professionals, and even some aspiring frontiersmen who struck out for the island's interior to establish plantations. European representatives of banking concerns, steamship lines, and trading companies also filtered through the Muslim South. Charles Ivins recalled debating military issues with a Scottish banker named Ian McDougal, who worked for the Charted Bank of India, Australia, and China while also serving as British consul.[58]

Cosmopolitan spaces like Zamboanga remained the exception. In 1913, the population of Mindanao-Sulu totaled 518,695. This included 324,816 Moros,

103,358 Lumad, and 85,148 Filipinos, numbers that the census broke down further to account for various tribal divisions. This left a small number of "Americans and foreigners." Zamboanga had 1,062 Chinese residents, 387 Americans and Europeans, and 343 Japanese. A further 3,584 Americans, Europeans, Chinese, and Japanese residents lived in other parts of the South, bringing the total number to around 5,376. Filipinization caused a decline in white residents during the following decades, while Japanese migration steadily increased until the Second World War.[59] Demographically limited despite efforts to grow a larger settler class, white colonials relied on intermediary figures to bridge ethnocultural divides. This category often included multiracial community leaders whose ambiguous status allowed them to move between the worlds of colonist and colonized.

In the Sulu Archipelago, the Schuck family filled this role. Patriarch Herman Leopold Schuck was a German trader-explorer based out of Singapore, who developed a friendship with Sultan Jamalul Alam in the 1860s. The Tausūg ruler liked Schuck enough to grant him land on the island of Jolo and in Sandakan Bay in North Borneo. The sea captain used these new allotments to create his own Singapore-based trade network, where he acquired products from a German-British consortium called the Labuan Trading Company. Schuck moved opium, firearms, tobacco, and other goods from Singapore to Tawi-Tawi, exchanging them for slaves and bartering those slaves for mother-of-pearl shell on Jolo. He served as an adviser to the sultan during negotiations leading to the 1878 treaty with Spain, ran a large plantation on Jolo, and maintained links with German colonial enterprises in Southeast Asia. After he died of cholera in 1887, his five sons, one of whom was from a Tausūg wife, remained in the archipelago.[60]

The Schuck brothers—Edward, Charles, Herman, William, and Julius—solidified their positions in Tausūg society by marrying local women. It is difficult to overstate how frequently U.S. colonial authorities turned to the Schucks after 1899. Few Americans had any knowledge of Sulu or its people, and the Schucks, bridging Western and native realms, were ideal middlemen. They variously acted as interpreters, advisers, guides, amateur police detectives, militia leaders, and government agents over the course of more than three decades. Edward, the oldest, was official translator during the discussions that precipitated the Bates Agreement. John Bates praised his "great influence with the natives."[61] The U.S. military used Herman Schuck as an interpreter and unofficial policeman on the island of Bongao, while Charles acted as liaison for Col. Joseph Duncan in the expedition that culminated in the 1906 Bud Dajo massacre. The 4th Cavalry and 6th Infantry staged the attack from the

Schuck family plantation southeast of Jolo town.[62] Charles and Julius also advised U.S. Army forces during a 1911 stand-off over disarmament that again drove Moros onto Dajo.[63] Deeply enmeshed in life on Jolo, the brothers and their wives likewise mediated disputes between local Moros.[64]

By the end of military rule, three of the Schuck brothers had died. Herman was beheaded in a dispute on Bongao, Edward passed away in 1912, and Charlie was murdered on Jolo in 1914.[65] The two remaining brothers, William and Julius, and the families of the deceased continued to play important roles in Sulu politics. William and Alexander Schuck served as special agents for the province of Sulu into the 1920s, making and breaking alliances with local political figures, the Bureau of Non-Christian Tribes, and members of the Philippine Constabulary.[66] Governor of Sulu in the 1930s, James Fugate complained bitterly about Julius Schuck and his Tausūg wife, Ruckaya, who involved themselves in government affairs.[67] The family's plantation remained in operation until the Second World War, and they also produced railway ties. Julpa Schuck, daughter of Edward, attended the elite Normal School in Manila and later translated fragments of traditional poetry from Sulu.[68]

Other interlocutors arrived with the U.S. military. Stefan Jurika, a Czech born in the Austro-Hungarian Empire, volunteered to fight in the Spanish-American War and was posted to the Southern Philippines. He settled in Sulu after leaving military service, opening a trading company on Jolo that later had branches in Zamboanga, Cotabato, and Davao. His business eventually became an official distributor for Colgate products—including "hair tonics, cosmetics, shampoos, and dental preparations"—and his bar on Jolo advertised itself as the "finest drinking place" in Sulu.[69] On his periodic trips to the United States and Europe, Jurika became a proselytizer of the Muslim South, arguing there had been "much misrepresentation [about] the mutinous disposition of the natives" in the U.S. press. His pitch was a familiar one: U.S. businesses should buy unprocessed native products from the Philippines and sell their finished manufactures back to the islands. He performed with such gusto that he became a representative for a variety of capitalist concerns, including steamship lines, the Milton G. Cooper Dry Goods Company, and the Goodyear Tire Company.[70] When he died in 1928, the trader had spent three decades in Mindanao-Sulu and become one of the most active merchants there.

Blanche Jurika, wife of Stefan, took over his businesses after his death. She opened a hardware and dry goods store in Zamboanga and founded a coconut plantation at Panabutan Bay, seventy miles northeast of the capital. The Zamboanga store carried items from all over the world and, unlike other Euro-American businesses, catered primarily to Moro customers. Risking alienation by transgressing the racial codes of colonial life, Jurika did sound business with the local Samal community. "Most of the Moros traded there," wrote Charles Ivins in the 1930s, "and it was one of the Zamboanga sights to watch [Jurika] and a group of native women haggle." Ivins, whose personal life was typically segregated, was surprised by Jurika's ability to "go anywhere" among the Moros "and not be afraid of personal violence."[71] She relocated to Manila in the late 1930s, writing a children's column for the *Manila Times* and presenting a radio program three times a week on KZRH. The Japanese military police uncovered Blanche Jurika's work for the resistance movement during the Second World War, and she was executed in Manila's North Cemetery in August 1944.[72]

The Chinese community in Mindanao-Sulu was centuries old but had grown rapidly in the nineteenth century.[73] Migratory waves emanating from South China—a result of famine, warfare, and limited social mobility—deepened the Southern Philippines' links to regional trade networks, with Chinese residents acting as local merchants and moneylenders. Although economically influential in some communities, the Chinese were culturally liminal, allowing them to function in intermediary roles between the Americans, Filipinos, Moros, and Lumad. Their livelihoods gave them cause to interact with each of these groups, becoming a useful Other for the authorities. Unarmed and outnumbered in the small islands of the Sulu Archipelago, Chinese merchants welcomed the U.S. presence, hoping it would protect them from jealous Moros. On Siasi, Chinese residents set off a "great number of firecrackers" to greet the Americans.[74] In Jolo, Ah Wah On (who adopted the colloquial name "Chino Charlie") catered to the U.S. penchant for "Moro curios" in his shop, which doubled as a tailor and a restaurant.[75] Although some colonial accounts emphasized Chinese racial difference, provincial governor Tasker Bliss claimed the group was "hard at work improving and developing the country."[76]

American colonials found a natural ally in Datu Piang, the multiracial leader of the Maguindanao Moros. Piang was born in 1846 to a Chinese father and a Maguindanao mother. His father, Tan Toy, was an Amoy trader who spent time in Dulawan and befriended the local ruler Datu Uto. Uto arranged for Tan to be married to a daughter of an ally and employed the trader as his adviser. Piang was the product of this marriage and raised in the orbit of Datu Uto's court.[77] During his early career, Piang served as minister of lands for Uto but later turned on his mentor, who was something of a tyrant. Piang sided with Moro oppositionists led by Uto's nephew Ali and helped overthrow the old datu in 1890. After Spain's ouster in 1899, he formed an ad hoc gov-

Figure 7.2 Datu Piang (third from right) and his retinue. The Maguindanao–Chinese leader rose to power in the Cotabato region during the chaos following Spanish rule. A reliable ally of the United States, he used his hybrid identity to negotiate complex regional politics. (Harris & Ewing Photographs, 1913, glass negative, LC-DIG-hec-02577. Library of Congress, Prints and Photographs Division)

ernment to oppose the rule of a Christian insurrecto junta. He executed twelve Filipino leaders and took steps to protect the Chinese merchants and traders in Cotabato. Although at times capricious, the regional strongman understood where power lay, raising the U.S. flag before U.S. Army troops arrived in Cotabato.[78]

John Bates and other military figures immediately recognized Piang as an important collaborator. A 1902 Philippine Commission report declared that the datu's "Chinese blood" made him a "shrewd businessman." He was "the only prominent Moro" who appreciated the "business opportunities" presented by the new colonial order.[79] Piang skillfully interpreted the prerogatives of American officials and prospered greatly in his commercial ventures as a result. In the early 1900s, he controlled much of the trade in Cotabato through a network of Chinese agents. His interests were diverse, ranging from rice farming to exports to photography studios. Piang's influence lasted until his death in the 1930s, and he cultivated important connections with figures like Leonard Wood, William Cameron Forbes, and Frank Carpenter. Toward the end of his life, the datu became an advocate for permanently separating Mindanao-Sulu from the remainder of the Philippines. Fearful of northern hegemony, Piang caricatured the Filipinos as cowards and villains.[80]

Datu Piang's unlikely rise to power in Cotabato reveals a level of fluidity in the class structures of Maguindanao society and also the importance of in-between actors to Euro-American colonizers. His nebulous ethnic identity and considerable natural abilities allowed him to negotiate not only the power dynamics of the Maguindanao elite but also those of two colonial regimes. Unlike more traditionally minded strongmen in the Southern Philippines, Piang understood that the integration of Southeast Asia into globalized colonial trade regimes signaled the end of regional autonomy. Attempts to regulate commerce, originating first from the European colonial powers and later from the Americans, curtailed the trade in slaves, imposed taxes on goods, and altered the movement of peoples. Piang and the Chinese traders he worked with adapted to these new realities better than most. Submitting to U.S. rule, they were able leverage the goodwill of U.S. military authorities to expand their commercial holdings, all while Piang still exercised the firm control of a local despot. Patricio Abinales identifies Piang as a transitional figure, linking a more independent nineteenth-century Maguindanao society to one increasingly subordinate to outside political power.[81]

Alongside families and individuals, regional porousness also shaped the colonial encounter in Mindanao-Sulu. Linkages with North Borneo illustrate this phenomenon. In 1878, the Austrian businessman Gustav von Overbeck secured far-reaching territorial rights there through negotiations with the sultan of Brunei and sultan of Sulu. Alfred and Edward Dent, British traders operating out of Shanghai and London, backed the deal, and William H. Treacher, the acting governor of Labuan, supervised negotiations. Overbeck sold his shares in North Borneo to the Dents in 1880, and they in turn petitioned the Foreign and Colonial Offices for a royal charter, which was granted in November 1881. The resulting British North Borneo Chartered Company, modeled on the East India Company, controlled nearly 10,800 square miles of land that it sought to commercially develop. Sulu's neighbor to the west became a British protectorate in 1888.[82]

The natives of the Sulu Archipelago saw little distinction between their islands and North Borneo. The lease or sale (depending on whom one asked) of Sabah was a revenue-generation scheme for native elites. For the average Tausūg or Samal traveling between Tawi-Tawi and Sandakan, impact was limited. Fleeing instability and insurrecto violence during the 1899 imperial transfer, some Mindanaoans sheltered in Sandakan. The Zamboangueno plantation owner Don Jose Alvarez y Sebastian traveled to the British colony by way of Jolo. Temporarily exiled, he received updates on his home from the Moros and Chinese who plied their wares between port settlements. In an interview with John Bates, Don Jose expressed his desire to return to Zamboanga and embrace U.S. sovereignty.[83] After the Spanish-American War, Zamboanga and Jolo maintained closer communication links to Sandakan than they did with Manila. This meant that the information, goods, and peoples passing through the Southern Philippines were often linked into British colonial nodes in Singapore, Hong Kong, and London.[84]

The sultans of Sulu always insisted they were merely renting Sabah to the British (at a rate of $5,000 per annum), although their ability to renege on the deal was nonexistent. During his negotiations with Sultan Kiram, John Bates contacted officials in North Borneo for assistance, attempting to secure the services of the academic Nicholas Belfield Dennys, who was then working in Sandakan as an interpreter. Dennys had authored a number of works, including *A Descriptive Dictionary of British Malaya* and a book that made cultural comparisons between Chinese folklore and that of "the Aryan and Semitic Races."[85] Kiram likewise utilized his North Borneo connections, calling on Hadji Usman, a Tausūg appointed as the sultan's representative on Siasi. Between 1881 and 1897, Usman was in the employ of the North Borneo Company as a maritime pilot. Fluent in English, Usman translated the meetings between Bates and the sultan, telling the former he was "very glad the Americans came" as "English and American rule" were "practically identical." He inquired about work with the new colonial government.[86]

Real and imagined territorial connections patterned life in the Sulu zone. Many business interests, including those of the Schuck family, straddled maritime borders. After the death of Herman Schuck, his sons started a coffee plantation in Borneo, where they grew Liberian beans through a combination of wage and slave labor.[87] Since Spanish control over Sulu had always been tentative, the British encouraged the channeling of trade through Sandakan, and traffic between these contiguous spaces was largely unregulated. U.S. attempts to create a more structured trade regime were slow moving. Beyond this, population transfers commonly occurred between Mindanao-Sulu and Borneo. Cycles of famine and epidemic led residents of the Sulu Archipelago to relocate to British territory, where many of them had familial and commercial connections.[88] Although these mobilities troubled Americans, they themselves looked to British possessions on Borneo for inspiration. The district governor of Sulu, Hugh Scott, compared U.S. efforts to those of James Brooke, who governed farther west in Sarawak. Rajah Brooke's efforts to reduce banditry and expand governance structures made the natives disposed to colonial rule, Scott believed. "In like manner the better class of people in Jolo feel thus towards the United States," he wrote.[89]

Illegal traffic between the two spaces irritated American officials. As early as June 1899, Commander Very of the USS *Castine* reported "illegal" movement between Sandakan and Mindanao.[90] Regulating the waters of the Sulu and Celebes Seas would make trade more profitable, decrease uncontrolled in- and out-migration, and eliminate the vices of gambling, opium, and prostitution from Mindanao-Sulu (thought to be of foreign import). Military authorities complained of dubious characters from North Borneo openly seeking business opportunities in Zamboanga and Jolo. A Japanese brothel owner in Sandakan named Otama, for instance, petitioned William Kobbé in 1901 to open up an "accommodation house" in Zamboanga and bring fifteen to twenty women to work there.[91] The smuggling of people and goods became so problematic in the Moro Province that the Jolo customs inspector E. L. Cook sent a plan to reorganize all of Sulu to his Manila superiors. Cook suggested large boats be put on constant patrol in the Sulu Sea, ensuring smaller crafts would come under government surveillance and be "forced to relinquish . . . illicit trade." He also encouraged expanded Constabulary backing for customs officials, effectively militarizing trade enforcement in the South.[92]

Slaving and smuggling, often intertwined, continued apace throughout the colonial period. At the end of his tenure in the Insular Government, Dean Worcester complained of persistent "slavery and peonage" in the Philippines, recalling earlier personal experiences at an open-air slave market where Dutch planters from Borneo purchased human wares from the Moros.[93] John C. Early complained of a "constant ingress of Chinese from Borneo through the southern islands." Coast guard ships patrolling the waters off of Mindanao were not fast enough to capture the quick vintas that brought in people and wares. Even when illegal migrants were apprehended, the government lacked funds to hold or deport them.[94] Various solutions surfaced, including travel passes to minimize the "smuggling of aliens between the southern islands and the colonies near Mindanao, like Borneo and the East Indies."[95]

Fugitives often used the demarcationist tendencies of colonial states for their own ends, slipping across invisible borders as a means of evading capture. Intercolonial policing and surveillance offered an imperfect solution to controlling difficult sea borders. Contact and coordination between the Americans and British benefited both parties and began in 1899 when the Philippine commissioner Jacob Gould Schurman made an inspection tour to North Borneo. There he met the British resident at Labuan, R. M. Little. Little became a contact for the U.S. Navy and tracked the circulation of Filipino nationalists through British territories. "I shall not allow Labuan to be made a centre for any intrigues with the Filipinos," he declared in a letter.[96] Information sharing between the two empires became standard.

Two examples illustrate the practice. In October 1902, Lt. George Duncan, stationed at Tawi-Tawi, received word from the police superintendent of Sandakan of a break-in at the museum there. Elephant tusks had been stolen, and Sandakan authorities placed the blame on Datu Tan Tong of Siminul. As Siminul was under U.S. control, Duncan made a search of Datu Tong's property on behalf of the British. Nothing was found, and Tan Tong requested he be allowed to travel to British territory to clear his name.[97] Another incident occurred in January 1905, when a mercenary and pirate named Pala, previously hired by Sultan Kiram to capture Panglima Hassan, raided a settlement in North Borneo. He and his men killed thirty-five people, returning to Jolo afterward. With him, Pala brought "a number of recruits from other islands, deserters from the Constabulary, and disorderly characters of all kinds." The group exploited public dislike of the cedula tax to foment unrest. Hugh Scott received an official arrest-and-extradition request from Whitehall in March and assembled a massive war party to move on Pala in early May. Native troops tracked down and killed the outlaw band in brutal close-quarters fighting, a precursor to expanded army and Constabulary sweeps across the island. Afterward, Governor Leonard Wood concluded Pala was "the head and front of the trouble," blaming the conflict on the massacre in North Borneo.[98]

Crimes committed across imperial boundaries persisted, as did coordinated responses to them. In April 1909, a group of seven Moros from Manuk Mangkaw traveled across the Celebes Sea to Sulawesi, where they robbed and killed two Dutch planters. They made the long voyage back to Sulu pursued by a Dutch gunboat, which was unable to catch them before they disembarked. Dutch authorities contacted the Constabulary detachment at Bongao, which was then reinforced by infantry companies from Jolo. While the Americans scoured Manuk Mangkaw for the fugitives, the Dutch gunboat patrolled surrounding waters. The partnership led to the capture of all the suspects involved, apart from the leader (who was apprehended a short time later by "friendly" Moros).[99] Intercolonial police actions provided a means of pooling resources and expertise in connected maritime environments, a ground-level analog to the exchanges that occurred in inspection tours and diplomatic communiqués.

Despite these regional exchanges, American impressions of neighboring empires were not always favorable. John C. Early wrote of North Borneo with a critical eye during a 1922 vacation there. Traveling with an assortment of colonial characters aboard a steamship to Sandakan, Early witnessed a Portuguese lieutenant beating Chinese prisoners who were destined for a penal colony in Timor. The American lamented the "thin veneer" of civility possessed by the "Latin" army officer. In Sandakan, Early denounced the British for living off the "wages of shame" by legalizing and regulating vice. The town itself was "quite unimproved," which outraged Early. The British at Sandakan had failed in their paternal mission, and since the colony was run like a business, "anything which did not pay was abandoned." The British kept their laborers in a state of ignorance as a "matter of policy," contradicting principles of uplift. This indifference to the moral mandates of colonialism, combined with the toleration of vice, encouraged a state of permanent dissipation in North Borneo. Chinese laborers openly smoked opium "with the consent and to the profit of the state" and frequently fled to the Philippines (by way of Sulu) when they grew unhappy with their work contracts. Early blamed the problem of porous boundaries in the Philippines on the mismanagement and moral decay of other colonies, suggesting that connection had its downsides.[100]

Pilgrims and Petitions

Moro links to the greater Middle East began centuries before the U.S. imperial occupation, with a shared Islamic faith serving as a connection point to the wider world. These linkages provided important bulwarks against the homogenizing tendencies of the colonial state and vexed American empire builders. Under the Spanish, Ottoman immigrants had settled in Manila and other parts of the archipelago. Primarily Druze and Maronite Christians from Syria, these refugees established themselves in the islands' merchant circles. Believing the Syrians would stabilize the South, Spanish authorities attempted to funnel them into Mindanao with limited success. More vexing to Spain were the Muslim missionary-traders who came to Moro lands through other channels. Bypassing Spanish influence, they enacted a "steady stream of counter-colonialism" in the region.[101]

American colonials looked to the Ottoman Empire for assistance. In 1899, Ambassador Oscar Straus met with Sultan Abdul Hamid II in Constantinople to discuss how to handle the Moros. Straus worried about "holy war" and implored the sultan to draft a message in support of the United States. The Ottoman potentate was unaware of the Moros and was surprised to learn that "considerable numbers" visited Mecca.[102] Straus presented the sultan with the 1796 Treaty of Tripoli, declaring that the United States intended to uphold its promise not to interfere with Muslim religious rights and touting the nation's record of friendship toward non-Christian peoples. Believing the ambassador's sincerity, Abdul Hamid drafted a message to the Moros prohibiting hostilities against the Americans so long as their religion was respected.[103]

Real and imagined linkages also drew Moros toward the Ottomans. As elsewhere, a mark of honor for prominent Tausūg men from Sulu was completing the costly and arduous trip to Mecca, which remained under Ottoman control until 1916. Sultan Kiram boasted that he had flown the flag of the sultanate while visiting the holy city in the 1890s, while the powerful Datu Jokanain spent most of early 1903 there.[104] Lanao datus revered the Ottoman sultan as leader of the *ummat al-Islamiyah*—the global Muslim community—and some believed they should direct fealty toward Constantinople instead of Washington. In 1902, Datu Gundar of Maciu wrote John Pershing that anticolonial Maranao groups looked to the "Sultan of Stanboul as the head of their government." If the Sultan was "not a friend of the Americans," they could not be either. Pershing assured the datu that cordial relations existed between the two empires, and Gundar promised to relay the message to anti-American leaders.[105] Outgunned and lacking resources, Maranao groups invoked Ottoman power in an attempt to stave off political marginalization and physical destruction. Presenting themselves as allied with a Muslim empire, datus hoped to gain better bargaining positions with the U.S. military.

The practice continued in the district for years. In April 1907, John McAuley Palmer received a series of letters from Datu Nurul Hakim, a prominent Maranao leader on the eastern shore of Lake Lanao. Hakim cautioned Palmer to "take into account the agreement of the Sultan of Istanbul with the Government . . . that the Government established in Lanao shall merely watch over Lanao and should not injure the inhabitants or change their customs." The datu claimed he had specific orders from Sultan Abdul Hamid II "not to let the Americans come to [his] *rancheria*," and declared his fealty to the Ottoman Empire. By exaggerating links to foreign authority, Hakim symbolically placed himself under Ottoman protection. This, he believed, increased Maranao bargaining power against the well-provisioned American forces at Camp Vicars and Camp Keithley. Palmer was unimpressed, seeing Hakim's posturing as a clumsy feint. The datu's next letter was an escalation. Presenting himself as a mere extension of Abdul Hamid's will, Hakim warned the Americans that an attack on his homestead at Rumayas was an attack on Ottoman "domain." Lanao's sovereignty now straddled imperial realms, if only notionally. Hakim threatened the lives of prominent Americans, including President Roosevelt, declaring that the colonial state could not "vanquish the Sultan of Istanbul."

Invoking Ottoman power failed, and U.S. Army and Philippine Constabulary troops destroyed Hakim's cotta soon thereafter.[106]

Other connections to the greater Middle East were more concrete. Religious tradition dictated able-bodied Muslims visit Mecca once in their lives. Hajj pilgrimages had long connected Southeast Asian Muslims to the wider Islamic world, but the practice expanded in the late nineteenth century. New transoceanic technologies made travel accessible to more people, with ships themselves becoming cosmopolitan sites of transfer.[107] As elsewhere, Moro men who made the long journey from the Southern Philippines to the Arabian Peninsula were accorded respect, taking the honorific title of hadji. Being able to connect oneself to the *ummah* lent religio-cultural authority to the pilgrim, setting them apart in Moro communities where most never traveled beyond Southeast Asia. Pilgrimages also provided access to inter-Islamic politics operating through and around Euro-American imperial designs. British, French, and Dutch colonial administrators all grappled with hajj mobilities, surveilling pilgrim networks for evidence of dangerous peoples and ideas.[108]

Traveling the nearly six thousand miles between Zamboanga and Mecca, through the South China Sea and across the Indian Ocean, was arduous. Hopeful pilgrims bunked in claustrophobically small and poorly maintained third-class compartments. Steamship companies routinely hired Arabic and Malay agents to advertise among the Moros, who spent large amounts to secure passage to Mecca. A characteristic journey looked like the one eleven pilgrims took from Lanao in 1930. At a cost of between ₱700 and ₱1,000 each, the Maranao group traveled by launch to Zamboanga and from there by steamer to Singapore. In Singapore, they boarded a larger ship that carried them across the Indian Ocean and up the Red Sea to Jeddah. A caravan took them overland to Mecca. The Maranao pilgrims spent twenty-seven days in the holy city praying at the Masjid al-Harem, the largest mosque in the world. The leader of the group, Datu Pambaya, wrote home to Lanao of life in the Arabian Peninsula. "It would be very fine if all the people in the world could trust each other as they do in Mecca," he declared.[109] In this cosmopolitan space, Moros came into contact with Muslims from the Middle East, South Asia, North Africa, and other areas of Southeast Asia, who introduced them to emerging political and religious movements.[110]

Like their European counterparts, American colonial administrators viewed the hajj with suspicion. John Pershing positioned himself against the practice while serving as governor of the Moro Province. Returning hadjis had an "exalted idea of their own importance" and considered themselves "above ordinary labor." Worse yet, the cost of the journey led to financial ruin for many.

Some Moros were "robbed and cheated" in the port cities along the way, while others returned with "loathsome diseases" that spread through Mindanao-Sulu. Pershing recommended that the government curtail the pilgrimages, except for those with proven financial resources.[111] His criticisms arose from a deeper antipathy toward Islam, but there is evidence that the journey was not an easy one. In the 1930s, groups of prospective hadjis occasionally appeared in Zamboanga and were lodged in schoolhouses due to lack of available hostels. The travelers sometimes fell victim to unscrupulous steamship agents, and many did not make it out of Southeast Asia. Other Moros called these pilgrims "Singapore *Hadjis* . . . an honorific hardly comparable to that of a bona fide Mecca *hadji*."[112]

For Christian imperialists, Moro connections to global Islam posed an existential challenge. Charles Brent worried that the United States was treating the "Moro problem" as a local issue when in reality it was a transimperial predicament. The Islamic world was a "unified and sensitive organ," the bishop believed: a conflagration in the Ottoman Empire had the potential to cause trouble in the Southern Philippines. Islam itself was a veritable "plague spot" in Europe, British India, and Southeast Asia, and Brent blamed "Arab priests" for transmitting the worst aspects of the faith to Moros. He called for an end to "Arabian immigration." In his mind, the Moros were pawns caught between the civilizing tendencies of the Americans and the fanaticism of Arabs and Ottoman Turks.[113] Even more fervent in his fantasies of spiritual reform, Frank Laubach argued (in his pre-Lanao days) for a "new assault on Mohammedanism" via the Southern Philippines. Moro disarmament presented a unique opportunity for conversion. Writing to Frank Carpenter in 1921, Laubach mapped a plan to convert the Tausūg of Sulu, who would then "turn down upon Borneo, Java (with its 30,000,000 of Mohammedans), Sumatra, the Straits Settlements and, perhaps, India." The missionary wrote in messianic terms, viewing his plan as "beginning the end of the Moslem regime."[114]

Not all visions of Islam were apocalyptic. Gen. William Kobbé studied temporal and spiritual authority in the Ottoman world and pored over a primer on Moro usage of the Arabic alphabet. He enlisted the aid of Najeeb Saleeby, whose early research on the Muslim sultanates made him valuable to successive colonial commanders. Saleeby and Kobbé discussed Moro understandings of Islam and the influence of Afghan hadjis in the region.[115] As school superintendent, Saleeby sparred with Leonard Wood over the role of Islamic religious education. His successor Charles Cameron openly advocated the use of foreign clerics, sending an Arabic teacher, Sheikh Mustafa Ahmed, on a recruitment trip through Sulu. The end goal was the establishment of a "Datu

School," where sons of prominent Moros could be taught Middle Eastern iterations of Islam alongside respect for secular authorities. In this dual system, Ahmed would instruct students on the Qur'an, and American teachers would lead classes in English on U.S. governance.[116] Although skeptical members of the provincial legislative council ultimately blocked its creation, the school represented a belief that Islam could be harnessed by the state. Saleeby continued consulting with officials in the Muslim South for decades. He provided commentary on Sultan Kiram's response to the 1915 Carpenter Agreement, situating the ruler's text within traditions of "Malayan sovereigns" and linking leadership and succession to socioreligious currents in the crumbling Ottoman Empire.[117]

More often, however, Americans identified global Islam as a threat and foreign Muslims as potential fifth columnists, spreading religious fanaticism to the detriment of the civilizing mission. Leonard Wood blamed resistance to U.S. rule during his tenure on "the Arab priest."[118] John Pershing was even more strident in his condemnations. "Arabian and other Mohammedan teachers" plagued the Moro Province, and their presence gave "occult inspiration" to native opposition. Government initiatives faltered because mosques and imams functioned as alternate power centers. That some Americans suggested using foreign Muslims for civilizational reform was "beyond belief" to Pershing, who opposed "any plan for the propagation of Mohammedanism through the prostitution of the public schools."[119]

The push and pull between integrating and rejecting "outside" Islamic influences coalesced in a sequence of events during the final years of the Moro Province. In 1911, John Finley, the district governor of Zamboanga and creator of the Moro Exchange system, developed an ambitious plan to use Islam for colonial ends. The inchoate version practiced by Moros generated opposition to the state, he decided, and required reform. Finley took it upon himself to be the voice of the Samal and Yakan Moros of the Zamboanga Peninsula and the island of Basilan. The Samal leadership (at his urging) bestowed on him the title of Tuan Maas, an honorific translating roughly to "teacher, sultan, and father." The following year, he convened a public meeting of Samal Moros at Taluksangay and had himself appointed *wakil mutalak* (plenipotentiary) of the region. Finley intended to travel to Constantinople on behalf of the Moros and deliver a petition to Sultan Mehmed V. He used the titles as a means of increasing his credibility.[120]

Written as a direct plea from the Moros of Zamboanga, the carefully crafted petition asked the Ottoman sultan to take a "wider and deeper interest" in Moro affairs and requested a representative to travel from the Sublime Porte

Figure 7.3 Datu Mandi (left) presents Col. John Park Finley with a petition from the Moros of the Zamboanga Peninsula requesting religious guidance from the Ottoman Empire—Taluksangay, May 1911. The petition set off an unusual sequence of events that ended in controversy. Datu Facundo, who traveled to St. Louis in 1904, is third from left. (Burton Norvell Harrison Family Papers, 1812–1926, box 38, Library of Congress, Manuscript Division)

to "examine" conditions in the Moro Province. The Ottoman agent would help Moros bring their "laws and customs" into agreement with U.S. governance and advise them on how to live a "truer and purer Mohammedan faith . . . without obstructing the laws of the State." Signed by sixty datus, the petition introduced Finley to the Ottoman potentate as "more than a father" and declared that the decision to name him Tuan Maas had occurred "spontaneously and unanimously." It concluded with florid praise for the sultan, who was the only individual that could help the Moros. Framed as a genuine appeal for political and religious guidance, the document closely mirrored Finley's own personal and public writings about Islam in the Philippines.[121]

"These people are wards of the government and as such children of the state. They should receive paternal care, more especially if they ask for it," Finley wrote to President Taft. "It is the burden of their petition and their call should be heeded." The plan stipulated that the Ottoman representative would be sent to Mindanao and placed in a position of moral leadership, guiding the Moros "through the instrumentality of modern Mohammedanism." This meant a domesticated version of Islam, stripped of its affiliation with rebellious datus and concerned with producing quiescent modern subjects. No longer would Moros be taught a "degraded" form of their faith by "fanatical native priests." Instead, the Ottoman agent would teach them adherence to provincial laws and modern sanitary practices. Finley expected a new spirit of temperance and industriousness to animate the Moros, leading them to respect the state monopoly on violence (ending juramentado attacks), develop their lands agriculturally, and curb social ills like gambling and theft.[122]

Finley suggested the individual selected for the job be "taken from a higher learning institution in the Ottoman Empire." The Moro Province would pay his salary, along with covering living expenses and accommodations. A title like "Moro Agent and Instructor" or "Traveling Moro Deputy" or "Provincial Moro Advisor" would be in order. The representative's service would last a year to eighteen months, with trained Moro datus assuming his duties afterward. U.S. officials in each district would ensure these ends were being pursued. The plan resembled the moral and commercial goals of Protestant reformers but translated through an Islamic intermediary more amenable to the Moros. Finley bolstered the scheme's legitimacy through reference to other empires. British, French, and Dutch rulers recognized native titles and customs, and it did "not appear to endanger the maintenance of proper control by the home government."[123]

Shortly after the petition was drafted, Governor John Pershing relieved Finley of his duties, and he departed for the United States on orders of the War Department. Skeptical of the Tuan Maas, Pershing made clear to Finley that any return to Zamboanga would be unwelcome. Finley was undeterred, traveling to Washington and meeting with an assortment of powerful figures, including President Taft, Secretary of War Henry Stimson, and Leonard Wood. He convinced them that the petition represented the Moro's genuine desire for guidance and received a personal letter of recommendation from Stimson.[124] Finley continued to Ottoman lands and in Constantinople received an audience with the sultan. The American's pitch convinced Mehmed to send a representative to the Southern Philippines. The chosen official was Sayyid Wajih b. Munib Zayd al-Kilani al-Nablusi. Originally from Ottoman Palestine, Wajih was a graduate of the theological school in Nablus and had also done training as a religious judge at the Qadi College in Constantinople. In 1913, he was an official for the Ottoman Shaykh al-Islam.[125] Finley returned to the Philippines in July 1913, meeting with the outgoing governor-general William Cameron Forbes. He tactfully omitted his arrangements to have an Ottoman religious teacher sent to Mindanao from the discussion.[126]

American military and civilian leaders reacted to Wajih's appearance in Mindanao at the end of January 1914 with surprise and dismay. The timing was not ideal. Anticipating the Wilson administration in Washington, Francis Burton Harrison had just replaced Forbes as governor-general. In the South, military rule was ending to make room for the civilian-led Department of Mindanao and Sulu. Finley and Wajih's appearance unsettled the new governor, Frank Carpenter, who cabled Manila to complain that their activities were "inopportune and probably perversive of public order." Despite his unfamiliarity with Muslim groups outside of Zamboanga, Finley requested transportation around the region, claiming he was "authorized by the Democratic Party . . . to teach the people here their Mohammedan catechism."[127] The military commander of the Philippines J. Franklin Bell was likewise apprehensive, viewing Wajih as an agent of Islamic revivalism and a "grave menace" to public order. That Finley wore his military uniform during his tour was of added concern. "It is plainly inappropriate for an Army officer to inject himself into the situation" in the service of "religious propaganda." Bell feared the mission would disrupt the "civilizing" efforts of the United States government and Christian missionary groups and actively worked to get Finley out of the colony.[128]

Carpenter's antipathy toward Finley's meddling was strong enough that he provided an account of the Wajih affair in the department's 1914 annual report. The governor placed Wajih in a category that included other foreign Muslim missionaries in the Philippines who arrived "independent of any superior ecclesiastical direction or control." Exacerbating matters were rumors spreading through the South that Constantinople was preparing to declare holy war against Christendom and that the Ottoman representative had traveled to Mindanao to foment rebellion. Calling Wajih a "Mohammaden propagandist" whose "reactionary and militant" presence would "prove fatal" to provincial progress, Carpenter advocated expulsion. Finley's high self-regard and belief that he could "redeem" the Moros became a liability when dealing with other colonial officials, who resented how he flouted bureaucratic norms and ignored government policies.[129]

Finley himself saw Wajih's visit as an unmitigated success and penned an account of it for the *Army and Navy Weekly*, a newspaper for active and retired servicemen in the Philippines. Although published without a byline, the article's level of detail and syntactical style clearly indicate authorship. It described Moros in Zamboanga flocking to the Wajih to kiss his hands and garments. "To them," wrote Finley, "it was as the coming of the Messiah; their hopes were at last fulfilled. Being Orientals their expressions of joy were the same as those of the crowds that followed Jesus in Galilee in days of old." The article described rapturous masses receiving the "Shaykh-al-Islam" of the Philippines wherever he ventured. Finley used the article to reassure skeptical American readers that greater links between the "Sublime Porte and Moroland" would improve colonial governance.[130]

Finley's plan to fuse Ottoman spiritual authority with U.S. colonial rule failed. The army transferred Finley back to the United States, and Wajih was "obliged" to leave the Philippines within a few months of his arrival. Back in Constantinople, the shaykh wrote to Secretary of War Lindley M. Garrison requesting funds to organize a return trip, perhaps unaware of the circumstances that led to his removal. The letter spoke of the "pitiful state" of the Moros and the desire of religious authorities in Constantinople to provide them with "instruction on the moral principles of our religion."[131] Rumors of Wajih's possible return on a battleship the following year circulated in the Philippines. Governor-General Harrison wrote to the Bureau of Insular Affairs, warning of the "embarrassment and possible consequences" of a second trip by the Ottoman agent. Harrison identified "a few Arabs, Turks, [and] Malays" as supporters of Wajih, rather than Moro groups. The desire to blame foreign Muslims for unrest in Mindanao–Sulu persisted.[132]

Undeterred by opposition to his mission, Wajih traveled to the United States in August 1915 hoping to secure a meeting with President Wilson.[133] The *New York Times* noted the shaykh's arrival. Moros would "become citizens of whom the United States [would] not be ashamed," Wajih told the *Times* reporter.[134] He continued seeking patronage. John Finley introduced the shaykh to the former district governor of Sulu, Hugh Scott, and Wajih himself wrote to Najeeb Saleeby requesting advice.[135] He received a terse response from the onetime Moro Province educator advising him to go through official channels before returning to the Philippines. He contacted Secretary Garrison once more to inform him that his Ottoman overseers did not know he had been asked to leave the Philippines on his previous journey. Spreading his "progressive and peaceful religious views to the American people" was of preeminent importance.[136]

The Bureau of Insular Affairs gave Wajih grudging permission to return to the Philippines against the protestations of officials there. They informed the shaykh that separation of church and state meant that the U.S. government had "no interest whatever in religious work in the world" or "disposition whatever to interfere with anyone in pursuit of such work." For that reason, the bureau could not "lend encouragement or aid to any particular missionary work in the islands."[137] As shown, North American Protestant missionaries often received a warmer reception when they traveled to Mindanao–Sulu. The bureau sought to marginalize Wajih, stripping him of any prestige gained through affiliation with the colonial state, but the planned second trip did not occur. In early 1916, Wajih al-Kilani fell ill while in Washington. He received treatment at the Hygeia Hospital and Sanitorium in Richmond, Virginia, where he died in early May. Writing two years later, a cynical Frank Carpenter wrote that Wajih's death was "timely" in that it eliminated him as a threat to public order in Mindanao-Sulu.[138]

The U.S. Army ensured annual reports from the Moro Province appeared on desks around the world. Lord Cromer received a copy, as did Bindon Blood, the military commander at Lahore, and Lionel Carden, the British minister in Havana. Dutch officials on Java kept abreast of developments in the archipelago, as did Wilhelm von Frihr of the German imperial army. Standard Oil officials, Panama Canal administrators, and the French ambassador to Spain likewise read the reports.[139] Even in death, major figures in colonial Moroland remained linked to their European peers. Eulogizing Leonard Wood and Charles Brent at Baguio in 1932, John Early declared that the former governor and the Episcopal bishop were "gentleman adventurers" in the spirit of Cecil Rhodes, T. E. Lawrence, and John Nicholson. As Nicholson was beloved by the Pashtuns of the Indian colonial frontier, Wood and Brent were "planted deep in the hearts" of Filipinos and Moros. Sentimentalism blurred boundaries and created unified moral histories of empire.[140]

Mindanao-Sulu was sequestered in imagination only. Americans serving there interacted with and drew from British, Dutch, French, Spanish, Portuguese, and Ottoman models, situating themselves as contributors to and competitors in a global imperial landscape. Inherited Spanish infrastructure provided the foundation for development projects, and Jesuit ethnographies and regional histories informed views of the Moros. An aspirational desire to emulate and surpass the successes of the British drove elites in Zamboanga, while inspection tours of Dutch and French colonies inspired administrative and cultural policies across the Moro Province. Personnel with experience in other colonial settings alternately aided constructive and destructive state impulses. Initiated under military rule, these exchanges continued in the civilian period, lasting well into the 1930s.

These interactivities took place amid a heterogeneous maritime environment with its own connections, forcing authorities to negotiate through hybridic interlocutors and coordinate across borders. The German Tausūg Schuck family provided cultural translation for the military on Jolo and took on politically significant roles on the island after 1914; Datu Piang bridged Maguindanao power structures with Chinese trading networks and was a reliable

American ally; and the Jurika family integrated themselves into the economic fabric of Mindanao-Sulu in ways that transient American officials could not. Ethnocultural connections between the Sulu Archipelago and North Borneo ensured that imperial borders were anything but secure. People moved from Sulu to the British Bornean possessions (and vice versa) regularly, frustrating territorial demarcation and necessitating ad hoc coordination. The unwillingness of some Moros to recognize new geographic boundaries troubled colonial officialdom, who sought control over how goods, peoples, and ideas moved through the Philippines.

Beyond their regional linkages to Borneo, Moros cultivated kinship with the wider Islamic world. During the early years of U.S. rule, this was often accomplished through reference to the Ottoman Empire. Datus facing grave military threats evoked the name of the Ottoman sultan as a warning to Americans and an expression of pan-Islamic solidarity. Middle Eastern imams provided religious instruction in Mindanao-Sulu, and Moros who could afford to do so often attempted the long hajj pilgrimage to Mecca. Those who made it became admired figures on their return to the Southern Philippines, their credibility bolstered by contact with the Islamic heartlands. These Muslim mobilities vexed leaders like John Pershing, who fretted about the pernicious influence of the "Mohammedan priest." Others like the educator Charles Cameron tried to channel global Islam toward colonial ends. The ultimate iteration of this came in the saga of John Finley and Shaykh Wajih, which drew together questions of interimperial exchange, religious freedom, and the utility of Islam in achieving colonial goals.

U.S. imperial power assumed many forms by the Progressive Era. It naturalized itself across vast swathes of North American territory, spread into Central America through protected zones and racialized labor, and manifested as formal colonial rule in parts of the Caribbean, South Pacific, and Southeast Asia. Persistent asymmetrical sovereignties underwrote the state's frequent spatial recalibrations, inscribing rule by difference from the slums of growing metropolitan cities to the rural villages of the Visayas. The silhouette of the imperial nation is becoming increasingly visible. With empire revealed, a key task involves resituating U.S. power within salient regional, supraregional, and global histories. The United States was a "nation among nations" but also an empire among empires—a fact more evident to early twentieth-century colonial officialdom than many contemporary historians. Its conquered, annexed, purchased, and usurped territories—and the peoples within—likewise had their own important and fluid links to the wider world. In Mindanao-Sulu, rulers and ruled often looked elsewhere.

Conclusion

Colonial Remains

In 1956, William Cameron Forbes lived in an apartment at the luxury Hotel Vendome in Boston's Back Bay neighborhood. Eighty-six years old, the former governor-general of the Philippines was preoccupied with colonial legacies. His nation's declining presence in the islands and a calamitous global conflict dimmed public memory of a once-prized colony. Six years prior, Forbes had commissioned a book to valorize U.S. achievements there. Written by his future biographer Arthur S. Pier, *American Apostles to the Philippines* celebrated many of the men responsible for colonial development in the Muslim South, including Leonard Wood, John Pershing, Charles Brent, Frank Carpenter, and Dean Worcester. The book brimmed with tales of heroic civilizing feats accomplished in the face of local resistance and anti-imperialist naysaying. "The page recording our adventure in the Philippines seems white and shining," its epilogue read.[1]

American Apostles received muted public response. Unsatisfied, Forbes began mapping a new project with Edward Bowditch, former vice-governor of the Moro Province, and the colonial medical specialist Victor Heiser.[2] The three represented a dwindling group of American elites who served in Southeast Asia during the early twentieth century. An ornery and demanding collaborator, Forbes pushed Bowditch and Heiser to remove "black shading" and "the reverse side of the medal" from their anecdotes and instead compose hagiographical portraits of Euro-American colonial modernizers.[3] The former governor-general called this group "the Brethren" and imagined them as transcendent figures. They had overcome inexperience, disease, and aggressive natives for the "cause of civilization."[4] Their ranks featured familiar names from Mindanao-Sulu. Wood, Brent, Pershing, Carpenter, and Worcester appeared again, as did Frank McCoy, James Fugate, George Langhorne, the Constabulary officers John White and Ole Waloe, and Bowditch himself.[5] Bowditch argued for the inclusion of women in the trio's "Philippine Valhalla," waxing poetic about Norse and Greek mythology as he made the case for the missionary socialite Caroline Spencer.[6]

The planned sequel to *American Apostles in the Philippines* was never published. It survives in drafts and correspondence between its creators. While tempting to dismiss as the legacy-building of aging men, the unfinished project also reveals a potent vision of empire. Forbes imagined "The Brethren" (its working title) making a case for U.S. extraterritorial power. The finished book was to include an essay exploring U.S. colonialism relative to other empires. The chapter would describe how the nation borrowed from and bettered upon European models. The authors contended that trusteeship and decolonization were natural outcomes of a four-decade march toward freedom in the Philippines. Having mastered the art of ruling foreign subjects, U.S. colonial administrators had kick-started decolonizing processes the world over. Unable to anticipate the denial of future decades, "The Brethren" encouraged Americans to embrace a model of imperial exceptionalism that placed their nation among *and* above other empires.[7] Forbes worded it in his own grandiose way: the "heroes" of the "Philippine saga" had written "a new page in colonial history."[8]

Forbes, Bowditch, and Heiser read the national mood incorrectly. In the rapidly decolonizing world of 1956, aged forms of colonial rule did not merit celebration. Predatory developmentalism and Cold War geopolitics replaced pith helmets and hill stations in the postwar era. The triumphalism of Forbes and his collaborators ran up against public indifference toward the "American Philippines." Critical evaluations of the U.S. legacy there had begun well before independence, as the project wound down in the Commonwealth era. "As I look about the streets of Zamboanga, I realize that we Americans have made a great many mistakes in the Philippines," Vic Hurley wrote in his 1935 memoirs. The plantation manager viewed colonial projects as failed experiments. Americans lacked a European understanding of race, he thought, lamenting the attempt to "implant an Occidental civilization in the lives of a race of brown Malays."[9]

Forbes's mythmaking and Hurley's sour racial essentialism represented differing conclusions on the same civilizing project. What did it all mean? At the end of the American period, there was hardly consensus on whether the "Moro problem"—now understood as the need to transform Muslims into quiescent national subjects—had been resolved. By the 1930s, a sequence of supposed turning points had come and gone, from disarmament campaigns in the Moro Province to political normalization in the late 1920s. Yet violence continued. The Philippine army repeatedly deployed to Mindanao during the Commonwealth era. Military planes bombed Maranao cottas in Lanao, and Filipino soldiers received shoot-to-kill directives.[10] American critics of Philippine independence positioned themselves as protectors of the Moros during these final years. Christian Filipinos were incapable of governing Muslims, the argument went, and Muslims also could not be trusted to govern themselves. If independence for the North was inevitable, perhaps Muslim-majority regions of Mindanao-Sulu could be partitioned and continue under U.S. tutelage.[11]

Americans continued to play important roles in the Muslim South well into the 1930s, although the high-water mark for white rule receded with the Moro Province in 1914. James Fugate, who administered Sulu, was the last American to hold a governorship in the South. He left office in 1936.[12] A nascent white settler movement that flourished in the first decades of the twentieth century fizzled out, the victim of poor planning and government indifference. The departure of Euro-American planters made way for other ethnic diasporas in Mindanao. By the end of the 1930s, nearly 18,000 Japanese migrants lived in Davao Province and dominated the hemp industry there.[13] This led to Filipino, Moro, and American complaints about the "land-hungry immigrant."[14] In the 1930s, the so-called Davao problem arose from fears of foreign control of Philippine markets and the growing regional designs of the Japanese Empire. Filipino nationalists urged greater migration from Luzon and the Visayas to counter the trend.[15]

In 1934, Governor-General Frank Murphy adopted the progressive language of the Roosevelt administration, promising a "new deal" for the Moros. He toured Mindanao-Sulu that year, reassuring Muslim groups that their religious rights would be respected in the impending Commonwealth of the Philippines.[16] He would have little ability to ensure this occurred. Throughout the 1920s and 1930s, Filipino political and cultural power brokers clashed over the Muslim South's future. Some, like Sergio Osmeña, believed the only roadblock to merging Christian and Muslim communities was continued U.S. rule. Removing colonialism would ensure integration. Others, like the Bureau of Non-Christian Tribes head Teofisto Guingona, remained skeptical. Channeling his American predecessors, Guingona emphasized the criminal nature of the Moro. "A nation cannot be built overnight," he wrote, arguing that decades of work remained before Muslims and Christians could have peaceable relations.[17] Filipino popular culture of the period inherited tropes of "Moro-land" as a prehistoric space of myth and danger, ensuring its frontier status crossed the colony-nation divide.[18]

Moro groups found themselves caught between these currents of Filipino nationalism and U.S. imperial revanchism. Petitions to President Franklin Roosevelt begged the Americans to stay. Sultan Aragon of Momungan "heartily opposed" independence as offered "through the hands of Christian Filipino leaders," while on Jolo local datus protested James Fugate's dismissal as governor, warning of "bloodshed" if a Filipino was appointed in his place.[19] Fears of Christian hegemony arose from real political shifts. Power struggles following Sultan Jamalul Kiram's death in 1936 allowed the Philippine government to quietly discontinue political recognition of the Sulu Sultanate. Datu Piang's passing in 1933 similarly reduced local autonomy in Cotabato. Anticipating new political realities, some younger Moros began using religious difference to stake a place within an emerging multiethnic state.[20] There was also a drive for greater Muslim presence in government bodies. This need was especially pressing in organizations like the Philippine Constabulary, which was dominated by Christians and had a fraught relationship with Moro communities.[21]

During the Second World War, many Muslims fought alongside Americans and Filipinos against the Japanese occupation. When the U.S. Army returned to Sulu in May 1945, Jolo datus welcomed them.[22] A year later, the United States relinquished sovereignty over the Philippines, leaving the Moros as minority groups on the fringes of a nation. Battles between state security forces and "outlaws" resumed. In December 1949, fifteen Constabulary officers died in a revolt against rigged elections on Jolo. The Philippine air force responded by dropping drums of gasoline on Tausūg rebels, killing at least thirty of them and echoing the violence of previous decades.[23]

There was no "Philippine Valhalla" in the postwar United States. The few U.S. newspaper stories run on the Moros after independence read much like those from the early twentieth century. The New York Times covered a 1950 visit to Lanao by Ambassador Myron Cowen, describing the "primitive" Maranao greeting the dignitaries with "shrill yells" and "war dances." The region's former status as a colonial possession received little notice. Gone were Pershing's punitive expeditions around the lake, John McAuley Palmer's urban designs for Dansalan, or Frank Laubach's experiments in missionary tutelage. Instead the article described the visit as the "first journey" through a "wild, remote area ever attempted by an American chief of mission."[24] The Second World War provided a convenient departure point, allowing the Southern Philippines to become a footnote in U.S. history. Imperial amnesia at once reclaimed American innocence and reified the South as a primal and unsullied frontier space. No longer a crucible for American ingenuity and will, Mindanao-Sulu was now a Philippine issue, where a newly independent nation enacted its own struggles against Muslim insurgents and communist guerillas. The colonial encounter transformed into narrow tales of military victories and failures in subsequent decades. More recently, Western commentators and policy makers have incorporated it into the War on Terror. Stripped of their histories, Bangsamoro struggles become means to illustrate the eternal threat of Islamic militancy.[25] At its nadir, this tendency spirals into violently racist mythomania where chain-e-mail histories inform presidential stump speeches and tweets.[26]

The postcolonial Philippine government benefitted from a settler exodus to Mindanao. Millions of Filipinos moved south in the decades following the Second World War, expanding national sovereignty claims in their wake. Some elite Moro families tied themselves to Manila and profited from new relationships with the North, but many Muslims and Lumad experienced these postwar years through cultural marginalization and physical displacement. New incursions from transnational capital, territorial manifestations of which grew out of the plantation economies of the colonial period, compounded these pressures.[27] There was widespread distrust toward the centralizing state, whose rhetoric of minority integration did not translate into genuine democratic action. What began as a series of clashes between Christian and Muslim militias in the late 1960s evolved into a decades-long conflict. Amidst this, Bangsamoro identity served as a means to weave together distinct Muslim groups alienated from the Philippine national body. Organizations like the Moro National Liberation Front and Moro Islamic Liberation Front rose in the 1970s and 1980s. Their struggle manifested in armed conflict against the Philippine military and state-aligned militias and also in modes of political and social activism.[28] The conflict has ebbed and flowed in recent decades but continues to raise challenging questions about identity, representation, integration, and self-determination in postcolonial societies.[29]

In October 2017, government security forces began mopping-up operations in the capital of Lanao Del Sur Province. Marawi, once known as Dansalan, had experienced five months of urban warfare—the most intense in the archipelago since the Second World War. Moro militants affiliated with Abu Sayyaf and ISIS seized control of the community, burning homes and terrorizing Christians, and the Philippine government responded with massive force. Targeted air strikes conducted with U.S. assistance reduced sections of Marawi to rubble, and building-to-building fighting left over a thousand people dead.

Displaced civilians numbered in the hundreds of thousands. Images of Marawi's Grand Mosque showed facades and domes pockmarked by countless rounds of ammunition. Entire neighborhoods were razed to the ground.[30] Newspaper reports inevitably stressed the ideological connections between armed Moros and the Islamic State in Syria and Iraq, rendering the struggle comprehensible to Western audiences habituated to Middle Eastern violence. Historical contextualization, where it appeared, rarely reached back further than the Cold War.[31] As in 1950, so in 2017: colonial empire did not merit attention.

Presentism allows us to recall these histories selectively. Decades of U.S. sovereignty in Mindanao-Sulu can be reduced to the "Moro War" or "Moro Rebellion" and told through a sequence of combat set pieces in which the Muslims of the Southern Philippines are cannon fodder and not much besides. State-building projects become "hearts and minds" operations instead of markers of prolonged colonial control. Transitional regimes blur the borders between imperial and national narratives. In 1919, the journalist José Melencio wrote that the "non-Christians" of the Philippines had been civilized "under the ambient air of Americanism." His aim was to flatter U.S. policy makers into granting the archipelago independence, but his evocative phrase also speaks to the ways in which colonialism permeates societies—its "ambience."[32] In its varied manifestations, the colonial state in Mindanao-Sulu took a comprehensive approach to civilizational transformation, in many cases creating perceptual frameworks and governance strategies that persisted after Philippine independence.

From its inception, U.S. rule in the Muslim South was predicated on notions of reform and reconfiguration. Informed by Spanish texts, North American continental expansion, and precolonial exploration, American colonial actors racialized Moros and validated conquest through prevailing civilizational indexes. They surveyed their new territories and deemed them unsullied frontier space in need of domestication. Moro and Lumad communities became sites to enact wide-ranging educational, legal, medical, and infrastructural programs. These initiatives occasionally flourished with collaboration from native leaders but more often faced degrees of contestation. Individually and collectively, Moros confronted the disorientations wrought by colonialism: the dismantling of pandita schools, erosion of customary law, decline of the datuship, overhaul of labor relations, and importation of settler communities. They did so in a host of ways, from petition writing to protest to armed resistance, and often faced harsh reprisals. American and Filipino officials alike stressed the disciplinary benefits of routinized state violence: "wholesome" lessons for "martial" peoples. Redemptive and exterminationist rationales dovetailed in spaces like Bud Dajo, where military forces killed hundreds of Tausūg Moros in 1906. Coercion also patterned daily life through detention practices, torture, and extrajudicial executions by state security organs.

Moros visited the United States, performing in the human zoos of international expositions, touring northeastern and midwestern cities as dignitaries, and enrolling in university programs. The perceived pedagogical benefits of these tours did not always translate into "tamed" colonial wards content to live under indefinite foreign control, however. Adventure books, radio serials, and films deepened the relationship between the U.S. public and the Muslim South, although they frequently reified long-standing tropes about Moro indolence and savagery. In the Southern Philippines, the indeterminacy (and at times imagined permanency) of rule led white colonials to design their homes, businesses, plantations, and clubs on those found in European colonies. Also shared were notions of tropical breakdown brought about by human and environmental threats. Mindanao-Sulu transformed into a proving ground, where the racial fitness and resolve of the Euro-American colonist was constantly tested.

Shades of exceptionalism colored the rhetoric of white colonials. In his notes for "The Brethren," William Cameron Forbes saw the United States as practicing a form of anticolonial imperialism distinct from traditional European models. From the vantage of 1956, he constructed a teleology linking benevolent assimilation in the Philippines to global decolonization. The reversals and deferrals on the archipelago's uneven path to independence vanished, replaced by a linear tutelary journey. Other empires existed in notes for "The Brethren" to illustrate U.S. improvements on their practices. In many ways, Forbes and his compatriots closed a loop, reproducing distancing strategies used in 1898 to distinguish the United States from Spain. A tidy narrative arc emerged, wherein the nation freed Spain's benighted subjects in the Caribbean Basin and Southeast Asia, perfected systems of colonial management, and solved the problem of imperialism itself. Over time, U.S. colonial empire receded from public view.[33]

The history of Mindanao-Sulu under U.S. rule tells a different story about the global production of colonial culture. Forbes himself traveled to Europe and North Africa to glean expertise from other empires—a practice he shared with many other Americans who served in the Philippines. The military officers responsible for the Moro Province visited the neighboring colonies of Southeast Asia, borrowing ideas about labor, punishment, and governance in the process. Teachers, engineers, soldiers, and merchants moved between imperial formations, stopping in the Muslim South and contributing their expertise to the civilizing mission before moving on. Western empires shared intelligence, coordinated security responses, and facilitated commerce between their colonies. Americans in the Southern Philippines operated amid peoples with their own connections, sometimes tapping into them for self-interested purposes. Moro groups cultivated links with Islamic Southeast Asia and the wider Muslim world, using cultural kinship as a block against the incursions of the colonial state.

We end at the beginning. In April 1899, as the U.S. military prepared to annex Mindanao and the Sulu Archipelago, the *Chicago Daily Tribune* published an article titled "All the Facts Concerning Our New Empire." The piece explained the Southern Philippines through its relationships with the wider world: Spain's struggles on Mindanao, Tausūg trade with Dutch planters on Java, civilizational development relative to the Ottoman Empire, and British native policies in North Borneo.[34] Before warships began cordoning off the waters of the Sulu Sea or John Bates negotiated with Sultan Kiram on Jolo, empire's boosters encouraged its practitioners to govern a region by looking abroad. In the coming decades, those responsible for administrating the South did just that. State imperatives and their responses emerged from regional particularities and national histories, but also from multidirectional exchanges extending beyond colony and metropole. Placed within global histories of empire, the contours of U.S. colonial rule in Mindanao-Sulu become more visible and less exceptional.

Notes

Introduction

1. Collectively, the indigenous Lumad are the second-largest population category in Mindanao. The term covers a diverse range of groups, each with their own cultural and linguistic variances. While Lumad actors appear in the following chapters, this project's primary focus is on U.S.-Moro relations. A comprehensive study of U.S.-Lumad relations in the colonial period remains unwritten. The most thorough study on Lumad interactions with Spanish colonialism is Paredes, *Mountain of Difference*. On designations between "Moro" and "Lumad" and the relations between the two groups, see Paredes, "Indigenous vs. Native," 168–70.

2. John P. Finley, "The Development of the District of Zamboanga," *Mindanao Herald*, February 3, 1909.

3. Finley, "Race Development," 367–68.

4. "Conversation with Major-General Leonard Wood, Governor-General of the Philippine Islands," folder 1, box 217, Leonard Wood Papers, Library of Congress, Washington, DC (hereafter LOC-MD); "Mr. Bryan's Position," *Mindanao Herald*, June 9, 1906.

5. Arolas Tulawie to American Chamber of Commerce (Manila), 1933, folder 31, box 28, Joseph Ralston Hayden Papers, 1899–1945, Bentley Historical Library, University of Michigan, Ann Arbor, Michigan (hereafter BHL).

6. Frederick Palmer, "Americanizing the Southern Philippines," *Collier's Weekly*, September 1, 1900.

7. Sermon, December 22, 1912, box 42, Burton Norvell Harrison Family Papers (hereafter BNHF Papers), 1812–1926, Manuscript Division, LOC-MD.

8. "Spirit of the Island Press," *Mindanao Herald*, February 17, 1906.

9. Examples include Arnold, *Moro War*; Bacevich, "Disagreeable Work," 41–45; Fulton, *Moroland*.

10. The literature includes a discipline-spanning array of analytical approaches. U.S. empire features in books and essays exploring overlapping aspects of globalization, capitalism, race, labor, territoriality, technology, migration, religion, biopolitics, the environment, colonial transfer, violence, domesticity, the environment, law and policing, and many other areas. A necessarily partial

list illustrating the diversity of recent conceptualizations includes Bender and Lipman, "Through the Looking Glass," 1–34; Bulmer-Thomas, *Empire in Retreat*, 1–15; DeLay, "Indian Polities," 927–42; Go, *Patterns of Empire*, 1–27; Greene, *Canal Builders*, 37–74; Hoganson, *Consumers' Imperium*, 13–56; Hopkins, *American Empire*, 10–42; Immerwahr, *Hide an Empire*, 3–19; Karuka, *Empire's Tracks*, 168–184; Kramer "Geopolitics of Mobility," 393–438; McCoy, *Policing America's Empire*, 15–58; Rosenberg and Fitzpatrick, "Introduction," 1–16; Tyrrell, *Reforming the World*, 13–27.

11. Kramer, "Power and Connection," 1348–49. Kramer's essay remains the best historiographical introduction to the topic of U.S. empire.

12. Ballantyne and Burton, "Reach of the Global," 285–305; Burbank and Cooper, *Empires in World History*, 1–22; Osterhammel, *Transformation of the World*, 392–468.

13. A useful typology appears in Osterhammel, *Colonialism*, 1–38.

14. Bjork, *Prairie Imperialists*, 169–204; Gowing, "Moros and Indians," 125–49.

15. Greenberg, *Wicked War*, 67–214; Frymer, *Building an American Empire*, 1–32; Hahn, *Nation without Borders*, 114–91;

16. Blower, "Nation of Outposts," 439–59; Gobat, *Empire by Invitation*, 1–11; Joyce, *Shaping of American Ethnography*, 1–10; Kaomea, "Education for Elimination," 123–44.

17. Colby, *Business of Empire*, 1–18; Gobat, *Confronting the American Dream*, 19–122; McGuinness, *Path of Empire*, 152–199; Renda, *Taking Haiti*, 10–38.

18. The notion of an "Indian problem" was familiar to Americans in the Southern Philippines. Solving racial issues through Christianization, commerce, and settlement has a long lineage in U.S. history. See, for early examples, Conroy-Krutz, *Christian Imperialism*, 19–50.

19. Lawrie, *Forging a Laboring Race*, 1–12; Jacobs, *White Mother*, 229–80.

20. Adas, "Improving on the Civilizing Mission?" 44–66; Go, *American Empire*, 25–54.

21. Recent works highlighting the diversity of these connections include Bender, *Animal Game*, 15–50; Bender, *Nation among Nations*, 182–245; Foster, *Projections of Power*, 73–109; Palen, *"Conspiracy" of Free Trade*, 1–32; Tyrrell, *Wasteful Nation*, 21–38; Zimmerman, *Alabama in Africa*, 112–54.

22. Exceptionalism still surfaces in claims that an imperial lens is the domain of the "pseudoscholarly" and the "postmodern." See Hoffman, *American Umpire*, 333–52. The limitations of the imperial—temporally, territorially, and conceptually—are discussed in Hopkins, *American Empire*, 10–21.

23. Debates over the eventual fate of the South feature in Suzuki, "Upholding Filipino Nationhood," 266–91. After returning to the Philippines to become governor-general, Leonard Wood gave an interview where he claimed only the American presence would prevent bloodshed between Moro and Christian Filipino populations. "Conversation with Major-General Leonard Wood, Governor-General of the Philippine Islands," folder 01, box 217, Leonard Wood Papers, 1825–1942, LOC-MD.

24. The wide-ranging works of Samuel K. Tan are notable. See, for examples, Tan, *Filipino Muslim Armed Struggle*; Tan, *Muslim South and Beyond*; Tan, *Sulu under American Military*; Tan, *Selected Essays*. Cesar Abid Majul's work on the Muslim South was likewise pathbreaking. See, for best example, Majul, *Muslims in the Philippines*. On Maguindanao, see Mastura, *Muslim-Filipino Experience*; Mastura, "Short History," 5–25.

25. Abinales, *Making Mindanao*; Abinales, *Orthodoxy and History*; Chanco, "Frontier Polities and Imaginaries," 111–33; Dacudao, "Ghost in the Machine," 209–26; Dacudao, "Abaca," 27–133.

26. The writings of Peter G. Gowing, who published extensively on the U.S. colonial state in the Southern Philippines and also lived there, are foundational. His major work is Gowing, *Mandate in Moroland*. The most recent book-length treatment on the topic comes from Michael Hawkins, who examines the construction of Moro identities by U.S. authorities. See Hawkins, *Making Moros*. Karine Walther integrates the Muslim South into the global story she tells about U.S.-Islamic relations in Walther, *Sacred Interests*. Other scholars have explored the region and period through varied

lenses, including education, ethnicity, media, violence, and transcultural connection. See, for illustrative examples, Federspiel, *Sultans, Shamans, and Saints*; Marr, "Diasporic Intelligences," 78–106; Milligan, *Islamic Identity*; Gedacht, "'Mohammedan Religion,'" 397–409.

27. Abinales and Amoroso, *State and Society*, 43; Beaujard, "Indian Ocean," 411–65.

28. Wade, "Early Age of Commerce," 258–65; Wendt and Nagel, "Southeast Asia and Oceania," 609–643.

29. Tan, *Sulu under American Military*, 3.

30. Hurley, *Swish of the Kris*, 39.

31. "Juramentados," *Mindanao Herald*, January 17, 1914.

32. Tan, *Sulu under American Military*, 6.

33. Mastura, "Short History," 9.

34. Warriner, "Traditional Authority," 51–56.

35. Non, "Moro Piracy," 413.

36. For examples, see Blair and Robertson, "Defeat of Moro Pirates," 215–26.

37. Non, "Moro Piracy," 408.

38. Warren, "Structure of Slavery," 112–24.

39. Tarling, "Establishment of Colonial Regimes," 27.

40. Abinales and Amoroso, *State and Society*, 70.

41. Abinales, "From *Orang Besar*," 200–210.

42. Tan, *Sulu under American Military*, 18–19.

43. Saleeby, *History of Sulu*, 243–44. The Spanish wrote their own histories of Mindanao and Sulu, often emphasizing the violence and savagery of the inhabitants. For examples, see Aguilar, *Mindanao*. Many of these chroniclers were Jesuit missionaries who accompanied military forces to the interior and were shocked by the resilience of Islamic resistance. The writings of the Jesuit Francisco Combés, originally published in 1667, reappeared in new editions in 1897 as Christian Filipinos mobilized against the Spanish colonial state. In an updated prologue, the civil servant and "Filipinologist" Wenceslao Retana urged readers to heed the words of Combés: "If the dominance of Spain in Mindanao was [then] a legitimate aspiration, we must now regard it as an urgent need." Combés, *Historia de Mindanao*. In 1862, the colonial administrator Agustin Santayana suggested administering the region separately from the rest of the Philippines. See Santayana, *La Isla de Mindanao*.

44. Jeremy Beckett, "Datus," 55.

45. Feuer, *America at War*, 214.

46. Elwell Otis to John Bates, July 3, 1899, folder 1, box 2, John C. Bates Papers, 1807–1922, United States Army Heritage and Education Center, Carlisle, Pennsylvania (hereafter USAHEC).

47. Memorandum, 1899, folder 9, box 2, John Bates Papers, USAHEC.

48. Abinales, "From *Orang Besar*," 200–210.

49. Datu Mandi to William Kobbé, September 10, 1900, folder 12, box 3, William A. Kobbé Papers, 1840–1931, USAHEC.

50. Yegar, *Between Integration and Secession*, 214. The final years of Spanish rule are discussed in Barrows, *Decade of American Government*, 154–59.

51. Adna Chaffee to Henry Corbin, May 4, 1902, box 11, Hugh A. Drum Papers, 1898–1951, USAHEC.

52. Interviews and Interrogations, 1902, box 319, John J. Pershing Papers, 1882–1971, LOC-MD. "Pershing Will Count the Moros He Has Left," *Manila Times*, February 14, 1903.

53. Gowing, *Mandate in Moroland*, 320.

54. Gowing, *Mandate in Moroland*, 112–17.

55. "Legislative Acts of the Moro Province, 1903–1906," box 216, Leonard Wood Papers, LOC-MD; Amoroso, "Inheriting the 'Moro Problem,'" 118–19.

56. "Writ for Man's Head," *Washington Post*, September 17, 1905.

57. Frank McCoy to His Mother, December 5, 1903, folder 4, box 15, Hermann Hagedorn Papers, 1912–1933, LOC-MD.

58. For an extensive but partial description of the events at Dajo, see White, *Bullets and Bolos*, 299–313.

59. Abinales, *Making Mindanao*, 69–77.

60. "Moro Murderers Free by Official Laxity," *Washington Post*, September 19, 1906; Diary of W. Cameron Forbes, Vol. 3, July 7, 1909, W. Cameron Forbes Papers, 1904–1946, LOC-MD.

61. Pershing, *Annual Report 1913*, 65. The events at Bud Bagsak are described in Hurley, *Swish of the Kris*, 121–23. A long list of violent encounters between Muslim groups and Christian Filipinos appears in Tan, *Filipino Muslim Armed Struggle*, 21–27.

62. John Pershing to J. Franklin Bell, November 1, 1913, box 41, BNHF Papers, LOC-MD.

63. Francis Burton Harrison to Lindley Garrison, November 25, 1941, box 41, BNHF Papers, LOC-MD. A paramilitary police force, the PC dealt with unrest in rural areas. During the military period, they had a sometimes tempestuous relationship with U.S. Army officials. An account of their role in the American Philippines is found in McCoy, *Policing America's Empire*, 59–230.

64. J. Franklin Bell to Francis Burton Harrison, November 20, 1913, box 41, BNHF Papers, LOC-MD.

65. A comprehensive breakdown of state authority in the Department of Mindanao and Sulu appears in Gowing, *Mandate in Moroland*, 260–69.

66. Harrison, *Corner-Stone of Philippine Independence*, 75–91; Gowing, *Mandate in Moroland*, 693–704. On economic development during this period, see Hartley, "American Participation."

67. Harrison, *Corner-Stone of Philippine Independence*, 121.

68. Memorandum, box 2, Edward Bowditch Papers, 1907–1957, Division of Rare and Manuscript Collections, Cornell University Library, Ithaca, New York (hereafter DRMC).

69. Agreement between the Governor General of the Philippine Islands and the Sultan of Sulu, March 22, 1915, box 1, Frank W. Carpenter Papers, 1884–1938, LOC-MD.

70. Gowing, *Mandate in Moroland*, 289–308.

71. Carpenter quoted in Gowing, *Mandate in Moroland*, 291; Yegar, *Between Integration and Secession*, 222–24.

72. "Act Making Certain Provisions Relating to the Operation of the Bureau of Non-Christian Tribes," February 20, 1917, box 1, Frank Carpenter Papers, LOC-MD.

73. Report, October 8, 1921, box 1, Dean C. Worcester Papers, 1887–1925, BHL.

74. Yegar, *Between Integration and Secession*, 227.

75. Abinales, *Making Mindanao*, 56.

76. Petition, July 13, 1934, folder 11, box 28, J. R. Hayden Papers, BHL.

77. Abinales, *Making Mindanao*, 58.

78. "Spirit of the Island Press," *Mindanao Herald*, June 23, 1906.

79. Fry, "Bacon Bill of 1926," 257–73.

80. Kratoska and Batson, "Nationalism and Modernist Reform," 264.

81. Abinales, *Making Mindanao*, 62–63.

82. Yegar, *Between Integration and Secession*, 231.

83. "The Crescent Promise," *Mindanao Herald*, November 24, 1906.

1. Imagining the Moro

1. Speech at Zamboanga Fair, February 1907, folder 5, box 43, Tasker H. Bliss Collection, 1829–1956, USAHEC.

2. Said, *Orientalism*, 50.

3. Gobat, "Invention of Latin America," 1345–48. See also Bose, *Hundred Horizons*, 1–36; Hoganson, *Consumers' Imperium*, 1–56; Hui, *Politics of Imagining Asia*, 10–63.

4. The constitution of Moro identity under U.S. authorities is also explored in McKenna, *Muslim Rulers and Rebels*, 105–10.

5. Zantop, *Colonial Fantasies*, 15. A rich body of literature links the ways that perception and fantasy helped chart the development of colonial policy. Examples of this include Bassin, *Imperial Visions*; Geiger, *Facing the Pacific*; Knellwolf, "Exotic Frontier," 10–30; Paxton, *Writing under the Raj*; Watts, *In This Remote Country*. The development of anticolonial or anti-imperial imaginations among subject populations is another consideration. See Anderson, *Under Three Flags*; and Makki, "Culture and Agency," 418–42.

6. Palmer, "Americanizing the Southern Philippines."

7. Untitled Draft, box 1, Carl Eugen Guthe Papers, 1919–1943, BHL.

8. Hunt, *Ideology*, 37.

9. Dwight, "Our Mohammedan Wards," 16.

10. Dalrymple, *Historical Collection*, 1–21; "Biographical Memoir," 186–87; Fry, *Alexander Dalrymple*, 47–48; Forrest, *Voyage to New Guinea*, 309–18. Dalrymple's efforts on behalf of the East India Company are examined in Warren, *Sulu Zone*, 18–27.

11. "Miscellaneous," *The American*, December 21, 1820.

12. "Borneo, Soo-Loo and Banca Company," *City Gazette and Commercial Daily Advertiser*, May 11, 1825.

13. Joyce, *Shaping of American Ethnography*, 10.

14. Wilkes, *Synopsis of the Cruise*, 39; Wilkes, *Narrative*, 348–53.

15. Wilkes, *Narrative*, 325.

16. Wilkes, *Narrative*, 330–31.

17. Jenkins, *Voyage*, 454–55.

18. Jenkins, *Voyage*, 342–43.

19. Clark, *Lights and Shadows*, 247; Pickering, *Races of Man*, 127. The Dutch shared similar preoccupations with "amuck" Malays. The practice of "Atjeh-Moorden" is analyzed in Kloos, "Crazy State," 25–65; and Winzeler, "Amok," 96–122.

20. Wilkes, *Narrative*, 348–55.

21. Their stockpiles eventually formed the backbone of the Smithsonian collections. See Adler, "From the Pacific," 70.

22. Wilkes, *Narrative*, 552

23. "The Sooloo Pirates," *The Albion*, June 21, 1851, 294; Almonte, "Adventure," 371; Kneeland, "Philippine Islands," 73–100; Steere, "Six Weeks," 289–94.

24. Steinmetz, *Devil's Handwriting*, 25.

25. Rice, *Dean Worcester's Fantasy Islands*, 5; Dean C. Worcester, "Spain in the Philippine Islands," *The Independent*, April 14, 1898. A thorough account of Worcester's time in the Philippines appears in Sullivan, *Exemplar of Americanism*.

26. Ferdinand Blumentritt (1853–1913) was a Prague-born professor of ethnology at the University of Leitmeritz. He maintained a long correspondence with José Rizal and, despite never visiting the islands, published extensively on the ethnographic composition of the Philippines. His classificatory schemes were taken up and modified by U.S. officials like Worcester and David Prescott

Barrows. For a brief summary of his work, including views on the Moros, see Blumentritt, *Philip-pines*. Blumentritt and nineteenth-century race science's role in the creation of Filipino national identity is explored in Aguilar, "Tracing Origins," 605–37.

27. Worcester, *Philippine Islands*, 175; Worcester, *Slavery and Peonage*, 5–6.

28. Bates referred to the "friendly relations that have so long existed between the Sultan's people and the people of the United States" in reference to the Wilkes Treaty—Memorandum, 1899, folder 9, box 2, John C. Bates Papers, USAHEC. A typical translation of a Spanish text was Baranera and Laist, *Handbook of the Philippine Islands*, 111–22. Baranera's work derives from his earlier text *Compen-dio de la Historia de Filipinas*. On Bates and the Malay states, see Metcalf, "From One Empire," 25–28.

29. "All the Facts Concerning Our New Empire," *Chicago Daily Tribune*, April 2, 1899; R. H. Little, "Details of the Sulu Compact," *Chicago Daily Tribune*, September 26, 1899; Benjamin, "Our Mohammedan Wards," 675–79.

30. "Wearing the Khaki: Diary of a High Private," 1901–1902, box 1, Walter L. Cutter Papers, 1898–1950, USAHEC. Although Cutter was likely unaware of them, Sudanese religious reformers did circulate through Southeast Asia during this period. These exchanges are discussed in Abush-ouk, "African Scholar," 23–50.

31. "Diary of Pirate-Hunting in the Sulu Archipelago," March 1, 1940, box 1, Charles D. Rhodes Papers, 1940–1949, USAHEC.

32. "Talk Made at Lunch of Fargo Rotary Club," June 18, 1941, folder 2, box 1, Matthew F. Steele Papers, 1880–1953, USAHEC.

33. Interview with Frank McCoy, June 7, 1929, folders 2 and 4, box 15, Hermann Hagedorn Papers, LOC-MD.

34. Salman, *Embarrassment of Slavery*, 1–99; Warren, "Structure of Slavery," 111–28; Non, "Moro Piracy," 401–19.

35. Hurley, *Swish of the Kris*, 7.

36. Cloman, *Myself*, 6–96.

37. White, *Bullets and Bolos*, 189–298.

38. "Moros Do Not Drink," *Boston Daily Globe*, May 13, 1900.

39. The study of Islamic syncretism in Southeast Asia has a long lineage in cultural anthropology, dating back to Geertz in *Islam Observed*. A useful recent study of hybridity and transregional connection is Mandal, *Becoming Arab*, 1–22.

40. Carpenter, *Annual Report 1914*, 354; "The Monkeys Have No Tails in Zamboanga," box 1, Charles F. Ivins Papers, 1933–1934, USAHEC.

41. Sterling Larrabee to Parents, June 18, 1912, box 1, Sterling Loop Larrabee Papers, 1909–1949, USAHEC.

42. Sermon, December 22, 1912, box 42, BNHF Papers, LOC-MD.

43. Dwight, "Our Mohammedan Wards," 27–28.

44. Hurley, *Swish of the Kris*, 75–78.

45. Brownell, "Turning Savages into Citizens," 925.

46. Pershing, *Annual Report 1913*, 64–65. For negative observations on the Filipino character, see also "Diary of a Twelve-Day Tour with Vice-Governor Hayden From Manila to Sulu and Back," September 10, 1935, box 8, Harley Harris Bartlett Papers, 1909–1960, BHL. The journalist Katherine Mayo emphasized these differences even more forcefully: "Between the Moros and the 'Indi-ans,' as the Spaniards called the tribes of the northern Archipelago, the newcomers found a wide difference, both in character and in status. The 'Indian' was a docile, light-brained child-savage, cribbed in his own small jungle range, without well-formed religious beliefs, without law or organized government, without books or written records, without any art save the most rudimentary. The 'Moro,' on the other hand, was a fighter, a sea-rover, a reader of the Koran and a devotee of

the Prophet. His civil laws, like those of his religion, with which they inseparably interlocked, were fixed and clear. His scheme of government and of official control, though simple, was mature. His better classes read and wrote their own languages, using the Hindu syllabaries and the Arabic alphabet. He had a definite system of education. His written records, histories, genealogies and religious works had been preserved for many hundreds of years, and the pride of a chief was in his collection of manuscripts." Mayo, *Isles of Fear*, 283.

47. Diary of Field Service in the Philippines, August 20, 1900, and July 20, 1901, box 1, William Kobbé Papers, USAHEC.

48. "The Sultan of Mindanao," *Atlanta Constitution*, June 17, 1900.

49. Taylor, "Powder Keg in Mindanao," 19.

50. *Eighth Army War Corps*, 21; Russel, *Woman's Journey*, 97–98.

51. "All the Facts Concerning Our New Empire," *Chicago Daily Tribune*, April 2, 1899.

52. Marr, "Diasporic Intelligences," 80–82. The Bureau of Non-Christian Affairs actively promoted ethnographic study, going so far as to provide guidelines. Amateur ethnologists like Maj. Robert Lee Bullard accumulated genealogical data in the Lake Lanao region dating back hundreds of years, compiled a Maranao vocabulary, and interviewed Moros on slavery and political terror. The surviving testimony of a girl enslaved by the Moros gives fascinating detail about the treatment of female slaves. "Genealogy of Moros by Priest Hadji Moro Mohammad," October 30, 1903, box 10, Robert Lee Bullard Papers, 1881–1955, LOC-MD; Undated Oral Testimonies on Moro Slavery, box 10, Robert Lee Bullard Papers, LOC-MD.

53. Gowing, *Mandate in Moroland*, 68.

54. Saleeby, *Studies in Moro History*, 32–33.

55. Saleeby, *History of Sulu*, 10–11.

56. Saleeby summarized his ideas on the Moros and colonial governance in a 1913 piece. In it he advocated on behalf of the Moros and argued for progressive policy changes. Saleeby, *Moro Problem*, 3.

57. Report on Sulu Moros, March 25, 1907, box 2, Edward Bowditch Papers, DRMC; Report on Moro Words, September 5, 1910, box 2, Edward Bowditch Papers, DRMC.

58. Stanley Koch Report, September 1, 1908, box 2, Edward Bowditch Papers, DRMC.

59. Smith, *Report on Sulu Moros*, 1–101.

60. Smith, *Report on Sulu Moros*, 32–64. After military rule, some American PC officers continued these modes of inquiry, albeit to a more limited extent. Maj. Guy O. Fort, who ran the regional Constabulary headquarters in Zamboanga during the 1920s, was "something of an amateur ethnographer." He composed a fifty-page manuscript featuring "questions of an ethnological nature" that he distributed to PC posts around the Southern Philippines. The anthropologist Carl Eugen Guthe visited Zamboanga in 1924 and wrote favorably about Fort's "scientific" approach. Diary, May 19, 1924, box 5, Carl Eugen Guthe Papers, BHL.

61. Elliot, *Vocabulary and Phrase Book*, 7.

62. Porter, *Primer and Vocabulary*.

63. Bartter, *English-Samal Vocabulary*; Buffum and Lynch, *Joloano Moro*. Americans also translated Spanish-language texts on Muslim dialects. See, for example, C. C. Smith, *Grammar of the Maguindanao*.

64. Harrison, *Corner-Stone of Philippine Independence*, 98–99.

65. Orosa, *Sulu Archipelago*, 72–78.

66. Hayden, "What Next," 634.

67. Kuder, "Moros," 126.

68. Richard Barry, "The End of Datto Ali," *Collier's Weekly*, June 9, 1906, 17–19.

69. Onuf, *Jefferson's Empire*, 46; Hinton, "Savages, Subjects, and Sovereigns," 440–46.

70. Preston, *Sword of the Spirit*, 138. Many works probe how these types of race thinking drove transcontinental expansion. See Blackhawk, *Violence over the Land*; Drinnon, *Facing West*; Horsman, *Race and Manifest Destiny*; Prucha, *Great Father*; Wolford, Benvenuto, and Hinton, *Colonial Genocide*.

71. Gedacht, "'Mohammedan Religion,'" 398–99; on Carlisle and Native education programs, see Schumacher, "Colonization through Education," 97–117.

72. Hunt and Levine, *Arc of Empire*, 11–12.

73. Carter, *Myth of the Western*, 1–2.

74. Ellingson, *Noble Savage*, 375.

75. A sustained consideration of frontier transfers is found in Bjork, *Prairie Imperialists*. For continuities in policy and comparatives between Christian Filipinos and Native Americans, see Williams, "United States Indian Policy," 828. British approaches to Malay peoples and their transimperial resonances are explored in detail in Amoroso, *Traditionalism*, 65–99; and Amoroso, "Inheriting the 'Moro Problem,'" 118–47.

76. Gowing, "Moros and Indians," 126–27.

77. Frank Carpenter to Adjutant General, September 17, 1932, box 1, Frank Carpenter Papers, LOC-MD. Other military officials who appear in this book participated in actions against the Native Americans, including John C. Bates, J. Franklin Bell, Adna R. Chaffee, George W. Davis, William August Kobbé, Elwell S. Otis, and Nelson Miles. See Williams, "United States Indian Policy," 828.

78. "Outline of the Life of Charles Everett MacDonald, New York University, Medical Class of 1896," March 10, 1936, folder 9, box 1, Charles E. MacDonald Papers, 1873–1936, USAHEC.

79. Journal, March 22, 1902, folder 7, box 1, Charles W. Hack Papers, 1800–1926, LOC-MD; Journal, December 21, 1901, folder 7, box 1, Charles W. Hack Papers, LOC-MD.

80. "Chapter 1: The Dato of the Malanos," folder 3, box 11, Hugh Drum Papers, USAHEC.

81. Wood and Bliss, *Annual Report 1906*, 44; Dphrepaulezz, "'Right Sort,'" 116.

82. Adas, *Prophets of Rebellion*, 183. For a discussion of Bolton's assassination, see Charbonneau, "'New West in Mindanao,'" 304–23.

83. Francis E. Leupp to Hugh Scott, November 5, 1903, folder 4, box 55, Hugh Lenox Scott Papers, 1582–1981, LOC-MD. Leupp himself was a great advocate of the civilizing mission in North America, going on to publish a book on the topic. Leupp, *Indian and His Problem*.

84. "Says Square Deal Will Win Moros," *New York Times*, December 26, 1913.

85. Bradford, *Scanning the Skies*, 17–18.

86. "Colonel Finley Gives Interesting Account of his Trip on Behalf of the Mohammedan Moros," *Army and Navy Weekly*, July 11, 1914; Finley and Churchill, *Subanu*.

87. Quoted in Hawkins, *Making Moros*, 20.

88. Finley, "Race Development," 352–60.

89. Kramer, *Blood of Government*, 285.

90. *Thirty-Fourth Annual Lake Mohonk Conference*, 4–6.

91. Scott, "Soldier's View," 121.

92. Brent, *Inspiration of Responsibility*, 154–56.

93. Melencio, *Arguments against Philippine Independence*, 27.

94. Juan F. Hilario, "Common Sense: A Filipino's View," *Manila Daily Bulletin*, October 20, 1932.

95. Nicholas Roosevelt, "Fighting Moros Are Like Our Indians," *New York Times*, September 12, 1926.

96. J. A. Hackett and J. H. Sutherland, "A Decennium," *Mindanao Herald*, February 3, 1909; "District of Lanao," *Mindanao Herald*, February 3, 1909.

97. Turner, *Frontier in American History*, 42.

98. Kohout, "From the Field," 138–202.

99. Adas, *Dominance by Design*, 153; Tyrrell, *Crisis*, 39–78.

100. On tabula rasa in British India, see Marriott, *Other Empire*, 133. The cartographic imagination figured heavily in colonial discourse around the world. Mapping or remapping physical geography was often a key feature of colonial control. See Craib, "Relocating Cartography," 481–90; Leibsohn, "Dentro y Fuera de los Muros," 229–51; Sato, "Imagined Peripheries," 119–145; Singaravelou, "Institutionalisation of 'Colonial Geography,'" 149–57.

101. Winichakul, *Siam Mapped*, 99.

102. Kirsch, "Insular Territories," 9–10.

103. Translated Spanish Text, box 319, John Pershing Papers, LOC-MD.

104. Report, April 20, 1903, folder 1, box 1, G. Soulard Turner Papers, April 20–May 13, 1903, USAHEC.

105. Edward Davis to Hugh Scott, December 1, 1903, folder 4, box 55, Hugh Scott Papers, LOC-MD; Leonard Wood to Hugh Scott, October 16, 1903, folder 3, box 55, Hugh Scott Papers, LOC-MD.

106. Roderick Dew to Commanding Officer, October 13, 1909, box 320, John Pershing Papers, LOC-MD.

107. Wood and Bliss, *Annual Report 1906*, 44.

108. Smith, "Geologic Reconnaissance," 473–74; "Mineral Wealth in Mindanao," *Mindanao Herald*, August 10, 1907.

109. The plan was first examined in Baylen and Moore, "Senator John Tyler Morgan," 65–75.

110. George W. Davis to Adna R. Chaffee, April 17, 1902, folder 1, box 1, George W. Davis Papers, 1896–1902, USAHEC; "Chapter 1: The Dato of the Malanos," folder 3, box 11, Hugh Drum Papers, LOC-MD. On African American soldiers in the Philippines, see Shellum, *Black Officer*.

111. George W. Davis to Adna R. Chaffee, April 17, 1902, folder 1, box 1, George W. Davis Papers, USAHEC.

112. Asaka, *Tropical Freedom*, 139–66.

113. George W. Davis to Adna R. Chaffee, April 17, 1902, folder 1, box 1, George W. Davis Papers, USAHEC; Colby, *Business of Empire*, 1–15.

114. The *Herald* believed indigenous labor on Mindanao would be built up under white guidance before importing other settler groups. Plans for Chinese, Italian, and Armenian migration also existed during this period, providing evidence of the frenzied desire to settle the region. "The District of Cotabato," *Mindanao Herald*, February 3, 1909; Charbonneau, "'New West in Mindanao,'" 313. Booker T. Washington engaged with global imperial formations elsewhere; see Zimmerman, *Alabama in Africa*, 20–65.

115. Carpenter, *Annual Report 1914*, 370.

116. Carpenter, *Annual Report 1914*, 372.

117. Frank Carpenter to Dean Worcester, May 13, 1914, box 1, Dean Worcester Papers, BHL.

118. James Fugate to N. J. Hollis, June 15, 1929, folder 28, box 29, J. R. Hayden Papers, BHL.

119. *Department of Mindanao and Sulu*, 17–19.

120. Roberto Villanueva, "Chain of Roads Luring Settlers to Mindanao to Be Finished Next June," *Manila Tribune*, August 2, 1936; "Sulu Sultan Urges Roads for Mindanao," *Manila Daily Bulletin*, August 3, 1931; "Gov't to Push Development of Mindanao," *Manila Tribune*, March 25, 1936.

121. "Cotabato: Largest and Most Fertile Province in the Philippine Islands," 26711–4, box 1123, General Classified Files 1898–1945 (1914–1945 Segment), Record Group 350.3—Entry 5. National Archives Building, College Park, Maryland (hereafter RG 350.3, NA-CP).

122. Frank Laubach to Mission Contributors, September 24, 1938, folder 6, box 2, Frank Laubach Collection, Special Collections Research Center, Syracuse University, New York (hereafter SCRC).

123. Ephraim, "Mindanao Plan," 411–18.

124. "Find Mindanao Ideal for Jews," *Manila Daily Bulletin*, July 3, 1939.

125. "Gen. Aguinaldo Opposes Jews as Colonists," *Manila Daily Bulletin*, April 28, 1939; "Boholanos Oppose Establishment of Jewish Colonies in Mindanao," *Manila Daily Bulletin*, June 5, 1939; "Jews in P. I. to Create Grave Race Problems," *Manila Daily Bulletin*, May 15, 1939; "N.Y. Colonization Experts to Survey Field for Jewish Immigrants," *Manila Daily Bulletin*, February 18, 1939.

126. Ephraim, "Mindanao Plan," 429.

127. The *New York Times* lauded the Moros for "fighting for their very existence, much as the American Indians of old" against a "wave of Filipino immigration" that would surely overwhelm them. "Our Own Mohammedans," *New York Times*, May 18, 1930. Likewise, the *Washington Post* praised Moro cultivation of their land and the organization of their government, in sharp contrast with some of the other writers found in this chapter. Katherine Mayo, "Wholesale Carnage in Moro Region is Prevented Only by Gen. Wood," *Washington Post*, January 3, 1925.

128. Gowing, "Moros and Indians," 143.

2. Courtrooms, Clinics, and Colonies

1. Tasker Bliss, "The Government of the Moro Province and its Problems," *Mindanao Herald*, February 3, 1909.

2. On race, class, and empire in the continental United States during the period under study, see Bender, *American Abyss*, 1–68; Huyssen, *Progressive Inequality*, 63–150; Streeby, *American Sensations*, 3-37.

3. Cooper, *Colonialism in Question*, 3–32; Gouda, *Dutch Culture Overseas*, 11–38.

4. On education, native intellectuals, and anticolonial movements, see Bhattacharya, *Sentinels of Culture*; Govaars, *Dutch Colonial Education*; Hansen, *How to Behave*; Saada, *Empire's Children*; Seth, *Subject Lessons*. On the colonial management of lands, see Ax et al., *Cultivating the Colonies*.

5. A comprehensive survey of colonial medicine is found in Chakrabarti, *Medicine and Empire*. Colonial law is likewise surveyed in Benton, *Law and Colonial Cultures*.

6. McClintock, *Imperial Leather*, 1–18.

7. Speech, January 3, 1914, box 2, Edward Bowditch Papers, DRMC.

8. Bliss, *Annual Report 1907*, 41–42.

9. "Act No. 39: An Act Temporarily to Provide for the Government of the Moros and Other Non-Christian Tribes," Legislative Acts Enacted by the Legislative Council of the Moro Province Council, February 19, 1904, box 216, Leonard Wood Papers, LOC-MD; Gowing, *Mandate in Moroland*, 116; Langhorne, *Annual Report 1904*, 6.

10. "List of Photographs and Other Records Pertaining to the Moros and Pagans of the Southern Philippines," 1912, folder 1, box 1, John P. Finley Papers, 1899–1912, USAHEC.

11. Bliss, *Annual Report 1907*, 42–46; Gowing, *Mandate in Moroland*, 545–46.

12. "Annual Report for Lanao District," June 30, 1907, folder 11, box 1, John McAuley Palmer Papers, 1863–1977, LOC-MD.

13. Sterling Larrabee to Charles Larrabee, November 29, 1911, folder 5, box 2, Sterling Loop Larrabee Papers, USAHEC.

14. Pershing, *Annual Report 1913*, 73.

15. J. Franklin Bell to Francis Burton Harrison, January 27, 1914, box 41, BNHF Papers, LOC-MD.

16. "Exhibit VIII—Sulu Codes, 1878, 1902," folder 28, box 29, J. R. Hayden Papers, BHL. For information on legal matters in the precolonial sultanate, see Warren, *Sulu Zone*, 215–51.

17. "Agreement between the Governor General of the Philippine Islands and the Sultan of Sulu," March 22, 1915, box 1, Frank Carpenter Papers, LOC-MD. In June 1935, Najeeb Saleeby provided commentary on a cyclical letter the sultan issued shortly after the 1915 agreement. The "curt and crude" letter of the sultan, Saleeby made clear, laid out regulations and fines—suggesting a continuation of temporal authority prohibited under the agreement. Najeeb Saleeby to J. R. Hayden, June 17, 1935, folder 2, box 30, J. R. Hayden Papers, BHL.

18. "Conference in My Office with Senator Hadji Butu," July 13, 1929, folder 28, box 28, J. R. Hayden Papers, BHL.

19. "Agama Court Problem," undated, folder 4, box 30, J. R. Hayden Papers, BHL; J. C. Early to Dwight Davis, December 18, 1930, folder 8, box 30, J. R. Hayden Papers, BHL.

20. Gulamu Rasul to Abad Santos, August 5, 1931, folder 8, box 30, J. R. Hayden Papers, BHL.

21. "Memorandum on Policy for the Province of Sulu," September 8, 1934, folder 4, box 30, J. R. Hayden Papers, BHL.

22. Frank Murphy to Jamalul Kiram, October 17, 1934, folder 3, box 30, J. R. Hayden Papers, BHL.

23. Filipino experts and officials dictating legal solutions to the "Moro problem" in the postwar period further alienated Muslim societies from the national government. See Abinales, "American Military Presence," 1–20; Abubakar, "Mindanao Peace Processes," 450–64; Abuza, "Moro Islamic Liberation Front," 453–79; George, *Revolt in Mindanao*.

24. William Howard Taft to Dean Worcester, November 30, 1907, box 1, Dean Worcester Papers, BHL. On networks of medical knowledge, see chap. 5, "Imperialism and the Globalization of Disease," in Chakrabarti, *Medicine and Empire*, 73–100; Coleborne and McCarthy, "Health and Place," 1–11.

25. Diary of Field Service in the Philippines, April 16–19, 1900, box 1, William Kobbé Papers, USAHEC.

26. George Barbour to Hugh Scott, October 14, 1903, folder 5, box 55, Hugh Scott Papers, LOC-MD.

27. Hugh Scott to Leonard Wood, August 17, 1903, folder 6, box 55, Hugh Scott Papers, LOC-MD; "Moros Attacked by Cholera," *Manila Times*, December 10, 1903; "Report on Intelligence-Gathering Trip from Cotabato to Lebac," April 20, 1903, folder 1, box 1, G. Soulard Turner Papers, USAHEC; Orville Wood to Frank McCoy, August 1, 1905, folder 2, box 11, Frank R. McCoy Papers, 1847–1957, LOC-MD; Thomas Darrah to Hermann Hagedorn, September 10, 1929, folders 2–3, box 15, Hermann Hagedorn Papers, LOC-MD.

28. Minutes of the Legislative Council of the Moro Province, January 7, 1905, folder 2, box 216, Leonard Wood Papers, LOC-MD.

29. Wood and Bliss, *Annual Report 1906*, 30–31; Charles Ewing to Tasker Bliss, August 6, 1906, folder 66, box 15, Tasker Bliss Collection, USAHEC.

30. Charles H. Brent, "Giving the Moro-Americans A Chance," *The Independent*, April 26, 1915.

31. *Upbuilding of the Wards of the Nation* (pamphlet), box 44, Charles Henry Brent Papers, 1860–1991, LOC-MD; *The Sixteenth Annual Report of the Missionary District of the Philippine Islands*, 30.

32. Pershing, *Annual Report 1913*, 37–43.

33. Carpenter, *Annual Report 1914*, 346.

34. Carpenter, *Annual Report 1914*, 325.

35. Wood and Forbes, *Report of the Special Mission*, 18.

36. George Lull to Dwight Davis, December 16, 1930, folder 29, box 28, J. R. Hayden Papers, BHL. A powerful typhoon in 1932 also exacerbated public health issues. See American Red Cross, *Sulu Archipelago Typhoon*, 6.

37. J. Scott McCormick to Luther Bewley, December 11, 1933, folder 24, box 29, J. R. Hayden Papers, BHL.

38. George Dunham to J.R. Hayden, April 2, 1934, folder 23, box 29, J. R. Hayden Papers, BHL.

39. "Annual Report of Provincial Governor for Lanao, 1932," January 27, 1933, folder 7, box 28, J. R. Hayden Papers, BHL.

40. On the rest of the Philippines see Anderson, *Colonial Pathologies*, 104–29.

41. Frank Laubach to John Laubach, March 23, 1933, folder 1, box 2, Frank Laubach Collection, SCRC; "Letter," *Lanao Progress*, September 1, 1933.

42. "Visiting Nurse," *Lanao Progress*, March 15, 1935. Nestlé marketed their products elsewhere in the Muslim world. The company's work in the Ottoman Empire, for example, helped set future marketing strategies in non-European countries. Activists have criticized the company's aggressive promotion of infant formula elsewhere. See Koese, "Nestlé," 724–61.

43. Frank Laubach to John Laubach, March 10, 1933, folder 1, box 2, Frank Laubach Collection, SCRC; Frank Laubach to John Laubach, March 23, 1933, folder 1, box 2, Frank Laubach Collection, SCRC.

44. See chap. 5, "Soft-Soaping Empire: Commodity Racism and Imperial Advertising," in McClintock, *Imperial Leather*, 207–31.

45. Report, 1925, box 82, Frank McCoy Papers, LOC-MD.

46. Teofisto Guingona to Frank Murphy, February 23, 1934, folder 8, box 29, J. R. Hayden Papers, BHL.

47. Act No. 55, Legislative Acts Enacted by the Legislative Council of the Moro Province, June 14, 1904, box 216, Leonard Wood Papers, LOC-MD.

48. Hawkins, *Making Moros*, 88.

49. Journal of W. Cameron Forbes, vol. 1, November 30, 1904, W. Cameron Forbes Papers, LOC-MD.

50. Brownell, "American Ideas of Citizenship," 979–81.

51. Brownell, "American Ideas of Citizenship," 983.

52. Report, October 31, 1910, folder 2, box 217, Leonard Wood Papers, LOC-MD.

53. "Memorandum on Activities at Zamboanga during Taft Visit," August 17–18, 1905, folder 3, box 11, Frank McCoy Papers, LOC-MD.

54. Brownell, "American Ideas of Citizenship," 983.

55. "Brief Report of the Basilan Campaign, 1907–1908," folder 6, box 217, Leonard Wood Papers, LOC-MD.

56. John P. Finley, "The Development of the District of Zamboanga," *Mindanao Herald*, February 3, 1909.

57. "Record of Business Conducted at Moro Exchanges and Trading Stores in the District of Zamboanga," June 30, 1911, box 1, folder 1, John Finley Papers, USAHEC.

58. Brownell, "Savages into Citizens," 929.

59. Finley, "District of Zamboanga."

60. Pershing, *Annual Report 1913*, 17–18.

61. "The Subjugation of the Moros and Pagans of the Southern Philippines through the Agency of Their Moral and Industrial Development," September 11, 1912, folder 1, box 1, John Finley Papers, USAHEC.

62. John P. Finley, "Commercial Awakening," 332. The exchanges received attention back in the United States. See "Teaching New York's Trade Tactics to the Moros," *Washington Post*, June 9, 1912.

63. John McAuley Palmer to Tasker Bliss, January 12, 1908, folder 11, box 1, John McAuley Palmer Papers, LOC-MD.

64. For an analysis of white settlement in Mindanao-Sulu, see Charbonneau, "'New West,'" 304–23.

65. Joseph Hayden to Betty Hayden, September 7, 1926, folder 26, box 28, J. R. Hayden Papers, BHL.

66. Hurley, *Southeast of Zamboanga*, 1–60.

67. Tan, *Filipino Muslim Armed Struggle*, 73–76.

68. Abinales, "State Authority," 247–282; Dacudao, "Ghost in the Machine," 29–33.

69. Leonard Wood to Tasker Bliss, July 5, 1906, folder 65, box 15, Tasker Bliss Collection, USAHEC; Leonard Wood to Tasker Bliss, December 1, 1906, folder 68, box 15, Tasker Bliss Collection, USAHEC; Bliss, *Annual Report—Fiscal Year 1907*, 35–36; Finley, "Race Development," 364.

70. Suzuki, "Upholding Filipino Nationhood," 268.

71. Eventually there were six settlements in the Cotabato Valley. See Gowing, *Mandate in Moroland*, 292.

72. "Report on Military Situation—Moro Province and Department Philippines," December 5, 1913, box 218, Leonard Wood Papers, LOC-MD; Carpenter, *Annual Report 1914*, 375.

73. Carpenter, *Annual Report 1914*, 377–78.

74. Frank Carpenter to Pascual de la Serna, March 20, 1914, box 1, Dean Worcester Papers, BHL.

75. Frank Carpenter to Dean Worcester, May 13, 1914, box 1, Dean Worcester Papers, BHL.

76. Photograph Collection, box 2, Edward Bowditch Papers, DRMC.

77. Frank Carpenter to Dean Worcester, May 13, 1914, box 1, Dean Worcester Papers, BHL.

78. Dean Worcester to Frank Carpenter, August 7, 1914, box 1, Dean Worcester Papers, BHL.

79. Gowing, *Mandate in Moroland*, 292–93.

80. Datu Piang to Calvin Coolidge, August 2, 1927, folder 33, box 28, J. R. Hayden Papers, BHL.

81. Report, 1930, folder 7, box 29, J. R. Hayden Papers, BHL.

82. "A Tentative Plan for the Development of Agricultural Colonies under the New Colonization Law," folder 6, box 29, J. R. Hayden Papers, BHL.

83. "Annual Report of the Director of the Bureau of Non-Christian Tribes for the Year 1934," March 11, 1935, box 28, folder 22, J. R. Hayden Papers, BHL.

84. "Government to Push Development of Mindanao," *Manila Tribune*, March 25, 1936.

85. "Subdivision of Huge Tracts of Land in Mindanao Endorsed by Dans," *Manila Daily Bulletin*, June 6, 1936.

86. Roberto Villanueva, "Chain of Roads Luring Settlers to Mindanao to Be Finished Next June," *Manila Tribune*, August 2, 1936; "Mindanao Land Surveys Will Open Region to 6,000 Families Next Year," *Manila Daily Bulletin*, September 8, 1936.

87. "Moros Ask for Homesteads," *Manila Daily Bulletin*, April 24, 1939.

88. "Makes Appeal to Till Lands," *Manila Daily Bulletin*, July 6, 1937.

89. Wernstedt and Simkins, "Migrations," 88.

90. Beckett, "Datus," 50.

91. Wernstedt and Simkins, "Migrations," 92.

92. Abinales, "State Authority," 329.

93. Wernstedt and Simkins, "Migrations," 95.

3. Civilizational Imperatives

1. Milligan, *Islamic Identity*, 41–42.

2. Milligan notes that it is "more appropriately called *makatib*—from the Arabic *kataba*, 'to read.'" Milligan, *Islamic Identity*, 33.

3. Smith, *Report on Sulu Moros*, 48.

4. Milligan, *Islamic Identity*, 43.

5. Elwell Otis to John Bates, July 3, 1899, folder 1, box 2, John Bates Papers, USAHEC.

6. Memorandum, 1899, folder 9, box 2, John Bates Papers, USAHEC.

7. Diary of Field Service in the Philippines, May 21, 1901, box 1, William Kobbé Papers, USAHEC.

8. Stephen Fuqua to Adjutant, September 30, 1903, folder 1, box 1, Joseph A. Marmon Papers, 1902–1932, USAHEC. According to Timothy Marr, in 1904 "only two out of 42 schools [in the province] were exclusively serving Moros." Marr, "Diasporic Intelligences," 85.

9. Marr, "Diasporic Intelligences," 84–85.

10. "Act No. 167: An Act to Require the Attendance of Children at the Public Schools," Legislative Acts Enacted by the Legislative Council of the Moro Province Council, June 20, 1906, box 216, Leonard Wood Papers, LOC-MD.

11. Speech, February 1907, folder 5, box 43, Tasker Bliss Collection, USAHEC.

12. Bliss, *Annual Report 1907*, 13–16.

13. James Reeves to Tasker Bliss, August 1, 1906, folder 65, box 15, Tasker Bliss Collection, USAHEC.

14. E.Z. Steever to Tasker Bliss, December 1, 1906, folder 68, box 15. Tasker Bliss Collection, USAHEC.

15. Charles Cameron to David Barrows, September 24, 1909, box 320, John Pershing Papers, LOC-MD.

16. Bliss, *Annual Report 1907*, 16–17. Cameron further observed: "Certain progress in civilization must be made before the schools, as ordinarily understood, can begin effective work. As a preparatory step, the wild man must establish communal relations and learn to be an orderly and useful member of society, however crude that society may be. Then and only then can the schools begin their task of individual and social development."

17. Female students represented only a fraction of this number. The 1913 provincial report praised the Cotabato Moro Girls' School, run by Anna Dworak, for teaching Maguindanao girls the domestic arts under "the elevating moral influence of the American Christian woman." Pershing, *Annual Report 1913*, 29–32.

18. Saleeby, *Moro Problem*, 29–31.

19. Milligan, *Islamic Identity*, 66; Bliss, *Annual Report 1907*, 36.

20. Milligan, *Islamic Identity*, 62; Charles R. Cameron, "The Schools of Moroland," *Mindanao Herald*, February 3, 1909, 35. Cameron followed his predecessor Saleeby's lead in attempting to document various aspects of Islamic culture in the Southern Philippines. In 1917, he published a compendium of Sulu-Arabic script. See Cameron, *Sulu Writing*.

21. Pershing, *Annual Report 1913*, 33.

22. Pershing, *Annual Report 1913*, 29–30.

23. Carpenter, *Annual Report 1914*, 350–54.

24. James McCall to Captain Gallman, January 16, 1914, box 41, BNHF Papers, LOC-MD.

25. Carpenter, *Annual Report 1914*, 351.

26. Development Program: Bureau of Non-Christian Tribes Scholarships, 1931, folder 2, box 30, J. R. Hayden Papers, BHL.

27. Teofisto Guingona to James Fugate, April 24, 1934, folder 24, box 28, J. R. Hayden Papers, BHL.

28. Gowa Mohammad to J. R. Hayden, July 24, 1935, folder 21, box 28, J. R. Hayden Papers, BHL; J. R. Hayden to Gowa Mohammad, July 30, 1935, folder 21, box 28, J. R. Hayden Papers, BHL.

29. Teofisto Guingona to Arolas Tulawie, July 23, 1920, folder 24, box 29, J. R. Hayden Papers, BHL.

30. "Moro Problem: Excerpt from Annual Report of the Provincial Governor of Lanao for the Year 1933," 1933, folder 9, box 28, J. R. Hayden Papers, BHL.

31. Anti-Catholicism and fears of conversion abounded during this period. Arolas Tulawie to Teofisto Guingona, August 12, 1920, folder 24, box 29, J. R. Hayden Papers, BHL.

32. Report, March 25, 1930, folder 14, box 29, J. R. Hayden Papers, BHL.

33. J. Scott McCormick to Luther Bewley, December 11, 1933, folder 24, box 29, J. R. Hayden Papers, BHL.

34. McKenna, *Muslim Rulers and Rebels*, 109; Kuder, "Moros in the Philippines," 126.

35. Kuder estimated prewar school figures in Cotabato, Lanao, and Sulu as follows: "7 secondary schools, 65–70 complete elementary schools, 250–300 primary schools, 1400–1500 teachers, and 60,000–65,000 pupils." Kuder, "Moros in the Philippines," 126.

36. "Development Plan for Mindanao-Sulu," 1934, folder 8, box 29, J. R. Hayden Papers, BHL; "Annual Report of the Director of the Bureau of Non-Christian Tribes for the Year 1934," March 11, 1935, folder 22, box 28, J. R. Hayden Papers, BHL.

37. Many scholars explore the influence of the Roman Catholic Church and its missionary orders in the Philippines. See Cornelio, "Popular Religion," 471–500. The Church presence in predominantly Muslim areas of Mindanao was limited but did exist. See Arcilla, "Philippine Revolution," 361–77.

38. Clymer, *Protestant Missionaries*, 153–90; Tyrrell, *Reforming the World*, 123–45.

39. "The Filipino Rose Has Its Thorn," *Hartford Courant*, June 30, 1898, 10.

40. Translated Spanish Text, box 319, John Pershing Papers, LOC-MD.

41. "A Few Facts about the Work of the Moro Educational Foundation," 1924, 28011, box 1277, General Classified Files 1898–1945 (1914–1945 Segment), RG 350.3, NA-CP.

42. Norbeck, "Charles Henry Brent," 164.

43. Foster, "Prohibition as Superiority," 253–73; chap. 7, "Opium and the Fashioning of the American Moral Empire," in Tyrrell, *Reforming the World*, 146–65.

44. "Proceedings of the Memorial Anniversary Dinner Held under the Auspices of the National Committee for the Moro School, Jolo, Philippine Islands and the Bishop Brent International Memorial Committee," December 17, 1939, 28011, box 1277, General Classified Files 1898–1945 (1914–1945 Segment), RG 350.3, NA-CP; Neill, "Charles Henry Brent," 158.

45. "Lorillard Spencer Is Dead," *New York Times*, March 15, 1912; "Mrs. L. Spencer Dies in Home at Newport," April 7, 1948; "Forsakes Society to Teach Murderous Moros," *New York Times*, December 14, 1913.

46. "Forsakes Society to Teach Murderous Moros," *New York Times*, December 14, 1913.

47. Journal of W. Cameron Forbes, vol. 4, February 5, 1911, W. Cameron Forbes Papers, LOC-MD.

48. Wainright, "Blue Wings over Sulu," 511. Another hagiographic account described Spencer and Brent disarming bandits by conversing with them. Slater, *Charles Henry Brent*, 23.

49. Caroline S. Spencer, "What the Golden Rule Has Taught the Moros," Pamphlet Reprinted by MEF from Newspaper Interviews, February 14 and 21, 1915, 28011, box 1277, General Classified Files 1898–1945 (1914–1945 Segment), RG 350.3, NA-CP; Carpenter, *Annual Report 1914*, 389.

50. "Upbuilding the Wards of the Nation," 1913, Charles Brent Papers, LOC-MD.

51. "School Works Magical Changes in the Moros," *New York Times*, April 27, 1924; J. W. Light to Caroline Spencer, September 4, 1920, 28011, box 1277, General Classified Files 1898–1945 (1914–1945 Segment), RG 350.3, NA-CP; "Upbuilding the Wards of the Nation," 1913, Charles Brent Papers, LOC-MD.

52. Photographs of the Willard Straight Agricultural School for Boys, 1910–1920s, 28011, box 1277, General Classified Files 1898–1945 (1914–1945 Segment), RG 350.3, NA-CP; MEF Press Material, 1930, 28011, box 1277, General Classified Files 1898–1945 (1914–1945 Segment), RG 350.3, NA-CP.

53. "Forsakes Society to Teach Murderous Moros," *New York Times*, December 14, 1913; "School Works Magical Changes in the Moros," *New York Times*, April 27, 1924; Eleanor Crosby Kemp, "Is the United States Educating the People of the Philippines?" *International Interpreter*, April 26, 1924. Reprinted as "Sound and Effective Educational Plan," 28011, box 1277, General Classified Files 1898–1945 (1914–1945 Segment), RG 350.3, NA-CP.

54. "Investments to Date on the Moro Educational Foundation," 1924, box 47, Charles Brent Papers, LOC-MD.

55. Arolas Tulawie to Teofisto Guingona, August 12, 1920, folder 24, box 29, J. R. Hayden Papers, BHL.

56. "Missionary District of the Philippine Islands," 1937, box 47, Charles Brent Papers, LOC-MD; Pickens, "Moros of the Philippines," 36.

57. MEF Press Material, 1930, 28011, box 1277, General Classified Files 1898–1945 (1914–1945 Segment), RG 350.3, NA-CP; "Missionary District of the Philippine Islands," 1937, box 47, Charles Brent Papers, LOC-MD.

58. "Necrology," *Michigan Alumnus*, June 10, 1939; Dumont, *Visayan Vignettes*, 23; Journal of W. Cameron Forbes, vol. 3, July 15, 1909, W. Cameron Forbes Papers, LOC-MD.

59. Charles Brent to Dean Worcester, September 26, 1914, box 1, Dean Worcester Papers, BHL; "The Sulu Press," 1924, box 47, Charles Brent Papers, LOC-MD; Carpenter, *Annual Report 1914*, 389.

60. "Motherhood," *Student Weekly*, March 7, 1925.

61. Authorities cleared PC officers of any fault as it was determined the suspect had been shot "while juramentado," a common claim in police records. "Insane Man Killed by Constabulary," *Student Weekly*, September 4, 1926; "School Notes," *Student Weekly*, March 7, 1925.

62. James Fugate to Caroline Spencer, November 5, 1924, folder 27, box 29, J. R. Hayden Papers, BHL; James Fugate to Charles Brent, June 17, 1924, folder 27, box 29, J. R. Hayden Papers, BHL; Charles Brent to James Fugate, June 24, 1924, folder 27, box 29, J. R. Hayden Papers, BHL; Frank Mosher to Charles Brent, June 2, 1924, folder 27, box 29, J. R. Hayden Papers, BHL.

63. James Fugate to Charles Brent, April 15, 1927, folder 27, box 29, J. R. Hayden Papers, BHL.

64. "Proceedings of the Memorial Anniversary Dinner Held under the Auspices of the National Committee for the Moro School, Jolo, Philippine Islands and the Bishop Brent International Memorial Committee," December 17, 1939, 28011, box 1277, General Classified Files 1898–1945 (1914–1945 Segment), RG 350.3, NA-CP.

65. "Proceedings," December 17, 1939, RG 350.3, NA-CP.

66. Charles Henry Brent, "The Romance of Missions and their Lack of Romance," *Philippine Presbyterian*, 1910. Clipping in box 44, Charles Brent Papers, LOC-MD.

67. "Proceedings," December 17, 1939, RG 350.3, NA-CP.

68. MEF Press Material, 1930, 28011, box 1277, General Classified Files 1898–1945 (1914–1945 Segment), RG 350.3, NA-CP.

69. A. C. Hudson, "Bishop Brent's Moro School, Wrecked by Typhoon, to Be Restored," *Washington Post*, December 2, 1932.

70. W. Cameron Forbes to Manuel Quezon, December 9, 1940, 28011, box 1277, General Classified Files 1898–1945 (1914–1945 Segment), RG 350.3, NA-CP; W. Cameron Forbes to Henry Stimson, January 13, 1941, 28011, box 1277, General Classified Files 1898–1945 (1914–1945 Segment), RG 350.3, NA-CP.

71. Richard Ely to E. A. Regnier, January 30, 1941, 28011, box 1277, General Classified Files 1898–1945 (1914–1945 Segment), RG 350.3, NA-CP.

72. On missionary education in Lanao, see Carter, "Implicit Evangelism," 73–96.

73. "Problems in Religious Education on the Island of Mindanao," March 24, 1913, folder 4, box 126, Frank Laubach Collection, SCRC.

74. His books included Laubach, *People of the Philippines*; and Laubach, *Rizal*.

75. Gowing, "Frank Charles Laubach," 59; Laubach, "What Shall We Do," 3–23.

76. Frank Laubach to *The Argus*, January 14, 1930, folder 3, box 1, Frank Laubach Collection, SCRC. *The Argus* was a newspaper published in Benton between 1892 and 1969. While in Lanao, Laubach began writing letters to the newspaper for publication in lieu of sending out multiple copies to various family members and friends.

77. Frank Laubach to *The Argus*, January 15, 1930, folder 3, box 1, Frank Laubach Collection, SCRC; Frank Laubach to *The Argus*, January 20, 1930, folder 3, box 1, Frank Laubach Collection, SCRC. Laubach's reflections on intercessory prayer continues to interest Christian groups.

78. Frank Laubach to John Laubach, April 22, 1930, folder 3, box 1, Frank Laubach Collection, SCRC.

79. This dichotomy was on full display when he met with prominent Maranao leaders in February 1930. He recounted the experience in a letter home: "Half of the distinguished friends out on the deck yonder are Mohammedan priests, who have been showing me the Koran and Mohammedan literature while I was genuinely interested. Twice a pandita especially interested in me, who called me his 'father', pointed to me and said to the other 'He is a Moslem.' I replied 'I am a friend of the Moslems' and smiled. It satisfied him. Suppose I said, 'I am a Christian minister.' Would I tell him the truth? No for what I would seem to say would be, 'I belong to the sect which hates and tries to destroy Moslems.' I am NOT a Christian—not that kind of Christian, for I love these Moslems. I want them to hang onto every fine thing in their religion, and I want them to endeavor to love the beauty of Jesus in addition—and I want the so-called Christian world to discover the love and begin to follow the beauty of Jesus." Frank Laubach to *The Argus*, March 1, 1930, folder 3, box 1, Frank Laubach Collection, SCRC.

80. *Lanao Progress*, September 1, 1934.

81. Frank Laubach to *The Argus*, 29 January 1930, box 1, folder 3, Frank Laubach Collection, SCRC.

82. "Method I: The Lanao Key System," folder 5, box 131, Frank Laubach Collection, SCRC; Gowing, "Frank Charles Laubach," 60.

83. Frank Laubach to J. R. Hayden, June 22, 1934, folder 11, box 28, J. R. Hayden Papers, BHL.

84. "Maranaw Folk School: Address to the Public," April 20, 1932, folder 5, box 131, Frank Laubach Collection, SCRC.

85. "Annual Report of Provincial Governor for Lanao, 1932," January 27, 1933, folder 7, box 28, J. R. Hayden Papers, BHL.

86. "Diary of a Twelve-Day Tour with Vice-Governor Hayden from Manila to Sulu and Back," September 11, 1935, box 8, Harley Harris Bartlett Papers, BHL; "Method I: The Lanao Key System," folder 5, box 131, Frank Laubach Collection, SCRC.

87. "Don't Drink, Maranaws!" *Lanao Progress*, October 15, 1940.

88. "Progress and Women," *Lanao Progress*, November 1, 1933.

89. "Do We Really Want a Dictatorship," *Lanao Progress*, October 15, 1940.

90. "Shark vs. Octopus," *Lanao Progress*, November 1, 1933; "Murder in His Eye," *Lanao Progress*, September 1, 1934. In the late 1930s the publication took on a youth focus, advertising itself as "wholesome, uplifting, educational, and cultural." "Lanao Progress: School Supplement," *Lanao Progress*, April 15, 1941.

91. Laubach, "Odyssey from Lanao," 459–68. Laubach's version was transcribed in verse, but an earlier telling in prose had appeared as Porter, "Story of Bantugan," 143–61.

92. "Diary of a Twelve-Day Tour with Vice-Governor Hayden from Manila to Sulu and Back," September 11, 1935, box 8, Harley Harris Bartlett Papers, BHL.

93. Reilly, "Collecting the People," 160–68; "The Literacy Laboratory in Lanao," folder 5, box 131, Frank Laubach Collection, SCRC; "Method I: The Lanao Key System," folder 5, box 131, Frank Laubach Collection, SCRC.

94. "Alphabet Is Taming Moros," *Boston Daily Globe*, July 13, 1931.

95. Arthur Mayhew to Frank Laubach, March 12, 1934, folder 11, box 28, J. R. Hayden Papers, BHL; Samuel T. Moyer to Frank Laubach, March 22, 1934, folder 11, box 28, J. R. Hayden Papers, BHL; Elaine Swenson to Frank Laubach, March 28, 1934, folder 11, box 28, J. R. Hayden Papers, BHL. On Arthur Mayhew, see Whitehead, *Colonial Educators*, 149–70.

96. "The Literacy Laboratory in Lanao," folder 5, box 131, Frank Laubach Collection, SCRC.

97. "Letters," *Lanao Progress*, July 1, 1935; "Progress of Literacy Campaign in Lanao Province, Philippine Islands, 1930–1934," 1934, folder 5, box 131, Frank Laubach Collection, SCRC.

98. Laubach, "Christianity and Islam," 47.

99. Laubach, "My Approach," 113–14.

100. Minutes of the Society of English-Speaking Youth, July–August 1934, folder 4, box 131, Frank Laubach Collection, SCRC; Laubach, *Planning Ahead*, 1.

101. Frank Laubach to David Mills, July 22, 1937, folder 6, box 2, Frank Laubach Collection, SCRC.

102. Laubach articulated his global vision in a 1951 book, discussing his experiences in Lanao in the context of social issues worldwide, the Cold War, and the need for literacy drives: Laubach, *Wake Up*. Biographies of Laubach published during his lifetime and after his death in 1970 are largely hagiographic. See, for instance, Roberts, *Champion*.

103. Henry Stimson to Hiram Bingham III, February 15, 1932, box 83, Frank McCoy Papers, LOC-MD.

104. Arolas Tulawie to American Chamber of Commerce, 1933, folder 31, box 28, J. R. Hayden Papers, BHL

4. Corrective Violence

1. "50 Moros Slain in Religious War," *Chicago Daily Tribune*, August 8, 1923.

2. Walter, *Colonial Violence*, 14–15.

3. Vann, "Of Pirates," 40–41.

4. Kramer, "Race-Making and Colonial Violence," 169–210.

5. Foucault, *Discipline and Punish*, 303–8.

6. Zinoman, *Colonial Bastille*, 6–7.

7. Americans experimented with modern penology and prison labor elsewhere in the Philippines and in their other colonies, as did European empires. On the U.S. colonial context, see Salman,

"'Prison That Makes Men,'" 116–30; Santiago-Valles, "American Penal Forms," 87–96. European colonial punishment and detention is explored in Brown, *Penal Power;* and Dikötter and Brown, *Cultures of Confinement.*

8. This was not uniquely American. On the close relationship between violence and the construction of racial difference in the British Empire, see Rand and Wagner, "Recruiting the 'Martial Races,'" 232–54; Wagner, "Savage Warfare," 217–35.

9. E. W. Chapman to J. R. Hayden, August 20, 1934, folder 1, box 30, J. R. Hayden Papers, BHL. Tabawan is in the Tawi-Tawi island group, a maritime border zone close to British North Borneo. Unreliable communications networks, resistance to secular education, and geographic isolation posed challenges to the U.S. colonial state. See Horvatich, "Martyr and the Mayor," 28–32.

10. Angeles, "Moros in the Media," 34.

11. Andriolo, "Murder by Suicide," 738.

12. Translated Spanish text, box 319, John Pershing Papers, LOC-MD.

13. Frank McCoy to His Mother, September 3, 1903, folder 2, box 15, Hermann Hagedorn Papers, LOC-MD. Charles Ivins related an identical story about John Pershing in "The Monkeys Have No Tails in Zamboanga," box 1, Charles Ivins Papers, USAHEC.

14. "Note and History of the Life of the Undersigned and His Relations with the Spaniards and Americans," September 10, 1900, folder 12, box 3, William Kobbé Papers, USAHEC.

15. Memorandum, Summer 1899, folder 9, box 2, John Bates Papers, USAHEC.

16. Frank McCoy to His Mother, September 3, 1903, folder 2, box 15, Hermann Hagedorn Papers, LOC-MD.

17. "Details of the Sulu Compact," *Chicago Daily Tribune,* September 26, 1899.

18. "Juramentados," *Mindanao Herald,* January 17, 1914.

19. Pershing, *Annual Report 1913,* 70–71.

20. "Insane Man Killed by Constabulary," *Student Weekly,* September 4, 1926; Memorandum, September 8, 1934, folder 4, box 30, J. R. Hayden Papers, BHL.

21. Russell, *Outlook for the Philippines,* 266.

22. Report, March 1913, box 38, BNHF Papers, LOC-MD.

23. "When Moros Run Amuck," *Washington Post,* January 14, 1912.

24. "Buried Pig with Moros," *New York Times,* December 22, 1903. The story still circulated decades later in vernacular stories about American daring in the Philippines. See "A Reasonable Profit: The Story of a Fight," *Boston Daily Globe,* November 27, 1927.

25. Hurley, *Swish of the Kris,* 119.

26. David Mikkelson, "General Pershing on How to Stop Islamic Terrorists," Snopes, accessed January 11, 2019, https://www.snopes.com/fact-check/general-pershing-stop-islamic-terrorists/. This practice has been mythologized and celebrated by Donald Trump and others in the post-9/11 era. The imperial resonances of the U.S. War on Terror are examined in Kramer, "Enemy You Can Depend On," 3–9.

27. White, *Bullets and Bolos,* 295.

28. White, *Bullets and Bolos,* 293.

29. Hurley, *Swish of the Kris,* 66–68.

30. Freer, *Philippine Experiences,* 266.

31. Laubach, "What Shall We Do," 15; Russel, *Woman's Journey,* 149; "The Monkeys Have No Tails in Zamboanga," box 1, Charles Ivins Papers, USAHEC.

32. Dale, "Religious Suicide," 56.

33. Adas, *Prophets of Rebellion,* 183.

34. Adna Chaffee to Henry Corbin, April 24, 1902, box 11, Hugh Drum Papers, USAHEC.

35. Adna Chaffee to Henry Corbin, May 13, 1902, box 11, Hugh Drum Papers, USAHEC.

36. "Pershing Takes Seven Moro Forts and Moves on the Sultan of Maciu," *Manila Cable-News*, November 23, 1902.

37. "Hundred Moros Killed; Pershing Captures Bacolod," *Chicago Evening Post*, April 10, 1903.

38. Hugh Scott to Mary Scott, November 16, 1903, folder 4, box 55, Hugh Scott Papers, LOC-MD; Hugh Scott to Leonard Wood, August 17, 1903, folder 6, box 55, Hugh Scott Papers, LOC-MD; Fulton, *Moroland*, 215.

39. White, *Bullets and Bolos*, 216; Fulton, *Moroland*, 246.

40. Hurley, *Swish of the Kris*, 91.

41. Leonard Wood to Tasker Bliss, April 16, 1906, folder 1, box 15, Tasker Bliss Collection, USAHEC.

42. Frank McCoy to J. J. Crittenden, November 1, 1905, folder 3, box 11, Frank McCoy Papers, LOC-MD; "Investigation Made by First Lieutenant Arthur Poilon, 14th Cavalry, Aid-de-Camp, per Verbal Instructions of the Department Commander," May 1906, folder 6, box 11, Frank Mc-Coy Papers, LOC-MD; George Langhorne to C. C. Gilbert, June 13, 1906, folder 6, box 11, Frank McCoy Papers, LOC-MD; Carpenter, *Annual Report 1914*, 338.

43. "History of Troop 'M' 14th Cavalry from its organization, April 25th 1901 to the present Date," January 17, 1906, folder 3, box 1, Marvin C. Hepler Papers, 1901–1969, USAHEC.

44. Langhorne, *Annual Report 1905*, 30.

45. Hurley, *Swish of the Kris*, 95.

46. Quoted in Fulton, *Honor for the Flag*, 96.

47. "Report of Engagement with the Moro Enemy on Bud Dajo, Island of Jolo," March 10, 1906, folder 6, box 217, Leonard Wood Papers, LOC-MD.

48. "Report of Engagement with the Moro Enemy on Bud Dajo, Island of Jolo," March 10, 1906, folder 6, box 217, Leonard Wood Papers, LOC-MD.

49. Fulton, *Honor for the Flag*, 153–54.

50. "Report of Engagement with the Moro Enemy on Bud Dajo, Island of Jolo," March 10, 1906, folder 6, box 217, Leonard Wood Papers, LOC-MD.

51. "Moros Slain in Fierce Battle," *Washington Post*, March 10, 1906.

52. "First Hand Story of the Jolo Fight," *Hartford Courant*, May 28, 1906; "Moros Tried Murder," *Washington Post*, March 21, 1906, 9.

53. Scott, *Some Memories*, 353; Wood and Bliss, *Annual Report 1906*, 3.

54. Hawkins, "Managing a Massacre," 102.

55. A Scathing Comment," *The Globe*, March 20, 1906; "The Latest Moro Slaughter," *The Nation*, March 15, 1906; "The 'Battle' at Jolo: Charges of Inhumanity in Congress," *Manchester Guardian*, March 16, 1906.

56. Storey, *Moro Massacre*, 1–3. A pamphlet adapted from a letter to the *Boston Daily Advertiser* by fellow Anti-Imperialist League member Edward Abbott was also distributed: Abbott, *Battle of the Crater*. The massacre of the Moros at Bud Dajo became part of a larger ongoing conversation about the relationship between United States and empire. See examples in Beaupre, "'What Are the Philippines,'" 711–27; Harris, "Women, Anti-Imperialism," 307–26; Tyrrell and Sexton, *Empire's Twin*.

57. Mark Twain, "Comments on the Moro Massacre, 12 and 14 March 1906," quoted in Zwick, *Weapons of Satire*, 168–78.

58. "'Fake' News of Jolo," *Hartford Courant*, March 20, 1906.

59. W. Morgan Shuster to Leonard Wood, May 23, 1906, folder 6, box 11, Frank McCoy Papers, LOC-MD. The contents of the letter mention that the photograph has "the appearance of having been taken from a broken negative which had been restored," suggesting that this was de-

rived from the glass plate negative Leonard Wood had "accidentally" broken. For more information on questions surrounding the photograph, see Fulton, *Honor for the Flag*, 51.

60. The photographs resembled those from colonial hunting expeditions and anticipated a darker turn in conflict imagery as the personal camera became more common in the following decades. The topic is discussed in Brower, "Trophy Shots," 21–22.

61. "The Week," *The Nation*, March 15, 1906; Byler, "Pacifying the Moros," 44.

62. Fulton, *Moroland*, 343; "Brief Report of the Basilan Campaign 1907–1908," folder 6, box 217, Leonard Wood Papers, LOC-MD; Amirell, "Pirates and Pearls," 46–47.

63. Amirell, "Pirates and Pearls," 48–49.

64. "Gun Boats on Man Hunt," *New York Times*, May 10, 1909.

65. "Diary of Pirate-Hunting in the Sulu Archipelago," 1909, box 1, Charles Rhodes Papers, USAHEC; Amirell, "Pirates and Pearls," 59–66.

66. Journal of W. Cameron Forbes, vol. 3, July 4–9, 1909, W. Cameron Forbes Papers, LOC-MD.

67. "When Our Own Pet Pirates Break Loose," *Atlanta Constitution*, June 25, 1911; "When Moros Run Amuck," *Washington Post*, January 14, 1912.

68. "A Moro Boy Talks of his Native Sululand," January 17, 1931, folder 10, box 30, J. R. Hayden Papers, BHL.

69. Constabulary Report, February 14, 1922, folder 27, box 28, J. R. Hayden Papers, BHL; Constabulary Report, February 6, 1923, folder 27, box 28, J. R. Hayden Papers, BHL

70. Pastor C. Soriano to PC Adjutant, December 10, 1920, folder 6, box 217, Leonard Wood Papers, LOC-MD.

71. Russell, *Outlook for the Philippines*, 277–78.

72. Report, January 3, 1921, folder 6, box 217, Leonard Wood Papers, LOC-MD.

73. C. E. Nathorst to Ole Waloe, January 21, 1921, folder 6, box 217, Leonard Wood Papers, LOC-MD.

74. C. E. Nathorst to Ole Waloe, September 8, 1921, folder 6, box 217, Leonard Wood Papers, LOC-MD.

75. C. E. Nathorst to Ole Waloe, September 9–12, 1921, folder 6, box 217, Leonard Wood Papers, LOC-MD; C. E. Nathorst to Ole Waloe, September 21, 1921, folder 6, box 217, Leonard Wood Papers, LOC-MD.

76. Constabulary Report, January 30, 1924, folder 27, box 28, J. R. Hayden Papers, BHL.

77. Constabulary Report, February 20, 1930, folder 27, box 28, J. R. Hayden Papers, BHL.

78. Constabulary Report, January 29, 1925, folder 27, box 28, J. R. Hayden Papers, BHL.

79. "Annual Report of Provincial Governor for Lanao, Year 1932," January 27, 1933, folder 7, box 28, J. R. Hayden Papers, BHL.

80. "Ambushed by Dimakaling," *Lanao Progress*, September 1, 1933.

81. Kawashima, "'Fearful Ruler of Lanao,'" 81.

82. Luther B. Bewley to Frank Murphy, July 2, 1934, folder 11, box 28, J. R. Hayden Papers, BHL.

83. "Dimakaling Followers Die," *Lanao Progress*, September 1, 1934.

84. Minutes of the Society of Educated Youth, August 6, 1934, folder 4, box 131, Frank Laubach Collection, SCRC.

85. "Diary of a Twelve-Day Tour with Vice-Governor Hayden from Manila to Sulu and Back," September 11, 1935, box 8, Harley Harris Bartlett Papers. BHL.

86. "Trail's End for Dimakaling," *Philippines Free Press*, November 30, 1935.

87. Hobsbawm, *Bandits*, 140–45.

88. Report, January 24, 1935, folder 1, box 30, J. R. Hayden Papers, BHL; Charles Cameron to David P. Barrows, September 24, 1909, box 320, John Pershing Papers, LOC-MD.

89. "Juramentado Kills Woman, Wounds Three," July 11, 1936, box 30, folder 11, J. R. Hayden Papers, BHL; "Moro in Jolo Runs Amuck," May 25, 1937, folder 1, box 29, J. R. Hayden Papers, BHL.

90. A large number of press clippings on crimes in Mindanao and Sulu are included in box 28, folders 16–17, J. R. Hayden Papers, BHL.

91. This was certainly the case on Jolo. One set of documents from the Sulu Sultanate features complaints about stolen horses, extortion rings, dead buffalos, cattle raids, opium sales, purloined slaves, and arson, not to mention local leaders on Jolo warning Americans to steer clear of internecine conflicts between them. See folders 1–8, set 1, Records of the Sultanate of the Sulu Archipelago, LOC-MD.

92. Diary of Field Service in the Philippines 1898–1901, May 9, 1900, William Kobbé Papers, USAHEC.

93. Stephen Fuqua to Adjutant, September 30, 1903. folder 1, box 1, Joseph Marmon Papers, USAHEC.

94. "Moro Murderers Free by Official Laxity," *Washington Post*, September 19, 1906.

95. Journal of W. Cameron Forbes, vol. 1, October 23, 1904, W. Cameron Forbes Papers, LOC-MD; Leonard Wood to W. Cameron Forbes, March 17, 1905, folder 1, box 11, Frank McCoy Papers, LOC-MD.

96. Leonard Wood to W. Cameron Forbes, March 18, 1905, folder 1, box 11, Frank McCoy Papers, LOC-MD.

97. Bliss, *Annual Report 1907*, 21.

98. "Public Works of the Moro Province," *Mindanao Herald*, February 3, 1909.

99. Bankoff, "Deportation," 444.

100. Bankoff, "Deportation," 454–55.

101. Frank G. Carpenter, "Moros Do Not Drink," *Boston Daily Globe*, May 13, 1900.

102. George Langhorne to Hugh Scott, folder 5, box 55, Hugh Scott Papers, LOC-MD.

103. Minutes of the Legislative Council of the Moro Province, September 29, 1905, folder 3, box 216, Leonard Wood Papers, LOC-MD.

104. Wood and Bliss, *Annual Report 1906*, 24; Bliss, *Annual Report 1908*, 16.

105. Wood and Bliss, *Annual Report 1906*, 85.

106. Hoyt, *Annual Report 1909*, 10.

107. Pershing, *Annual Report 1913*, 112.

108. Pershing, *Annual Report 1913*, 15.

109. W. H. Dade to Judge Ingersoll, November 14, 1913, box 41, BNHF Papers, LOC-MD.

110. Pershing, *Annual Report 1913*, 14.

111. Carpenter, *Annual Report 1914*, 355.

112. Russell, *Outlook for the Philippines*, 58–59.

113. Carpenter, *Annual Report 1914*, 355.

114. J. R. Hayden to Betty Hayden, September 17, 1926, folder 26, box 28, J. R. Hayden Papers, BHL.

115. Laubach, "What Shall We Do," 18–19.

116. "A Tentative Plan for the Development of Agricultural Colonies under the New Colonization Law," folder 6, box 29, J. R. Hayden Papers, BHL.

117. Juan C. Orendain, "Davao Colony Is Model Work in Penology," *Manila Daily Bulletin*, April 25, 1936.

118. "The Administration of Justice in the Philippine Islands," 1921, box 82, Frank McCoy Papers, LOC-MD; LawPhil Project (Philippine Laws and Jurisdiction Databank), "The United States Vs. Jose I. Baluyot," accessed November 2, 2014, http://www.lawphil.net/judjuris/juri1919/nov1919/gr_l-14476_1919.html.

119. Wood and Forbes, *Report*, 27–28.

120. "Administration of Justice," 1921, box 82, Frank McCoy Papers, LOC-MD.

121. J. R. Hayden to Frank Murphy, April 20, 1934, folder 9, box 30, J. R. Hayden Papers, BHL.

122. "Administration of Justice," 1921, box 82, Frank McCoy Papers, LOC-MD; C. E. Nathorst to Ole Waloe, September 12, 1921, folder 6, box 217, Leonard Wood Papers, LOC-MD.

123. J. J. Heffington to Teopisto Guingona, August 3, 1934, folder 12, box 28, J. R. Hayden Papers, BHL.

124. Edward M. Kuder to J. R. Hayden, April 12, 1934, folder 24, box 28, J. R. Hayden Papers, BHL.

125. J. J. Heffington to Teopisto Guingona, August 3, 1934, folder 12, box 28, J. R. Hayden Papers, BHL.

126. "Scenes in a War 350 Years Old That Americans Are about to End," *Washington Post*, July 22, 1913.

127. Pershing, *Annual Report 1913*, 68.

128. "Annual Report the Governor Lanao for the Year Ending December 31, 1937," folder 8, box 28, J. R. Hayden Papers, BHL. They were no better in the 1920s, when Hayden claimed the school superintendent was not able to make his inspection tours without an armed escort. Hayden, "What Next," 642.

129. Werth, *Cannibal Island*, 178.

130. Minnie Schultz to Mission Contributors, January 8, 1938, folder 6, box 2, Frank Laubach Collection, SCRC; Frank Laubach to Mission Contributors, April 8, 1938, folder 6, box 2, Frank Laubach Collection, SCRC.

5. Tropical Idylls

1. "The Monkeys Have No Tails in Zamboanga," box 1, Charles Ivins Papers, USAHEC.

2. Alidio, "'When I Get Home,'" 105–22; Anderson, *Colonial Pathologies*, 1–13; Bankoff, "First Impressions," 261–80; Bender, *American Abyss*, 40–99; Schumacher, "On the Frontier," 127–42.

3. Zantop, *Colonial Fantasies*, 14.

4. Stoler, "Intimidations of Empire," 7.

5. Bender, *American Abyss*, 44. See also Driver and Martins, *Tropical Visions*.

6. Brownell, "American Ideas of Citizenship," 978.

7. Chang and King, "Genealogy of Tropical Architecture," 287–97.

8. Asaka, *Tropical Freedom*, 1–20; Lake and Reynolds, *Global Colour Line*, 1–12.

9. Kennedy, *Magic Mountains*, 226; Pradhan, "Empire in the Hills," 33–91.

10. McKenna, *American Imperial Pastoral*, 15–18.

11. Brody, *Visualizing American Empire*, 149; Duque, "Modern Tropical Architecture," 261–71; Schumacher, "Creating Imperial Spaces," 59–75.

12. "Extracts from Letters of Commander Very, U.S.S. 'Castine,'" May 24, 1899, folder 3, box 2, John Bates Papers, USAHEC; H. M. Reeve to John Bates, July 31, 1899, folder 3, box 2, John Bates Papers, USAHEC.

13. Langhorne, *Annual Report 1904*, 15–17.

14. Wood and Bliss, *Annual Report 1906*, 7.

15. Carpenter, "Moros Do Not Drink."

16. Bliss, *Annual Report 1907*, 23.

17. "American Residents of Zamboanga, together with Europeans," box 320, John Pershing Papers, LOC-MD.

18. "'The Key to the Orient': The Growing Port of Zamboanga," 26715, box 1123, General Classified Files 1898–1945 (1914–1945 Segment), RG 350.3, NA-CP.

19. "The Monkeys Have No Tails in Zamboanga," box 1, Charles Ivins Papers, USAHEC; Chang and King, "Genealogy of Tropical Architecture," 286.

20. "The Monkeys Have No Tails in Zamboanga," box 1, Charles Ivins Papers, USAHEC.

21. J. R. Hayden to Betty Hayden, September 17, 1926, folder 26, box 28, J. R. Hayden Papers, BHL.

22. "In the Philippines," December 14, 1901, box 1, Walter Cutter Papers, USAHEC.

23. J. R. Hayden to Betty Hayden, September 17, 1926, folder 26, box 28, J. R. Hayden Papers, BHL.

24. "In the Philippines," December 14, 1901, box 1, Walter Cutter Papers, USAHEC.

25. "The Monkeys Have No Tails in Zamboanga,", box 1, Charles Ivins Papers, USAHEC.

26. Bliss, *Annual Report 1907*, 26.

27. Bliss, *Annual Report 1907*, 26.

28. John McAuley Palmer to J. P. Jervey, February 13, 1907, folder 11, box 1, John McAuley Palmer Papers, LOC-MD.

29. Tasker Bliss to John McAuley Palmer, July 3, 1907, folder 11, box 1, John McAuley Palmer Papers, LOC-MD; John McAuley Palmer to Tasker Bliss, July 13, 1907, folder 11, box 1, John McAuley Palmer Papers, LOC-MD.

30. John McAuley Palmer to Martin Geary, March 4, 1907, folder 11, box 1, John McAuley Palmer Papers, LOC-MD.

31. John McAuley Palmer to Tasker Bliss, January 12, 1908, folder 11, box 1, John McAuley Palmer Papers, LOC-MD.

32. John McAuley Palmer to Martin Geary, March 4, 1907, folder 11, box 1, John McAuley Palmer Papers, LOC-MD.

33. Pershing, *Annual Report 1911*, 14–15; Pershing, *Annual Report 1913*, 25–28, 37–40.

34. J. R. Hayden to Betty Hayden, September 12, 1926, folder 26, box 28, J. R. Hayden Papers, BHL; "The Apostleship of Sunset Cox," *La Opinion y el Comercio*, July 16, 1926.

35. S. S. Schier, "The Lake Empire of Lanao," *Philippines Free Press*, July 26, 1941.

36. "The Monkeys Have No Tails in Zamboanga," box 1, Charles Ivins Papers, USAHEC.

37. A 2017 confrontation between ISIS / Abu Sayyaf–affiliated fighters and the Philippine Army devastated Marawi. On the destruction of the city and its appearance in news media, see Panzo, "Framing the War," 149–53.

38. Interview with Mrs. Dorey, May 1, 1930, folder 2, box 15, Hermann Hagedorn Papers, LOC-MD; Interview with Mrs. Dorey, May 1, 1930, folder 4, box 17, Hermann Hagedorn Papers, LOC-MD.

39. W. Seymour Howell to Howard Howell, August 31, 1902, box 1, Howell-Taylor Family Papers, 1641–1951, USAHEC.

40. "Memorandum: On the Entertainment in Honor of the Honorable Secretary of War, William H. Taft," August 17–18, 1905, box 11, folder 3, Frank McCoy Papers, LOC-MD.

41. Diary, May 18, 1924, box 5, Carl Eugen Guthe Papers, BHL.

42. "The Monkeys Have No Tails in Zamboanga," box 1, Charles Ivins Papers, USAHEC.

43. Jenks, *Death Stalks*, 191–92.

44. "The Monkeys Have No Tails in Zamboanga," box 1, Charles Ivins Papers, USAHEC.

45. "Order of the Kris," *Manila Times*, December 27, 1902.

46. "The Monkeys Have No Tails in Zamboanga," box 1, Charles Ivins Papers, USAHEC.

47. "Wearing the Khaki: Diary of a High Private," November–December 1901, box 1, Walter Cutter Papers, USAHEC.

48. "23rd Infantry Mess Thirteenth Anniversary Dinner—Menu," December 4, 1909, folder 9, box 11, Hugh Drum Papers, USAHEC; "Rare Bits," December 4, 1909, folder 9, box 11, Hugh Drum Papers, USAHEC.

49. Protschky, "Colonial Table," 356.

50. "The Monkeys Have No Tails in Zamboanga," box 1, Charles Ivins Papers, USAHEC.

51. "Zamboanga Planters Association Meets," *Mindanao Herald*, November 16, 1907, 1; "Davao Planters Doing Things," *Mindanao Herald*, March 30, 1907; "Mr. Beardsley Talks of Davao," *Mindanao Herald*, February 22, 1908.

52. "The Yellow Peril," *Twenty-Third Infantry Lantaka*, November 20, 1909; "Personals," *Twenty-Third Infantry Bolo*, April 9, 1907.

53. "The Belle of Jolo," *Jolo Howler*, January 1, 1902.

54. "Spring Fashions for Jolo," *Jolo Howler*, January 1, 1902.

55. The most comprehensive listing of American songs from the colonial Philippines is found in Walsh, *Tin Pan Alley*. Walsh's notations on the songs about the Southern Philippines are extensive and useful. See, for examples, pages 151–52 on Moro cross-dressing or pages 193–95 on Datu Ali.

56. Antolihao, *Playing*, 1–30; Guttmann, *Games and Empires*, 171–88.

57. Journal of W. Cameron Forbes, vol. 3, July 10, 1909, W. Cameron Forbes Papers, LOC-MD; Journal of W. Cameron Forbes, vol. 4, March 5–7, 1910, W. Cameron Forbes Papers, LOC-MD.

58. Baseball was a recurrent feature throughout U.S. extraterritorial possessions. See Pope, "Rethinking Sport," 92–120; Kramer, *Blood of Government*, 386; Elias, *Empire Strikes Out*; Gems, *Athletic Crusade*.

59. N. M. Green to Frank McCoy, March 25, 1906, folder 5, box 11, Frank McCoy Papers, LOC-MD; "Battalion League," *Twenty-Third Infantry Lantaka*, November 20, 1909.

60. Report, January 11, 1910, folder 5, box 3, Matthew Steele Papers, USAHEC.

61. "No Title," *Twenty-Third Infantry Lantaka*, April 9, 1907.

62. "The Monkeys Have No Tails in Zamboanga," box 1, Charles Ivins Papers, USAHEC.

63. Worcester, "Non-Christian Peoples," 1252–55.

64. Jenks, *Death Stalks*, 177–79.

65. "The Monkeys Have No Tails in Zamboanga," box 1, Charles Ivins Papers, USAHEC.

66. Barrows, *Circular of Information Instructions*, 8; Fred J. Passmore to J. R. Hayden, September 17, 1934, folder 11, box 28, J. R. Hayden Papers, BHL.

67. Journal, June 22, 1902, folder 7, box 1, Charles Hack Papers, LOC-MD; "List of Artifacts in Hack's Collection," 1919–1926, folder 9, box 1, Charles Hack Papers, LOC-MD.

68. Journal of W. Cameron Forbes, vol. 3, July 13, 1909, W. Cameron Forbes Papers, USAHEC; W. Seymour Howell to Wife, February 22, 1903, box 1, Howell-Taylor Papers, USAHEC; J. R. Hayden to Betty Hayden, September 17, 1926, folder 26, box 28, J. R. Hayden Papers, BHL.

69. "Advertisement: Jos. S. Johnston," *Mindanao Herald*, February 3, 1909.

70. Rice, *Dean Worcester's Fantasy Islands*, 1–39.

71. Thompson, *Eye for the Tropics*, 7.

72. Sterling Larrabee to Parents, June 18, 1912, box 1, Sterling Loop Larrabee Papers, USAHEC.

73. "20 Moro Outlaws Killed in Battle," *New York Herald*, February 19, 1911.

74. Sterling Larrabee to Parents, August 4, 1911, box 1, Sterling Loop Larrabee Papers, USA-HEC.

75. "Photographs—Moros," box 10, Robert Lee Bullard Papers, LOC-MD; Personal photographs affixed to *Report of the Special Mission to the Philippines*, 1921, box 82, Frank McCoy Papers, LOC-MD.

76. Levine, "States of Undress," 206–7; Tuason, "Ideology of Empire," 34–53.

77. The American neurologist George Miller Beard popularized the idea of neurasthenia. His work on the topic includes Beard and Rockwell, *Practical Treatise*.

78. Anderson, *Colonial Pathologies*, 139–53.

79. For European examples, see Crozier, "What Was Tropical," 546–47; Reinkowski and Thum, *Helpless Imperialists*; Rogers, *Jungle Fever*.

80. Langhorne, *Annual Report 1904*, 21.

81. Journal, June 2, 1902, folder 7, box 1, Charles Hack Papers, LOC-MD.

82. Journal, June–September 1902, folder 7, box 1, Charles Hack Papers, LOC-MD.

83. Journal, September 30, 1902, folder 7, box 1, Charles Hack Papers, LOC-MD.

84. McKenna, *American Imperial Pastoral*, 22–23.

85. "Mindanao Troops May Be Relieved," *Manila Times*, February 14, 1903.

86. "Philippinitis," *Twenty-Third Infantry Lantaka*, November 20, 1909.

87. "News Notes," *Twenty-Third Infantry Lantaka*, November 20, 1909.

88. Memorandum, February 24, 1908, folder 9, box 217, Leonard Wood Papers, LOC-MD.

89. "Report on Shortening Philippines Tour of Duty," September 8, 1914, folder 3, box 217, Leonard Wood Papers, LOC-MD.

90. "Memorandum Regarding Government Service of Frank W. Carpenter," October 1915, box 1, Frank Carpenter Papers, LOC-MD.

91. Francis Burton Harrison to Lindley Garrison, November 5, 1915, box 1, Frank Carpenter Papers, LOC-MD.

92. Frank Carpenter to Richard B. Wigglesworth, February 20, 1935, box 1, Frank Carpenter Papers; United States Senate, Committee on Territories and Insular Affairs, *Frank W. Carpenter* (S. 1699), by Henry Cabot Lodge Jr. (Washington: United States Government Printing Office, 1937).

93. James Fugate to J. R. Hayden, 1932, folder 30, box 29, J. R. Hayden Papers, BHL.

94. "Diary of a Twelve-Day Tour with Vice-Governor Hayden from Manila to Sulu and Back," September 14, 1935, box 8, Harley Harris Bartlett Papers, BHL.

95. James Fugate to J. R. Hayden, December 28, 1933, folder 29, box 29, J. R. Hayden Papers, BHL.

96. "The Monkeys Have No Tails in Zamboanga," box 1, Charles Ivins Papers, USAHEC.

97. "The Monkeys Have No Tails in Zamboanga," box 1, Charles Ivins Papers, USAHEC. Cross-cultural intimate relationships in the Southern Philippines are explored in Winkelmann, "Rethinking the Sexual Geography," 39–76.

98. "The Monkeys Have No Tails in Zamboanga," box 1, Charles Ivins Papers, USAHEC.

99. Hurley, *Southeast of Zamboanga*, 21.

100. Hurley, *Southeast of Zamboanga*, 32–34.

101. Aldrich, "Colonial Man," 136. A rich body of literature attends to imperial masculinities and femininities, including Aldrich, *Colonialism and Homosexuality*; Anderson, "Trespass Speaks," 1342–70; Cruz, *Transpacific Femininities*; Fischer-Tiné and Gehrmann, *Empires and Boundaries*; Mills, *Gender and Colonial Space*; Pante, "Collision of Masculinities," 253–73; Woollacott, *Gender and Empire*.

102. Hurley, *Southeast of Zamboanga*, 27.

103. Hurley, *Southeast of Zamboanga*, 219.

104. Hurley, *Southeast of Zamboanga*, 228–29.

105. Arthur Ruhl, "No Place for a White Man," *Saturday Review of Literature*, June 1, 1935.

106. Bashford, *Imperial Hygiene*, 188.

107. "The Monkeys Have No Tails in Zamboanga," box 1, Charles Ivins Papers, USAHEC. Ivins wrote his candid unpublished memoirs in the 1960s and 1970s following his retirement. Attached to the manuscript is a short newspaper article from September 1980 from the *St. Petersburg Times* detailing the Ivinses' deaths. Suffering from severe dementia and mobility issues, Vivian was confined to a care facility. It was there that Charles, diagnosed with terminal cancer, shot her and himself, leaving behind a note at his apartment imploring friends and family to regard the deaths "not as an act of violence, but as an act of love." For more information, see Coffman, *Regulars*, 426.

108. Protschky, "Seductive Landscapes," 391; Brody, *Visualizing American Empire*, 141.

6. Moros in America

1. Williams, *Uncle Bob*, 278–79. Race thinking affected both pro- and anti-imperial discourses in the United States. Both sides argued from the commonly held belief that Anglo-Saxon societies represented the pinnacles of progress but differed in their notions of civilizational responsibility and assessments of the danger posed by racial Others to the body politic. See Baldoz, *Third Asiatic Invasion*, 22–23.

2. Williams, *Uncle Bob*, 280.

3. Cohn, *Colonialism*, 10.

4. Bennett, *Pasts beyond Memory*, 19.

5. Bhabha, *Location of Culture*, 86.

6. McClintock, *Imperial Leather*, 58.

7. Bennett, *Pasts beyond Memory*, 14

8. McGrane, *Beyond Anthropology*, 111.

9. On U.S. fairs, see Gilbert, *Whose Fair?*; Gleach, "Pocahontas at the Fair," 419–45; Kramer, "Making Concessions," 74–114; Miller, "Incoherencies of Empire," 39–62; Rogers, "Colonial Imitation," 347–67; Rydell, *World's a Fair*; Rydell, Findling, and Pelle, *Fair America*.

10. Domosh, "'Civilized' Commerce," 189–97.

11. Moore, "Mapping Empire," 115.

12. Moore, "Mapping Empire," 121.

13. "Filipino Village," *Atlanta Constitution*, January 20, 1901; "The Pan-American Exposition: The Ethnological Building," *Phrenological Journal and Science of Health* (April 1901): 3–4.

14. C. H. Huttig to Charles Reeves, December 10, 1901, folder 12, box 2, Charles Monroe Reeves Papers, State Historical Society of Missouri, Columbia, Missouri (hereafter SHSM-C); "States, Territories, and Possessions," folder 12, box 2, Charles Monroe Reeves Papers, SHSM-C.

15. *Report of the Philippine Exposition Board*, 6; Wilson, "Philippines at St. Louis," 3–5.

16. Soderstrom, "Family Trees," 179–80.

17. "Dr. Gustavo Niederlein—Special Commissioner of Philippine Islands for the World's Fair," *World's Fair Bulletin* 3, no. 12 (1902): 30; *Circular Letter of Governor Taft*, 11.

18. Jenks, *Death Stalks*, 171.

19. Guy T. Viskniskki, "The Filipino Conquest of America," *Toledo Times-Bee*, July 17, 1904, Louisiana Purchase Exposition Scrapbook 196, Missouri History Museum Library and Research Center, St. Louis, Missouri (hereafter LPE Scrapbook [#], MHM-LRC).

20. Jenks, *Death Stalks*, 189.

21. "Interesting Relics for World's Fair," *Binghampton Leader-Chronicle*, October 10, 1903, LPE Scrapbook 113, MHM-LRC; "Huge Exhibit by Isles," *Chicago Record-Herald*, October 22, 1904, LPE Scrapbook 196, MHM-LRC.

22. The Philippine Reservation was the largest single exhibit at the exposition, costing over a $1,000,000 (close to $30,000,000 by present valuation), with nearly one hundred buildings, 75,000 exhibits, and 1,100 people on display. Herbert S. Stone, "Philippine Exposition: World's Fair, St. Louis, 1904," SHSM-C.

23. Rydell, *World's a Fair*, 157.

24. *Report of the Philippine Exposition Board*, 34. A listing of the names of Moro participants is included in Parezo and Fowler, *Anthropology Goes*, 415–16.

25. Francis, *Universal Exposition of 1904*, 571; *Report of the Philippine Exposition Board*, 34–35.

26. "Free Pictorial Map of the Philippine Exposition," folder 154, Louisiana Purchase Exposition Collection, SHSM-C; *Daily Official Program—World's Fair, 25 April 1904* (St. Louis: St. Louis World's Fair Program Co., 1904).

27. Francis, *Universal Exposition of 1904*, 571; Wolcott Calkins, "Teaching the Brown Man," *Boston Evening Transcript*, April 27, 1904, LPE Scrapbook 196, MHM-LRC.

28. *Report of the Philippine Exposition Board*, 571.

29. Wilson, *Official Catalogue of Exhibits*, 262–71; Herbert S. Stone, "Philippine Exposition: World's Fair, St. Louis, 1904," SHSM-C.

30. Wilson, *Official Catalogue of Exhibits*, 293; Herbert S. Stone, "Philippine Exposition: World's Fair, St. Louis, 1904," SHSM-C.

31. Martha L. Root, "In the Philippines and on the Pike," *Pittsburgh Dispatch*, June 26, 1904, LPE Scrapbook 196, MHM-LRC.

32. William E. Curtis, "The Curtis Letter," *New York Globe*, August 3, 1904, LPE Scrapbook 196, MHM-LRC. Like Niederlein, Curtis participated in other world's fairs, heading the Latin American Department and Historical Section at the World's Columbian Exposition in Chicago in 1893 and directing the Columbian Historical Exposition in Madrid, overseeing a wide array of Americana there. See "William E. Curtis of the Chicago Record-Herald—Lecture Tour," box 82, Redpath Chautauqua Collection, University of Iowa Libraries Special Collections Department, Iowa City, Iowa.

33. "Savages at the Fair as Snobs," *Washington Post*, September 10, 1904.

34. "Dowie's Agent Gives up Moros as Bad Job," *St. Louis Republic*, May 13, 1904.

35. "The Philippine Display," *World's Fair Bulletin* 3, no. 7 (1902): 21.

36. W. J. McGee, "Anthropology," *World's Fair Bulletin* 5, no. 4 (1904): 4.

37. Parezo and Fowler, *Anthropology Goes*, 39.

38. McGee, "Strange Races of Men," 5188.

39. McGee, "Strange Races of Men," 5185.

40. McGee, "Strange Races of Men," 5188.

41. Francis E. Leupp, "Hints for Fair Visitors," *New York Evening Post*, July 2, 1904, LPE Scrapbook 196, MHM-LRC.

42. "The President of the United States Visits the World's Fair," *World's Fair Bulletin* 6, no. 2 (1904): 3.

43. *Report of the Philippine Exposition Board*, 48.

44. "Awards," *World's Fair Bulletin* 6, no. 1 (1904): 20; *Report of the Philippine Exposition Board*, 42; "No Shower Baths during Hot Days," *St. Louis Republic*, July 29, 1904.

45. William E. Curtis, "Huge Exhibit by Isles," *Chicago Record-Herald*, October 22, 1904, LPE Scrapbook 196, MHM-LRC.

46. Kramer, "Making Concessions," 78–79, 106–8.

47. Herbert S. Stone, "Philippine Exposition: World's Fair, St. Louis, 1904," SHSM-C.

48. Rydell, *World's a Fair*, 174.

49. Bennett, *Pasts beyond Memory*, 9.

50. Bliss, *Annual Report 1907*, 34; Kramer, *Blood of Government*, 340.

51. Ram, "White but Not Quite," 736.

52. Lahiri, "Performing Identity," 409; Ram, "White but Not Quite," 736.

53. Anderson, "Going through the Motions," 711–12.

54. Francis, *Universal Exposition of 1904*, 571; "Igorrotes to Be Clad," *Washington Post*, August 9, 1904; "Igorrotes on Way," *Washington Post*, August 8, 1904.

55. "Igorrotes to Be Clad," *Washington Post*, August 9, 1904.

56. "Dattos See Capital," *Washington Post*, August 10, 1904.

57. Hawkins, *Making Moros*, 125.

58. "Dattos See Capital," *Washington Post*, August 10, 1904.

59. "Dattos See Capital," *Washington Post*, August 10, 1904; "Filipinos Return from Washington," *St. Louis Republic*, August 10, 1904.

60. "Dattos See Capital," *Washington Post*, August 10, 1904.

61. "At the White House," *Washington Evening Star*, November 2, 1907.

62. "Moro Datto Comes Here," *Washington Post*, August 2, 1907; "Too Much Matrimony," *Washington Post*, October 13, 1907.

63. Elwell Otis to John Bates, July 3, 1899, folder 1, box 2, John Bates Papers, USAHEC; Gianakos, "George Ade's Critique," 223–25.

64. Jamalul Kiram to O. J. Sweet, September 16, 1901, folder 1, box 55, Hugh Scott Papers, LOC-MD.

65. J. Franklin Bell to Francis Burton Harrison, January 1914, box 41, Burton Norvell Harrison Family Papers, LOC-MD.

66. "Sultan Sails Hither," *Los Angeles Times*, July 24, 1910.

67. "Sultan of Sulu Is Here to See Taft," *Boston Daily Globe*, September 24, 1910.

68. "New York's Marvels Awe Sultan of Sulu," *New York Times*, September 25, 1910.

69. "New York's Awe Sultan of Sulu," *New York Times*, September 25, 1910; "Hadji Takes Pickles with His Ice Cream," *Boston Daily Globe*, September 26, 1910.

70. "Chicago's Pants Win Sulu Sultan," *Chicago Daily Tribune*, October 1, 1910.

71. Rovine, "Colonialism's Clothing," 44.

72. "Chicago's Pants Win Sulu Sultan," *Chicago Daily Tribune*, October 1, 1910.

73. Levine, "States of Undress," 212–13.

74. "Sultan Has to Wait," *Washington Post*, September 27, 1910.

75. "Whole World One Big School to Him Says Sulu Sultan," *Christian Science Monitor*, October 6, 1910.

76. "The Sultan's Manners," *Washington Post*, September 28, 1910.

77. "What the Sultan Is Taking to Sulu," *Christian Science Monitor*, October 20, 1910; "The Lure of America for the Far East Is Growing," *New York Times*, October 2, 1910.

78. Pershing, *Annual Report 1913*, 70–71.

79. Angeles, "Philippine Muslim Women," 212–13.

80. Pershing, *Annual Report 1913*, 29–30.

81. Carpenter, *Annual Report 1914*, 351.

82. Angeles, "Philippine Muslim Women," 213.

83. "Development Program: Bureau of Non-Christian Tribes Scholarships," 1931, folder 2, box 30, J. R. Hayden Papers, BHL.

84. Stockwell, "Leaders, Dissidents," 487–507; Bryant, "Social Networks and Empire," 39–66.

85. The *Chicago Daily Tribune* reported the two were "stunned" by the "enchanted world" of Chicago but also noted they felt "more at home" when taken to the city's busy markets, which reminded Kiram of "the cock fights at home." "Glories of Loop Amaze 2 Little Filipino Maids," *Chicago Daily Tribune*, August 28, 1919; "They Find Chicago a Wonder City," *Chicago Daily Tribune*, August 28, 1919.

86. "Princess of Sulu Visits Washington on Way to Illinois College Where She Hopes to Learn about America," *Washington Herald*, September 8, 1920.

87. "Rise of Princess Recalls Coed Days," *Boston Daily Globe*, March 31, 1932.

88. Gedacht, "Holy War," 450.

89. "That Wild Little Sulu Flapper We Couldn't Tame," *Atlanta Constitution*, March 6, 1927.

90. Dwight, "Our Mohammedan Wards," 16.

91. Orosa, *Sulu Archipelago*, 54; Constabulary Report, March 19, 1927, folder 27, box 28, J. R. Hayden Papers, BHL.

92. "Princess Missing after Moro Battle," *Washington Post*, February 3, 1927; "Sultana of Sulu, Once U. I. Co-Ed, Stalks Bandits," *Chicago Daily Tribune*, February 6, 1938.

93. Elizabeth Walker, "Moro Princess Explains Her Reversion to Type," *Los Angeles Times*, February 6, 1927; Elizabeth Walker, "Co-Ed from Chicago Holds Sulu Island in Defiance of America," *Boston Daily Globe*, February 6, 1927.

94. L. B. Johnson, "Co-Ed Reveals How Royal Dreams Faded," *Chicago Daily Tribune*, February 9, 1927; "Moro Princess Outcast," *Los Angeles Times*, February 7, 1927.

95. Margaret C. Stoll, "Voice of the People: A Portrait of Princess Tarhata," *Chicago Daily Tribune*, February 18, 1927.

96. "Princess Blames Moore," *Los Angeles Times*, February 18, 1927.

97. Elizabeth Walker, "Moro Princess Explains Her Reversion to Type," *Los Angeles Times*, February 6, 1927. Other elite Muslims filtered into the United States. Abdullah, son of the Maguindanao ruler Datu Piang, visited San Francisco in 1912, ostensibly "hunting" for an American bride. Gulamu Rasul, a member of Kiram's retinue in 1910, returned to U.S. shores in 1919 to study at George Washington University. He eventually married an American woman named Alma Stewart. See Richard Barry, "Datto Abdulah Piang—Wife Hunting in America," *Evening Standard*, March 6, 1912; "Capital Girl Stirs Ire of Moro Wife," *Washington Post*, March 30, 1922.

98. Kolb, "George Ade (1866–1944)," 157–58; Salman, *Embarrassment of Slavery*, 45–46. Characteristic examples of the playwright's newspaper work are found in Ade, *Fables in Slang*.

99. Gianakos, "George Ade's Critique," 223–25.

100. Coyle, *George Ade*, 55.

101. Ade, *Sultan of Sulu*, 12.

102. Ade, *Sultan of Sulu*, 25–26.

103. George Barbour to Hugh Scott, October 18, 1903, folder 5, box 55, Hugh Scott Papers, LOC-MD.

104. Angeles, "Moros in the Media," 42–43.

105. Kutzer, *Empire's Children*, 14.

106. Little, *Francisco the Filipino*.

107. Stuart, *Adventures of Piang*, 4.

108. "Latest Works of Fiction," *New York Times*, October 7, 1917. Stuart was not the only writer of fanciful tales about the Moros. See also Meek, *Monkeys Have No Tails*.

109. Other writers made genuine attempts to compile the popular folk tales of Mindanao. Mabel Cole, who spent four years in the Philippines with her ethnologist husband, transcribed some in her book Cole, *Philippine Folk Tales*.

110. Stuart, *Adventures of Piang*, 160.

111. Stuart, *Adventures of Piang*, 191.

112. Stuart, *Adventures of Piang*, 223. Finley's own descriptions of the celebrations are strikingly similar to Stuart's: "As the vast assemblage drew near to the Zamboanga dock, the hum of voices, the shouts of command, the swish of paddles, all coupled with the noise of *agongs* and *lantakas* made indescribable din and a scene of matchless barbaric splendor." Finley, "Race Development," 343–44.

113. Hancock, *Uncle Sam's Boys*, 122–24. Hancock's contributions to the war preparedness movement are cataloged in Frank, "Advocating War Preparedness," 215–31.

114. Hancock, *Uncle Sam's Boys*, 199.

115. Hancock, *Uncle Sam's Boys*, 251–53.

116. Dunning, *On the Air*, 353–55.

117. "A New Adventure," *Jack Armstrong, the All-American Boy*, January 6, 1941, tape 156, American Radio Collection, 1931–1972, SHSM-C.

118. "Moro Peddler," *Jack Armstrong, the All-American Boy*, January 17, 1941, tape 157, American Radio Collection, SHSM-C; "Anothing Talking Trick," *Jack Armstrong, the All-American Boy*, January 20, 1941, tape 157, American Radio Collection, SHSM-C; "After Hidden Guns," *Jack Armstrong, the All-American Boy*, January 21, 1941, tape 157, American Radio Collection, SHSM-C.

119. "Gary Cooper Cast in 'The Real Glory,'" *Atlanta Constitution*, April 2, 1939; "'Glory' Up to Start," *Variety*, April 19, 1939.

120. Clifford, *The Real Glory*. The film was based on a novel by Charles L. Clifford, a prolific writer of adventure stories who published frequently in magazines like *The Red Book* (now *Redbook*), *Cosmopolitan*, and *Adventure*. His identity remains a matter of speculation, with some claiming Clifford was a pseudonym of Vic Hurley, author of *The Swish of the Kris* and *Jungle Patrol*.

121. "Withdraw 'Real Glory' after Gov't Request," *BoxOffice*, September 13, 1942.

122. *The Real Glory*, directed by Henry Hathaway (1939; Los Angeles: MGM Movie Legends Collection, 2007), DVD.

123. Hathaway, *The Real Glory*.

124. Hathaway, *The Real Glory*.

125. Hathaway, *The Real Glory*.

126. Nelson B. Bell, "There Is Enough of It for All in 'Real Glory'," *Washington Post*, November 6, 1939; Mae Tinee, "'The Real Glory' Has Good Cast in Good Story," *Chicago Daily Tribune*, November 4, 1939; "The Real Glory," *Hartford Courant*, June 19, 1942.

127. The afterlives of the fair are explored in Parezo and Fowler, *Anthropology Goes*, 358–90.

128. Yegar, *Between Integration and Secession*, 231.

129. "Sulu Princess Claims Islands in South Seas; Calls on British to Give Them to Philippines," *New York Times*, March 30, 1930; Akuk Sangkula to Frank Murphy, January 6, 1934, folder 34, box 29, J. R. Hayden Papers, BHL; "Sulu Princess Offers to Visit Outlaws, Try to End Killings," *Boston Daily Globe*, March 13, 1941; "Sulu Princess Gets Posts," *New York Times*, December 6, 1947.

130. National Historical Institute, *Historical Markers: Regions V–X11* (Manila, PI, 1994), 82.

131. Recent histories of Asian migration to the United States probe the contours of colonial and national citizenship. See Baldoz and Ayala, "Bordering of America," 76–105; Kramer, "Imperial Openings," 317–47.

7. Imperial Interactivities

1. José Rizal, "Filipinas Dentro De Cien Años—IV," *La Solidaridad*, January 31, 1890.

2. Spanish intra-imperial relationships are illustrated in Bjork, "Link," 25–50. Sulu and Mindanao participated in supraregional networks through their role in maritime trade; see Warren, "Structure of Slavery," 111–28.

3. Saunier, *Transnational History*, 7; Adas, "From Settler Colony," 1692–1720; Schumacher, "United States," 278–303. The global dimensions of U.S. territorial expansion feature heavily in McCoy and Scarano, *Colonial Crucible*.

4. Deacon, Russell, and Woolacott, *Transnational Lives*, 10.

5. Ballantyne and Burton, "Reach of the Global," 296.

6. Ewen, "Lost in Translation?" 174.

7. Harris, *God's Arbiters*, 3–37.

8. Hoganson, *Fighting for American Manhood*, 15–42.

9. Anduaga, "Spanish Jesuits," 519–21; Warren, "Scientific Superman," 508–19; Lumba, "Imperial Standards," 603–28.

10. Foreman, "Spain," 32–33.

11. Baranera and Laist, *Handbook*, 111–22.

12. Baranera, *Compendio de la Historia de Filipinas*, 120–21.

13. Translated Spanish Text, box 319, John Pershing Papers, LOC-MD.

14. The missionaries existed in a tentative position between government and rebel forces during the Philippine revolution. The final group of Jesuits departed Mindanao in April 1900. On this topic, see Arcilla, "Jesuits," 296–315.

15. Cano, "Evidence," 27–30. For an illustrative example of the collection, see Blair and Roberston, *Philippine Islands, 1493–1898*, vol. 1.

16. Memorandum, 1899, folder 9, box 2, John Bates Papers, USAHEC.

17. Interview, August 14, 1899, folder 1, box 2, John Bates Papers, USAHEC.

18. Elwell Otis to John Bates, July 3, 1899, folder 1, box 2, John Bates Papers, USAHEC; Elwell Otis to John Bates, July 1, 1899, folder 1, box 2, John Bates Papers, USAHEC.

19. "Wearing the Khaki: Diary of a High Private," 1901–1902, box 1, Walter Cutter Papers, USAHEC.

20. "Appendix V: The Moros of the Philippines," in Davis, *Annual Report 1902*, 117–49.

21. John Finley to John Pershing, January 1, 1910, box 320, John Pershing Papers, LOC-MD; Report, September 8, 1934, folder 4, box 30, J. R. Hayden Papers, BHL.

22. "Military Spain," box 83, Frank McCoy Papers, LOC-MD.

23. Speech, February 1907, folder 5, box 43, Tasker Bliss Collection, USAHEC.

24. Arolas Tulawie to Teopisto Guingona, August 12, 1920, folder 24, box 29, J. R. Hayden Papers, BHL.

25. "Interview with Datu Piang of Dulawan," September 1926, folder 26, box 28, J. R. Hayden Papers, BHL.

26. Kramer, "Empires, Exceptions," 1326; Schumacher, "American Way of Empire," 42.

27. Tyrrell, "Regulation of Alcohol," 539–69; Wertz, "Idealism, Imperialism," 467–99.

28. Charles Brent to Frank McCoy, April 17, 1905, folder 1, box 11, Frank McCoy Papers, LOC-MD.

29. "Bishop Brent at Zamboanga," *Hartford Courant*, January 15, 1913; Brent, *Inspiration of Responsibility*, 161–64.

30. Lord, *Proconsuls*, 79.

31. Journal of W. Cameron Forbes, vol. 3, January 1909, W. Cameron Forbes Papers, LOC-MD.

32. Bacevich, *Diplomat in Khaki*, 22–23.

33. McCoy, quoted in Bacevich, *Diplomat in Khaki*, 26.

34. Bacevich, *Diplomat in Khaki*, 27; Interview, June 7, 1929, folder 4, box 15, Hermann Hagedorn Papers, LOC-MD.

35. Frank McCoy to Margaret McCoy, September 3, 1903, folder 2, box 15, Hermann Hagedorn Papers, LOC-MD.

36. Notes, February 7, 1906, folder 4, box 11, Frank McCoy Papers, LOC-MD.

37. Interview, June 8, 1929, folder 2, box 15, Hermann Hagedorn Papers, LOC-MD.

38. Tasker Bliss to Eleanor Bliss, July 9, 1906, folder 3, box 22, Tasker Bliss Collection, USA-HEC.

39. Richard Barry to Leonard Wood, January 12, 1906, folder 3, box 15, Hermann Hagedorn Papers, LOC-MD.

40. John P. Finley, "The Non-Christians of the Southern Islands of the Philippines—Their Self-Government and Industrial Development," paper given at Lake Mohonk, October 24, 1912, box 38, BNHF Papers, LOC- MD.

41. John McAuley Palmer to Tasker Bliss, January 12, 1908, folder 11, box 1, John McAuley Palmer Papers, LOC-MD.

42. George W. Davis to Adna R. Chaffee, April 17, 1902, folder 1, box 1, George Davis Papers, USAHEC; Davis, *Annual Report 1903*, 12.

43. Davis, *Annual Report 1903*, 106–10.

44. Francis Burton Harrison to Lindley Garrison, April 4, 1915, box 42, BNHF Papers, LOC-MD.

45. Rosenberg, "Transnational Currents," 919–20.

46. "Lieutenant Preuss Wounded in Action," box 1, Sterling Loop Larrabee Papers, USAHEC; Vic Hurley, *Jungle Patrol*, 286–87; Pershing, *My Life*, 572; Fulton, *Moroland*, 407–9.

47. Vic Hurley, *Jungle Patrol*, 287; Pershing, *Annual Report 1913*, 56.

48. Report, 1911, folder 2, box 2, Sterling Loop Larrabee Papers, USAHEC; "The Horseman's Album: A Tribute to Sterling Loop Larrabee, Master of the Old Dominion Foxhounds," January 1935, folder 3, box 2, Sterling Loop Larrabee Papers, USAHEC; Fulton, *Moroland*, 408.

49. Preuss was listed as killed in action in 1915 but later cropped up in U.S. Expeditionary Force documents as an "agent" in Spain in 1917–1918. He was also reported to be in the United States in the 1920s. "Shuster's Gendarmerie in Persia," August 1912, folder 2, box 2, Sterling Loop Larrabee Papers, USAHEC; John J. Pershing, *My Life*, 573.

50. Research Notes for "The Brethren," 1956, box 1, Edward Bowditch Papers, DRMC.

51. Memorandum, 1941, folder 1, box 2, Sterling Loop Larrabee Papers, USAHEC.

52. Adas, *Dominance by Design*, 150.

53. "Gentlemen Adventurers," February 1932, box 1, John Early Papers, BHL.

54. Speech, April 14, 1931, 18865–55, box 916, General Classified Files 1898–1945 (1914–1945 Segment), RG 350.3, NA-CP.

55. Dwight F. Davis to Patrick J. Hurley, 18865–55, box 916, General Classified Files 1898–1945 (1914–1945 Segment), RG 350.3, NA-CP. Anne Foster examines Davis's trip within the context of intelligence gathering and anticommunism in her work. See Foster, *Projections of Power*, 39–41.

56. Warren, "Sulu Zone," 177–83; Tagliacozzo, *Secret Trades, Porous Borders*, 307–9.

57. Non, "Moro Piracy," 401–10.

58. "The Monkeys Have No Tails in Zamboanga," box 1, Charles Ivins Papers, USAHEC.

59. Pershing, *Annual Report 1913*, 50–53. The 1913 census was the first conducted in Mindanao and Sulu since the nationwide one in 1903.

60. Schult, "Sulu and Germany," 80–99. The most comprehensive account of Herman Schuck's life is found in Montemayor, *Captain Herman Leopold Schuck*. Schuck ran into trouble with the Spanish for dealing arms to the Sulu Sultanate; see Orosa, *Sulu Archipelago*, 116.

61. Report, August 21, 1899, folder 1, box 2, John Bates Papers, USAHEC. Najeeb Saleeby was less enthused with Edward Schuck, whom he accused of distorting the translation of the agreement, thereby increasing tensions between the Americans and the Moros. Proceedings, December 13, 1903, folder 6, box 55, Hugh Scott Papers, LOC-MD.

62. Cloman, *Myself*, 100; Report, March 10, 1906, folder 6, box 217, Leonard Wood Papers, LOC-MD. Charlie Schuck assisted in the hunt for the pirate Jikiri in 1908–1909, suffering a gunshot wound to the leg and abdomen during an encounter on Pata Island. Diary, June 4–5, 1909, box 1, Charles Rhodes Papers, USAHEC.

63. Matthew Steele to Stella Steele, December 23, 1911, folder 1, box 12, Matthew Steele Papers, USAHEC.

64. Diary of Field Service in the Philippines, November 2, 1900, box 1, William Kobbé Papers, USAHEC; Proceedings, December 13, 1903, folder 6, box 55, Hugh Scott Papers, LOC-MD.

65. On Herman, see Cloman, *Myself*, 86. On Eddy, see Carl Garmson to J. R. Hayden, May 10, 1934, folder 21, box 28, J. R. Hayden Papers, BHL. On Charles, see Hurley, *Swish of the Kris*, 125.

66. Villamor, *Census*, 378; James Fugate to Henry L. Stimson, September 1, 1928, folder 28, box 29, J. R. Hayden Papers, BHL.

67. James Fugate to J. R. Hayden, December 28, 1933, folder 29, box 29, J. R. Hayden Papers, BHL

68. Report, March 25, 1930, folder 14, box 29, J. R. Hayden Papers, BHL; Manuel, "Philippine Folk Epics," 18; Reilly, "Collecting the People," 146.

69. *Program of the Jolo Agricultural and Industrial Fair*, 1; "Advertisement," *Mindanao Herald*, January 17, 1914.

70. "People Met in Hotel Lobbies," *Washington Post*, July 17, 1907; "Wonderful Pearl of Great Value from Sulu," *Washington Post*, February 3, 1907; "Filipino Buyer Urges Closer Trade Contact," *Los Angeles Times*, June 27, 1923.

71. "The Monkeys Have No Tails in Zamboanga," box 1, Charles Ivins Papers, USAHEC.

72. "Just Little Things," 40; Jurika, "A Philippine Odyssey," 4–5. See also Parsons, "Life in Moroland—Part I," 77–95; Parsons, "A Life in Moroland—Part II," 31–41; "U.S. Civilians Slain in Manila," *Cass City Chronicle*, July 27, 1945.

73. The anthropologist Charles Eugen Guthe found antique Chinese trading goods and graves during his expeditions in the Southern Philippines in the 1920s, surmising that intermarriage between Chinese traders and local families must have been common long before European contact. "University of Michigan Philippines Expedition," *Manila Times*, May 13, 1925.

74. John Bates to Adjutant General, September 27, 1899, folder 6, box 2, John Bates Papers, USAHEC.

75. *Program of the Jolo Agricultural and Industrial Fair*, 10.

76. Bliss, *Annual Report 1907*, 23.

77. Abinales, "From *Orang Besar*," 200; McKenna, *Muslim Rulers and Rebels*, 91–92. Datu Uto's rule is surveyed in Ileto, *Magindanao, 1860–1888*.

78. John Bates to 8th Army Chief of Staff, December 17, 1899, folder 13, box 2, John Bates Papers, USAHEC.

79. Quoted in Beckett, "Datus," 57.

80. Datu Piang to Calvin Coolidge, August 26, 1927, folder 33, box 28, J. R. Hayden Papers, BHL.

81. Abinales, "From *Orang Besar*," 208.

82. Doolittle, "Colliding Discourses," 99–100; Tarling, "Establishment of Colonial Regimes," 9–28.

83. Interview, September 6, 1899, folder 6, box 2, John Bates Papers, USAHEC.

84. Hurley, *Swish of the Kris*, 79–80. Information from Manila was so scarce during the Spanish-American War that "at one time, the Spanish padres of Zamboanga received word that Boston had been captured by the troops of Spain."

85. John Bates to Adjutant General, August 21, 1899, folder 1, box 2, John Bates Papers, USA-HEC; Dennys, *Descriptive Dictionary*; Dennys, *Folk-Lore of China*.

86. Interviews, July 31, 1899, folder 3, box 2, John Bates Papers, USAHEC; John Bates to Adjutant General, September 27, 1899, folder 6, box 2, John Bates Papers, USAHEC.

87. Frank G. Carpenter, "Coffee in the Philippines," *Boston Daily Globe*, July 29, 1900.

88. Charles Cameron to Dean Worcester, May 19, 1913, box 1, Dean Worcester Papers, BHL.

89. "Killing of Moros," *Washington Post*, March 20, 1906.

90. Extracts from Letters of Commander Very, June 15, 1899, folder 3, box 2, John Bates Papers USAHEC.

91. Otama to William Kobbé, February 27, 1901, folder 7, box 3, William Kobbé Papers, US-AHEC.

92. E. L. Cook to W. Morgan Shuster, August 11, 1906, folder 66, box 15, Tasker Bliss Collection, USAHEC.

93. Dean Worcester, "What Would Lincoln Do? Slave Trading under the Stars and Stripes," *Semi-Monthly Magazine*, January 11, 1914.

94. John C. Early to Dwight F. Davis, December 20, 1930, folder 29, box 28, J. R. Hayden Papers, BHL.

95. "Passes for Moros," August 29, 1926, folder 11, box 30, J. R. Hayden Papers, BHL.

96. R. M. Little to Commander (Signature Illegible), August 23, 1899, box 1, folder 2, John Bates Papers, USAHEC; Kramer, "Empires, Exceptions," 1352. On R. M. Little, see Singh, *Making of Sabah*, 198–201.

97. George Duncan to Adjutant General, November 1, 1902, folder 3, box 55, Hugh Scott Papers, LOC-MD.

98. Leonard Wood to Military Secretary, May 22, 1905, folder 2, box 11, Frank McCoy Papers, LOC-MD; Fulton, *Moroland*, 242–44.

99. Pershing, *Annual Report 1910*, 19–20.

100. "Reminiscences of John C. Early," 1920s, box 1, John Early Papers, BHL.

101. Blumi, *Ottoman Refugees*, 109–11.

102. Finley, "Mohammedan Problem," 357–58.

103. Finley, "Mohammedan Problem," 357–58.

104. Conference Proceedings, August 14, 1899, folder 1, box 2, John Bates Papers, USAHEC; Davis, *Annual Report 1903*, 109.

105. Interviews, June 21, 1902, box 319, John Pershing Papers, LOC-MD.

106. Hakim's letters to Palmer are quoted at length in correspondence between Palmer and J. P. Jervey, the officer who replaced George T. Langhorne as provincial secretary for the Moro Province in late 1906. John McAuley Palmer to J. P. Jervey, 20 April 1907, folder 11, box 1, John McAuley Palmer Papers, LOC-MD.

107. Mobilities in the Dutch Empire underpinned colonial and anticolonial activities alike. See Alexanderson, *Subversive Seas*, 1–28.

108. Worcester, "Non-Christian Peoples," 1227.

109. Frank Laubach to *The Argus*, January 15, 1930, folder 3, box 1, Frank Laubach Collection, SCRC.

110. Matias Cuadra, working for the Bureau of Non-Christian Tribes, believed the Moros had learned modern methods of commerce and agriculture from these journeys. Matias Cuadra to G. K. Raval, folder 4, box 126, Frank Laubach Collection, SCRC.

111. Pershing, *Annual Report 1913*, 58–59.

112. "The Monkeys Have No Tails in Zamboanga," box 1, Charles Ivins Papers, USAHEC.

113. Sermon, December 22, 1912, box 42, BNHF Papers, LOC-MD.

114. Frank Laubach to Frank Carpenter, September 23, 1921, box 1, Frank Carpenter Papers, LOC-MD.

115. Najeeb Saleeby to William Kobbé, August 11, 1901, folder 7, box 3, William Kobbé Papers, USAHEC.

116. School Prospectus, September 24, 1906, box 320, John Pershing Papers, LOC-MD; Charles Cameron to David Barrows, September 24, 1909, box 320, John Pershing Papers, LOC-MD.

117. Commentary, June 17, 1935, folder 2, box 30, J. R. Hayden Papers, BHL.

118. Wood and Bliss, *Annual Report 1906*, 9.

119. Pershing, *Annual Report 1913*, 33.

120. Meeting Minutes, March 29, 1912, folder 1, box 1, John Finley Papers, USAHEC.

121. Meeting Minutes, March 29, 1912, folder 1, box 1, John Finley Papers, USAHEC.

122. "A Review of the Moro Petition, Its Origin, Scope and Purpose, and How Its Object May Be Realized in Aid of the American System of Control," 1912, folder 1, box 1, John Finley Papers, USAHEC.

123. "A Review of the Moro Petition, Its Origin, Scope and Purpose, and How Its Object May Be Realized in Aid of the American System of Control," 1912, folder 1, box 1, John Finley Papers, USAHEC.

124. Edward Bowditch to J. Franklin Bell, February 5, 1914, box 41, BNHF Papers, LOC-MD.

125. "Colonel Finley Gives Interesting Account of His Trip to Turkey on Behalf of the Mohammedan Moros," *Army and Navy Weekly* 1, no. 10 (1914): 1; Gedacht, "Holy War," 459. Recent scholarship has examined Wajih's visit to the Philippines from multiple analytical angles; see, for examples, Gedacht, "'Shaykh al-Islām,'" 172–202; Clarence-Smith, "Wajih al-Kilani," 172–92; Kawashima, *"White Man's Burden."*

126. Edward Bowditch to J. Franklin Bell, February 5, 1914, box 41, BNHF Papers, LOC-MD.

127. Frank Carpenter to Francis Burton Harrison, February 8, 1914, box 41, BNHF Papers, LOC-MD.

128. J. Franklin Bell to Francis Burton Harrison, February 11, 1914, box 41, BNHF Papers, LOC-MD.

129. Carpenter, *Annual Report 1914*, 391–93.

130. "Colonel Finley Gives Interesting Account of His Trip to Turkey on Behalf of the Mohammedan Moros," *Army and Navy Weekly* 1, no. 10 (1914): 11.

131. Wajih al-Kilani to Lindley Garrison, September 23, 1914, 2509, box 1025, General Classified Files 1898–1945 (1914–1945 Segment), RG 350.3, NA-CP.

132. Francis Burton Harrison to Insular Bureau, June 26, 1915, 2509, box 1025, General Classified Files 1898–1945 (1914–1945 Segment), RG 350.3, NA-CP.

133. Wajih al-Kilani to Woodrow Wilson, September 2, 1915, 2509, box 1025, General Classified Files 1898–1945 (1914–1945 Segment), RG 350.3, NA-CP.

134. "Sheikh Here to Lecture," *New York Times*, August 13, 1915.

135. John Finley to Hugh Scott, September 23, 1915, 2509, box 1025, General Classified Files 1898–1945 (1914–1945 Segment), RG 350.3, NA-CP.

136. Wajih Gilani to Lindley Garrison, October 23, 1915, 2509, box 1025, General Classified Files 1898–1945 (1914–1945 Segment), RG 350.3, NA-CP.

137. T. L. Hurt to Francis Burton Harrison, February 1916, 2509, box 1025, General Classified Files 1898–1945 (1914–1945 Segment), RG 350.3, NA-CP.

138. Frank Carpenter to Carl Moore, June 1, 1918, 2509, box 1025, General Classified Files 1898–1945 (1914–1945 Segment), RG 350.3, NA-CP.

139. Mailing List, 1900s, folder 4, box 217, Leonard Wood Papers, LOC-MD.

140. "Gentlemen Adventurers," February 1932, box 1, John Early Papers, BHL.

Conclusion

1. Pier, *American Apostles*, 152.

2. Forbes, *Philippine Islands*. The revised edition of the book was published by Harvard University Press in 1945.

3. W. Cameron Forbes to Edward Bowditch, April 11, 1956, box 1, Edward Bowditch Papers, DRMC

4. Memorandum, June 28, 1956, box 1, Edward Bowditch Papers, DRMC; "Genesis of the Philippine Valhalla," 1956, box 1, Edward Bowditch Papers, DRMC.

5. Research Notes, 1956, box 1, Edward Bowditch Papers, DRMC.

6. Edward Bowditch to W. Cameron Forbes and Victor Heiser, November 2, 1956, box 1, Edward Bowditch Papers, DRMC.

7. Essay, 1956, box 1, Edward Bowditch Papers, DRMC.

8. Memorandum, June 28, 1956, box 1, Edward Bowditch Papers, DRMC.

9. Hurley, *Southeast of Zamboanga*, 30.

10. "Rush More Soldiers to Lanao Area," *Manila Tribune*, April 8, 1937; "Six Outlaws Die as Troops Attack Cotta," *Manila Tribune*, April 30, 1907; "Planes Join Moro Battle," *New York Times*, December 3, 1937.

11. Carl N. Taylor, "Powder Keg in Mindanao," *Today Magazine*, March 7, 1936; Glazer, "Moros as a Political Factor," 78–79.

12. Fugate retired to Cotabato to manage the grounds of an Episcopal mission. He was murdered there by a disgruntled former employee in 1938. Friends and former colleagues lauded him as a transformative figure and blamed "ungrateful" natives for his death. "Fugate Murdered in Moro Province," *New York Times*, December 16, 1938; H. F. Cameron to Isaac Fugate, May 9, 1939, folder 1, James Fugate Correspondence, 1937–1939, BHL; H. F. Cameron to Isaac Fugate, June 14, 1939, folder 1, Fugate Correspondence, BHL.

13. Yu-Jose and Dacudao, "Visible Japanese," 104.

14. "Non-Christians of Davao," September 3, 1930, folder 1, box 28, J. R. Hayden Papers, BHL.

15. "Japanese and Filipino Pioneers in Davao," August 23, 1930, box 28, folder 1, J. R. Hayden Papers, BHL; Abinales, *Making Mindanao*, 81–86; Juan C. Orendain, "Exploit Lands in Davao to Prevent Japanese Expansion while P. I. Seeks Solution, Assemblyman Suggests," *Manila Daily Bulletin*, May 25, 1936; Dacudao, "Davao," 5–6.

16. Robert Aura Smith, "Murphy Returns to Manila Determined to Place Fresh Emphasis upon Problems Discovered during Trip of Inspection through Southern Provinces," *Manila Daily Bulletin*, March 12, 1934; E. E. Bomar, "Filipino-Moro Amity Encouraged by Gov. Murphy," *Manila Daily Bulletin*, June 19, 1934; Brands, *Bound to Empire*, 163.

17. Teofisto Guingona to Teofilo Sison, September 27, 1933, folder 3, box 30, J. R. Hayden Papers, BHL.

18. Retizos, "Maguindanao Pearls," *Philippine Magazine*, 179–89.

19. Sultan of Momungan to Franklin Roosevelt, May 26, 1934, folder 11, box 28, J. R. Hayden Papers, BHL; Jolo Datus to Frank Murphy, folder 32, box 29, J. R. Hayden Papers, BHL.

20. Abinales, *Making Mindanao*, 61–65; Thomas, "Muslims but Filipinos," 239–88.

21. Ibra Gundarangin to J. R. Hayden, April 10, 1934, folder 24, box 28, J. R. Hayden Papers, BHL.

22. Richard C. Bergholz, "Sultan of Sulu, Who Surrendered Moros to Pershing in 1913, Greets Americans Loyally This Time—and Gets Another Gun," *Washington Post*, May 20, 1945.

23. "Outlaws Slay 15 Police in Philippines," *Washington Post*, December 16, 1949; "Philippine Planes Wreck Moro Camp," *Los Angeles Times*, December 26, 1949.

24. Tillman Durdin, "Americans Hailed in Visit to Moros," *New York Times*, June 10, 1950.

25. The tendency grew after the events of September 11, 2001. For examples spanning the past two decades, see Raymond Bonner, "Threats and Responses: Southeast Asia; Philippine Camps Are Training Al Qaeda's Allies, Officials Say," *New York Times*, May 31, 2003; Preeti Bhattacharji, "Terrorism Havens: Philippines," Council on Foreign Relations, June 1, 2009, accessed April 7, 2019, https://www.cfr.org/backgrounder/terrorism-havens-philippines; Per Liljas, "ISIS is Making Inroads in the Southern Philippines and the Implications for Asia Are Alarming," April 14, 2016, *Time*, accessed March 10, 2019, http://time.com/4293395/isis-zamboanga-mindanao-moro-islamist-terrorist-asia-philippines-abu-sayyaf/.

26. Hasian, *President Trump*, 107–33.

27. Chanco, "Frontier Polities and Imaginaries," 119–20.

28. Adam, "Bringing Grievances Back In," 1–5.

29. Buendia, "State-Moro Armed Conflict," 131–32; Imbong, "Neoliberalism and the Moro," 80; San Juan, "Ethnic Identity," 411–18; Soriano and Sreekumar, "Multiple Transcripts," 1037–38.

30. Shibani Mahtani, "Philippine Forces Cleared This City of Islamist Militants in 2017; It's Still a Ghost Town," *Washington Post*, February 1, 2019; Alan Taylor, "A Victory against ISIS in the Philippines Leaves a City Destroyed," *The Atlantic*, October 25, 2017, accessed March 15, 2019, https://www.theatlantic.com/photo/2017/10/a-victory-against-isis-in-the-philippines-leaves-a-city-destroyed/543963/.

31. Patrick B. Johnston and Colin P. Clarke, "Is the Philippines the Next Caliphate?" *Foreign Policy*, accessed April 7, 2019, https://foreignpolicy.com/2017/11/27/is-the-philippines-the-next-caliphate/; Felipe Villamor, "ISIS Threat in Philippines Spreads in Remote Battles," *New York Times*, October 23, 2017.

32. Melencio, *Arguments against Philippine Independence*, 11.

33. Memorandum, June 28, 1956, box 1, Edward Bowditch Papers, DRMC.

34. "All the Facts Concerning Our New Empire," *Chicago Daily Tribune*, April 2, 1899.

Glossary

agama—religion or religious (here, religious courts)

agung—vertically suspended gongs; used in musical performance

barong—leaf-shaped bladed weapon

bejuco—a type of climbing vine

bichara—a large meeting or assembly

bolo—a knife similar to a machete

capitazes—"captains"; used to describe native policemen

carabao—domesticated water buffalo

cotta—a fortification

datu—chief, ruler, or sovereign

fellahin—Egyptian peasantry

igud—a gambling game

jihad—a struggle for a religious principal or belief (contextual)

juramentado—derived from the Spanish for "one who takes an oath"; used to describe Moro warriors who died while committing ritualized violence against foreign occupiers

kris—a bladed weapon with a distinctive asymmetrical shape

lantaka—a type of cannon used by indigenous groups in Southeast Asia

mujahid—someone engaged in jihad

pandita—religious leader within a Moro community

parang sabil—the idea of defending liberty against colonizing forces

rancheria—a small, rural settlement; holdover term from Spanish period

souk—a marketplace or bazaar

tarsilas—Moro royal genealogies; from the Arabic *silsila*, or "name chain"

ummah—community, in this case a global religious one

vinta—traditional single-sailed boat used in the Southern Philippines

Zamboangueño—creole ethnolinguistic group on the Zamboanga Peninsula

Bibliography

Archival Sources

Bentley Historical Library
(Ann Arbor, MI)

Harley Harris Bartlett Papers
John C. Early Papers
James Fugate Correspondence
Carl Eugen Guthe Papers
Joseph Ralston Hayden Papers
Dean C. Worcester Papers

Division of Rare and Manuscript Collections, Cornell University Library
(Ithaca, NY)

Edward Bowditch Papers

Library of Congress, Manuscript Division
(Washington, DC)

Charles Henry Brent Papers
Burton Norvell Harrison Family Papers
Robert Lee Bullard Papers
Frank W. Carpenter Papers
W. Cameron Forbes Papers
Charles W. Hack Papers
Hermann Hagedorn Papers

John McAuley Palmer Papers
Frank R. McCoy Papers
John J. Pershing Papers
Records of the Sultanate of the Sulu Archipelago
Hugh Lenox Scott Papers
Leonard Wood Papers

Missouri History Museum Library and Research Center
(St. Louis, MO)

Louisiana Purchase Exposition Scrapbooks

National Archives
(College Park, MD)

Record Group 350.3—Entry 5: Bureau of Insular Affairs

Special Collections Research Center, Syracuse University Library
(Syracuse, NY)

Frank Laubach Collection

State Historical Society of Missouri
(Columbia, MO)

American Radio Collection
Charles Monroe Reeves Papers
The Louisiana Purchase Exposition Collection

University of Iowa Libraries Special Collections Department
(Iowa City, IA)

Redpath Chautauqua Collection

U.S. Army Heritage and Education Center
(Carlisle, PA)

John C. Bates Papers
Tasker H. Bliss Collection
Walter L. Cutter Papers
George W. Davis Papers
Hugh A. Drum Papers
John P. Finley Papers
Marvin C. Hepler Papers

Howell-Taylor Family Papers
Charles F. Ivins Papers
William A. Kobbé Papers
Sterling Loop Larrabee Papers
Charles E. MacDonald Papers
Joseph A. Marmon Papers
Charles D. Rhodes Papers
Matthew F. Steele Papers
G. Soulard Turner Papers

Newspapers, Weeklies, Newsletters, and Pamphlets

The Albion
The American
Army and Navy Weekly
Atlanta Constitution
The Atlantic
Binghamton Leader-Chronicle
Boston Daily Globe
Boston Evening Transcript
BoxOffice
Bulletin of the American Historical Collection
Cass City Chronicle
Chicago Daily Tribune
Chicago Evening Post
Chicago Record-Herald
Christian Science Monitor
City Gazette and Commercial Daily Advertiser
Collier's Weekly
Daily Official Program—World's Fair
Evening Standard
Foreign Policy
The Forum
The Globe
Hartford Courant
The Independent
International Interpreter
Jolo Howler
Lanao Progress
La Opinion y el Comercio
La Solidaridad
Los Angeles Times

Manchester Guardian
Manila Cable-News
Manila Daily Bulletin
Manila Times
Manila Tribune
The Michigan Alumnus
Mindanao Herald
The Nation
New York Evening Post
New York Globe
New York Herald
New York Times
Philippine Presbyterian
Philippines Free Press
Pittsburgh Dispatch
Saturday Review of Literature
Semi-Monthly Magazine
St. Louis Republic
The Student Weekly
Time
Today Magazine
Toledo Times-Bee
Twenty-Third Infantry Bolo
Twenty-Third Infantry Lantaka
Variety
Washington Evening Star
Washington Herald
Washington Post
World's Fair Bulletin

Published Primary Sources

Abbott, Edward. *The Battle of the Crater: Letter in the Boston Daily Advertiser, March 20, 1906*. Boston: Anti-Imperialist League, 1906.

Ade, George. *Fables in Slang*. Chicago: Herbert Stone, 1899.

———. *The Sultan of Sulu: An Original Satire in Two Acts*. New York: R. H. Russell, 1903.

Aguilar, José Nieto. *Mindanao—Su Historia y Geographia*. Madrid: Imprenta del Cuerpo Administrativo del Eiército, 1894.

Almonte, Bernard. "An Adventure in the Sooloo Sea." *Frank Leslie's Popular Monthly* 33 (1892): 369–73.

American Red Cross. *The Sulu Archipelago Typhoon: Official Report of Relief Work in Jolo and Cagayan de Sulu*. Manila: Philippines Chapter—American Red Cross, 1932.

Baranera, Francisco. *Compendio de la Historia de Filipinas*. Manila: Establecimiento Tipo-Litografico de M. Perez, 1884.

Baranera, Francisco, and Alexander Laist. *Handbook of the Philippine Islands*. Manila: William Partier, 1890.

Barrows, David Prescott. *Circular of Information Instructions for Volunteer Field Workers—the Museum of Ethnology, Natural History and Commerce*. Manila: Bureau of Non-Christian Tribes, 1901.

Bartter, Frances E. *English-Samal Vocabulary*. Zamboanga, Philippines: Sulu Press, 1921.

Beard, George M., and A. D. Rockwell. *A Practical Treatise on Nervous Exhaustion (Neurasthenia), Its Symptoms, Nature, Sequences, Treatment*. New York: E. B. Treat, 1889.

Benjamin, Anna N. "Our Mohammedan Wards in Sulu." *The Outlook*, November 18, 1899, 675–79.

"Biographical Memoir of Alexander Dalrymple, Esq. Late Hydrographer to the Admiralty." *Naval Chronicle* 35 (1816): 186–87.

Blair, Emma H., and James A. Robertson, eds. *The Philippine Islands, 1493–1898*. Vol. 1. Cleveland: Arthur H. Clark, 1903.

——. *The Philippine Islands, 1493–1898*. Vol. 27. Cleveland: Arthur H. Clark, 1903.

Bliss, Tasker. *The Annual Report of the Governor of the Moro Province—for the fiscal Year Ended June 30, 1907*. Manila: Bureau of Printing, 1907.

——. *The Annual Report of the Governor of the Moro Province—for the Fiscal Year Ended June 30, 1908*. Zamboanga, Philippines: Mindanao Herald, 1908.

Blumentritt, Ferdinand. *The Philippines: A Summary Account of Their Ethnographical, Historical and Political Conditions*. Chicago: Donohue Brothers, 1900.

Brent, Charles H. *The Inspiration of Responsibility and Other Papers*. New York: Longmans, Green, 1915.

Brownell, Atherton. "Turning Savage into Citizens." *The Outlook*, December 24, 1910, 921–31.

——. "What American Ideas of Citizenship May Do for Oriental Peoples: A Moro Experiment." *The Outlook*, December 23, 1905, 975–84.

Buffum, Katharine G., and Charles Lynch. *Joloano Moro*. Manila: E. C. McCullough, 1914.

Butterfield, Kenyon. "Toward a Literate Rural World." *Journal of Adult Education* 4, no. 4 (1932): 383–88.

Cameron, Charles R. *Sulu Writing: An Explanation of the Sulu-Arabic Script as Employed in Writing the Sulu Language of the Southern Philippines*. Zamboanga, Philippines: Sulu Press, 1917.

Carpenter, Frank W. *Report of the Governor of the Department of Mindanao and Sulu (Philippine Islands) 1914*. Washington, DC: Government Printing Office, 1916.

Circular Letter of Governor Taft and Information and Instructions for the Preparation of the Philippine Exhibit for the Louisiana Purchase Exposition to Be Held at St Louis, Mo, 1904. Manila: Bureau of Public Printing, 1904.

Clark, Joseph G. *Lights and Shadows of Sailor Life*. Boston: John Putnam, 1847.

Clifford, Charles L. *The Real Glory*. London: Heinemann, 1937.

Cloman, Sydney A. *Myself and a Few Moros*. New York: Doubleday, Page, 1923.

Cole, Mabel Cook. *Philippine Folk Tales*. Chicago: A. C. McClurg, 1916.

Combés, Franciso. *Historia de Mindanao y Jolo*. Madrid: n.p., 1897.

Dalrymple, Alexander. *An Historical Collection of the Several Voyages and Discoveries in the South Pacific Ocean.* Vol. 1. London: J. Nourse, 1770.

Dennys, N. B. *The Folk-Lore of China.* London: Trubner, 1876.

———. *A Descriptive Dictionary of British Malaya.* London: London and China Telegraph Office, 1894.

The Department of Mindanao and Sulu at the Second Philippine Exposition. Zamboanga, Philippines: Mindanao Herald, 1914.

Dwight, Henry O. "Our Mohammedan Wards." *The Forum,* March 1900, 16.

Eighth Army War Corps Songs. Manila: Freedom, 1899.

Elliot, Charles Winslow. *A Vocabulary and Phrase Book of the Lanao Moro Dialect.* Manila: Bureau of Printing, 1913.

Finley, John P. "The Commercial Awakening of the Moro and Pagan." *North American Review* 197 (1913): 325–34.

———. "Race Development by Industrial Means among the Moros and Pagans of the Southern Philippines." *Journal of Race Development* 3, no. 3 (1913): 343–68.

Finley, John P., and William Churchill. *The Subanu: Studies of a Sub-Visayan Mountain Folk of Mindanao.* Washington, DC: Carnegie Institution of Washington, 1913.

Forbes, William Cameron. *The Philippine Islands.* New York: Houghton Mifflin, 1928.

Foreman, John. "Spain and the Philippine Islands." *Contemporary Review* 74 (1898): 20–33.

Forrest, Thomas. *A Voyage to New Guinea, and the Moluccas, from Balambangan.* London: J. Robson, 1780.

Francis, David R. *The Universal Exposition of 1904.* Vol. 1. St. Louis: Louisiana Purchase Exposition, 1913.

Freer, William B. *The Philippine Experiences of an American Teacher.* New York: Charles Scribner's Sons, 1906.

Glazer, Sydney. "The Moros as a Political Factor in Philippine Independence." *Pacific Affairs* 14, no. 1 (1941): 78–90.

Hancock, H. Irving. *Uncle Sam's Boys in the Philippines; or, Following the Flag against the Moros.* Philadelphia: Henry Altemus, 1912.

Harrison, Francis Buron. *The Corner-Stone of Philippine Independence: A Narrative of Seven Years.* New York: Century, 1922.

Hayden, Joseph Ralston. "What Next for the Moro?" *Foreign Affairs* 6, no. 4 (1928): 633–44.

Hoyt, Ralph. *Annual Report of Colonel Ralph W. Hoyt, 25th United States Infantry, Governor of the Moro Province, for the Fiscal Year Ended June 30, 1909.* Zamboanga, Philippines: Mindanao Herald, 1909.

Hurley, Vic. *Southeast of Zamboanga.* New York: E. P. Dutton, 1935.

———. *The Swish of the Kris: The Story of the Moros.* New York: E. P. Dutton, 1936.

———. *Jungle Patrol: The Story of the Philippine Constabulary.* New York: E. P. Dutton, 1938.

Jenkins, John S. *Voyage of the U.S. Exploring Squadron.* Auburn, NY: Alden and Beardsley, 1855.

Jenks, Maud Huntley. *Death Stalks the Philippine Wilds: Letters of Maud Huntley Jenks.* Minneapolis: Lund, 1951.

"Just Little Things." *American Chamber of Commerce Journal* 20, no. 2 (1940): 40.

Kneeland, Samuel. "The Philippine Islands: Their Physical Characteristics, Customs of the People, Products, Earthquake Phenomena, and Savage Tribes." *Journal of the American Geographical Society of New York* 15, no. 2 (1883): 73–100.

Kuder, Edward M. "The Moros in the Philippines." *Far Eastern Quarterly* 4, no. 2 (1945): 119–26.

Langhorne, George T. *Annual Report of the Governor of the Moro Province—September 1, 1903, to August 31, 1904.* Washington, DC: Government Printing Office, 1904.

Laubach, Frank C. "What Shall We Do with the Moros?" *Envelope Series* 24, no. 3 (1921): 3–23.

———. *The People of the Philippines: Their Religious Progress and Preparation for Spiritual Leadership in the Far East.* New York: George H. Doran, 1925.

———. "An Odyssey from Lanao, pt. III." *Philippine Public Schools* (1930): 459–68.

———. "Christianity and Islam in Lanao." *Muslim World* 25, no. 1 (1935): 45–49.

———. *Rizal: Man and Martyr.* Manila: Community, 1936.

———. *Planning Ahead for Better Christian-Moslem Relations.* Lanao, Philippines: American Board of Foreign Commissioners for Foreign Missions in the Philippine Islands, 1942.

———. "My Approach to the Moros." *Muslim World* 36, no. 2 (1946): 113–14.

———. *Wake Up or Blow Up—America: Lift the World or Lose it!* New York: Fleming H. Revell, 1951.

Leupp, Francis E. *The Indian and His Problem.* New York: Charles Scribner's Sons, 1910.

Little, Burtis M. *Francisco the Filipino.* New York: American Book, 1915.

Mayo, Katharine. *The Isles of Fear: The Truth about the Philippines.* New York: Harcourt, Brace, 1925.

McGee, W. J. "Strange Races of Men." *World's Work* (August 1904): 5185–88.

Meek, S. P. *The Monkeys Have No Tails in Zamboanga.* New York: William Morrow, 1935.

Melencio, José P. *Arguments against Philippine Independence and their Answers.* Washington, DC: Philippines Press Bureau, 1919.

Miller, Hunter, ed. *Treaties and Other International Acts of the United States of America.* Vol. 2. Washington, DC: Government Printing Office, 1931.

Neill, Stephen C. "Charles Henry Brent." *Canadian Journal of Theology* 8, no. 3 (1962): 153–71.

Orosa, Sixto Y. *The Sulu Archipelago and Its People.* Yonkers, NY: World Book, 1931.

"The Pan-American Exposition: The Ethnological Building." *Phrenological Journal and Science of Health* (April 1901): 3–4.

Pershing, John J. *Annual Report of Brigadier General John J. Pershing, U.S. Army, Governor of the Moro Province, for the Year Ending August 31, 1910.* Zamboanga, Philippines: Mindanao Herald, 1911.

———. *Annual Report of Brigadier General John J. Pershing, U.S. Army, Governor of the Moro Province, for the year Ending June 30, 1911.* Zamboanga, Philippines: Mindanao Herald, 1911.

———. *Annual Report of the Governor of the Moro Province, for the Fiscal Year Ended June 30, 1913.* Zamboanga, Philippines: Mindanao Herald Publishing Co., 1913.

———. *My Life before the War, 1860–1917: A Memoir.* Edited by John T. Greenwood. Lexington: University Press of Kentucky, 2013.

Pickens, Claude L. "With the Moros of the Philippines." *Muslim World* 30, no. 1 (1940): 360–40.

Pickering, Charles. *The Races of Man and Their Geographical Distribution*. Philadelphia: C. Sherman, 1848.

Pier, Arthur S. *American Apostles in the Philippines*. Boston: Beacon, 1950.

Porter, Ralph S. "The Story of Bantugan." *Journal of American Folklore* 15, no. 58 (1902): 143–61.

———. *A Primer and Vocabulary of the Moro Dialect (Magindanau)*. Washington, DC: Government Printing Office, 1903.

Program of the Jolo Agricultural and Industrial Fair. Jolo, Philippines: R. B. Hayes, 1906.

The Real Glory. Directed by Henry Hathaway. 1939. Los Angeles: MGM Movie Legends Collection, 2007. DVD.

Report of the Philippine Exposition Board to the St. Louis Purchase Exposition. St. Louis: Greeley, 1904.

Report of the Thirty-Fourth Annual Lake Mohonk Conference on the Indian and Other Dependent Peoples. Lake Mohonk, NY: Lake Mohonk Conference on the Indian and Other Dependent Peoples, 1916.

Retizos, Isidro L. "Maguindanao Pearls." *Philippine Magazine* 28, no. 4 (1931): 179–89.

Roberts, Helen M. *Champion of the Silent Billion: The Story of Frank C. Laubach, Apostle of Literacy*. St. Paul: Macalaster Park, 1961.

Russel, Florence Kimball. *A Woman's Journey through the Philippines*. Boston: L. C. Page, 1907.

Russell, Charles Edward. *The Outlook for the Philippines*. New York: Century, 1922.

Saleeby, Najeeb. *Studies in Moro History, Law, and Religion*. Manila: Bureau of Public Printing, 1905.

———. *The History of Sulu*. Manila: Bureau of Printing, 1908.

———. *The Moro Problem: An Academic Discussion of the History and Solution of the Problem of the Government of the Moros of the Philippine Islands*. Manila: E. C. McCullough, 1913.

Scott, Hugh L. "A Soldier's View of the Philippine Question." In *Proceedings of the Twenty-Fifth Annual Meeting of the Lake Mohonk Conference of Friends of the Indian and Other Dependent Peoples*, edited by Lilian D. Powers, 119–22. Lake Mohonk, NY: Lake Mohonk Conference, 1907.

———. *Some Memories of a Soldier*. New York: Century, 1928.

Santayana, Agustin. *La Isla de Mindanao su Historia y su Estado Presente*. Madrid: Imprenta de Alhambra y Comp, 1862.

The Sixteenth Annual Report of the Missionary District of the Philippine Islands. Manila: Printing Committee, 1920.

Slater, Eleanor. *Charles Henry Brent—Everybody's Bishop*. Milwaukee: Morehouse, 1932.

Smith, C. C., trans. *A Grammar of the Maguindanao Tongue according to the Manner of Speaking It in the Interior of the South Coast of the Island of Mindanao*. Washington, DC: Government Printing Office, 1906.

Smith, E. L. *Report on Sulu Moros*. Manila: E. C. McCullough, 1908.

Smith, Warren D. "A Geologic Reconnaissance of the Island of Mindanao and the Sulu Archipelago." *Philippine Journal of Science* 3 (1908): 473–99.

Steere, Joseph Beal. "Six Weeks in Southern Mindanao." *American Naturalist* 22, no. 256 (1888): 289–94.

Storey, Moorfield. *The Moro Massacre*. Boston: Anti-Imperialist League, 1906.

Stuart, Florence Partello. *The Adventures of Piang the Moro Jungle Boy*. New York: Century, 1917.

Taylor, Carl N. "Powder Keg in Mindanao." *Today Magazine*, March 7, 1936, 19.

Turner, Frederick Jackson. *The Frontier in American History*. New York: Henry Holt, 1921.

Upbuilding the Wards of the Nation: The Work of Charles H. Brent, of the Philippine Islands. New York: Harmony Club of America, 1913.

Villamor, Ignacio. *Census of the Philippine Islands: Appendix to Volume I—Organization, Census Acts, and Regulations*. Manila: Bureau of Printing, 1920.

Wainright, Fonrose. "Blue Wings over Sulu." *Survey Graphic* 18, no. 8 (1939): 485–91, 509–12.

White, John R. *Bullets and Bolos: Fifteen Years in the Philippine Islands*. New York: Century, 1928.

Wilkes, Charles. *Synopsis of the Cruise of the U.S. Exploring Expedition, 1838–1842*. Washington, DC: Peter Force, 1842.

———. *Narrative of the United States Exploring Expedition*. Vol. 5. Philadelphia: C. Sherman, 1844.

Williams, Herschel. *Uncle Bob and Aunt Becky's Strange Adventures at the World's Great Exposition*. Chicago: Laird and Lee, 1904.

Wilson, W. P. *Official Catalogue of Exhibits—Philippine Government*. St. Louis: Official Catalogue, 1904.

———. "The Philippines at St. Louis." *The Booklovers Magazine* 4, no. 1 (1904): 3–16.

Wood, Leonard, and Tasker Bliss. *Annual Report Department of Mindanao—July 1, 1905 to June 30, 1906*. Manila: Bureau of Printing, 1906.

Wood, Leonard, and W. Cameron Forbes. *Report of the Special Mission on Investigation to the Philippine Islands*. Manila: Bureau of Printing, 1921.

Worcester, Dean C. *The Philippine Islands and Their People*. New York: Macmillan, 1898.

———. "The Non-Christian Peoples of the Philippine Islands." *National Geographic* 24, no. 2 (1913): 1157–256.

———. *Slavery and Peonage in the Philippine Islands*. Manila: Bureau of Printing, 1913.

Secondary Sources

Abinales, Patricio N. "State Authority and Local Power in the Southern Philippines, 1900–1972." PhD diss., Cornell University, 1997.

———. "From *Orang Besar* to Colonial Big Man: Datu Piang of Cotabato and the American Colonial State." In *Lives at the Margin: Biography of Filipinos Obscure, Ordinary, and Heroic*, edited by Alfred W. McCoy, 193–227. Quezon City, Philippines: Ateneo de Manila University Press, 2000.

——. *Making Mindanao: Cotabato and Lanao in the Formation of the Philippine Nation-State.* Quezon City, Philippines: Ateneo de Manila University Press, 2000.

——. "American Military Presence in the Southern Philippines: A Comparative Overview." *East West Center Working Papers, Politics and Security Series* 7 (2004): 1–20.

——. *Orthodoxy and History in the Muslim-Mindanao Narrative.* Quezon City, Philippines: Ateneo de Manila University Press, 2010.

Abinales, Patricio N., and Donna J. Amoroso. *State and Society in the Philippines.* New York: Rowman & Littlefield, 2005.

Abubakar, Carmen A. "Review of the Mindanao Peace Processes." *Inter-Asia Cultural Studies* 5, no. 3 (2004): 450–64.

Abuzza, Zachary. "The Moro Islamic Liberation Front at 20: State of the Revolution." *Studies in Conflict and Terrorism* 28 (2005): 453–79.

Adam, Jeroen. "Bringing Grievances Back In: Towards an Alternative Understanding of the Rise of the Moro Islamic Liberation Front in the Philippines." *Bijdragen Tot De Taal-, Land- En Volkenkunde* 174 (2018): 1–23.

Adas, Michael. *Prophets of Rebellion: Millenarian Protest Movements against the European Colonial Order.* Chapel Hill: University of North Carolina Press, 1979.

——. "Improving on the Civilizing Mission? Assumptions of United States Exceptionalism in the Colonization of the Philippines." *Itinerario* 22, no. 4 (1998): 44–66.

——. "From Settler Colony to Global Hegemon: Integrating the Exceptionalist Narrative of the American Experience into World History." *American Historical Review* 106, no. 5 (2001): 1692–720.

——. *Dominance by Design: Technological Imperatives in America's Civilizing Mission.* Cambridge, MA: Harvard University Press, 2007.

Adler, Anthony. "From the Pacific to the Patent Office: The U.S. Exploring Expedition and the Origins of America's First National Museum." *Journal of the History of Collections* 23, no. 1 (2011): 49–74.

Aguilar, Filomeno V. "Tracing Origins: 'Ilustrado' Nationalism and the Racial Science of Migration Waves." *Journal of Asian Studies* 64, no. 3 (2005): 605–37.

Aldrich, Robert. *Colonialism and Homosexuality.* New York: Routledge, 2002.

——. "Colonial Man." In *French Masculinities: History, Culture and Politics,* edited by Christopher E. Forth and Bertrand Taithe, 123–40. New York: Palgrave Macmillan, 2007.

Alexanderson, Kris. *Subversive Seas: Anticolonial Networks across the Twentieth-Century Dutch Empire.* Cambridge: Cambridge University Press, 2019.

Alidio, Kimberly. "'When I Get Home, I Want to Forget': Memory and Amnesia in the Occupied Philippines, 1901–1904." *Social Text* 59 (1999): 105–22.

Amirell, Stefan Eklöf. "Pirates and Pearls: Jikiri and the Challenge to Maritime Security and American Sovereignty in the Sulu Archipelago, 1907–1909." *International Journal of Maritime History* 29, no. 1 (2017): 44–67.

Amoroso, Donna J. "Inheriting the 'Moro Problem': Muslim Authority and Colonial Rule in British Malaya and the Philippines." In *The American Colonial State in the Philippines: Global Perspectives,* edited by Julian Go and Anne L. Foster, 118–47. Durham, NC: Duke University Press, 2003.

———. *Traditionalism and the Ascendency of the Malay Ruling Class.* Singapore: NUS Press, 2014.

Anderson, Benedict. *Under Three Flags: Anarchism and the Anti-Colonial Imagination.* New York: Verso, 2006.

Anderson, Warwick. "The Trespass Speaks: White Masculinity and Colonial Breakdown." *American Historical Review* 102, no. 5 (1997): 1342–70.

———. "Going through the Motions: American Public Health and Colonial 'Mimicry,'" *American Literary History* 14, no. 4 (2003): 686–719.

———. *Colonial Pathologies: American Tropical Medicine, Race, and Hygiene in the Philippines.* Durham, NC: Duke University Press, 2006.

Andriolo, Karin. "Murder by Suicide: Episodes from Muslim History." *American Anthropologist* 104, no. 3 (2002): 734–42.

Anduaga, Aitor. "Spanish Jesuits in the Philippines: Geophysical Research and Synergies between Science, Education and Trade, 1865–1898." *Annals of Science* 71, no. 4 (2014): 497–521.

Angeles, Vivienne S. M. "Philippine Muslim Women: Tradition and Change." In *Islam, Gender, and Social Change,* edited by Yvonne Yazbeck Hadda and John L. Esposito, 209–34. Oxford: Oxford University Press, 1994.

———. "Moros in the Media and Beyond: Representations of Philippine Muslims." *Contemporary Islam* 4, no. 1 (2010): 29–53.

Antolihao, Lou. *Playing with the Big Boys: Basketball, American Imperialism, and Subaltern Discourse in the Philippines.* Lincoln: University of Nebraska Press, 2015.

Arcilla, José S. "The Philippine Revolution and the Jesuit Missions in Mindanao, 1896–1900." *Archivum Historicum Societatis Jesu* 47 (1978): 361–77.

———. "The Jesuits during the Philippine Revolution." *Philippine Studies* 35, no. 3 (1987): 296–315.

Arnold, James R. *The Moro War: How America Battled a Muslim Insurgency in the Philippine Jungle, 1902–1913.* New York: Bloomsbury, 2011.

Asaka, Ikuko. *Tropical Freedom: Climate, Settler Colonialism, and Black Exclusion in the Age of Emancipation.* Durham, NC: Duke University Press, 2017.

Ax, Christina Folke, Niels Brimnes, Niklas Thode Jensen, and Karen Oslund, eds. *Cultivating the Colonies: Colonial States and their Environmental Legacies.* Athens: Ohio University Press, 2011.

Bacevich, Andrew J. *Diplomat in Khaki: Major General Frank Ross McCoy and American Foreign Policy, 1898–1949.* Lawrence: University Press of Kansas, 1989.

———. "Disagreeable Work: Pacifying the Moros, 1903–1906." *Military Review* 85, no. 3 (2005): 41–45.

Baldoz, Rick. *The Third Asiatic Invasion: Empire and Migration in Filipino America, 1898–1946.* New York: New York University Press, 2011.

Baldoz, Rock, and César Ayala. "The Bordering of America: Colonialism and Citizenship in the Philippines and Puerto Rico." *Centro Journal* 25, no. 1 (2013): 76–105.

Ballantyne, Tony, and Antoinette Burton. "Empires and the Reach of the Global." In *A World Connecting: 1870–1945,* edited by Emily Rosenberg, 285–434. Cambridge, MA: Harvard University Press, 2012.

Bankoff, Greg. "Deportation and the Prison Colony of San Ramon, 1870–1898." *Philippine Studies* 39, no. 4 (1991): 443–57.

———. "First Impressions: Diarists, Scientists, Imperialists and the Management of the Environment in the American Pacific, 1899–1902." *Journal of Pacific History* 44, no. 3 (2009): 261–80.

Barrows, David Prescott. *A Decade of American Government in the Philippines, 1903–1913.* New York: World Books, 1914.

Bashford, Alison. *Imperial Hygiene: A Critical History of Colonialism, Nationalism and Public Health.* New York: Palgrave MacMillan, 2004.

Bassin, Mark. *Imperial Visions: Nationalist Imagination and Geographic Expansion in the Russian Far East, 1840–1865.* Cambridge: Cambridge University Press, 1999.

Baylen, Joseph O., and John Hammond Moore. "Senator John Tyler Morgan and Negro Colonization in the Philippines, 1901 to 1902." *Phylon* 29, no. 1 (1968): 65–75.

Beaujard, Philippe. "The Indian Ocean in Eurasian and African World-Systems before the Sixteenth Century." *Journal of World History* 16, no. 4 (2005): 411–65.

Beaupre, Myles. "'What Are the Philippines Going to Do to Us?' E. L. Godkin on Democracy, Empire, and Anti-Imperialism." *Journal of American Studies* 46, no. 3 (2012): 711–27.

Beckett, Jeremy. "The Datus of the Rio Grande de Cotabato under Colonial Rule." *Asian Studies* 5 (1977): 46–64.

Bender, Daniel E. *The Animal Game: Searching for Wildness at the American Zoo.* Cambridge, MA: Harvard University Press, 2008.

———. *American Abyss: Savagery and Civilization in the Age of Industry.* Ithaca, NY: Cornell University Press, 2009.

Bender, Daniel E., and Jana K. Lipman, "Through the Looking Glass: U.S. Empire through the Lens of Labor History." In *Making the Empire Work: Labor and United States Imperialism,* edited by Daniel E. Bender and Jana K. Lipman, 1–34. New York: New York University Press 2015.

Bender, Daniel E., and Jana K. Lipman, eds. *Making the Empire Work: Labor and United States Imperialism.* New York: New York University Press, 2015.

Bender, Thomas. *A Nation among Nations: America's Place in World History.* New York: Hill and Wang, 2006.

Bennet, Tony. *Pasts beyond Memory: Evolution, Museums, Colonialism.* New York: Routledge, 1994.

Benton, Laura. *Law and Colonial Cultures: Legal Regimes in World History, 1400–1900.* Cambridge: Cambridge University Press, 2001.

Bhabha, Homi K. *The Location of Culture.* New York: Routledge, 1994.

Bhattacharya, Tithi. *Sentinels of Culture: Class, Education, and the Colonial Intellectual in Bengal, 1848–55.* Oxford: Oxford University Press, 2005.

Bjork, Katharine. "The Link that Kept the Philippines Spanish: Mexican Merchant Interests and the Manila Trade, 1571–1815." *Journal of World History* 9, no. 1 (1998): 25–50.

———. *Prairie Imperialists: The Indian Country Origins of American Empire.* Philadelphia: University of Pennsylvania Press, 2018.

Blackhawk, Ned. *Violence over the Land: Indians and Empires in the Early American West.* Cambridge: Harvard University Press, 2006.

Blower, Brooke L. "Nation of Outposts: Forts, Factories, Bases, and the Making of American Power." *Diplomatic History* 41, no. 3 (2017): 439–59.

Blumi, Isa. *Ottoman Refugees, 1878–1939: Migration in a Post-Imperial World.* London: Bloomsbury, 2013.

Bose, Sugata. *A Hundred Horizons: The Indian Ocean in the Age of Global Empire.* Cambridge, MA: Harvard University Press, 2011.

Bradford, Marlene. *Scanning the Skies: A History of Tornado Forecasting.* Norman: University of Oklahoma Press, 2001.

Brands, H. W. *Bound to Empire: The United States and the Philippines, 1890–1990.* Oxford: Oxford University Press, 1992.

Brody, David. *Visualizing American Empire: Orientalism and Imperialism in the Philippines.* Chicago: University of Chicago Press, 2010.

Brower, Matthew. "Trophy Shots: Early North American Photographs of Nonhuman Animals and the Display of Masculine Prowess." *Society and Animals* 13, no. 1 (2005): 13–32.

Brown, Mark. *Penal Power and Colonial Rule.* New York: Routledge, 2014.

Bryant, Kelly Duke. "Social Networks and Empire: Senegalese Students in France in the Late Nineteenth Century." *French Colonial History* 15, no. 1 (2014): 39–66.

Buendia, Rizal G. "The State-Moro Armed Conflict in the Philippines: Unresolved National Question or Question of Governance?" *Asian Journal of Political Science* 13, no. 1 (2005): 109–38.

Bulmer-Thomas, Victor. *Empire in Retreat: The Past, Present, and Future of the United States.* New Haven, CT: Yale University Press, 2018.

Burbank, Jane, and Frederick Cooper. *Empires in World History: Power and the Politics of Difference.* Princeton, NJ: Princeton University Press, 2000.

Cano, Gloria. "Evidence for the Deliberate Distortion of the Spanish Philippine Colonial Historical Record in *The Philippine Islands 1493–1898.*" *Journal of Southeast Asian Studies* 39, no. 1 (2008): 1–30.

Carter, Bentley G. "Implicit Evangelism: American Education among the Muslim Maranao." *Pilipinas* 12 (1989): 73–96.

Carter, Matthew. *Myth of the Western: New Perspectives on Hollywood's Frontier Narrative.* Edinburgh: Edinburgh University Press, 2014.

Chakrabarti, Pratik. *Medicine and Empire: 1600–1960.* New York: Palgrave Macmillan, 2013.

Chanco, Christopher John. "Frontier Polities and Imaginaries: The Reproduction of Settler Colonial Space in the Southern Philippines." *Settler Colonial Studies* 7, no. 1 (2017): 111–33.

Chang, Jiat-Hwee, and Anthony D. King. "Towards a Genealogy of Tropical Architecture: Historical Fragments of Power-Knowledge, Built Environment and Climate in the British Colonial Territories." *Singapore Journal of Tropical Geography* 32 (2011): 283–300.

Charbonneau, Oliver. "'A New West in Mindanao': Settler Fantasies on the U.S. Imperial Fringe." *Journal of the Gilded Age and Progressive Era* 18, no. 3 (2019): 304–23.

Clarence-Smith, William G. "Wajih al-Kilani, Shaykh al-Islam of the Philippines and Notable of Nazareth, 1913–1916." In *Nazareth History and Cultural Heritage: Proceedings of the 2nd International Conference, Nazareth, July 2–5, 2012,* edited by Mahmoud Yazbak and Sharif Sharif, 172–92. Nazareth, Israel: Municipality of Nazareth Academic Publications, 2013.

Clymer, Kenton J. *Protestant Missionaries in the Philippines, 1898–1916: An Inquiry into the American Colonial Mentality.* Chicago: University of Illinois Press, 1986.

Coffman, Edward M. *The Regulars: The American Army, 1898–1941.* Cambridge, MA: Harvard University Press, 2004.

Cohn, Bernard S. *Colonialism and Its Forms of Knowledge: The British in India.* Princeton, NJ: Princeton University Press, 1996.

Colby, Jason M. *The Business of Empire: United Fruit, Race, and U.S. Expansion in Central America.* Ithaca, NY: Cornell University Press, 2011.

Coleborne, Catharine, and Angela McCarthy. "Health and Place in Historical Perspective: Medicine, Ethnicity, and Colonial Identities." *Australian and New Zealand Society of the History of Medicine* 14, no. 1 (2012): 1–11.

Conroy-Krutz, Emily. *Christian Imperialism: Converting the World in the Early American Republic.* Ithaca, NY: Cornell University Press, 2015.

Cooper, Frederick. *Colonialism in Question: Theory, Knowledge, History.* Berkeley: University of California Press, 2005.

Cornelio, Jayeel S. "Popular Religion and the Turn to Everyday Authenticity: Reflections on the Contemporary Study of Philippine Catholicism." *Philippine Studies* 62, no. 3/4 (2014): 471–500.

Coyle, Lee. *George Ade.* New York: Twayne, 1964.

Craib, Raymond B. "Relocating Cartography." *Postcolonial Studies* 12, no. 4 (2009): 481–90.

Crozier, Anna. "What Was Tropical about Tropical Neurasthenia? The Utility of the Diagnosis in the Management of British East Africa." *Journal of the History of Medicine and Allied Sciences* 64, no. 4 (2009): 518–48.

Cruz, Denise. *Transpacific Femininities: The Making of the Modern Filipina.* Durham, NC: Duke University Press, 2012.

Dacudao, Patricia Irene. "Ghost in the Machine: Mechanization in a Philippine Frontier, 1898–1941." In *Travelling Goods, Travelling Moods: Varieties of Cultural Appropriation (1850–1950),* edited by Christian Huck and Stefan Bauernschmidt, 209–26. Frankfurt: Campus Verlag, 2012.

——. "Abaca: The Socio-economic and Cultural Transformation of Frontier Davao, 1898–1941." PhD diss., Murdoch University, 2017.

Dale, Stephen Frederic. "Religious Suicide in Islamic Asia: Anticolonial Terrorism in India, Indonesia, and the Philippines." *Journal of Conflict Resolution* 32, no. 1 (1988): 37–59.

Deacon, Desley, Penny Russell, and Angela Woolacott, eds. *Transnational Lives: Biographies of Global Modernity, 1700–Present.* New York: Palgrave Macmillan, 2010.

DeLay, Brian. "Indian Polities, Empire, and the History of American Foreign Relations." *Diplomatic History* 39, no. 5 (2015): 927–42.

Dikötter, Frank, and Ian Brown, eds. *Cultures of Confinement: A History of the Prison in Africa, Asia and Latin America.* Ithaca, NY: Cornell University Press, 2007.

Domosh, Mona. "A 'Civilized' Commerce: Gender, 'Race,' and Empire at the 1893 Chicago Exposition." *Cultural Geographies* 9, no. 2 (2002): 181–201.

Doolitte, Amity. "Colliding Discourses: Western Land Laws and Native Customary Rights in North Borneo, 1881–1918." *Journal of Southeast Asian Studies* 34, no. 1 (2003): 97–126.

Dphrepaulezz, Omar. "'The Right Sort of White Men': General Leonard Wood and the U.S. Army in the Southern Philippines, 1898–1906." PhD diss., University of Connecticut, 2013.

Drinnon, Richard. *Facing West: The Metaphysics of Indian-Hating and Empire-Building.* Minneapolis: University of Minnesota Press, 1980.

Driver, Felix, and Luciana Martins, eds. *Tropical Visions in an Age of Empire.* Chicago: University of Chicago Press, 2005.

Dumont, Jean-Paul. *Visayan Vignettes: Ethnographic Traces of a Philippine Island.* Chicago: University of Chicago Press, 1992.

Dunning, John. *On the Air: The Encyclopedia of Old-Time Radio.* Oxford: Oxford University Press, 2003.

Duque, Estela. "Modern Tropical Architecture: Medicalization of Space in Early Twentieth-Century Philippines." *Architectural Research Quarterly* 13, no. 3/4 (2009): 261–71.

Elias, Robert. *The Empire Strikes Out: How Baseball Sold U.S. Foreign Policy and Promoted the American Way Abroad.* New York: New Press, 2010.

Ellingson, Ter. *The Myth of the Noble Savage.* Berkeley: University of California Press, 2001.

Ephraim, Frank. "The Mindanao Plan: Political Obstacles to Jewish Refugee Settlement." *Holocaust and Genocide Studies* 20, no. 3 (2006): 410–36.

Ewen, Shane. "Lost in Translation? Mapping, Molding, and Managing the Transnational Municipal Moment." In *Another Global City: Historical Explorations into the Transnational Municipal Moment, 1850–2000,* edited by Pierre-Yves Saunier and Shane Ewen, 173–84. New York: Palgrave Macmillan, 2008.

Federspiel, Howard M. *Sultans, Shamans, and Saints: Islam and Muslims in Southeast Asia.* Honolulu: University of Hawaii Press, 2007.

Feuer, A. B. *America at War: The Philippines, 1898–1913.* Westport, CT: Praeger, 2002.

Fischer-Tiné, Harald, and Susanne Gehrmann, eds. *Empires and Boundaries: Rethinking Race, Class, and Gender in Colonial Settings.* New York: Routledge, 2009.

Foster, Anne L. "Prohibition as Superiority: Policing Opium in South-East Asia, 1898–1925." *International History Review* 22, no. 2 (2000): 253–73.

———. *Projections of Power: The United States and Europe in Colonial Southeast Asia, 1919–1941.* Durham, NC: Duke University Press, 2010.

Foucault, Michel. *Discipline and Punish: The Birth of the Prison.* New York: Vintage, 1995.

Frank, Elizabeth S. "Advocating War Preparedness: H. Irving Hancock's *Conquest of the United States* Series." In *Pioneers, Passionate Ladies, and Private Eyes: Dime Novels, Series Books, and Paperbacks*, edited by Larry Sullivan and Lydia Cushman Schurman, 215–31. Binghamton, NY: Haworth, 1996.

Fry, Howard T. *Alexander Dalrymple (1737–1808) and the Expansion of British Trade.* New York: Routledge, 1970.

———. "The Bacon Bill of 1926: New Light on an Exercise in Divide-and-Rule." *Philippine Studies* 26, no. 3 (1978): 257–73.

Frymer, Paul. *Building an American Empire: The Era of Territorial and Political Expansion.* Princeton, NJ: Princeton University Press, 2017.

Fulton, Robert. *Honor for the Flag: The Battle for Bud Dajo—1906 and the Moro Massacre.* Bend, OR: Tumalo Creek, 2009.

———. *Moroland: The History of Uncle Sam and the Moros, 1899–1920.* Bend, OR: Tumalo Creek, 2011.

Gedacht, Joshua. "'Mohammedan Religion Made It Necessary to Fire': Massacres on the American Imperial Frontier from South Dakota to the Southern Philippines." In *Colonial Crucible: Empire in the Making of the Modern American State*, edited by Alfred W. McCoy and Francisco A. Scarano, 397–409. Madison: University of Wisconsin Press, 2009.

———. "Holy War, Progress, and 'Modern Mohammedans' in Colonial Southeast Asia." *Muslim World* 105, no. 4 (2015): 446–71.

———. "The 'Shaykh al-Islām of the Philippines' and Coercive Cosmopolitanism in an Age of Global Empire." In *Challenging Cosmopolitanism: Coercion, Mobility and Displacement in Islamic Asia*, edited by Joshua Gedacht and R. Michael Feener, 172–202. Edinburgh: University of Edinburg Press, 2018.

Geertz, Clifford. *Islam Observed: Religious Development in Morocco and Indonesia.* New Haven, CT: Yale University Press, 2018.

Geiger, Jeffrey. *Facing the Pacific: Polynesia and the U.S. Imperial Imagination.* Honolulu: University of Hawaii Press, 2007.

Gems, Gerald R. *The Athletic Crusade: Sport and American Cultural Imperialism.* Lincoln: University of Nebraska Press, 2006.

George, T. J. S. *Revolt in Mindanao: The Rise of Islam in Philippine Politics.* Oxford: Oxford University Press, 1980.

Gianakos, Perry E. "George Ade's Critique of Benevolent Assimilation." *Diplomatic History* 7, no. 3 (1983): 223–38.

Gilbert, James. *Whose Fair? Experience, Memory, and the History of the Great St. Louis Exposition.* Chicago: University of Chicago Press, 2009.

Go, Julian. *American Empire and the Politics of Meaning: Elite Political Cultures in the Philippines and Puerto Rico during U.S. Colonialism.* Durham, NC: Duke University Press, 2008.

———. *Patterns of Empire: The British and American Empires, 1688 to the Present.* Cambridge: Cambridge University Press, 2011.

Gobat, Michel. *Confronting the American Dream: Nicaragua under U.S. Imperial Rule.* Durham, NC: Duke University Press, 2005.

———. "The Invention of Latin America: A Transnational History of Anti-Imperialism, Democracy, and Race." *American Historical Review* 118, no. 5 (2013): 1345–75.

———. *Empire by Invitation: William Walker and Manifest Destiny in Central America.* Cambridge, MA: Harvard University Press, 2018.

Gouda, Frances. *Dutch Culture Overseas: Colonial Practice in the Netherlands Indies, 1900–1942.* Amsterdam: University of Amsterdam Press, 1995.

Govaars, Ming. *Dutch Colonial Education: The Chinese Experience in Indonesia, 1900–1942.* Singapore: Chinese Heritage Centre, 2005.

Gowing, Peter G. "Mandate in Moroland: The American Governor of Muslim Filipinos, 1899–1920." PhD diss., University of Syracuse, 1968.

———. "Moros and Indians: Commonalities of Purpose, Policy and Practice in American Government of Two Hostile Subject Peoples." *Philippine Quarterly of Culture and Society* 8, no. 2/3 (1980): 125–49.

———. "The Legacy of Frank Charles Laubach." *International Bulletin of Missionary Research* 7, no. 2 (1983): 58–62.

———. *Mandate in Moroland: The American Government of Muslim Filipinos, 1899–1920.* Quezon City, Philippines: New Day, 1983.

Gleach, Frederic W. "Pocahontas at the Fair: Crafting Identities at the 1907 Jamestown Exposition." *Ethnohistory* 50, no. 3 (2003): 419–45.

Greenberg, Amy S. *A Wicked War: Polk, Clay, Lincoln, and the 1846 U.S. Invasion of Mexico.* New York: Alfred A. Knopf, 2012.

Greene, Julie. *The Canal Builders: Making America's Empire at the Panama Canal.* New York: Penguin, 2009.

Guttmann, Allen. *Games and Empires: Modern Sports and Cultural Imperialism.* New York: Columbia University Press, 1994.

Hahn, Steven. *A Nation without Borders: The United States and Its World in an Age of Civil Wars, 1830–1910.* New York: Viking, 2016.

Hansen, Anne Ruth. *How to Behave: Buddhism and Modernity in Colonial Cambodia, 1860–1930.* Honolulu: University of Hawaii Press, 2007.

Harris, Susan K. "Women, Anti-Imperialism, and America's Christian Mission Abroad: The Impact of the Philippine American War." In *Becoming Visible: Women's Changing Presence in Late Nineteenth Century America,* edited by Alison Easton, R. J. Ellis, Janet Floyd, and Lindsay Traub, 307–26. Amsterdam: Rodopi, 2010.

———. *God's Arbiters: Americans and the Philippines, 1898–1902.* Oxford: Oxford University Press, 2011.

Hartley, Douglas Thompson Kellie. "American Participation in the Economic Development of Mindanao and Sulu, 1899–1930." PhD diss., James Cook University of North Queensland, 1983.

Hasian, Marouf A., Jr. *President Trump and General Pershing: Remembrances of the "Moro" Insurrection in the Age of Post-Truths.* New York: Palgrave Pivot, 2018.

Hawkins, Michael C. "Managing a Massacre: Savagery, Civility, and Gender in Moro Province in the Wake of Bud Dajo." *Philippine Studies* 59, no. 1 (2011): 83–105.

———. *Making Moros: Imperial Historicism and American Military Rule in the Philippines' Muslim South.* DeKalb: University of Northern Illinois, 2013.

Hinton, Alex. "Savages, Subjects, and Sovereigns: Conjunctions of Modernity, Genocide, and Colonialism." In *Empire, Colony, Genocide: Conquest, Occupation, and Subaltern*

Resistance in World History, edited by A. Dirk Moses, 440–60. Oxford: Berghahn Books, 2008.

Hobsbawm, Eric. *Bandits*. London: Weidenfield & Nicolson, 2000.

Hoffman, Elizabeth Cobbs. *American Umpire*. Cambridge, MA: Harvard University Press, 2013.

Hoganson, Kristen L. *Fighting for American Manhood: How Gender Politics Provoked the Spanish-American and Philippine-American Wars*. New Haven, CT: Yale University Press, 2000.

——. *Consumers' Imperium: The Global Production of American Domesticity, 1865–1920*. Chapel Hill: University of North Carolina Press, 2007.

Hopkins, Bernard. *American Empire: A Global History*. Princeton, NJ: Princeton University Press, 2018.

Horsman, Reginald. *Race and Manifest Destiny: The Origins of American Racial Anglo-Saxonism*. Cambridge, MA: Harvard University Press, 1981.

Horvatich, Patricia. "The Martyr and the Mayor: On the Politics of Identity in the Southern Philippines." In *Cultural Citizenship in Island Southeast Asia: Nation and Belonging in the Hinterlands*, edited by Renato Rosaldo, 16–43. Berkeley: University of California Press, 2003.

Hui, Wang. *The Politics of Imagining Asia*. Cambridge, MA: Harvard University Press, 2011.

Hunt, Michael H. *Ideology and U.S. Foreign Policy*. New Haven, CT: Yale University Press, 1987.

Hunt, Michael H., and Steven I. Levine. *Arc of Empire: America's Wars in Asia from the Philippines to Vietnam*. Chapel Hill: University of North Carolina Press, 2012.

Huyssen, David. *Progressive Inequality: Rich and Poor in New York, 1890–1920*. Cambridge, MA: Harvard University Press, 2014.

Ileto, Reynaldo Clemeña. *Magindanao, 1860–1888: The Career of Datu Uto of Buayan*. Manila: Anvil Vintage, 2007.

Imbong, Regletto Aldrich. "Neoliberalism and the Moro Struggle in the Southern Philippines." *Journal for the Study of Religions and Ideologies* 17, no. 51 (2018): 69–84.

Immerwahr, Daniel. *How to Hide an Empire: A History of the Greater United States*. New York: Farrar, Straus, and Giroux, 2019.

Jacobs, Margaret D. *White Mother to a Dark Race: Settler Colonialism, Maternalism, and the Removal of Indigenous Children in the American West and Australia, 1880–1940*. Lincoln: University of Nebraska Press, 2009.

Joyce, Barry Alan. *The Shaping of American Ethnography: The Wilkes Exploring Expedition*. Lincoln: University of Nebraska Press, 2001.

Jurika, Louis. "A Philippine Odyssey." *Beyond the Wire* 4, no. 1 (2011): 4–5.

Kaomea, Julie. "Education for Elimination in Nineteenth-Century Hawai'i: Settler Colonialism and the Native Hawaiian Chiefs' Children's Boarding School." *History of Education Quarterly* 54, no. 2 (2014): 123–44.

Karuka, Manu. *Empire's Tracks: Indigenous Nations, Chinese Works, and the Transcontinental Railroad*. Berkeley: University of California Press, 2019.

Kawashima, Midori. "The Uprising of the 'Fearful Ruler of Laneo': Banditry and the Internalization of Violence in a Southern Philippine Muslim Society during the

1930s." In *Popular Movements and Democratization in the Muslim World*, edited by Masatochi Kisaichi, 78–99. New York: Routledge, 2006.

——. *The "White Man's Burden" and the Islamic Movement in the Philippines: The Petition of the Zamboanga Muslim Leaders to the Ottoman Empire in 1912*. Monograph Series 17. Tokyo: Institute of Asian Cultures, Sophia University, 2014.

Kennedy, Dane Keith. *The Magic Mountains: Hill Stations and the British Raj*. Berkeley: University of California Press, 1996.

Kirsch, Scott. "Insular Territories: U.S. Colonial Science, Geopolitics, and the (Re)Mapping of the Philippines." *Geographical Journal* 182, no. 1 (2016): 2–14.

Kloos, David. "A Crazy State: Violence, Psychiatry, and Colonialism in Aceh, Indonesia, ca. 1910–1942." *Bildragen tot de Taal-, Land-, en Volkenrunde* 170, no. 1 (2014): 25–65.

Knellwolf, Christa. "The Exotic Frontier of the Imperial Imagination." *Eighteenth-Century Life* 26, no. 3 (2002): 10–30.

Koese, Yavuz. "Nestlé in the Ottoman Empire: Global Marketing with Local Flavor, 1870–1927." *Enterprise and Society* 9, no. 4 (2008): 724–61.

Kohout, Amy Lee. "From the Field: Nature and Work on American Frontiers, 1876–1909." PhD diss., Cornell University, 2015.

Kolb, Harold H. "George Ade (1866–1944)." *American Literary Realism* 4, no. 2 (1971): 157–69.

Kramer, Paul A. "Making Concessions: Race and Empire Revisited at the Philippines Exposition, St. Louis, 1901–1905." *Radical History Review* 73 (1999): 74–114.

——. "Empires, Exceptions, and Anglo-Saxons: Race and Rule between the British and United States Empires, 1880–1910." *Journal of American History* 88, no. 4 (2002): 1315–53.

——. *The Blood of Government: Race, Empire, the United States, and the Philippines*. Chapel Hill: University of North Carolina Press, 2006.

——. "Race-Making and Colonial Violence in the U.S. Empire: The Philippine-American War as Race War." *Diplomatic History* 30, no. 2 (2006): 169–210.

——. "Power and Connection: Imperial Histories of the United States in the World." *American Historical Review* 116, no. 5 (2011): 1348–91.

——. "Imperial Openings: Civilization, Exemption, and the Geopolitics of Mobility in the History of Chinese Exclusion, 1868–1910." *Journal of the Gilded Age and Progressive Era* 14, no. 3 (2015): 317–47.

——. "An Enemy You Can Depend On: Trump, Pershing's Bullets, and the Folklore of the War on Terror." *Asia-Pacific Journal* 15, no. 4 (2017): 3–9.

——. "The Geopolitics of Mobility: Immigration Policy and American Global Power in the Long Twentieth Century." *American Historical Review* 123, no. 2 (2018): 393–438.

Kratoska, Paul, and Ben Batson. "Nationalism and Modernist Reform." In *The Cambridge History of Southeast Asia*, vol. 2, edited by Nicholas Tarling, 249–324. Cambridge: Cambridge University Press, 1992.

Kutzer, M. Daphne. *Empire's Children: Empire and Imperialism in Classic Children's Books*. London: Routledge, 2002.

Labi, Hadji Sarip Riwarung. "Dimakaling—Hero or Outlaw? A View from a Meranao Folk Song." *Journal of Sophia Asian Studies* 27 (2009): 161–80.

Lahiri, Shompa. "Performing Identity: Colonial Migrants, Passing and Mimicry between the Wars." *Cultural Geographies* 10, no. 4 (2003): 408–23.

Lake, Marilyn, and Henry Reynolds. *Drawing the Global Colour Line: White Men's Countries and the Challenge of Racial Equality.* Cambridge: Cambridge University Press, 2008.

Lawrie, Paul R. D. *Forging a Laboring Race: The African American Worker in the Progressive Imagination.* New York: New York University Press, 2016.

Levine, Philippa. "States of Undress: Nakedness and the Colonial Imagination." *Victorian Studies* 50, no. 2 (2008): 189–219.

Liebsohn, Dana. "*Dentro y fuera de los muros*: Manila, Ethnicity, and Colonial Cartography." *Ethnohistory* 62, no. 2 (2014): 229–51.

Lord, Carnes. *Proconsuls: Delegated Political-Military Leadership from Rome to America Today.* Cambridge: Cambridge University Press, 2012.

Lumba, Allan E. S. "Imperial Standards: Colonial Currencies, Racial Capacities, and Economic Knowledge during the Philippine-American War," *Diplomatic History* 39, no. 4 (2015): 603–28.

Majul, Cesar Abid. *Muslims in the Philippines.* Quezon City, Philippines: University of the Philippines Press, 1973.

Makki, Fouad. "Culture and Agency in a Colonial Public Sphere: Religion and the Anti-Colonial Imagination in 1940s Eritrea." *Social History* 36, no. 4 (2011): 418–42.

Mandal, Sumit Kumar. *Becoming Arab: Creole Histories and Modern Identity in the Malay World.* Cambridge: Cambridge University Press, 2018.

Manuel, E. Arsenio. "A Survey of Philippine Folk Epics." *Asian Folklore Studies* 22 (1963): 1–76.

Marr, Timothy. "Diasporic Intelligences in the American Philippine Empire: The Transnational Career of Dr. Najeeb Mitry Saleeby." *Mashria and Mahjar* 2, no. 1 (2014): 78–106.

Marriott, John. *The Other Empire: Metropolis, India and Progress in the Colonial Imagination.* Manchester: Manchester University Press, 2003.

Mastura, Michael O. "A Short History of Cotabato City and Its Historic Places." In *Cotabato City Guidebook*, edited by Simeon F. Millan, 5–25. General Santos City, Philippines: Simeon F. Millan, 1979.

——. *Muslim-Filipino Experience: A Collection of Essays.* Marawi City, Philippines: Mindanao State University Research Center, 1982.

McClintock, Anne. *Imperial Leather: Race, Gender, and Sexuality in the Colonial Contest.* London: Routledge, 1995.

McCoy, Alfred W. *Policing America's Empire: The United States, the Philippines, and the Rise of the Surveillance State.* Madison: University of Wisconsin Press, 2009.

McCoy, Alfred W., and Francisco A. Scarano, eds. *Colonial Crucible: Empire in the Making of the Modern American State.* Madison: University of Wisconsin Press, 2009.

McGrane, Bernard. *Beyond Anthropology: Society and the Other.* New York: Columbia University Press, 1989.

McGuinness, Aims. *Path of Empire: Panama and the California Gold Rush.* Ithaca, NY: Cornell University Press, 2009.

McKenna, Rebecca Tinio. *American Imperial Pastoral: The Architecture of US Colonialism in the Philippines*. Chicago: University of Chicago Press, 2017.

McKenna, Thomas M. *Muslim Rulers and Rebels: Everyday Politics and Armed Separatism in the Southern Philippines*. Berkeley: University of California Press, 1998

Metcalf, Thomas R. "From One Empire to Another: The Influence of the Raj on American Colonialism in the Philippines." *Ab Imperio* 3 (2012): 25–41.

Miller, Bonnie M. "The Incoherencies of Empire: The 'Imperial' Image of the Indian at the Omaha World's Fairs of 1898–1899." *American Studies* 49, no. 3/4 (2008): 39–62.

Milligan, Jeffrey Ayala. *Islamic Identity, Postcoloniality, and Educational Policy: Schooling and Ethno-religious Conflict in the Southern Philippines*. New York: Palgrave Macmillan, 2005.

Mills, Sara. *Gender and Colonial Space*. Manchester: Manchester University Press, 2005.

Montemayor, Michael Schuck. *Captain Herman Leopold Schuck: The Saga of a German Sea Captain in 19th-Century Sulu-Sulawesi Seas*. Honolulu: University of Hawaii Press, 2006.

Moore, Sarah J. "Mapping Empire in Omaha and Buffalo: World's Fairs and the Spanish-American War." *Bilingual Review* 25, no. 1 (2000): 111–26.

Non, Domingo M. "Moro Piracy during the Spanish Period and Its Impact." *Southeast Asian Studies* 30, no. 4 (1993): 401–19.

Norbeck, Mark D. "The Legacy of Charles Henry Brent." *International Bulletin of Missionary Research* 20, no. 4 (1996): 163–68.

Onuf, Peter S. *Jefferson's Empire: The Language of American Nationhood*. Charlottesville: University of Virginia Press, 2000.

Osterhammel, Jürgen. *Colonialism: A Theoretical Overview*. Princeton, NJ: Markus Wiener, 2005.

———. *The Transformation of the World: A Global History of the Nineteenth Century*. Princeton, NJ: Princeton University Press, 2015.

Palen, Marc-William. *The "Conspiracy" of Free Trade: The Anglo-American Struggle over Empire and Economic Globalisation, 1846–1896*. Cambridge: Cambridge University Press, 2016.

Pante, Michael D. "A Collision of Masculinities: Men, Modernity, and Urban Transportation in American-Colonial Manila." *Asian Studies Review* 38, no. 2 (2014): 253–73.

Panzo, Maria T. B. "Framing the War: The Marawi Siege as Seen through Television Documentaries." *Asian Politics and Policy* 10, no. 1 (2018): 149–53.

Paredes, Oona. *A Mountain of Difference: The Lumad in Early Colonial Mindanao*. Ithaca, NY: Southest Asia Program Publications, Cornell University, 2013.

———. "Indigenous vs. Native: Negotiating the Place of Lumads in the Bangsamoro Homeland." *Asian Ethnicity* 16, no. 2 (2015): 166–185.

Parezo, Nancy J., and Don D. Fowler. *Anthropology Goes to the Fair: The 1904 Louisiana Purchase Exposition*. Lincoln: University of Nebraska Press, 2007.

Parsons, Katsy Jurika. "A Life in Moroland: A Memory of Blanche Walker Jurika by Her Daughter—Part 1." *Bulletin of the American Historical Collection* (January-March 2004): 77–95.

——. "A Life in Moroland: A Memoir of Blanche Walker Jurika by Her Daughter—Part 2." *Bulletin of the American Historical Collection* (April-June 2005): 31–41.

Paxton, Nancy L. *Writing under the Raj: Gender, Race, and Rape in the British Colonial Imagination, 1830–1947.* New Brunswick, NJ: Rutgers University Press, 1999.

Pope, Steven W. "Rethinking Sport, Empire, and American Exceptionalism." *Sport History Review* 38 (2007): 92–120.

Pradhan, Queeny. "Empire in the Hills: The Making of Hill Stations in Colonial India." *Studies in History* 23, no. 1 (2007): 33–91.

Preston, Andrew. *Sword of the Spirit, Shield of the Faith: Religion in American War and Diplomacy.* New York: Knopf, 2012.

Protschky, Susie. "The Colonial Table: Food, Culture and Dutch Identity in Colonial Indonesia." *Australian Journal of Politics and History* 54, no. 3 (2008): 346–57.

——. "Seductive Landscapes: Gender, Race and European Representations of Nature in the Dutch East Indies." *Gender and History* 20, no. 2 (2008): 372–98.

Prucha, Francis Paul. *The Great Father: The United States Government and the American Indians.* 2 vols. Lincoln: University of Nebraska Press, 1984.

Rand, Gavin, and Kim A. Wagner. "Recruiting the 'Martial Races': Identities and Military Service in Colonial." *Patterns of Prejudice* 46, no. 3/4 (2012): 232–54

Ram, Mori. "White but Not Quite: Normalizing Colonial Conquests through Spatial Mimicry." *Antipode* 46, no. 3 (2014): 736–53.

Reilly, Brandon Joseph. "Collecting the People: Textualizing Epics in Philippine History from the Sixteenth Century to the Twenty-First." PhD diss., University of California, Los Angeles, 2013.

Reinkowski, Maurus, and Gregor Thum, eds. *Helpless Imperialists: Imperial Failure, Fear and Radicalization.* Göttingen, Germany: Vandenhoeck & Ruprecht, 2013.

Renda, Mary. *Taking Haiti: Military Occupation and the Culture of U.S. Imperialism.* Chapel Hill: University of North Carolina Press, 2011.

Rice, Mark. *Dean Worcester's Fantasy Islands: Photography, Film, and the Colonial Philippines.* Ann Arbor: University of Michigan Press, 2014.

Rogers, Charlotte. *Jungle Fever: Exploring Madness and Medicine in Twentieth-Century Tropical Narratives.* Nashville, TN: Vanderbilt University Press, 2012.

Rogers, Randal. "Colonial Imitation and Racial Insubordination: Photography at the Louisiana Purchase Exhibition of 1904." *History of Photography* 32, no. 4 (2008): 347–67.

Rovine, Victoria L. "Colonialism's Clothing: Africa, France, and the Deployment of Fashion." *Design Issues* 25, no. 3 (2009): 44–61.

Rosenberg, Emily S. "Transnational Currents in a Shrinking World." In *A World Connecting, 1870–1945*, edited by Emily Rosenberg, 815–996. Cambridge, MA: Harvard University Press, 2012.

Rosenberg, Emily S., and Shanon Fitzpatrick. "Introduction." In *Body and Nation: The Global Realm of U.S. Body Politics*, 1–16. Durham, NC: Duke University Press, 2014.

Rydell, Robert. *All the World's a Fair: Visions of Empire at American International Expositions, 1876–1916.* Chicago: University of Chicago Press, 1984.

Rydell, Robert, John Findling, and Kimberly Pelle, eds. *Fair America: World's Fairs in the United States*. Washington, DC: Smithsonian Books, 2000.

Saada, Emmanuelle. *Empire's Children: Race, Filiation, and Citizenship in the French Colonies*. Chicago: University of Chicago Press, 2012.

Said, Edward. *Orientalism*. London: Penguin, 1977.

Salman, Michael. *The Embarrassment of Slavery: Controversies over Bondage and Nationalism in the American Colonial Philippines*. Berkeley: University of California Press, 2001.

———. "'The Prison that Makes Men Free': The Iwahig Penal Colony and the Simulacra of the American State in the Philippines." In *Colonial Crucible: Empire in the Making of the Modern American State*, edited by Alfred W. McCoy and Francisco A. Scarano, 116–30. Madison: University of Wisconsin Press, 2009.

San Juan, E., Jr. "Ethnic Identity and Popular Sovereignty: Notes on the Moro Struggle in the Philippines." *Ethnicities* 6, no. 3 (2006): 391–422.

Santiago-Valles, Kevin. "American Penal Forms and Colonial Spanish Custodial-Regulatory Practices in Fin de Siècle Puerto Rico." In *Colonial Crucible: Empire in the Making of the Modern American State*, edited by Alfred W. McCoy and Francisco A. Scarano, 87–96. Madison: University of Wisconsin Press, 2009.

Sato, Masayuki. "Imagined Peripheries: The World and Its Peoples in Japanese Cartographic Imagination." *Diogenes* 44, no. 173 (1996): 119–45.

Saunier, Pierre-Yves. *Transnational History*. New York: Palgrave Macmillan, 2013.

Schult, Volker. "Sulu and Germany in the Late Nineteenth Century." *Philippine Studies* 48, no. 1 (2000): 80–108.

Schumacher, Frank. "The American Way of Empire: National Tradition and Transatlantic Adaptation in America's Search for Imperial Identity, 1898–1910." *GHI Bulletin* 31 (2002): 35–50.

———. "Creating Imperial Spaces: Baguio and the American Empire in the Philippines, 1898–1920." In *Taking Up Space: New Approaches to American History*, edited by Anke Ortlepp and Christopher Ribbat, 59–75. Trier, Denmark: WVT, 2004.

———. "On the Frontier of Civilization: Deliberations of Exceptionalism and Environmental Determinism in the Creation of America's Tropical Empire, 1890–1910." In *Frontiers and Boundaries in U.S. History*, edited by Cornelius A. van Minnen and Sylvia L. Hilton, 127–42. Amsterdam: VU University Press, 2004.

———. "Colonization through Education: A Comparative Exploration of Ideologies, Practices, and Cultural Memories of 'Aboriginal Schools' in the United States and Canada." *Zeitschrift für Kanada-Studien* 26, no. 2 (2006): 97–117.

———. "The United States: Empire as a Way of Life?" In *The Age of Empires*, edited by Robert Aldrich, 278–303. London: Thames & Hudson, 2007.

Seth, Sanjay. *Subject Lessons: The Western Education of Colonial India*. Durham, NC: Duke University Press, 2007.

Shellum, Brian G. *Black Officer in a Buffalo Soldier Regiment*. Lincoln: University of Nebraska Press, 2010.

Singarayelou, Pierre. "The Insitutionalisation of Colonial Geography in France, 1880–1940." *Journal of Historical Geography* 37, no. 2 (2011): 149–57.

Singh, D. S. Ranjit. *The Making of Sabah, 1865–1941: The Dynamics of Indigenous Society.* Kuala Lumpur: University of Malaya Press, 2000.

Soderstrom, Mark. "Family Trees and Timber Rights: Albert E. Jenks, Americanization, and the Rise of Anthropology at the University of Minnesota." *Journal of the Gilded Age and Progressive Era* 3, no. 2 (2004): 176–204.

Soriano, Cheryll Ruth, and T. T. Sreekumar. "Multiple Transcripts as Political Strategy: Social Media and Conflicting Identities of the Moro Liberation Movement in the Philippines." *Media, Culture and Society* 34, no. 8 (2012): 1028–39.

Steinmetz, George. *The Devil's Handwriting: Precoloniality and the German Colonial State in Qingdao, Samoa, and Southwest Africa.* Chicago: University of Chicago Press, 2007.

Stoler, Ann Laura. "Intimidations of Empire: Predicaments of the Tactile and Unseen." In *Haunted by Empire: Geographies of Intimacy in North American History*, edited by Ann Laura Stoler, 1–22. Durham, NC: Duke University Press, 2006.

Stockwell, A. J. "Leaders, Dissidents and the Disappointed: Colonial Students in Britain as Empire Ended." *Journal of Imperial and Commonwealth History* 36, no. 3 (2008): 487–507.

Streeby, Shelley. *American Sensations: Class, Empire, and the Production of Popular Culture.* Berkeley: University of California Press, 2002.

Sullivan, Rodney J. *Exemplar of Americanism: The Philippine Career of Dean C. Worcester.* Ann Arbor: University of Michigan Press, 1991.

Suzuki, Nobutaka. "Upholding Filipino Nationhood: The Debate over Mindanao in the Philippine Legislature, 1907–1913." *Journal of Southeast Asian Studies* 44, no. 2 (2013): 266–91.

Tagliacozzo, Eric. *Secret Trades, Porous Borders: Smuggling and States along a Southeast Asian Frontier, 1865–1915.* New Haven, CT: Yale University Press, 2005.

Tan, Samuel K. *Sulu under American Military Rule, 1899–1913.* Quezon City, Philippines: University of the Philippines, 1968.

———. *The Filipino Muslim Armed Struggle.* Manila: Filipinas Foundation, 1977.

———. *Selected Essays on Filipino Muslims.* Marawi City, Philippines: Mindanao State University Research Center, 1982.

———. *The Muslim South and Beyond.* Quezon City, Philippines: University of the Philippine Press, 2010.

Tarling, Nicholas. "The Establishment of Colonial Regimes." In *The Cambridge History of Southeast Asia*, vol. 2, edited by Nicholas Tarling, 213–28. Cambridge: Cambridge University Press, 1992.

Thomas, Ralph Benjamin. "Muslims but Filipinos: The Integration of Philippine Muslims, 1917–1946." PhD diss., University of Pennsylvania, 1971.

Thompson, Krista. *An Eye for the Tropics: Tourism, Photography, and Framing the Caribbean Picturesque.* Durham, NC: Duke University Press, 2006.

Tuason, Julie A. "The Ideology of Empire in *National Geographic* Magazine's Coverage of the Philippines, 1898–1908." *Geographical Review* 89, no. 1 (1999): 34–53.

Tyrrell, Ian. "The Regulation of Alcohol and Other Drugs in a Colonial Context: United States Policy Towards the Philippines, c. 1898–1910." *Contemporary Drug Problems* 35 (2008): 539–69.

———. *Reforming the World: The Creation of America's Moral Empire*. Princeton, NJ: Princeton University Press, 2010.

———. *Crisis of the Wasteful Nation: Empire and Conservation in Theodore Roosevelt's America*. Chicago: University of Chicago Press, 2015.

Tyrrell, Ian, and Jay Sexton, eds. *Empire's Twin: U.S. Anti-Imperialism from the Founding Era to the Age of Terrorism*. Ithaca, NY: Cornell University Press, 2015.

Vann, Michael G. "Of Pirates, Postcards, and Public Beheadings: The Pedagogic Execution in French Colonial Indochina." *Historical Reflection* 36, no. 2 (2010): 39–58.

Wade, Geoff. "An Early Age of Commerce in Southeast Asia, 900–1300 CE." *Journal of Southeast Asian Studies* 40, no. 2 (2009): 221–65.

Wagner, Kim A. "Savage Warfare: Violence and the Rule of Difference in Early British Counterinsurgency." *History Journal Workshop* 85 (2019): 217–35.

Walsh Thomas P. *Tin Pan Alley and the Philippines: American Songs of War and Love, 1898–1946—a Resource Guide*. Lanham, MD: Scarecrow, 2013.

Walter, Dierk. *Colonial Violence: European Empires and the Use of Force*. Oxford: Oxford University Press, 2017.

Walther, Karine V. *Sacred Interests: The United States and the Islamic World, 1821–1921*. Chapel Hill: University of North Carolina Press, 2015.

Warren, James Francis. "The Sulu Zone, the World Capitalist Economy and the Historical Imagination: Problematizing Global-Local Interconnections and Interdependencies." *Southeast Asian Studies* 35, no. 2 (1997): 177–222.

———. "The Structure of Slavery in the Sulu Zone in the Late Eighteenth and Nineteenth Centuries." *Slavery and Abolition* 24, no. 2 (2003): 111–28.

———. *The Sulu Zone, 1768–1898: The Dynamics of External Trade, Slavery, and Ethnicity in the Transformation of a Southeast Asian Maritime State*. 2nd ed. Singapore: NUS Press, 2007.

———. "Scientific Superman: Father José Algué, Jesuit Meteorology, and the Philippines under American Rule, 1897–1924." In *Colonial Crucible: Empire in the Making of the Modern American State*, edited by Alfred W. McCoy and Francisco A. Scarano, 508–19. Madison: University of Wisconsin Press, 2009.

Warriner, Charles K. "Traditional Authority and the Modern State: The Case of the Maranao of the Philippines." *Social Problems* 12, no. 1 (1964): 51–56.

Watts, Edward. *In This Remote Country: French Colonial Culture in the Anglo-American Imagination, 1760–1860*. Chapel Hill: University of North Carolina Press, 2006.

Wendt, Reinhard, and Jürgen C. Nagel. "Southeast Asia and Oceania." In *Empires and Encounters, 1350–1750*, edited by Wolfgang Reinhard, 555–738. Cambridge, MA: Harvard University Press, 2015.

Wernstedt, Frederick L., and Paul D. Simkins. "Migrations and the Settlement of Mindanao." *Journal of Asian Studies* 25, no. 1 (1965): 83–103.

Werth, Nicolas. *Cannibal Island: Death in a Siberian Gulag*. Princeton, NJ: Princeton University Press, 2007.

Wertz, Daniel J. P. "Idealism, Imperialism, and Internationalism: Opium Politics in the Colonial Philippines, 1898–1925." *Modern Asian Studies* 47, no. 2 (2013): 467–99.

Whitehead, Clive. *Colonial Educators: The British Indian and Colonial Education Serve, 1858–1983*. London: I. B. Tauris, 2003.

Williams, Walter L. "United States Indian Policy and the Debate over Philippine Annexation: Implications for the Origins of American Imperialism." *Journal of American History* 66, no. 4 (1980): 810–31.

Winichakul, Thongchai. *Siam Mapped: A History of the Geo-body of a Nation*. Honolulu: University of Hawaii Press, 1994.

Winkelmann, Tessa Ong. "Rethinking the Sexual Geography of American Empire in the Philippines: Interracial Intimacies in Mindanao and the Cordilleras, 1898–1921." In *Gendering the Trans-Pacific World: Diaspora, Empire, and Race*, edited by Catherine Ceniza Choy and Judy Tzu-Chun Wu, 39–76. Leiden, Netherlands: Brill, 2017.

Winzeler, R. L. "Amok: Historical, Psychological, and Cultural Perspectives." In *The Emotions of Culture: A Malay Perspective*, edited by W. J. Karim, 96–122. Oxford: Oxford University Press, 1990.

Woolford, Andrew, Jeff Benvenuto, and Alexander Laban Hinton, eds. *Colonial Genocide in Indigenous North America*. Durham, NC: Duke University Press, 2014.

Woollacott, Angela. *Gender and Empire*. New York: Palgrave Macmillan, 2006.

Yegar, Moshe. *Between Integration and Secession: The Muslim Communities of the Southern Philippines, Southern Thailand, and Western Burma/Myanmar*. Lanham, MD: Lexington Books, 2002.

Yu-Jose, Lydie N., and Patricia Irene Dacudao. "Visible Japanese and Invisible Filipino: Narratives of the Development of Davao, 1900s–1930s." *Philippine Studies* 63, no. 1 (2015): 101–29.

Zantop, Susanne. *Colonial Fantasies: Conquest, Family, and Nation in Precolonial Germany, 1770–1870*. Durham, NC: Duke University Press, 1997.

Zimmerman, Andrew. *Alabama in Africa: Booker T. Washington, the German Empire, and the Globalization of the New South*. Princeton, NJ: Princeton University Press, 2010.

Zinoman, Peter. *The Colonial Bastille: A History of Imprisonment in Vietnam, 1862–1940*. Berkeley: University of California Press, 2001.

Zwick, Jim, ed. *Mark Twain's Weapons of Satire: Anti-Imperialist Writings on the Philippine-American War*. Syracuse, NY: Syracuse University Press, 1992.

Index